A History of
Credit & Power in
the Western World

Scott B. MacDonald
Albert L. Gastmann

A History of
Credit & Power in
the Western World

Transaction Publishers
New Brunswick (U.S.A.) and London (U.K.)

Library of Congress Number: 2001027042
ISBN: 0-7658-0085-3
Printed in the United States of America

Library of Congress Cataloging-in-Publication Data

MacDonald, Scott B.
   A history of credit and power in the western world / Scott B. MacDonald and Albert L. Gastmann.
       p. cm.
   Includes bibliographical references and index.
       ISBN 0-7658-0085-3 (cloth : alk. paper)
   1. Credit—History. 2. Finance—History. 3. Finance, Public—History. 4. Power (Social sciences)—History. 5. Political science—Economic aspects—History. 6. Economic history. 7. World history. I. Gastmann, Albert L. II. Title.

HG3701 .M177 20001
332.7—dc21   2001027042

Contents

Preface

A thousand blinking lights illuminate the trading floors on Wall Street, the City of London, and Tokyo. Those lights throw up vast amounts of information that reflect the flow of trillions of dollars of credit into the global economy. There is no place on the planet that the flickering lights do not cast a ray—a ray that links the ups and downs of stock exchanges in Buenos Aires, Rabat, Moscow, and Kuala Lumpur with their more mature cousins in London, Tokyo, and New York. And beyond the many bourses of the world are the banks, credit unions, insurance companies, and rating agencies. Presiding over this game of blinking lights and creditworthiness are the guardians of the globalized economy—central banks, ministries of finance, the Bank for International Settlements, and the International Monetary Fund. The game of credit at the dawn of the twenty-first century is global, touching almost all aspects of modern life, and is a major force in determining who has political power in a rapidly changing international system.

Rapid change always brings about a certain sense of excitement, the thrill of adventure, but also some degree of trepidation. Clearly this was the case at the end of the Cold War. This put the planet on a new track. Gone was the familiar world of bipolarity, red phones, and ICBMs (Inter-Continental Ballistic Missiles), abruptly replaced by a strange new world of the Internet, e-commerce, and Palm Pilots. What had seemed clear about the course of human relations suddenly and rudely became unclear. The "New World Order" was defined by a U.S.-led war against Iraq, bloody ethnic strife in Bosnia and Rwanda, and religious turmoil in Central Asia. One aspect of the evolving global system in the early twenty-first century that is often overlooked in grandiose discourses about the brave new world of hegemons, emerging markets, and digital economies is the role of credit. As the world becomes a smaller place, an increasingly larger number of people have access to credit or want it. Without easy credit the developed world could not keep expanding as rapidly as it does. Fortunately, in much of the post-industrial world there is an army of companies actively peddling it. In the emerging market economies of China, Russia, India, and Brazil, credit is desired usually because of low local levels of savings or underdeveloped capital markets or a combination of both. Credit functions as a critical building block for developing greater national and individual wealth. At the same time, too much credit can be bad as exemplified by the banking crises in the Nordic countries in the late 1980s and early 1990s and the Asian contagion in 1997-1998. The latter crisis hit banks, finance companies and corporations in Southeast Asia, Korea, and Japan and spread into Russia and in the 1998-1999 period into Latin America.[1] In both the cases of the Nordic banks and their Asian counterparts too much credit had been pumped into economic systems at a time of deregulation, which, when confidence in the market fled, turned into a massive financial panic.

The purpose of this book is to examine the interplay between credit and power. While there is a considerable amount written on money and how to make it (something we're all interested in), few efforts have been made to examine the role of credit and its interrelationship with the rise and fall of the great powers. We firmly believe in the complementary nature of power and credit. As the Reverend C.C. Colton noted in 1823: "There are two things that bestow consequence; great possessions, or great debts. Julius Caesar consented to be millions of sectaries worse than nothing, in order to be everything; he borrowed large sums to pay his officers, to quell sedition in his troops, who had mutinied for want of pay, and thus forced his partisans to anticipate their own success only through that of their commander."[2] Consequently, in the broad historical range, this book examines the evolution of credit in the Western world and its relationship to power from the European trade fairs of the late Middle Ages to Cyberspace in the early twenty-first century. At the core of the relationship between the nation-state and credit is the issue of power and how it is changing at the end of the twentieth century. Six major themes dominate:

1. There is a direct relationship between credit and power. The wealth represented by credit augments political power.

2. Along the same lines, different kinds of political power promote different kinds of economic behavior. For example, the advancement of a functioning modern credit system found fertile soil in the more open

political systems of the Netherlands, Switzerland, Britain, and the United States than in the autocratic Ottoman, Austro-Hungarian, and Russian empires.

3.   Throughout much of the development of credit, certain societal groups were able to embrace the dynamics of the relationship between credit and trade in a much more holistic way than others. There is a certain degree of truth to the importance of culture in economic determination. This point should not be overstated as it is one factor among many that helped to propel at different points the Jews, Italians, Dutch, English, and Americans to the commanding heights of the Western credit system.

4.   The Western credit system evolved in tandem with the development of the nation-state.

5.   The development of a Western-based, but ultimately global credit system occurred with considerable volatility. There is no straight line in the spread of Western-based credit uses, but many stops and goes.

6.   Over time, we witness the spread of credit from being the privilege of the wealthy and the powerful to being available to vast numbers of North Americans, Japanese, and Europeans.

This book took several years to write. The authors wish to thank a number of people who helped the creative process along. They include Dr. Jonathan Lemco (at Vanguard), Professor Barry Rosen at Baruch College in New York City, Borden Painter, Professor of History at Trinity College, and Mark Gross at AIG, all of whom read through various parts of the manuscript and offered valuable criticisms. Thanks are also extended to Matt Burnell at Merrill Lynch, Allerton "Tony" Smith of Credit Suisse First Boston, Betty Hanson, Professor of Political Science at the University of Connecticut, Amin Aladin at Aladdin Capital LLC, George Marshman and Joe Schlim at Aladdin Capital, Keith Rabin at KWR International, and David Levey at Moody's Investor Service. The White Plains Public Library and Trinity College Library were both extremely helpful in locating books and articles.

Scott B. MacDonald wishes to thank his wife, Kateri Scott-MacDonald for all her help during the long hours of work that went into finishing the book. He also extends thanks to his two children, Alistair and Estelle, for all their countless distractions that pointed out that there is more to life than endless work.

Notes

1.   For more information about the Nordic banking crises, see Burkhard Drees and Ceyla Pazabasioglu, *The Nordic Banking Crises: Pitfalls in Financial Liberalization?* (Washington, DC: International Monetary Fund, 1998) and Goran Lind and Anna-Karin Nedersjo, "The Banking Sector in 1993," *Quarterly Review*, Sveriges Riksbank (Sweden), Vol. 2 (June), pp. 24-35.
2.   Quoted from Kevin Jackson, ed., *The Oxford Book of Money* (New York: Oxford University Press, 1996), p. 229.

Part 1

Introduction

1

Introduction

Beautiful Credit. The foundation of modern society. Who shall say that this is not the golden age of natural trust, of unlimited reliance upon human promises?
—Mark Twain and Charles Dudley Warner, The Gilded Age, p. 243

A well-maintained irrigation system brings an adequate supply of water to thirsty crops in the field. It can make a dusty and sun-baked field green and verdant, capable of producing food for the hungry. In a sense, every drop of water is precious. A poorly maintained irrigation system wastes water and often results in crop failure. Much of the same can be said of credit in the global economic system: efficient allocation and use produces positive results in economic development benefiting the majority of citizens; poor allocation and misuse leads to corruption, graft, and economic and financial collapses. Under these circumstances only a handful at the top benefit.

At the beginning of the twenty-first century the global economic system is supported by an international credit system. That credit system is hardly perfect, but it does provide badly needed capital for a host of users, ranging from national and subnational (states, provinces, and municipalities) governments in the Americas, Asia, the Middle East and Europe, and in parts of Africa to Fortune 500 corporations and the myriad of small enterprises and households the world over. Although the objectives of governments, multinational corporations, and individuals are different, the need for credit is the same. In a sense, credit is like water. It is a key wellspring of life—in this case, economic life. Without credit, most businesses would find it difficult to function, and certainly many governments would be forced to scale down their operations and reduce expenditures (certainly not a bad idea in some cases). Consequently, a well-run credit system is essential for the flow of goods and services around the planet as well as for helping families and individuals realize their dreams. Calls for a new "international financial architecture," which reverberated in the late 1990s, reflect that the international organization of credit is hardly a fine-tuned and well-structured system. Rather it is highly volatile, often spooked by rumors, and given to periodic panics. The market is the main primeval force that determines who gets what and why. While the international credit market is hardly perfect, it is better than any alternatives that have been tried, such as the failed efforts of the Soviet Union's command economy to strategically allocate credit.

This book is a history of credit, spanning several centuries of human endeavor and focusing mainly on Western Europe and the United States. Other great cultures, such as the Chinese and Indians, developed sophisticated economic systems, but none created financial infrastructures capable of giving birth to highly efficient credit systems that are still with us. The approach used is close to financial history, modified by a healthy dose of political science, complemented by social history. A central strand among the major themes of the book is the relationship between the evolution of credit and power—simply stated, who has what and why, or who is a creditor and who a debtor? This book does not seek to provide a comprehensive narrative account of Western civilization. That task has been undertaken much more competently by others.

Six major themes run through the book. First and foremost is the thesis that there is a direct relationship between credit and power. The wealth represented by credit augments political power. Yet for a credit market to work in an efficient manner, it is essential that power provides political stability and the rule of law. The rule of law remains a core necessity, as reflected by the deeply rooted development problems suffered by Russia, Ukraine, and Indonesia in the 1990s.

The second theme is that different kinds of political power promote different kinds of economic behavior.[1] A functioning modern credit system found more fertile soil in the northern Italian city-states, in the cities of the Holland and Flanders, and in England than on the Russian steppes, the Anatolian highlands, or the Balkans. Politics decidedly was a factor as the leadership elites in the former areas regarded economic activity, in particular, trade, important. In the latter regions, local leadership elites were more rooted in agriculture and property-ownership than entrepreneurship and augmentation of one's wealth through commerce. This difference was evident in policies adopted by the various governments as well as who had influence in each political system. It was also evident in the willingness of some leadership elites to surrender or relegate the function of credit to minorities.

The third theme is cultural. Throughout much of the history of credit certain societal groups were able to embrace more readily the workings of credit and its relationship to trade and commerce. This point should be neither overstated nor understated. However, the involvement of such groups as the northern Italians, Jews, Dutch, French Protestants, Scots, English, and Americans cannot be easily dismissed. Why did these societal or cultural groups—sometimes as minorities—rise to the top in providing credit in a particular economy and hence hold some degree of political power or, at least, influence?

A considerable amount of literature, based on the works of Max Weber, Talcott Parsons, Florence Kluckhohn, and George Foster, argues that "progress-prone" societies are rational, ascetic, ethical, universalist, achievement-oriented, activist, future-oriented, and egalitarian. These societies also seek a balance between group and individual interests and observe life as a positive-sum game. In contrast, "progress-resistant" societies are fatalistic, particularistic, ascriptive, passive, individualistic and familistic, past- or present-oriented, and hierarchical. They perceive life as a zero-sum game. According to one study, examples of progress-prone societies include Western Europe, North America, China, Taiwan, Korea, Japan, Hong Kong, Singapore, and East Asian immigrants in the United States, Southeast Asia, Brazil, and elsewhere.[2] It also extends to successful religious or ethnic groups such as Jews, Quakers, Mormons, Armenians, Sikhs, and Jains.

We observe this cultural theme in the treatment of Protestants by Max Weber. In his 1904 book, *The Protestant Ethic and the Spirit of Capitalism*, Weber argued that the break with the Roman Catholic Church during the Reformation encouraged the rise of capitalism by relieving it of its anxieties, its scruples, or, in others, its bad conscience. For Weber, there is a direct link between the early Protestant reformers and the Puritans and the Americans. Evidence of this linkage came in the form of one of the founders of the United States, Benjamin Franklin, who coined such capitalist sayings as, "Remember that time is money...Remember that credit is money...Remember that money is of a prolific generating nature" (*Advice to a Young Tradesman*).

What we can take away from the cultural dimension is that culture does have an impact in shaping both political and economic behavior. In the case of credit, culture is important from the standpoint of how a particular group regarded the idea of usury, the extension of credit, and its use in daily life. For example, was credit to be used to purchase consumer goods or was it for developing a productive enterprise? Taking this one step further, culture helped establish the perceptual lens through which groups like the Jews, Catholics, and Protestants regarded credit as a force to promote development through rationalization, efficiency, and stability.

The fourth theme of the book is that the Western credit system evolved in tandem with the development of the nation-state, in particular with the Netherlands, the United Kingdom, Germany, France and the United States. If in the seventeenth and eighteenth centuries first Holland and then England developed successful credit systems this was due to the legal system they had. Other critical factors that helped stimulate a working credit market were a system of strong public finances (that included a government debt market), a strong complementary position in trade, and a commanding position in capital markets via a stock market, supported by strong banks. To this could be added an open political system, which allowed a degree of creativity to flow freely. Creativity remains a key force in the development of new financial instruments that help give the global credit market depth and sophistication.

The fifth theme is that the historical development of the global credit market is hardly a smooth line. It is rather a history of considerable volatility, with the crash of more than one famous banking house and the dishonor of default shaking many governments, as well as the short memories of investors. Humankind has demonstrated an amazing ability to repeatedly stampede itself into financial crises, starting with Dutch Tulipmania and continuing through the financial crises of the early twenty-first century. The pattern that appears evident is one of credit expansion in a period of economic growth and prosperity, followed by over-extension of both prime borrowers and lenders, then a crisis of confidence and a crash. After the dust settles, there is a gradual rebirth of the credit activity. Indeed, the words of economists Barry Eichengreen and Albert Fishlow in examining Mexico's financial problems in December 1994 and early 1995 strike a chord: "This characterization of the historical record implies, of course, that smooth capital transfers are the norm and disruptions to international financial flows the punctuation marks. The opposite might also be argued: debt-servicing difficulties, the suspension of voluntary lending, and calls for third-party intervention—the constituents of which are called debt crises—are the normal state of affairs."[3]

The sixth and final theme is the spread of credit from being the privilege of the wealthy and the powerful to being available to vast numbers of North Americans, Japanese, and Europeans. The traditional banking families, like the Fuggers, Welsers, and Rothschilds, did not make their fortunes lending to the unwashed masses, and certainly this was true of the initial American creditors, as well. Rather their business was to supply credit to governments, and later to major companies, such as railways, steelmakers, and other heavy industries. It was only in the second and third decades of the twentieth century that this process of spreading credit down through the ranks developed. Following the Second World War it expanded rapidly. It happened through the creation of credit unions, the actions of commercial banks (sometimes pushed by governments), and most significantly through the credit card.

What is Credit?

What then is credit? According to *The Harper Collins Dictionary of Economics*, credit is defined as follows: "Loans and other deferred payment methods made available to consumers and companies to enable them to purchase goods and services, raw materials, and components."[4] In this respect, credit is a form of money, but a deferred type of money and not necessarily in a tangible form, though it is often guaranteed by something, that is, money in the bank, gold, or some tangible good. As James Grant notes of the distinction between money and credit: "The money supply can be counted, and so can the supply of debt. However the potential supply of debt can only be imagined."[5] The actual word "credit" comes from the Latin *credere*, meaning to trust. This trust allows credit to be created and used, while a lack of trust can destroy it. Consequently, credit works because of trust and confidence in the parties involved, which is further related to the concept of a legal or value system that upholds a contract between parties as legal and binding.

The trust or confidence factor cannot be easily dismissed. Francis Fukuyama in his book, *Trust: The Social Virtues and the Creation of Property*, noted, "Thus, economic activity represents a crucial part of social life and is knit together by a wide variety of norms, rules, moral obligations, and other habits that together shape the society...one of the most important lessons we can learn from an examination of economic life is that a nation's well-being, as well as its ability to compete, is conditioned by a single, pervasive cultural characteristic: the level of trust inherent in the society."[6]

In his book, *Golden Fetters: The Gold Standard and the Great Depression 1919-1939*, Barry Eichengreen added two other elements that are important in any economic activity: The stability of the pre-war gold standard "was the result of two factors, credibility and co-operation."[7] The point he makes is that governments of the major industrial countries worked together to make certain that the system of international currency flows remained supported by the gold standard. Eichengreen also stated, "The very credibility of the official commitment to gold meant that this commitment was rarely tested."[8] In our story about credit, the concept of credibility and cooperation play most significant roles.

Related to credit is the concept of leverage. Leverage often refers to power or influence. In the financial sense, leverage refers to "money borrowed to increase the return on invested capital."[9] Stated in another fashion, leverage is when money or credit is borrowed, put to work and provides a profit. For example, a company has $10 million. It wishes to expand and needs more than the $10 million. It goes to a bank and borrows seven times its $10 million, giving it a leverage position of $70 million. Although the money is borrowed and must be paid back at some date, if its application is done well, it allows both repayment and a net gain. Leveraging is an important concept used in modern corporate finance and over time has become an accepted and normal business practice.

To our definition of credit should be added wealth generation. Credit does not come out of thin air nor is it a crop that can be harvested. There must be some form of economic activity, such as trade, that generates a surplus of money. That surplus thus becomes the source of credit to be borrowed. In a sense, credit provides the situation by which surplus money is made available at a cost to people or institutions with a credit deficit. Consequently, the idea of wealth generation is important when thinking about credit.

Our last introductory point about credit is that it has been around for a long time. Indeed, one of the earliest references to credit activities was the Code of Hammurabi. Drawn up by the ancient Babylonian king Hammurabi (1726-1686 B.C.), the code contains about 150 paragraphs dealing with nearly all cases arising from loans, interest, pledges, guarantees, and the presence of evidence.[10] In today's world, credit is a key lubricant of international commerce. Massive amounts of global, regional, and local commerce of goods and services depend on a credit system that supports a "buy now-pay later" mode of operation. Those societies that have easy access to credit prosper and occupy a leading position in the present world. Consequently, those who control it are powerful. How does all this fit into our world at the beginning of the twenty-first century?

Five Periods of Credit

This volume covers the period between the start of recorded history and the twenty-first century. We break down the history of credit into five broad periods. The first period is early pre-modern and is defined by the earliest references to banking and credit arrangements as exemplified by the Code of Hammurabi around 1726 B.C. The pre-modern period continues through the end of the Roman Empire and entails the creation of money and the growing use of credit in trade throughout Europe and parts of the Middle East and Asia. According to the New Testament, Jesus threw the moneylenders out of the Temple. Credit, though used in the Roman economy, was not yet a major force. As Robert S. Lopez notes, "Credit was a will-o'-the-wisp when it was not usurious pawnbrokering; the prudent, conservative spirit of Roman society could hardly conceive wealth otherwise than a tangible collection of fields, houses, cattle, slaves, movable objects or hard cash."[11] It is important to underscore that when the Roman Empire geared up for war and its expenses exceeded its revenues it did not borrow from its citizens, instead it opted for currency debasement and extraordinary taxation.

The second period is that of late pre-modern which begins with the fall of Rome and continues until the eleventh century, when barbarian invasions led to an almost complete breakdown in credit networks in the West. The bright lights of civilization in terms of the organization of international credit came from the Byzantine Empire and the newly established Islamic states in the Middle East and Africa and parts of Asia (China and India) still engaged in transnational trade. For Western Europe, this period ended and the early modern commenced in the late twelfth century when trade stimulated a renewal of international credit in the Italian city-states. These city-states were strategically located between a Europe that was gradually reviving and the Levant, believed to be the source of exotic spices and other goods. During this period trade fairs became key to facilitating trade and stimulating new credit arrangements. The Crusades also played an important role in stimulating commerce and credit, in particular, when looking at the part played by the Knights Templar in facilitating credit. The early modern period stretches from about 1090 to around 1500.

The fourth period is modern, which incorporates the rise of credit in the Low Countries, in particular the cities of Bruges, Antwerp, and Amsterdam in the 1500s, and extends through the rise of London and New York as the major international credit hubs. Through this sweep of four centuries there was a steady push to internationalize credit. Indeed, the term "financial capitalism," as used by Larry Neal in his *The Rise of Financial Capitalism*, describes the rise of a class of capitalists, who derived their power and influence from financial activities, which often included the ownership of industrial pursuits.[12] Although there were efforts to stop this process of internationalizing credit, and periodic violence (such as the First World War) made the regular functioning of international credit networks at times impossible, the overall trend was incorporation of the community of nations into the global economy, urbanization, and technological innovations, all of which helped make credit accessible around the planet to an increasingly larger segment of the population.

A distinguishing point between the modern and preceding periods in the history of credit was a significant shift, beginning with the Dutch and continuing with the British and Americans: for the first time in history there was a convergence of sound public finances, strong positions in trade, and the creation and growth of capital markets. The turn to improved public finances, most notable in England, was essential as it also meant the development of a more professional civil service than had existed prior, essential for record keeping, efficient use of proceeds, and upholding the rule of law. Unlike the Romans before them, the Dutch, but much more so the English and American governments, were willing and able to borrow from their publics. This helped create a foundation for the modern international financial system based on the rule of law. Capital markets that had before lacked depth, began to take on a structured form of existence.

It is also important to underscore the historical continuity between what happened with the development of credit in the Low Countries, in particular Holland, and how that process continued in England and the United States. A number of historians such as Eric Hobsbawm, Fernard Braudel, Violet Barbor, and Immanuel Wallerstein have regarded the Dutch experience as "essentially backward looking, the culmination of something with no future."[13]   Braudel pronounced, "The emergence of Amsterdam prolonged the old pattern; took place, logically enough, according to the old rule," while Hobsbawm cautioned against the temptation "to exaggerate the 'modernity' of the Dutch."[14] We regard the Dutch as formulating an important stage in the evolution of the history of credit. In the great sweep of history, we must agree with Dutch historians Jan de Vries and Ad van der Woude that the Dutch economy was not the last stage of the old European economy, but "the first modern economy," defined by the following features:

- markets, for both commodities and the factors of production (land, labor, and capital), which are reasonably free and pervasive;

- agricultural productivity adequate to support a complex social and occupational structure that allows for a far-reaching division of labor;

- a state which in its policy-making and enforcement is attentive to property rights, to freedom of movement and contract and, at the same time, is not indifferent to the material conditions of the lives of most inhabitants; and

- a level of technology and organization capable of sustained development and of supporting a material culture of sufficient variety to sustain market-oriented consumer behavior.[15]

The creation of the first modern economy was a critical stepping-stone for the emergence of an international credit system. Consequently, the Dutch period is a pivotal in our story.

The fifth and last period is the global one in which the organization of markets has become international. This period begins in the early 1990s and reflects the linkages of almost all points of the map— what impacts one market may send shock waves rippling through others. This was made painfully evident in the Asian contagion of 1997-98, which initially hit Asia and then subsequently rippled outward to savage the economies of Russia, South Africa, and Brazil. The main driving forces in the globalization of credit are advances in technology and financial innovations as well as the relative decline of New York before competitors Tokyo and London. This period also mirrors the deepening democratization of credit in North America, Europe, and parts of Asia.

Our Perceptual Lens

The history of credit must be seen through the following perceptual lens. For the purposes of this book, the capability to govern is defined as having three components—the power of the word, the sword, and the purse. Spokesmen of religious doctrines and political beliefs are often the most powerful forces in shaping the cultural concepts on which political decisions for society are made. The influence of religious leaders in the politics of the Middle East and South Asia (Saudi Arabia, Iran, and Afghanistan) and the influence of leaders expounding nationalist viewpoints can be observed all over the world. In many cases those who propagate popular political theories and values have brought about revolution, much as Robespierre and the Jacobins did with France in the nineteenth century and Adolf Hitler and the Nazis in Germany in the twentieth century. A third example of the power of the word are the followers of new Marxist theories of economics as in the cases of Lenin and Mao Zedong, who radically changed the structure of their societies and governments.

As to the power of the sword, empires of the past have usually been the creation of military leaders, such as Alexander the Great and Genghis Khan. Clearly, in the early Middle Ages military leaders of the tribal peoples of Western Europe laid the foundations for the feudal kingdoms in the latter part of that age. However, to maintain these kingdoms their rulers needed the Church and its power of the word. By the end of the twelfth century, the Church's power was such that the word of the Pope persuaded kings and nobles to place their military forces at the disposal of the Church. Those forces were needed by the Papacy to reconquer the Holy Land after Jerusalem fell to the forces of Muslim Seljuk Turks, who refused the Christian pilgrims access to Palestine. At first it was the religious order of the Knights Templar with its establishments in Europe and the Middle

East, who shaped the financial structure to undertake this crusading enterprise. At about the same time, the merchants of the Italian city-states began to participate in the same enterprise. It was the power of the purse of these merchants that in the following centuries helped elevate them to the ruling elite of the Italian city-states and to become a major force in the politics of the rulers of Europe. The Medicis, in particular, had enormous political influential as they provided credit to the various rulers of Europe, especially France in the latter Middle Ages.

Even now, when the power of credit seems to give some national leaders immense political power internationally, it behooves one to remember that the power of the word and the power of the sword remain as constant companions in shaping the politics of the world. As Karl Polanyi wrote, "Power had precedence over profit. However closely their realms interpenetrated, ultimately it was war that laid down the law to business."[16]

It is also important to clarify one additional factor. Although the book is focused on the history of Western credit, we have also taken into consideration how the Western system became the global credit system. It was Western trade that caused Asians and Africans, however reluctant, to adopt financial institutions and practices based on Western models. Chapter 13 focuses on Asian and other non-Western present-day economic practices and difficulties. Although Islamic and other regional forms of banking existed and still exist, credit institutions in the world today are largely based on Western concepts. This is not to argue that Asians lacked their own financial networks: until the seventeenth century, China[17] had a stable social system ensuring prosperity and well being. China and some other non-Western civilizations were in advance of the Western Europe of that day, but nowhere else did there develop a cash and credit system as sophisticated as that of Europe. Credit culture is Western in origin, although it has spread around the planet. Consequently, we take a page from the eminent British historian J.M. Roberts, who wrote of Europe and its place in history:

> World history, if that is the story to be told, and not the history of some parts of it, has in fact to be understood over the last few centuries in Eurocentric terms. Europe was the original source of the most powerful of the prime movers of world history for most of that time. The history of other parts of the world or other peoples during those same centuries is obviously worthy of study for excellent reasons quite other than its connection with European expansion...and for a little while, European history's impact on the world was much greater than that of Asia, Africa, or the Americas.[18]

In the same sense, we argue that modern credit evolved from a Western, largely European background, hence the thrust of our story. At the same time, we do not seek to dismiss easily the evolution of credit in Asia, Africa, or the Americas until these areas are themselves woven into the growing international system. While the story of credit remains Western-dominated, hubbing around New York and the International Monetary Fund-World Bank in Washington, DC, there are other pulls that could in time change the direction of the story.

Notes

1.   This view has been advanced by the late economist Mancur Olson, most recently in his last book completed before his death in 1998, *Power and Prosperity: Outgrowing Communist and Capitalist Dictatorships* (New York: Basic Books, 2000). For a brief, yet worthwhile view of his ideas, see "Out of Anarchy," *The Economist*, February 19, 2000, p. 79.
2.   Lawrence E. Harrison, *The Pan-American Dream: Do Latin America's Cultural Values Discourage True Partnership with the United States and Canada?* (New York: Basic Books, 1997), p. 33.
3.   Barry Eichengreen and Albert Fishlow, *Contending with Capital Flows: What is Different About the 1990s?* (New York: A Council on Foreign Relations Paper, 1996), p. 1.
4.   C. Pass, B. Lowes, L. Davies, and S.J. Kronish, *The Harper Collins Dictionary of Economics* (New York: Harper Collins, 1991), p. 105. Edward Chancellor provides another definition: "Yet credit, unlike gold, could be created and destroyed. It had no utility and its value depended on an act of belief from which it derived its name (Latin: *credere, creditum*, to believe). Credit was in constant flux, elusive, independent, and uncontrollable...Credit was the Siamese twin of speculation; they were born at the same time and exhibited the same nature; inextricably linked, they could never be separated." *Devil Take the Hindmost: A History of Financial Speculation* (New York: Farrar, Straus and Giroux, 1999), p. 32.
5.   James Grant, *Money of the Mind: Borrowing and Lending in America from the Civil War to Michael Milken* (New York: Farrar, Straus Giroux, 1992), p. 6.
6.   Francis Fukuyama, *Trust: The Social Virtues and the Creation of Prosperity* (New York: Free Press Paperbacks, 1995), p. 7.
7.   Barry Eichengreen, *Golden Fetters: The Gold Standard and the Great Depression, 1919-1939* (New York: Oxford University Press, 1995), p. 5.
8.   Ibid.
9.   Thomas Fitch, *Dictionary of Banking Terms* (New York: Barron's 1997), p. 224.
10.   Roger Orsingher, *Banks of the World* (New York: Walker and Company, 1967), p. viii.
11.   Robert S. Lopez, *The Commercial Revolution of the Middle Ages, 950-1350* (New York: Cambridge University Press, 1976), p. 10.
12.   See Larry Neal, *The Rise of Financial Capitalism: International Capital Markets in the Age of Reason* (Cambridge: Cambridge University Press, 1990).
13.   Jan de Vries and Ad van der Woude, *The First Modern Economy: Success, Failure, and Perseverance of the Dutch Economy, 1500-1815* (New York: Cambridge University Press, 1997), p. 1.

14.   Fernard Braudel, *The Perspective of the World, Vol. 3: Civilization and Capitalism, 15th-18th Century* (New York: Harper & Row, Publishers, 1984), p. 175, and E.J. Hobsbawm, "The Crisis of the 17th Century—II" *Past and Present* 6 (1954): 54.
15.   De Vries and van der Woude, *The First Modern Economy*, p. 693.
16.   Karl Polanyi, *The Great Transformation: The Political and Economic Origins of Our Time* (Boston: Beacon Press, 1957), p. 12.
17.   "Prosperity and well being in China under the Ming Dynasty 1368-1641 was far in front of any contemporary state." Wells, H.G. *The New and Revised Outline of History* (Garden City, NY: Doubleday and Co., 1931), p. 583.
18.   J.M. Roberts, *The Penguin History of Europe* (New York: Penguin Books, 1996), p. 666.

Part 2

Early Pre-Modern Credit Period

2

The Ancient Mediterranean World

When contemplating the exploits of Macedonia's Alexander the Great, Carthage's Hannibal, or Rome's Julius Caesar, the idea of credit does not immediately come to mind. Instead, the image is of conquering armies, heroic adventures, and the rise and fall of empires. Moreover, the intellectual life of Antiquity is dominated by the works of Socrates, Plato, Tacitus, and Livy, not the contemporary equivalents of Bill Gates or Michael Milken. Economic life rotated around labor and those commanding it—be it in the agricultural or military field. Troops and workers were often raised by levy, while during the Roman period taxes were used to pay the troops and run the state, the dominant economic force. Usury existed in a limited form and credit was a pale vapor of what it would later become. As M.I. Finley noted in his *The Ancient Economy*, "There was endless moneylending among both Greeks and Romans, as we have seen, but all lenders were rigidly bound by the actual amount of cash on hand; there was not, in other hands, any machinery for the *creation of credit* through negotiable instruments."[1] Yet, something of a credit system existed, providing a foundation for the development of the modern Western credit system, based on cities, the rule of law, and an ongoing dynamic of change oriented to spreading the uses of credit to an ever-widening swath of humanity.

Egypt and Mesopotamia

What is significant about the ancient world is the transmission of the idea of credit and the complementary ideas of the rule of law and central authority from the cities of Mesopotamia and Egypt to Athens and Rome, which are regarded as the bedrocks of modern Western civilization. In the early chapters of human history ideas about trade, coinage, banking and credit witnessed a genesis from the Fertile Crescent (built around the Tigris and Euphrates rivers) and Egypt to the Syrian coastal cities that gave birth to the Phoenicians and Carthaginians, to Greece and Rome. Although credit was not a major factor in the economies of the ancient world, the idea gradually evolved, crossed borders and ultimately converged with the historical factors in Western Europe. How did credit evolve?

According to *The Oxford Classical Dictionary*, credit was "the temporary transfer of property rights over money or goods," and "was central to the functioning of ancient society."[2] To this was added, "The great majority of credit operations would have been informal transactions between relations, neighbors and friends, marked by the absence of interest, security or written agreement." Burt Edwards notes credit was used in the civilizations of Babylon, Assyria, and Egypt:

> In ancient times there were three main scenarios. First and mainly, some people had a surplus of product and others had a need for it but not the immediate means to pay. Secondly, agricultural economies had seasonal ups and downs, which affected buyers' timing of payments. Thirdly, when goods were conveyed long distances, or into other countries, buyers wanted to see the shipments before paying. A period of trust was inevitable.[3]

Key to the development of the modern concept of credit was trade. Egypt and Mesopotamia, both centered on large rivers, were blessed with adequate water sources and fertile land, which produced an overabundance of grain. The latter region also had a surplus of wool derived from numerous flocks of sheep. As these early societies became settled, with a wealthy and powerful ruling class and large pool of workers, imports became necessary for further development. On the one hand, there were certain staples needed to maintain society. Both Egypt and Mesopotamia lacked timber and a number of metals as well as certain stones, such as marble. Timber was of particular importance for shipbuilding and was essential in completing the construction of temples, palaces, and wealthy estates. On the other hand, the upper class, in its quest to reinforce its stature in society, was usually interested in obtaining that which was rare, beautiful, and different, in short, the luxury import.

The need for imports soon sent keen-minded traders out into the world. These early entrepreneurs came to learn the routes across the desolate Syrian Desert to the Mediterranean coast, through the passes of the Zagros Mountains into Iran and as far north as Lake Van in

Armenia, and in time to China. It is known that the northern Mesopotamian city of Ashur was active in shipping tin, originally obtained in Afghanistan, and woolen textiles to the city of Kanesh, 700 miles away, where the goods were exchanged for other goods and silver. The traders also plied trade routes as far as the Indus River valley in modern day India and down the Red Sea along the African coastline. As Samuel Noah Kramer noted of the early Mesopotamian traders: "They plied the Persian Gulf in boats, reaching far-off India, and crossed the Arabian Sea to trade with Somaliland and Ethiopia in Africa. In exchange for the grain, wool and textiles that made up their loan or cargo they brought back gold, silver, copper and lead, such badly needed timber as cedar and cypress, and luxury items that included ivory, pearls and shells, as well as malachite, carnelian, lapis lazuli, and other semiprecious stones."[4]

While the Mesopotamians traded to their north and south, they also traded with Egypt via Syria. For the Egyptians this trade was significant and it complemented trade down the Red Sea with Punt. Punt, which is thought to be around the Horn of Africa, was a source of myrrh, ebony wood, ivory, cinnamon wood, eye-paint, monkeys, panther skins, and slaves. Additionally, the Egyptian state was the dominant force in developing trade with Nubia, present-day Sudan. Many of the same products were obtained from Nubia as well as gold and elephant tusks.

Considering the development of trade throughout the Middle East and into the Mediterranean in the west and the Indus River region in the east, an intriguing question is how trade was actually conducted. Coinage did not yet exist and the idea of credit was at best rudimentary. There were no banks to rush off to and cash in a traveler's check. In an essay entitled "Marketless Trading in Hammurabi's Time," Karl Polanyi advanced the idea that in the absence of money as a means of exchange there was often a large-scale public storage of staples with the concomitant practice of carrying debt accounts of individuals, and accompanying clearing practices. As he pointed out, "Though money is not used as a means of exchange, it may well be employed as a standard as well as a means of payment, different goods being used for different purposes. Brokerage and auction are then the usual devices for arranging an exchange."[5]

Polanyi's view is partially supported by an Egyptian document arising from a lawsuit shortly after 1300 B.C. The document depicts how a merchant had gone from house to house attempting to sell a

Syrian slave-girl. Finally the wife of an official purchased the slave-girl. The price was agreed in terms of silver, but was paid in various cloths, garments, and bronze vessels, each item being separately valued. The text makes special reference to the bronze vessels that were obtained from neighbors. As Professor H.W.F. Saggs noted, "This suggests that neighbors were accustomed to borrow and lend amongst themselves, keeping a tally of debits and credits, so that when it suddenly became necessary to pay for a purchase made outside the community, the purchaser could call for goods from those with whom he or she had a credit balance."[6] In an actual exchange, therefore, it was not necessary for the standard of value to be physically present or to be a part of the exchange, as long as the commodities involved could be valued in relation to it.[7] On this basis barter and even credit transactions preceded the use of coins.

Location was also a factor. Credit transactions at an early stage gravitated to cities. Civilization in Mesopotamia was based on the city and economic development flowed from that experience. Although Egypt's earlier civilization was more pastoral in nature, Mesopotamia lacked political unity and resembled a patchwork of independent city-states. Between circa 3500-2500 B.C. Mesopotamia and the surrounding regions (Syria, Turkey, Lebanon, Jordan and Israel) were made up of hundreds of independent city-states. From around 2500 B.C. forward some of the dominant city-states sought to establish empires. Nonetheless, most cities kept their individual character. While this did little to foster political unity or stability (as there were many rebellions against imperial authority), cities were to maintain a central role in fostering trade and credit, something that would be evident through later Hellenistic and Roman periods and into modern society.

A second interrelationship of credit transactions and cities was the often close relationship between the merchants and temples. Every city had temples and at an early stage it appears that a strong link developed between religious authorities and merchants. In particular, religious authorities could make income from merchant activities taking place under their roof. In their gratitude, the merchants often gave offerings to the particular god under whose roof they were conducting business. Among the many contributions were large amounts of gold and silver.[8] From the merchant standpoint, temples had many attributes. Although close affiliation with a particular religious organization might limit one's freedom of action, temples, usually located in a central location in major urban areas and usually secure with guards and priests, were hence a safe place to conduct business and leave goods. Often temples for a particular god were found in many cities, providing a safe harbor when one traveled abroad. Because of the linkage to trade, temples often functioned as clearinghouses for trading accounts. At some point, grain and specie were loaned from temples, helping tofacilitate trade and commercial exchanges.

Two other important ideas emerged from the Fertile Crescent and Egyptian civilizations—the rule of law and the rule of central authority, which was usually in the form of a divine ruler, whether king or pharaoh. The two ideas are complementary as the king upheld the rule of law. Stated in another fashion, the law was the king's. As one scholar of the ancient world noted, "…the giving of justice was an essential function of the ruler, whether king or tribal ruler."[9] As mentioned earlier, one of the best-known cases of law was the Code of Hammurabi of Babylonia during the second millennium B.C. As writing emerged with early civilization, beginning in Sumer with the use of simple pictographs on clay tablets sometime before 3000 B.C., it allowed the recording of laws. Altogether King Hammurabi's code contains 300 clauses of law, some of which pertain to credit and debt. This reflects a desire to make credit and debt practices more uniform and part of the system of law, which guided society.

King Hammurabi was not alone in the formulation of laws. Assyrian, Hittite, and Eshnunna laws dealt with an entire range of economic and social concerns, including property rights and transactions, marriage rights, contracts and payment to a builder, and penalties for default of obligations. This was an important development as it established a foundation for the idea of the codification of law for later civilizations, in particular the Greeks and Romans.

One area that the earliest civilizations in the Middle East failed to develop was money, coins in particular. Before the invention of metallic coins a number of other commodities had functioned as standards of value, the most fundamental use of money, and also as media of exchange. Coins greatly simplified commercial transactions and allowed the expansion of the market system to many groups who otherwise would have remained isolated in a closed subsistence economy.[10]

The oldest surviving coins date back to the seventh century B.C. and come from Asia Minor. According to some sources, something similar to money can be found in Mesopotamia, China, and Egypt, but coins were not actually used in an extensive sense until the rise of Lydia in Asia Minor between 640 and 630 B.C. As Jack Weatherford wrote in his history of money, "The genius of the Lydian kings can be seen in their recognition of the need for very small and easily transported ingots worth no more than a few days' labor or a small part of a farmer's harvest. By making these small ingots in a standardized size and weight, and by stamping on them an emblem that verified their worth to even the illiterate, the kings of Lydia exponentially expanded the possibilities of commercial enterprise."[11] It is also important to stress that there was a certain level of trust that the coins, first made of electrum (a natural alloy of gold and silver found in the alluvial valleys of Anatolia), had real value. As a standardized medium of exchange, there was trust that the coins had value, backed by the authority of the kingdom. During 547-546 B.C., Lydia's King Croesus launched a bloody and unsuccessful campaign to conquer the Persian Empire. Despite Croesus' execution by the Persian king Cyrus the Great, by being forced to swallow molten gold, the idea of coins caught on and were soon part and parcel of the Greek and Roman economies.

With coins adopted and a money economy created, changes came about in the whole structure of society as it affects and subjugates all institutions of the social system to new relationships. As Alpha Behn, a seventeenth-century dramatist who spent part of her younger years in Suriname, where she could observe tribes untouched by a money culture, wrote in her play, *The River*, in 1677: "Money speaks sense in a language all nations understand."[12] When coins became part and parcel of the economy of ancient Greece they set into motion a new basis for social structure where the power of the state was based on economic and not military power. This became particularly important as the dynamic of history changed from Persia to the Greek city-states. As Weatherford noted, "The great struggle between the market cities of Greece and the empire of Persia represented a clash between the old and new systems of creating wealth. It represented a clash between the market system based on democratic principles and a tributary system based on autocratic power, and it was a clash that has erupted repeatedly in history right up to the modern day."[13]

The Greeks and Credit

The Greeks emerged as great traders in the Mediterranean, having outposts and colonies from the Black Sea to modern France. There are historical records on the use of credit in Athens during the fourth century B.C., suggesting that sources of credit extended beyond family and friends to encompass professional moneylenders, bankers, and usurers. At that time, there was a multiple of currencies, and trade between city-states in the region was important. Coins provided the means for lending, and trade created a constant need for money changing. Throughout much of the Greek world temples often took deposits and lent money.[14] The temples provided a convenient place of exchange, considering that almost all Greek towns had them and that they were often centrally located and close to the market. It is important to add that temples were usually part of the state governmental structure and, with only the exception of certain national religious shrines, they exercised limited freedom.[15] Consequently, it could be argued that the state (as it stood) was supportive of having a credit system functioning under its wing.

It is important to emphasize that the money lent came from the temple's own funds. Deposits were left untouched in the lending business. Also plying their trade were moneylenders who lent from their own resources and specialized in short-term loans of small sums of coins.

Another group involved with pre-modern credit operations in Athens were the "bankers." Banking in the Greek world appears to have evolved out of professional money changing, which was closely linked to trade. Indeed, the word *trapeziles* or banker refers to the *trapeza* or the changer's table. The Athenian banker was known to receive money on deposit and lend it to merchants at interest rates that varied from 12 to 30 percent according to the risk.[16] In Athens, during the fourth century B.C., the names of some twenty bankers are known.[17] Although bankers existed, there was no integrated banking system or system of credit. That would take a long time to develop. Bankers who plied their trade did so limited to the confines of their city-state.

We also know that banking and moneylending services were not always appreciated in ancient Greece. Plato, the famous Greek philosopher, articulated his hostility towards the establishment of formal credit agreements as they implied a lack of trust. His pupil,

Aristotle (384-322 B.C.), was to comment, "Of the two sorts of money-making one, as I have just said, is part of household management, the other is retail trade: the former is necessary and honorable, the latter a kind of exchange which is justly censured; for it is unnatural, and a mode by which men gain from one another. The most hated sort, and with the greatest reason, is usury, which makes a gain out of money itself, and not from the natural use of it."[18] Plato and Aristotle would hardly be alone in the sweep of history in their antipathy of those involved in credit and money.

Credit instruments were also in evidence in Ptolemaic Egypt. Surviving papyri indicate that a system of bills of exchange was in use. Bills of exchange, which are still in use as a standard credit instrument, are payment orders written by one person to another, directing the latter to pay a certain amount of money at a future date to a third party. Ptolemaic Egypt had a range of banking institutions and a network of royal or state banks.

What was significant about the use of credit and banking in Greece (and Ptolemaic Egypt) was the continuity of the basic ideas. From the earliest civilizations the idea of credit was transmuted to the Greeks and then to the Romans. As historian Will Durant noted of the Greek bankers: "He takes his methods from the Near East, improves them, and passes them on to Rome, which hands them down to modern Europe."[19]

Rome

Credit became more institutionalized during the Roman Empire. At its high point in the first and second centuries A.D., the Roman Empire held sway over most of Western Europe, the Mediterranean basin, and much of the Middle East. The empire extended from the Black Sea and the Euphrates to the Atlantic coast of Europe and ancient Britain. At the beginning of the Christian era the entire population was between 50-60 million, much of it in rural areas, surrounding five to six swollen administrative capitals of which Rome was the main star.[20] The Roman peace meant a reduction in piracy, the construction of roads and ports linking the far-flung parts of the empire, and the standardization of law. The Roman legal system, in particular, provided for strict enforcement of contracts and property rights and prompt (and usually equitable) settlement of disputes.[21] Old barriers to trade were removed and the empire traded under one political and administrative system. In essence, *Pax Romana* functioned as an extensive (albeit rudimentary) free trade zone, which expanded Mediterranean trade to unprecedented levels. Roman rule meant that goods could be moved from the Levant to Rome or from Rome to London without concern for pirates or other disruptions. Moreover, the Roman Empire at its peak provided for one currency, which helped facilitate trade. Even the barbarian peoples surrounding the Roman Empire found coinage useful as is reflected by the experience of the Celts, who, for a long period, occupied the lands north of the Roman Empire from the Balkans to Gaul. With law more formalized and predictable, a Roman credit system functioned, though it was to remain relatively rudimentary, especially in the area of private sector finance and there would be no development of major capital markets.

As there was a fair amount of trade, the Romans needed and had a credit system based on trust in the rule of the law that allowed obligations to be made between parties at one part of the empire with parties at the other end. There was a rudimentary system in place that was structured around banking interests. Usury was a part of daily life. Bank accounts existed during the republic and early empire, though they are not evident in the late Empire.[22] Moreover, there was some degree of specialization from the first century B.C. on. Moneylending was the domain of the *nummularii* and credit facilities were offered to those purchasing goods at auction by the *coactores argentarii*. The *argentarii* handled changing, deposit, and credit functions.

Generally speaking, involvement in credit was not held in high regard and the upper end of Roman society was not drawn to these activities. The situation was probably not helped by the large number of foreigners, namely Greeks and Syrians, involved in credit. In fact, in Gaul (modern France), the words for Syrian and banker were synonyms.[23] Moreover, the clients of the *nummularii, argentarii,* and *coactores argentarii* did not include the Roman elite, who usually had their own safe deposits and sources of credit (much of it derived from wealth in land). As historian Robert Lopez stated, "Credit, at any rate, played a modest role in the Roman economy. Lending money at interest was not illegal, but was regarded as still more despicable than engaging in trade; for, as the philosophers taught, money is not consumed by the user and unlike trees, does not bear fruit."[24]

Roman achievements were mainly in the military and administrative spheres, with the economic dimension somewhat lagging as reflected by the agricultural sector, which operated at mostly close to self-sufficiency levels.[25] This was mirrored in Roman society, which consisted of an immense and impoverished peasantry and a relatively small wealthy urban class engaged in a variety of business activities, including estate management and trade. The Roman government relied heavily upon taxes to raise revenues. There was no national debt or trade in Roman Empire bonds. In the late empire (fourth century) the costs of the defense of Rome against barbarian invaders mounted considerably, which resulted in heavier taxation. Lactantius, a Roman historian, observed cynically that the number of men who were supported by the taxes was larger than the number of those who paid them.[26]

One major problem for the Roman economy was a low level of industrial productivity, which was related to the use of credit, and was due to inadequate mechanization. While machines of various types were invented and were used in ambitious projects, such as public buildings, hydraulic works, and highway construction, their widespread application was limited because of a lack of capital. The problem was in large part attitudinal. As Lopez depicts, "All this, however, required capital, and capital was in the hands of landowners who had no mind for industry (or, at most, drafted their slaves and tenants to make bricks, tools, and other agricultural implements for their own large estates); of merchants who could spare little beyond their investment in commerce proper; and of a government whose economic goals went no further than insuring stability, peace and bread for all."[27]

Another problem for the development of a more broader-gauged credit system was the ongoing problem of the debasement of coins. The Romans were often hard-pressed to maintain sizeable armies in the field. One option to remedy this, of course, was taxation. Taxation was frequently resorted to as a means of raising cash for the state. The other option was to cheat on the currency. The Roman state, especially in the latter stages of the empire, frequently debased currency, hoping to make gains through providing cheaper currency while seeking to maintain the same prices. This undermined the idea of trust, essential to credit.

Out of the ancient world, the Romans emerged with a rudimentary credit system based on trust in the rule of law that allowed obligations to be made between parties at one end of the empire with parties at the other end. The Romans, like the Greeks before them, also made use of money, which provided a fluid medium for trade and helped advance new ideas in the realm of finance—people began to borrow to buy and speculation began to emerge. Moreover, in the fourth century corporations were created to assist the state to raise revenues. Although shares of these companies were traded in a market in Rome, the economy was increasingly dominated by the state and promotion of a private-sector-led credit system was not a priority.[28] Private-sector financial markets remained somewhat underdeveloped and it would be for future merchants to develop a more sophisticated system.

Conclusion

The contribution of the pre-modern period of credit development was the creation and spread of ideas pertaining to credit and the following—trade, coins, and other mediums of exchange, the rule of law and central authority. Although the ensuing fall of the Roman Empire and the Dark Ages would follow, the fundamental ideas necessary for a revolution in the use of credit were already evident.

Notes

1. M.I. Finley, *The Ancient Economy* (Berkeley and Los Angeles: University of California Press, 1973), p. 141.
2. Simon Hornblower and Anthony Spawforth, editors, *The Oxford Classical Dictionary* (New York: Oxford University Press, 1996), p. 407.
3. Burt Edwards, "The History and Future of Credit," in Burt Edwards, ed., *Credit Management Handbook* (Aldershot, U.K.: Gower Publishing Company Limited, 1997), p. 5.
4. Samuel Noah Kramer, *Cradle of Civilization* (New York: Time Inc., 1967), p. 85.
5. Karl Polanyi, "Marketless Trading in Hammurabi's Time," in Karl Polanyi, Conrad M. Arensberg and Harry W. Pearson, eds., *Trade and Markets in Early Empires: Economies in History and Theory* (New York: The Free Press, 1957), p. 14.
6. H.W.F. Saggs, *Civilization Before Greece and Rome* (New Haven, CT: Yale University Press, 1989), p. 138.
7. Rondo Cameron, *A Concise Economic History of the World: From Paleolithic Times to the Present* (New York: Oxford University Press, 1997), p. 35.
8. Robert Sobol, *The Pursuit of Wealth: The Incredible Story of Money Throughout the Ages* (New York: McGraw Hill, 2000), p. 8.
9. Saggs, *Civilization Before Greece and Rome*, p. 156.
10. Cameron, *A Concise Economic History of the World*, p. 35.
11. Jack Weatherford, *The History of Money* (New York: Three Rivers Press, 1997) pp. 30-31.
12. Ibid., p. 11.
13. Ibid., p. 34.
14. Hornblower and Spawforth, *The Oxford Classical Dictionary*, p. 232.
15. Sobel, *The Pursuit of Wealth*, p. 11.

16. Will Durant, *The Life of Greece* (New York: Simon and Schuster, 1939), p. 274.
17. Hornblower and Spawforth, *The Oxford Classical Dictionary*, p. 407.
18. Quoted in Jackson, *The Oxford Book of Money*, p. 244.
19. Durant, *The Life of Greece*, p. 274.
20. Finley, *The Ancient Economy*, p. 30.
21. Cameron, *A Concise Economic History of the World*, p. 37.
22. Paul Veyne, *The Roman Empire* (Cambridge, MA: The Belknap Press of the Harvard University Press, 1997), p. 147.
23. Will Durant, *Caesar and Christ: A History of Roman Civilization and of Christianity from Their Beginnings to A.D. 325* (New York: Simon and Schuster, 1944), p. 320.
24. Robert S. Lopez, *The Commercial Revolution of the Middle Ages, 950-1350* (New York: Cambridge University Press, 1976), p. 10.
25. Jonathan Barron Baskin and Paul J. Miranti, Jr., *A History of Corporate Finance* (New York: Cambridge University Press, 1997), p. 320.
26. J.P.V.D. Balsdon, *Rome: The Story of a Empire* (New York: McGraw-Hill Book Company, 1970), p. 225.
27. Lopez, *The Commercial Revolution of the Middle Ages*, p. 9.
28. Tenney Frank, *An Economic History of Rome* (Baltimore, MD: Johns Hopkins University Press, 1927), p. 194.

3

Byzantine Christians and Muslims

In the aftermath of the fall of the Roman Empire, Visigoths, Vandals, Franks, and many other peoples swarming across the old imperial frontiers, overran Western Europe. Although the Roman Empire lived on in the east in the form of the Byzantine Empire until it was extinguished in 1453 by the Ottoman Turks, most of the Roman Empire in the West had crumbled a thousand years earlier. In A.D. 376 the Goths crossed the Danube; in 406 the Vandals and Suevi crossed the Rhine. In 410 the Visigoths sacked Rome and in 455 the Vandals sacked Rome again. In 476 the last western Roman emperor, Romulus Augustulus, was deposed. It was at the end of the fifth century that the Franks established themselves on the lower Rhine and by the eighth century had occupied most of present-day France, forming the Frankish Merovingian kingdom. While the Byzantine Empire struggled on in the east, the old Roman world was further shattered by the Arab conquests of the seventh and eighth centuries that swept through the Middle East and North Africa and into Spain. Finally, in 732 Frankish forces routed the Muslim invader from Spain at Poitiers, France, thus ending their threat. From then until the coming of the Seljuks two hundred years later, there was a certain amount of economic understanding between Christians and Muslims.

By now the basis for a Christian (namely Catholic) Western Europe had been established, as had been an Islamic Middle East and North Africa, as well as an Orthodox Christian Europe under the Byzantine Empire in the Balkans and Asia Minor. However, the history of credit in Western Europe entered a bleak period, leaving the continuity of credit systems in the hands of Byzantine Christians and Muslims. This point will be discussed in this chapter, and the Jewish contribution in the following chapter.

Darkness in the West

In Western Europe, considering the upheaval in the world and the breakdown in the rule of law, concerns about personal safety encouraged the rise of the mutually supportive feudal and manorial systems, first noticeable in the sixth century in the Frankish Merovingian kingdom. Simply stated, life became a matter of survival and the concept of existence beyond the confines of the local village or urban center diminished considerably. As this system spread through much of Western Europe, its economic mode was largely agricultural, with estates headed by nobles who were basically military men. In return to pledging loyalty to a monarch, these nobles were granted suzerainty over their territories. For that granting of suzerainty, the nobles were obligated to raise soldiers for the monarch during war. Although the nobility was sustained by the output of serfs, the surpluses were minimal and broader markets were lacking. Consequently, from the fifth to the eleventh century practically no major financial mechanisms existed to facilitate the transformation of savings into investment.[1]

Some trade existed in the Mediterranean among North African, Jewish, and Greek merchants, who placed considerable emphasis on reputation in their conduct of trade. However, in Catholic Europe these examples of trade and credit were hardly in existence and often were held hostage to political and social upheaval, and of course, they lagged well behind the more developed Byzantine and Islamic worlds of the times.[2]

Byzantine Christians

The Byzantine Empire was decidedly the bright light for Christendom during the darkest days of the Middle Ages.[3] While Western European cities were depopulated and economic life stagnated, Constantinople entertained a sophisticated and intricate court life. Byzantine armies held sway over a large area of the Balkans, Spain, Asia Minor, much of Anatolia and Armenia and for brief periods Egypt, parts of North Africa, and a sizeable part of Italy. Founded in A.D. 330 by Constantine the Great, Constantinople and its empire also functioned as a long-standing shield against encroaching Islamic invaders and was an important trade partner. In fact, one group of traders who maintained some ties to the West, mainly along the Mediterranean coast, was Byzantine merchants (also referred to as Greeks), whose fortunes were often reflected in the ups and downs of imperial armies. The Byzantine Empire also had a community of Jews, who were active in long-distance trading, more of which will be discussed in the next chapter.

Despite the grandeur of Constantinople, Byzantium's contribution to the history of credit was meager. Clearly, the empire of the east was an extension of the late Roman Empire and as such, its ruling classes held many of the same attitudes about money lending and credit. As Lopez noted, "Her basic economic assets and liabilities also bore a Roman stamp: on the active side of the balance, a skillful agriculture of the intensive Mediterranean type, a diversified industry, an active commerce based on cash and to a smaller amount credit, a good number of accessible towns; on the passive side, high taxation, little mechanization, and deep-rooted biases against nonagricultural pursuits."[4] Indeed, there was a preference to use taxation to raise money for the state. The result was that while what was preserved of the ancient economic organization was sufficient to keep the Byzantine Empire economically well ahead of the Catholic West until the tenth century, it was not enough to provide the critical catalyst of change that more efficient use of credit was able to provide. In a sense, this left the Byzantine Empire in an economic straitjacket, which became progressively tighter as foreign powers encroached and chipped away rich agricultural lands necessary for the functioning of the ancient Roman economy. Chief among those chipping away at the Byzantine Empire were its ultimate historical heirs, the Turks, a central Asian people converted to Islam.

The Islamic World

The Islamic world was also initially more advanced in terms of commerce and finance compared to Western Europe during much of the Middle Ages. Beginning in the seventh century, Arab conquests brought a sea of change in terms of economic and political life in the Middle East. In 630 Muhammad captured Mecca, while his followers were to go on and capture Jerusalem in 638 from the Byzantines. The Sassanian Empire (that held sway in Persia) was obliterated and its longtime foe, the Byzantine Empire, was driven back. As Islamic historian Ira M. Lapidus stated, "By the unification

of the former Sassanian and Byzantine parts of the Middle East into
one polity, political and strategic barriers to trade were removed,
and the foundations for a major commercial revival were laid."[5] The
new Islamic empire did not stop after storming into Persia and Syria
and Egypt. North Africa was conquered between 643 and 711, while
Spain was overrun between 711 and 759. Arab armies even pushed
into Central Asia, taking Bukhara in 712 and Samarkand in 713.

The Islamic conquests established a virtual free-trade zone throughout much of the Mediterranean and into Western Asia. This was of
critical importance to the new imperial elite, who were keenly aware
of the advantages of trade and looked upon commerce in a favorable light. New cities arose out of the nuclei of Arab garrisons, which
helped stimulate the flow of trade and a new cosmopolitan culture.
Moreover, old routes that had fallen into disuse were now reopened.
Consequently, trade along the Silk Road through Central Asia increased as the Arabs and Chinese (under the T'ang [618-907] and
Sung dynasties [960-1280]) pacified the area, and there was an in-
tensification of maritime trade across the Indian Ocean, in particular
with South Asia and East Africa.[6] At the same time, the renewed
unity of the Mediterranean under *Pax Islamica* was somewhat reminis-
cent of its ancient unity under *Pax Romana* of the first and second
centuries.

Most importantly, the new Arab elite was also willing to let non-
Muslim and non-Arab merchants prosper within the empire. This
meant that Jews, such as the highly successful Radhaniya merchants
(financed by Jewish bankers in Baghdad during the ninth and tenth
centuries), Nestorian and Coptic Christians, and Persians were allowed to maintain their ancient cultural and trade networks within
the confines of an integrated imperial system.[7] As one authority on
Indian Ocean trade indicated, "The great age of Middle Eastern
merchants and sailors had begun. Arab, Persian, Christian and Jewish merchants from the Middle East now traveled to the farthest
reaches of the Indian Ocean."[8]

Revival in the commercial fortunes of the Islamic world required
credit. In fact, the Arab world in medieval times developed its own
system of credit that did not lack in sophistication. The records of
the Cairo Geniza indicate that by the eleventh century, credit operations constituted an integral element of Mediterranean and Indian
Ocean commerce. Moreover, on the basis of non-documentary Muslim sources it has been suggested that as early as the late eighth

century, credit arrangements of various types were an important element of both trade and industry in the Middle East.[9] Prior to Islam's explosion out of the Arabian Peninsula, the use of two coinages, gold in the Byzantine Empire and silver in the Sassanid Empire, provided a basis of trade and credit.[10] After the Arabs swept out of their desert lands, they carried Islam and some form of political stability across North Africa and into Spain in one direction and to Indonesia and the borders of China and India in the other direction. Arabic became the universal language and Islam the ideological glue to a new world drawn closer together. All of this provided a foundation for interregional trade that made considerable use of the Indian Ocean as a major route of commerce, while Central Asia under the Mongols revived the silk routes. As historian Bernard Lewis noted, "With a degree of physical as well as social and intellectual mobility unparalleled in ancient and medieval times, the Islamic World developed a far-flung network of communications by both land and water."[11]

Trade became an important part of the Islamic world. Considering the long distances involved, there emerged a pressing need for credit. Merchants in one city might have agents in another, and though organized banks in the modern sense did not exist, the drawing of bills was used. Another method used was the *mudaraba* arrangement under which an investor entrusted goods or capital to someone who used them for trade and then returned to the investor his capital together with an agreed share of the profits.[12]

Credit played an important role in the Islamic world, despite the Koran's specific prohibition against usury: "God has permitted buying and selling and forbidden usury...those who [after warning] revert to usury are doomed to everlasting hellfire..." Not exactly a ringing endorsement to charge interest! In fact, this prohibition was absolute, meaning that straightforward interest-bearing cash loans, speculative transactions, and certain forms of delayed payment were beyond the pale of Islamic law. Yet, like the Christians and Jews who were also opposed to usury, ways were found to respect the law and provide credit. As Abraham L. Udovitch stated, "Various legal fictions, based primarily on the model of the 'double-scale' were, if not enthusiastically endorsed by the religious lawyers, at least not declared invalid. Furthermore, the urban populations of the medieval Islamic world included commercially active Christian and Jewish minorities. While Christians and Jews may have been inhibited from conducting usurious practices within their own religious communities, no such constraints affected their economic contacts with each other or with commercial colleagues from the dominant Muslim communities."[13] Consequently, the Arab world was able to organize credit, investment, partnerships, and banking, which meant that in the high Middle Ages, it was much more advanced in finance than Europe. The Islamic world, however, was unable to maintain its more advanced standing. By the late Middle Ages, it was in decline, its once finely tuned international credit network disrupted.

The decline in the Islamic world's credit system was due to a number of factors. One was a decline in Arab power. Arab power probably crested in 732 when Charles Martel defeated the Moors at Poitiers. At that stage, the Arab world stretched from Central Asia to Spain. By the time of Caliph Haroun-al-Raschid's death in 809, Arab unity was a thing of the past and it was to be around two hundred years before the forces of Islam were to rally under first the Seljuk Turks and later the Ottoman Turks.

When the Islamic world was under "Arab" control commerce bloomed and merchants were influential in the governing process. When this Arab world of the Caliphate weakened it was conquered by the Seljuk Turks—good fighters, but not traders. The Arab decline was the result of a number of reasons, including infighting, corruption, and a series of external threats, such as the Mongols and Seljuk Turks. These forces combined to sap the vigor of the Arab Islamic world and leave it in a state of dissolution and weakness, ripe for the assault of a revitalized Christian Western Europe in the forms of the First Crusade in 1096, the reconquest of Spain, and Italian military raids against North Africa.

Equally significant in the decline in the Islamic world's credit system was the increasing domination of the state by military aristocracies (such as the Seljuks) that had little interest in commerce and production. This was certainly the case of Seljuk Turks, who came from Central Asia, conquered Persia, captured Baghdad in 1050, and in 1071 routed a large Byzantine army and captured the Byzantine emperor. The power of the sword was very much the dominant force, especially as it was supported by the power of the word—to fight against the nonbelievers was righteous. Trading with the Seljuks was not so good. This led to a decline in Middle Eastern agriculture and industry, which, in turn, meant that the region was unable to provide an exportable surplus of commodities essential to maintain a strong position in trade that helped generate surplus credit. At the same time, Middle Eastern traders were forced increasingly to rely upon transit trade between Europe and the Far East. As Lewis noted, "Meanwhile, technological, financial and commercial advances in Western Europe provided Western traders with the means, the resources and skills to dominate Middle Eastern markets, to which access was, if anything, facilitated by the unity and stability of the Ottoman Empire. Ottoman armies ruled the land, and Ottoman fleets for a while dominated the seas; but the European merchant, quietly and peacefully, captured the markets."[14]

Another factor was the exhaustion or loss to invaders of mines and precious metals in the Sudan and sub-Saharan Africa, a situation that left the Islamic states short of money at a time when their European competitors were discovering new sources of gold and silver in the Americas. The vigor of commerce and credit in the Islamic states was also sapped by the Black Death and a series of highly destructive invasions, including those of the Mongols in the East and the Hilali Bedouin in North Africa.[15] The combination of these forces was to have a profound historical impact—at a time when the Christian West was slowly beginning to put the pieces into place for a transnational credit system that would continue to advance through innovations in methods and institutions, the Islamic world was increasingly coming under the weight of the power of the sword and the word, while that of the purse was relegated to a distant and increasingly ineffectual (at least in globally competitive terms) third place. What this meant was that there was no build up of a legal system to help the merchant class in its range of activities, including credit transactions.

One last point must be made regarding the Islamic credit system and its decline. In the eighth, ninth, and tenth centuries, the Arab Muslims and Christians could work together in Palestine. Despite the initial conquest by the sword, the Arabs did have a penchant for trade and were relatively tolerant of other religious groups. In this environment a credit system could function. This situation changed with the invasion of most of Asia Minor by the Seljuk Turks in the 1070s. The Seljuks were primarily soldiers and more fundamentalist in their views of Islam and were not content to maintain peaceful coexistence with the Christians. As one observer said of the Seljuks, "They caused a great revival of vigour in Islam, and they turned the minds of the Moslem world once more in the direction of a religious war against Christiandom."[16] The more fanatical struggle between Islam and Christianity that escalated in the eleventh century was to be a critical factor in the development of a modern credit system in Western Europe.

Conclusion

Despite the sometimes-popular perception that the fall of the Roman Empire was followed by a complete halt in civilization in Europe for the next several centuries, the reality of it is different. Western Europe did falter and its political and economic development was retarded by the advent of feudalism, a system not oriented to capitalism. Yet, for all the clamor over the Dark Ages, the concept of credit was maintained by Byzantine Christians and Muslims. Although there were no great advances in the practice of credit, the essential thing is that trade continued and the need for formal arrangements of commerce remained. Western Europe's institutions were incapable of providing the basic level of trust for a stable credit system. This state of affairs would begin to change in the eleventh and twelfth centuries, during which time the momentum in political and economic power slowly shifted from the eastern Mediterranean to Italy and then northward. However, within the West some degree of knowledge about credit survived in the hands of the Jews, who are the subject of our next chapter.

Notes

1.   Carlo M. Cipolla, *Before the Industrial Revolution: European Society and Economy, 1000-1700* (New York: W. W. Norton & Company, 1976), p. 183.
2.   Some variety of credit arrangements were known and practiced in the medieval Islamic world. It was the main force in the development of the robust regional and international trade of the Middle East. See A.L. Udovitch, "Banking Islamic," in *The Dictionary of the Middle Ages, Volume 2* (New York: Charles Scribner's Sons, 1983), p. 79.
3.   As historian Peter Brown noted, "Even on the distant shores of the western Mediterranean, Byzantine outposts in the West were like mirrors, casting the light of the eastern Mediterranean far into the darkness of early medieval northern Europe. Isolated and grandiloquent, the kingdom of Visigothic Spain nevertheless moved to the rhythms of Byzantine life: its rulers eyed the eastern empire closely as a model and as a potential menace. In northern Europe, every great church was hung with Byzantine silks; liturgical books were written Byzantine papyrus; relics were cased in Bzyantine silverwork..." Peter Brown, *The World of Late Antiquity, A.D. 150-750* (New York: W. W. Norton & Company, 1989), p. 158.

4. Robert S. Lopez, *The Commercial Revolution of the Middle Ages*, 950-1350 (New York: Cambridge University Press, 1976), p. 23.

5. Ira M. Lapidus, *A History of Islamic Societies* (Cambridge: Cambridge University Press, 1991), pp. 45-46. He was also to clarify that the benefits of such a change in the Middle East were not generally beneficial. "Thus, the net effect of the Arab conquests and empire was prosperity in Iran, a redistribution of the pattern of development in Iraq, and the economic decline of Mesopotamia and Egypt," p. 48.

6. Kenneth McPherson, *The Indian Ocean: A History of People and The Sea* (Delhi: Oxford University Press, 1995), p. 97. Also see K.N. Chaudhuri, *Trade and Civilization in the Indian Ocean: An Economic History from the Rise of Islam to 1750* (Cambridge, UK: Cambridge University Press, 1985).

7. Ibid., p. 96.

8. Ibid.

9. Abraham Udovitch, "Bankers without Banks: Commerce, Banking, and Society in the Islamic World of the Middle Ages," in Center for Medieval and Renaissance Studies, *The Dawn of Modern Banking* (New Haven, CT: Yale University Press, 1979), p. 261.

10. According to Bernard Lewis, "The need to conduct large-scale trade over vast areas produced a class of money-changers, functioning in almost every major commercial centre, and ultimately to the development of a ramified and sophisticated system of banking." In *The Middle East: A Brief History of the Last 2,000 Years* (New York: Scribner, 1995), p. 172.

11. Ibid., p. 173.

12. Albert Hourani, *A History of the Arab Peoples* (New York: Warner Books, 1991), p. 112.

13. Udovitch, "Bankers without Banks," *The Dawn of Modern Banking*, p. 258. Hourani also noted, "Jews of the Muslim cities also played an important part in long-distance trade with the ports of the Mediterranean Europe and, until Mamluk times, with those of the Indian Ocean. Among the crafts, those concerned with drugs and with gold and silver tended to be in the hands of Jews or Christians, working for themselves or for Muslims." Hourani, *A History of the Arab Peoples*, p. 118.

14. Lewis, *The Middle East*, p. 178.

15. As Peter Mansfield noted of the Mongols, "In the beginning of the thirteenth century, the Muslim world had to face a new and terrifying threat: the Mongols. Like the nomadic Turkish tribes before them, the Mongols burst out of central Asia into the rich lands of the Fertile Crescent. In 1220 Genghis Khan seized Persia; in 1243 his successors routed the entire Seljuk army and went on to occupy the sultanate of Rum. In 1258 Genghis Khan's grandson Hulagu captured Baghdad and eliminated the last ghostly relic of the Abbasid caliphate, as his armies completed the destruction of the great irrigation works of Mesopotamia." *A History of the Middle East* (New York: Viking, 1991), p. 22.

16. H.G. Wells, *Outline of History* (Garden City, NY: Garden City Publishing Co., 1931), p. 628.

4

The Jewish Bridge

While credit mechanisms survived and found ready use in the Islamic world in the early and mid-Middle Ages, Western Europe lost the political and economic integration that had developed under the Romans. The fall of the Roman Empire created a massive disruption in trade, and the rudimentary credit system that had existed largely folded. Central authority vanished and took many years to be reestablished with a completely different cast of characters. What trade that did exist in Western Europe in the early Middle Ages was tenuous and usually came in the form of itinerant Jewish, Syrian, or Greek merchants. The Jews, in fact, prospered in early medieval Europe because of their positions as merchants and moneylenders in an agrarian society. Spread throughout the former Western Roman Empire as well as throughout the new Islamic world, the Jews functioned as a bridge between the credit systems of the ancient world and the development of a modern credit system in the West. While their contribution should not be overstated, it cannot be ignored. The flow of ideas about credit and trade, the rules of law and central authority are all at play with the Jews and the significant role they played during the early and mid-Middle Ages.

The Diaspora and Islam

During the second half of the first century A.D., unsuccessful rebellions against the Romans had resulted in the destruction of the Jewish Temple in Palestine and the accelerated development of larger communities outside the homeland, in what is described as the Diaspora. Jews had long existed outside of Palestine, as evidenced by the Babylonian Exile and the captivity in Egypt. The reasons for the Diaspora are many: overpopulation in Judea in the early Seleucid period moved migrants to other parts of Israel and Egypt (in particular Alexandria); new waves of migration from those communities went to Asia Minor and Cyrenaica (modern-day Libya); and forced waves of migration caused by religious persecutions preceding the Hasmonean Revolt in Judea (167-164 B.C.) and the destruction of the Jerusalem Temple in A.D. 70 by the Romans. By the last days of the Roman Empire, Jewish settlement was spread throughout the Mediterranean, the Middle East, and possibly as far as the Malabar and Coromondel coasts of India. In Western Europe their settlement was sparse, concentrated along a line leading roughly from Barcelona to Narbonne and Marseilles, in addition to communities in Italy.

Despite the great disruptions associated with the end of the Roman Empire in the west and the eventual Islamic invasions in the Middle East and North Africa, the Jews were able to maintain their overseas links, which made them an important middleman community between Christians and Muslim lands. Although the Diaspora left large numbers of Jews outside of their traditional homeland, it also established an international network conducive to trade and credit operations. When commercial activity picked up between the ninth and eleventh centuries it was the Jewish merchants in European towns who conducted regional and international trade in such commodities as cloth, grain, salt, slaves, and wine. As one historian noted, "They enjoyed the great advantage of commercial contacts with Jewish communities in Islamic and Byzantine cities, and shared with these communities a familiarity with accounting techniques, commercial contracts, and other business methods otherwise unknown in the West."[1]

Equally significant, the Islamic invasions brought new opportunities for the Jews. As the Arabs formed new urban centers and established new seats of central authority, Jews clustered around such places as Basra in Iraq and Malaga and Seville in Spain and found employment in the newly formed Arab courts. Indeed, the position of the Jews in Muslim Spain until the end of the eleventh century was more favorable than in any other part of Western Europe, with Arab princes virtually accepting them as equals.[2]

In the Islamic world, the Jews made a significant shift from being a predominantly rural and agricultural people to becoming urban dwellers. This was due to the new Islamic world imposed by the Arabs. While the Arabs were tolerant of other monotheistic religions (i.e., Judaism and Christianity) and allowed relative freedom of worship, such tolerance came with an economic cost. Non-Muslims were forced to pay discriminatory land and other taxes, but converts to Islam were exempt. Jane S. Gerber observed the result:

> Economic incentives combined with religious disincentives to drive the Jews off the land. Formerly, the Jews had been a primarily rural people. Whole provinces of Iraq were abandoned as Jews flocked to the cities, unable to compete with newly converted Muslim cultivators who were not subject to discriminatory land taxes, poll taxes and self-imposed religious tithes that made agriculture economically unfeasible for Jews....One of the results of the Muslim conquests was the decisive transformation of the Jews into an urban people.[3]

Another offshoot of the Islamic conquests was the elevation of trade over agriculture as a professional pursuit. Specifically, trade was not regarded with disdain in the Islamic world; rather it was looked upon in a positive light. Muhammad, the great prophet and founder of the Islamic religion, had been a merchant from the commercial oasis of Mecca in the Arabian Desert. In the *Pax Islamic* world during the ninth through the twelfth centuries, Jews, like their Muslim rulers, traveled far and wide, commuting regularly between Spain, Sicily, North Africa, the eastern shores of the Mediterranean, and the Indian Ocean. Indeed, the Jews, along with Middle Eastern Muslims, maintained a role of intermediary in the trade of spices from South Asia during the thirteenth century.

The Jews were also able to benefit from the imposition of central authority throughout the Islamic world. Muslim troops provided law enforcement in the cities and patrols in the countryside and along trade routes, while lighthouses were constructed to help shipping. Islamic law, strengthened by the universality of the Arabic language, reinforced a sense of a single unifying central authority in which people could put their trust. This helped Jewish merchant families (often in partnership with Muslims) to move back and forth between rival kingdoms.[4]

The structure of the business unit used by the Jews was the family, which was considered the ideal form of business partnership, with ties of blood superceding ties of marriage.[5] As trade cut across many political borders, the network of Jewish communities and families provided a natural network for trade. The fact that Hebrew was understood in educated Jewish circles throughout the medieval world provided Jewish merchants with their own *lingua franca* that reinforced the sense of community.

One example of a Jewish international trading company was the Radhanites, who were based in either southern France or Spain (under the Muslims). The Radhanites' activities stretched across several continents and they had branches in a number of major ports. They used four land and sea routes. As one source notes, "One went northward through Europe via Prague, Bulgaria and the land of the Khazars in the Crimea. Two proceeded along the Mediterranean littoral and ended in Iran and Iraq (the trip from Cordoba to Baghdad normally took a year). The fourth went by sea and land all the way to China."[6]

The Jews working in the Islamic world and in parts of Western Europe had another important point in their favor. As Gerber points out, "It appears that the Jews were among the first to understand the importance of credit and its utility in long-distance trade."[7] This was manifest in the innovative use of letters of credit, known as *suftafa*. Although the *suftafa* were not as sophisticated as later letters of credit, they allowed Jewish merchants an opportunity to conduct business over long distances. It is thought that the development of this early capitalist instrument originated among Jewish bankers in Baghdad.

The relationship between the Jews and Islam would continue for a long time. In 1492, when the Jews were expelled from Spain, a large number went either to the Muslim lands in North Africa or to the seat of the Ottoman Empire of the Turks, Istanbul. In both cases, they were generally welcomed and became part of the merchant and banking communities.

The Western Experience

Although the Roman Empire fell, the Jewish communities throughout Western Europe continued to survive and, in some cases, even prosper. In fact, Jewish settlement (in small numbers) gradually moved north into central and northern France in the sixth century and by the eighth century had reached the edge of the Rhineland. It could be said that there was a convergence in the interests of the German rulers of Europe and the small Jewish communities sprinkled throughout France, Italy, the Low Lands (present-day Belgium, Netherlands, and Luxembourg), and Germany. Although this convergence of interests would weaken in the tenth and eleventh centuries, it set a pattern of Jewish involvement in credit, not to mention making the Jews an urban people in the west much as they had become in the east.

For the newly empowered German kingdoms, the Jews represented an important pool of talent. From the Jewish standpoint, farming (with its growing prohibitions from the Church pertaining to the right of Jews to retain in their employ or under their roof, Christian domestics, serfs, and slaves), was increasingly less attractive. While such activities as goldsmithing and dyeing attracted a few, most Jews preferred commerce first and after that, lending. Trade was a profession in which profits were potentially great (as well as the risks) and the competition minimal in the early Middle Ages as many Christians were still deterred from commercial endeavor by the lingering stigma that Roman society had attached to it.[8] As medieval authority Norman Cantor states of the Jews in Western Europe at this time, "They played an important role in whatever international trade still existed between western Europe and the Mediterranean after the sixth century. They suffered occasional persecution, particularly in Visigothic Spain, but, by and large, the Germanic kings found their services as merchants and moneylenders too useful to allow fanatical bishops to foment pogroms against them."[9] Consequently, the newly established Germanic kingdoms guaranteed all subjects equal freedom and protection, which meant that Jewish-Christian relations in Western Europe during the early Middle Ages were generally tranquil.[10] Moreover, there was an effort made on the part of local leaders to attract Jewish settlers, which included the granting of privileges and charters, which essentially provided the legal basis for the existence of Jewish communities in European cities.[11] It should be added that some of the more enlightened popes called for restraint in the treatment of the Jews.

The high point of Jewish prominence in long-distance trade in both Christian and Muslim countries occurred in the tenth and early eleventh centuries.[12] Consequently, they played an important role in whatever international trade still existed between Catholic Western Europe and the more advanced world beyond it—the Islamic states, the Byzantine Empire, and India and China. But the Jewish role in international trade declined in the eleventh century, due to the growth of Christian piety, which led to an increase in judophobia. This, in turn, led to pogroms. Additionally, as feudal institutions emerged that required the oath of loyalty to either a lord or a guild, the distinct culture of the Jews living in a predominantly Christian world guaranteed their discrimination. By the mid-eleventh century, the Jewish involvement in trade had notably declined before the advance of rising Christian competition, in particular from the rising Italian trading republics.

While the Jewish role in international trade declined, the Jewish role in credit was to expand during the eleventh and early twelfth centuries; by the latter period, their main economic resource was usury. By the High Middle Ages, most Jews seem to have abandoned commerce in favor of exploiting the capital acquired through their previously successful trading.[13] This shift was due partially to the proliferation of feudal institutions, which made it difficult for Jews to hold land or enter merchant guilds, which came to have a major role in international trade.[14] At this point international trade was recovering and the need for credit was growing. At the same time, moneylending and credit could be highly profitable enterprises and served as a venue for wealthy Jewish merchants to use their earnings from trade. Additionally, moneylending was not a time-consuming business, such as agriculture, goldsmithing or dyeing, and gave the elite within the Jewish community time for the study and reflection of the Torah and Talmud.

While Christians moved into trade (especially the northern Italians who are the subject of chapter 5), the Church remained opposed to the idea of making profits through interest from lending money to others. Much of Church thinking was rooted in a past shaped by a pastoral and agricultural life, centered about small village communities, not in a world of long-distance trade. Simply stated, usury was unlawful, sinful, and downright un-Christian. However, there was an economic need that the Jews could fulfill. As the feudal age increasingly impinged on Jewish rights, prohibiting them from many agrarian and commercial livelihoods, the door to moneylending and credit opened.

Before plunging into the world of credit, the Jews also faced a moral problem. Usury was also frowned upon within Judaism. Jewish rabbis, however, took a pragmatic approach to this dilemma. After considerable thought, the rabbis took the biblical injunction against usury to mean that it referred only to relations between members of the Jewish community and that usurious practices were permitted between Jew and gentile.[15] In other words, it was a sin for a Jew to lend to another Jew, but it was not a sin for a Jew to lend to a Christian. In like fashion, the Church observed the relationship in much of the same light. After all, it was stated in the New Testament of the Bible, Matthew 21.12: "Then Jesus entered the temple and drove out all who were selling and buying in the temple, and He overturned the tables of the money changers and the seats of those who sold doves. He said to them, 'It is written, my house shall be called a house of prayer; but you are making it a den of robbers.'" Moneylenders in the temple were not looked upon in a positive light, a view that was upheld by other voices in the Church. Consequently, the "sinful" commerce in money and credit was left to the Jews, hence maintaining the protection of Christians from such practices. The Church naturally turned a blind eye to the expansion of Italian merchant-bankers and the activities of the Knights Templars, both of which were actively engaged in the twelfth century in credit operations.

The Jewish shift to credit had both a positive and negative side. On the positive side, the Church's opposition to usury for a period made the Jew the only creditor in the neighborhood, city or region. This meant that whenever any great scheme was under consideration, the services of the local Jewish creditor were sought. His role was critical, considering that the two major occupations of the Middle Ages were fighting and building, both of which were costly. This was evident in the fact that Jewish credit helped finance the Crusades and was sometimes used by ecclesiastical foundations in building new churches. Consequently, the transition of Europe from a barter-economy to a money-economy, during the two and a half centuries following the First Crusade, was facilitated by the Jew's role as creditor.[16]

On the negative side, the linkage of the Jew and lending created a strong public perception. Licensed to lend, the Jews became cursed as "bloodsuckers" and "usurers" living off the debts of the Christians.[17] As Professor Kenneth Stow of Haifa University comments, "Lending was perceived as a Jewish act; lenders themselves were considered (even legally) to be Jews. Edward I scornfully labeled English lenders 'Judaizers' (although this did not prevent him, and other rulers as well, from tolerating and financially benefiting from their activities), and in Bruges (Flanders), Italian lenders were as socially segregated as were Jews."[18]

Along with the negative perceptions, the Jewish role in credit held obvious dangers. Clients included profligate nobles, bankrupt churchmen, and expanding royal governments as well as individuals from the lower and middle social ranks. Such a clientele carried considerable risk, and chances of repayment were often questionable. This fact led Jewish lenders to charge high interest rates, sometimes as much as 50 percent of the principal.[19] Although the Jewish lenders were not alone in such practices, they were an easily identifiable minority. Needless to say, such practices did little to endear Jewish lenders to the public, who often pledged real estate or personal items against the loan. As Christian piety increased in the early eleventh century, the view vis-à-vis the Jews hardened. In 1096, as Christiandom geared up for the First Crusade, anti-Jewish violence broke out and destroyed the flourishing Jewish communities of Mainz, Worms, and Cologne, while communities were attacked in Treves, Prague, and Rouen. The same fervor leveled against the Muslims was leveled against the other non-Christian people—the Jews or Christ-killers, often referred to as the enemies within Christiandom.[20]

Despite such attacks, the Jewish role in finance continued. However, this made the Jewish lender that much more dependent on central authority as the only protection against massacre. As Cantor notes, "By 1200 the Jews in western Europe were in effect the slaves of royal and ducal governments. They were allowed to engage in usurious practices and to preserve their religion and hence protected from mass murder, but in return they were mercilessly taxed by royal treasuries that used them as parasites to draw money out of the outraged populace."[21]

Decline

The Jewish role in credit was not to disappear, but it did decline during the twelfth and thirteenth centuries. This decline coincided with increasing anti-Jewish actions. Jews were killed in incidents at Blois in 1171 and Brie in 1192 that involved French nobility, partially incited by clerics. At the Fourth Lateran Council of the Church of 1215, it was prescribed to ghettoize the Jews and that all members of that religious community should wear a yellow label as an emblem of their pariah status. While the Church became more strident against the Jews, feeding into latent popular mistrust, new competition emerged in the financial world. Both the Knights Templar and the northern Italian city-states produced Christian financial institutions that offered the same services as Jewish lenders. The rise of this competition did not entirely eclipse the Jewish creditor, but it did reduce the scope of his operations. The Jews were now forced to restrict themselves in most cases to lending money on pledge and similar petty transactions, basically pawnbroking.[22]

The Jews were also hit hard by expulsions. By the 1290s, the kings of England and France expelled the Jews to satisfy the demands of popular hatred as well as to enrich their treasuries by seizing Jewish property.[23] This was hardly the end of such actions. In 1391, Spanish society expelled the Jews or converted them, sending many back to the Islamic east, notably the Ottoman Empire where they were welcome. Spanish and Portuguese Jews, known as Sephardic Jews, also went in the next century to Holland, where in the seventeenth century they would play a significant role in overseas trade and credit.

In the fourteenth and fifteenth centuries, many Jews moved eastward to Germany and eventually into Eastern Europe. Others remained in Italy, where they continued to be a factor in moneylending.[24] Although the Jews were able to maintain a role in finance throughout Europe, they were restricted to a small range of commercial activities and forced to live in well-marked ghettos. Moreover, they were forced to remain closely tied to local royal families for both business and protection. Ironically, the long trek of the Jews in Western Europe and their movement through Germany set the stage for the rise of two significant international powers in credit in the nineteenth and early twentieth centuries—the Rothchilds in Frankfurt and the Warburgs in Hamburg.

Conclusion

Between the fall of Rome in the fifth century and the commercial revival of Europe in the eleventh century, credit operations were carried on by Jews. The Jewish role should not be overstated: the Jewish providers of credit were generally family businesses tied initially to international trade and commerce. The widespread settlement of Jewish communities throughout the ancient Roman world also helped this process of trade and credit. The Islamic conquest reactivated part of the old Roman world, giving it the rule of law necessary to facilitate trade and credit.

In the West, conditions were radically different, as the old order was swept away and a new one took a long period to become institutionalized. In this fluid environment, the Jews were one of the few communities willing and able to conduct trade beyond local borders and use credit. In this, they made a massive contribution to the development of a modern credit system. Clearly, the capitalist mentality that coincides with the principal tenets of the Jewish religion helped make this group a factor. At the same time, it would be an overstatement to give them credit for inventing capitalism or re-inventing it, as proposed by historian and radical anti-Semite Werner Sombart in his *Die Juden und das Wirtschaftsleben* (1922). We concur with another historian, Fernard Braudel, who stated, "If the Jews had invented or re-invented it, it could only have been in collaboration with many other people."[25]

The role played in the West by the Jew was to deteriorate as Christian society became more rooted in the various kingdoms. As central authority grew, the rule of law become more political, much to the advantage of the Christian majority. Many of the earlier privileges granted to Jews as incentives to settle in a particular location were gradually eroded. Ultimately, for their services the Jews were protected from the masses by the power of the sword, wielded by a Christian ruler. But this was hardly a favorable relationship for the Jew, considering the prohibitions he faced in living accommodations, professions and travel. Moreover, royal protection could be fickle as it was sometimes forced to bow to public opinion, which was sometimes incited by the clergy against the Jews. It was no mistake that the kings of England and France would expel Jews and confiscate their property in 1290. It is ironic that the same fate would befall both the northern Italian banks and the Knights Templar in the years to come.

Notes

1.   C. Warren Hollister, *Medieval Europe: A Short History* (New York: Alfred A. Knopf, 1982), pp. 151-152.
2.   Norman F. Cantor, *The Civilization of the Middle Ages* (New York: Harper Collins, 1993), p. 364.
3.   Jane Gerber, "My Heart is in the East…", in Nicholas de Lange, ed., *The Illustrated History of the Jewish People* (New York: Harcourt Brace and Company, 1997), p. 149.
4.   Ibid., p. 151.
5.   Ibid.
6.   Ibid., p. 152.
7.   Ibid.
8.   Kenneth Stow, *Alienated Minority: The Jews of Medieval Latin Europe*, (Cambridge, MA: Harvard University Press, 1992), p. 215.
9.   Cantor, *The Civilization of the Middle Ages*, p. 364.
10.   Ora Limar, "A Rejected People," in Nicholas de Lange, ed., *The Illustrated History of the Jewish People*, p. 96.
11.   Ibid., p. 99.
12.   Lopez, *The Commercial Revolution in the Middle Ages*, p. 61.
13.   Stow, *Alienated Minority*, p. 216.

14. Cantor, *The Civilization of the Middle Ages*, p. 365. Also see Robert Bonfil, "Aliens Within: The Jews and Antijudaism," in Brady, Oberman, and Tracy, eds.., *Handbook of European History, 1400-1600*, pp. 269-271.

15. Ibid.

16. Cecil Roth, *A History of the Jews: From Earliest Times Through the Six Day War* (New York: Schocken Books, 1971), p. 194.

17. John Cornwall, *Hitler's Pope: The Secret History of Pius XII* (New York: Viking Press, 1999), p. 25.

18. Stow, *Alienated Minority*, p. 211.

19. Cantor, *The Civilization of the Middle Ages*, p. 365.

20. Simon Lloyd, "The Crusading Movement, 1096-1274," in Jonathan Riley-Smith, ed., *The Oxford History of the Crusades* (New York: Oxford University Press, 1999), p. 66.

21. Ibid., p. 366.

22. Roth, *A History of the Jews*, p. 195.

23. See Sophia Menache, "The King, the Church, and the Jews: Some Considerations on the Expulsions from England and France," *Journal of Medieval History* (1987), Vol. 13, pp. 223-236.

24. See Robert Bonfil, "Jewish Lenders in Italy during the Renaissance: An Economic Force?" *Pa'amin* (1990), Vol. 41, pp. 58-64.

25. Fernand Braudel, *The Wheels of Commerce: Civilization & Capitalism 15th-18th Century* (Berkeley: University of California Press, 1991), pp. 159-160.

Part 3

Early Modern Credit Period

5

Trade Fairs and The Knights Templar

In the early modern period of credit history, we observe the direct relationship between credit and power, the evolution of the credit system in tandem with the development of the nation-state, and the ongoing challenge of volatility in credit markets (such as they were). Credit was also very much the domain of the wealthy and powerful. As the period of invasions gradually subsided in Western Europe and the Franks established a stable kingdom by 732, life patterns became more settled. By the early eleventh century, the old feudal system was slowly opening up to the larger world. The pressures on Western Europe to move beyond localized trade included the survival of the Byzantine Empire, the limited maintenance of trade within the west and with the east, and trade and war with the various Muslim states in the Middle East and North Africa. The process of "opening up" was first noticeable in Italy's maritime cities. By the eleventh century the interior towns of the peninsula were also experiencing growing trade, industry, and mercantile activity. A certain amount of impetus was given these developments through the Crusades that started in 1096 and the advent of large trade fairs, which drew merchants from all over Europe. From Italy, the "commercial revolution" spread to the rest of Europe. It is important to clarify that the awakening of Europe refers to Christian Europe. As noted in the previous chapter, the Jews maintained both trade and credit activities here during the early and mid-Middle Ages. Although Christian merchants and lenders initially lagged behind their Jewish counterparts, they caught up rapidly by the twelfth century, becoming the dominant force.

There are five factors to be considered in the development of credit in the late Middle Ages. First and foremost, the political situation improved. Though far from stable, political institutions and geographically represented political entities took form and provided a relative degree of central authority and rule of law. Secondly, a number of regions, namely northern Italy and Flanders, underwent important socioeconomic changes that set the stage for an explosion of trade and commerce. The third factor, which is directly related, was the advent of the trade fair, which was a considerable stimulus for the development of credit instruments. Fourth, the long period of Italian dominance in trading created a surplus of capital that gave way to the development of merchant banking. And, the fifth factor is the nature of the commercial revolution itself, stimulated by the trade fairs and encouraged by the northern Italians, as it gradually spread north to encompass a greater community of peoples from the Hanse on the Baltic, the English, and the Germans. These five factors are the focus of this chapter, although a more comprehensive treatment of the Italians follows in chapter 6.

Important Pre-Conditions: Socioeconomic and Political Changes in the Late Middle Ages

Although Western Europe was to remain a region of political tensions and divided loyalties, a degree of relative stability was notable by the early 700s. The Franks had settled in what would later emerge as France and Germany. The Lombards held most of northern Italy, the Venetians were emerging as a city-state of influence in the Adriatic, the Papacy dominated central Italy and the Normans occupied Sicily and parts of southern Italy. Beyond these borders the Arabs held sway over most of the Iberian Peninsula, North Africa, and most of the Middle East, while the Byzantine Empire controlled Asia Minor, most of Anatolia and parts of the Balkans and Italy. In 732, Charles Martel, the "Hammer," defeated the Arabs at the Battle of Tours, hence containing the Islamic threat to the West from Spain. At the same time, this helped Charles and his family, the Carolingians, gain greater power in France and Germany. The Hammer's grandson, Charlemagne, became king of the Franks in 768 and he pushed the borders of Christian Europe deeper into Germany by conquering the Saxons and integrating the region into his kingdom. He also destroyed the Kingdom of the Lombards, raided Muslim Spain, and by 800 was crowned in Rome as the Emperor of the Holy Roman Empire. Although peoples from the East, such as the Magyars and Avars,

continued to threaten Western Europe, the days of large-scale barbarian invasions were over and lasting political and cultural entities
were forming.[1]

Another important political development was a new form of government established by the Anglo-Norman monarchy under William
the Conqueror and his sons following the conquest of England in
1066. As Cantor noted, "William and his sons were able to advance
English royal institutions to a point of perfection and efficiency hitherto unknown in medieval Europe. They ended up by developing a
new kind of medieval kingship that relied upon administration and
law to unify the realm, allowing them to dispense with the traditional ideological basis of monarchy."[2] The Norman kings presided
over the complete feudalization of their English realm, which clearly
placed the king at the apex of the power pyramid, backed by the full
weight of law. This increased the reach of the crown in terms of
financial resources, as the new royal line was able to more efficiently
tax its subjects, while reinforcing the central authority of the royal
government. Though a considerable distance from the governing
apparatus of the modern nation-state, the new feudal state established by William the Conqueror and his sons set an example to
other kings on the continent who were interested in establishing the
same type of powerful central authority.

The shift to a relatively more stable political environment occurred
roughly at the same time the commercial revolution took off. When
the pattern of low population, low consumption, and low production was broken by demographic expansion, conditions proved apt
for the economic revitalization of the West. Why and when this occurred no one is exactly certain, but it was significant in helping to
develop towns, which in time came to sponsor trade fairs, and which
in turn proved critical to the evolution of modern credit. Towns began to grow because of a better food supply, as more land was
brought under cultivation and farming techniques improved (as did
governments). One offshoot was that as cash crops for expanding
markets emerged, the self-sufficient manor became a unit producing for sale. It found markets in towns, the number or which expanded steadily between 1100 and 1300.[3]

Another important development was the revival of the use of coins.
Coins were minted during the Carolingian era, but only gained in
significance in the economic life of Europe in the thirteenth century.
The gold and silver coins minted in Italy (Florence, in 1251) be-

came the standard for setting prices and other economic activities. It is important to emphasize that the conversion of precious metal to coin facilitated commercial development by helping to expand Europe's credit base.

A number of the older-established cities like Paris, Venice, Florence and Genoa benefited from these trends, but it appears the main gainers were those urban centers linked to emerging markets. As historian Roberts commented, "They provided markets, or lay on great trade-routes such as the Meuse and Rhine, or were grouped in an area of specialized production, such as Flanders, where already in the late twelfth century Ypres, Arras and Ghent were famous textile centers, or Tuscany, another cloth-producing region." [4] Other cities, such as Bordeaux, benefited from trade in wine, a major cross-border product, while Genoa, Venice, and Bruges evolved as metropolitan centers for maritime activities, providing goods and services to the hinterland.

There was also a sociopolitical element to the establishment of towns in the tenth and eleventh centuries. In many cases, poorer knights and more prosperous peasants took up residence in towns and became merchants and artisans. It is highly plausible that the development of the tenth-century cities, which gained momentum in the eleventh and twelfth centuries, lay exclusively in international trade. In his essay, *Medieval Cities*, Henri Pirenne contended that merchants who engaged in international trade gathered for protection under the walls of a "burgh," a fortress belonging to some lay or ecclesiastical prince.[5] Such "burgers" went on to make their town into a center for commerce. In time, as the burgers (who became the bourgeois) expanded in number, they constructed the walls themselves. In cities, which emerged as the commercial centers in Flanders and northern Italy, real political power belonged to the bourgeois, in particular, a small oligarchy of great entrepreneurs who controlled the merchant guilds and dominated the town government.[6] The involvement of entrepreneurial traders was to have an enormous impact on the development of credit. As already demonstrated during the very early civilizations and carried through to Roman times, traders expanded a society's horizons by forcing open the door to the broader world. This resulted in the movement of ideas as well as goods. The same was to happen with the advent of trade fairs in Western Europe as well as with the Crusades, both of which play a significant role in the history of credit.

The Trade Fairs

It is probable that it was in the Flemish cities that the first staple of medieval European international trade was developed.[7] The late tenth-century peasants, who drained the marshes of Flanders, quickly detected that the recovered land was unsuitable for crops but highly suitable for sheep. This allowed them to obtain enough wool to produce cloth for export. Consequently, the towns of Ghent and Ypres emerged as great weaving centers. By 1050 the first internal trade routes developed, linking Flanders across Europe to northern Italy (another textile-producing region), with the meeting ground for Flemish and Italian merchants being the county of Champagne, whose ruler in the twelfth century was to sponsor an annual international fair in his territory.[8] The fairs rotated almost continuously throughout the year among the four towns of Provins, Troyes, Lagny, and Bar-sur-Aube.

The fair originally had its beginning as a religious custom, which brought people together from various parts of Europe for the celebration of a local saint. Fairs provided a critical mass of both customers and merchants for trade, with different locations and their own particular saints providing a calendar of feast dates around which a progression or cycle of fairs could be constructed.[9] In Flanders, a cycle of fairs emerged around the mid-eleventh century and early twelfth century, revolving around the towns of Ypres, Lille, Mesen, Torhout, and Bruges.

The trade fairs in Champagne, however, emerged as the major event. What is significant is that local political power recognized the benefit of such activities and helped establish the necessary rule of law and concomitant stability for trade fairs to flourish. As John Chown noted, "Rulers, notably the Counts of Champagne, set out deliberately to offer *conduits des foires* (safe conducts and protection) to visiting merchants and to encourage their activities. *Custodes rundiarum*, 'guards of the fairs' maintained order. Treaties with neighboring potentates, such as the Duke of Burgundy, extended protection for the journey to and from the fair." [10] The counts also provided merchandising facilities and special commercial courts.

The trade fair appears to have gained important momentum in 1174 when Milanese merchants started to participate in the Champagne trade fairs. The Italians bought cloth from Flanders and Arras, which they then exported to the East, and traded more exotic, high value and easily portable wares from the Mediterranean. Having penetrated much of the Mediterranean and benefited from the Crusader kingdoms, they had many exotic goods to trade (though the volume of such goods was not large). The Milanese were soon joined by other Italians and by 1180 the pattern of trade was established. As historian Robert-Henri Bautier states, there was a certain pattern in each fair: "...to begin with there was a week during which merchandise was exempt from taxes; then there was the cloth fair, then the leather fair and the avoirs du poids (goods sold by weight: wax, cotton, spices, etc.); finally came the concluding stage when debts incurred during the fair were settled. The complete cycle lasted from fifteen days to two full months for each fair." [11]

Trade Fairs and Credit

What made the trade fairs work was the system of credit. In particular, credit was used in settling large international transactions without the physical expense and risk of transporting coined or uncoined bullion. It should be noted that money in circulation consisted largely of minted coins. The balance of trade was in favor of the Italians, which meant that the trade in goods was not enough to make up the difference. The solution—at least initially—was to make up the difference in both bullion and coins. Yet there were problems associated with transporting coins. First, there was the cost of actual transport; second, armed guards, and third, tolls. Moreover, once the money arrived, the person receiving it had to verify the worth of each coin due to concerns about possible debasement.

Coins also represented a problem from the standpoint of their multiplicity. Most regions in Western Europe used the Carolingian monetary system of pounds, shillings, and pence. This apparent unity, however, camouflaged an almost baffling disunity of actual monies. As economic historian Rondo Cameron expressed, "For one thing, the Genoese lira did not have the same value as the English pound, the French livre, or even the Milanese or Pisan lire. More fundamentally, both the pound and shilling were mere monies of account; no actual coins of those values were struck until very late in the Middle Ages."[12] The lack of monetary unity, the absence of coins of significant value (most were pennies), and the frequent debasement of coinage by financially hard-pressed rulers did little to make the coin a favored medium of exchange. It was not until the gold florin in 1252 that Europe had a relatively stable currency with which to conduct commerce. By then credit was well-established and favored in long-distance trade, such as that of the trade fairs. Considering the problems associated with transporting such valuable, yet heavy items, Europe's businessmen were innovative. As Hunt and Murray noted, "In this connection the international fairs transcended themselves as merchants developed a payment system based on credit instruments called *lettres de faire*, or fair letters. These documents recognized sales of merchandise, but often specified payment at a later fair, when the total of debits and credits for a season would be computed and a final reckoning made between buyers and sellers."[13]

From the fair letters, there was a short distance to travel to the most important financial innovation of the late Middle Ages, the bill of exchange. It is important to note that the bills of exchange were not merchandise, but a currency transaction secured by the assets of the drawer. It is believed that the earliest version of a bill of exchange was in Genoa late in the twelfth century, about the time of the great trade fairs. According to Hunt and Murray, bills of exchange avoided the cost of transporting specie, provided a practical mechanism for international credit and currency exchange, and finessed the church's prohibition against usury. One such bill of exchange was discovered among the papers of Francesco di Marco Datini, a fourteenth-century Tuscan merchant:[14]

In the name of God, the 12th of February 1395. Pay at usance*, by this first of exchange, to Giovanni Asoperdo L306 13s.4d. Barcelonesi, which are for 400 florins received here from Bartolemeo Garzoni, at 15s.4d. per florin. Pay and charge our account there and reply.

God keep you.

Francesco and Andrea, greetings from Genoa.

Accepted March 13.

*Usance was the time customarily allowed for the payment of a bill of exchange. The usance between Genoa and Barcelona was 20 days.

The above transaction involved four parties, the borrower and lender in the town of issue and the borrower's correspondent (the payer) and the lender's representative (the payee) in the town of repayment. The difference in dates, called "usance," normally reflected the generally accepted time required to move goods between the two locations, in this case twenty days between Genoa and Barcelona. It could also be a negotiated figure. The bills, themselves, however, could move much more quickly. Also negotiated were the exchange rates, with the objective of giving the issuer a reasonable profit on the deal.[15]

Although the Champagne trade fairs were to decline, the bills of exchange were only to increase in use. Credit worked in the trade fair system because of the rule of law that supported it as well as a healthy degree of self-regulation. Contracts made at one fair were valid and could be enforced anywhere in the system, especially as they created their own legal system for the settlement and arbitration of crimes.[16] There came into existence an effective and well-staffed private enterprise legal system established by merchants. The system was effective and worked as follows:

> If a merchant refused to recognize the jurisdiction, the dispute was reported to his own city or state. If they failed to enforce a judgement, the fair officials could pronounce the "interdict of the fairs" against the offending city, all of whose merchants, and not only the offender, would be banned. This sort of lay excommunication was a very peaceful deterrent. The general community of merchants had a strong interest in enforcing the system: in a closely-knit community self regulation works splendidly.[17]

The trade fairs spread as the benefits of trade and a working credit system became evident. Beyond the cloth trade between Flanders and Italy, northern trade routes developed connecting Bruges in Flanders to Cologne. Close ties were furthermore developed with trade fairs that linked the English wool industry, putting St. Ives, St. Giles, Winchester, and St. Botolph on the map. Bruges was also connected primarily by the Hanseatic League to the mercantile cities of the Baltic Sea through which the traders reached Novgorod in Russia.

The Church and Christian Credit

As trade took off in the Commercial Revolution, the demand for credit became overwhelming. This was to force the Church to change its views. It was one thing when the Church allowed the Jews to extend credit, but what about when those resources were inadequate and lending became a profitable enterprise? In the old, closed economies of the feudal system large amounts of credit were not needed and the Church's power was considerable. Henry Pirenne noted that the Church was "an indispensable money-lender of the period," supplying credit against land to neighboring lords. As he stated, "When it prohibited usury for religious reasons, the Church therefore rendered a signal service to the agrarian society....It saved it from the affliction of consumption debts from which the ancient world suffered so severely." [18]

But times changed. Though Europe was still predominantly agrarian, a new urban-based economy, founded on trade and commerce was emerging and was giving no evidence of being short-lived. Obviously, the pragmatic side of the Church allowed certain loopholes that were useful for the institution to survive. One such loophole was outlined by St. Thomas Aquinas, who made allowance for the "just price." Simply stated, if a creditor could prove that some damage had been caused to him (for example, by slowness in repaying a debt), it was legal for the debtor to pay him compensation. This proved to have a very wide interpretation, as in practice it served to authorize the taking of interest under the name of compensation or sometimes a gift.[19]

As the world changed, the revival of trade and commerce, as well as the rise of power of local kings and princes, posed tough challenges to the Church's power. Although the Church permitted a number of loopholes that allowed interest to be charged, it sought to halt the slide toward widespread usury. What evolved was a business community operating from Italy to Flanders and London that adapted by inventing new "loopholes," which the canon lawyers then sought to close. At the end of the day, the Roman Catholic Church fought a losing battle. As Chown aptly noted, "The legal and moral system was quite out of line with the needs of commerce."[20] While the local merchants and, in time, bankers continued to develop their businesses, the Church's ability to sway conditions to its line of thinking diminished and the issue of usury was eclipsed by more important concerns of the Church and its relations to kings and princes.

Northern Europe's Involvement in Trade Fairs

Northern Europe was not be to left out of the Commercial Revolution and involvement in trade fairs. Although Scandinavian military and economic power collapsed between the late eleventh and late thirteenth centuries, the German Hanseatic League arose, creating a network of mercantile cities along the Baltic and North Seas, spreading trade and credit.[21] The Hanseatic League was one of the earliest attempts at federalism. The League itself was gradually established in the mid-twelfth century to help these northern German cities to trade among themselves and Western Europe, and eventually included almost 200 cities and towns. It also differed with some of the other leagues formed by German cities, such as the Swabian League, as it encompassed not only cities, but also associations formed by German merchants abroad, as in London and Bruges. It was also a factor in helping spread Christianity in the north, initially in the form of crusade in Latvia and Estonia. The Hanseatic League lasted until 1660 as a force, helping to provide the necessary political stability to facilitate trade, while also acting as a police force to curb pirate activities in the North Sea and the Baltic. Lubeck was almost always at the center of Hanse activities and other important members included Brunswick, Bremen, Hamburg, Dortmund, and Cologne, as well as the Wendish towns of Luneburg, Wismar, Rostock, and Straslund. Additionally, in the east were Danzig, Riga, Borpat, and Reval.

Northern and northeastern Europe, in a sense, were a frontier in the twelfth and thirteenth centuries. After all, it had been in the ninth century that the Vikings had burst out of Scandinavia attacking the Frankish kingdoms in France and Germany and the Celtic and Saxon peoples of the British Isles and sending out raiding and settler-missions across the Northern Atlantic to Iceland and Greenland.[22] In time, the North's political situation settled and contacts with the rest of Europe brought Christianity. Rape and pillage were gradually bypassed by trade and commerce. The Hanse played a key role in bringing the north into the emerging European-wide trade and credit systems.

The Hanse also played a role in financing Edward III of England. The English monarch was constantly in need of money to carry on his war against France. In 1345, he repudiated his substantial debt to the Italian merchant-banking houses of the Bardi and Peruzzi. Although this wiped Edward's slate clean of the Italians, he was now lacking creditors. Into this void stepped the Hanse merchants, who were willing to assume the role of chief source of credit. The Hanse merchants advanced Edward III large sums of money in exchange for trading privileges and, over time, the management of export duties at different ports, and for several years management of the valuable tin mines of Cornwall.[23] Edward III's financial needs were so great that at one point the crown jewels were pledged in Cologne, a Hanse city.

At the same time, it should be noted the Hanse versions of contracts and its credit organization were less developed than those of the Italians. Hanse merchants did use bills of exchange in their trade between Bruges and Lubeck as early as the 1290s. However, after the formal creation of the Hansetic League in 1370, its assemblies or "diets" imposed increasingly severe restrictions and even bans on bills of exchange and other credit transactions.[24] It was believed that these transactions promoted fraud and price instability.

Decline of the Trade Fairs

By the late thirteenth century, trade fairs were in decline. Simply stated, the system was too successful. The credit mechanisms that had developed during the trade fairs now allowed the merchants to remain at home and operate through a network of correspondents. Furthermore, products, which had earlier been transported overland within Europe due to the lack of safety in maritime routes, now enjoyed the revival of sea trade between England and Flanders to Italy and points East. One stimulus to the revival of water transport was that France's King Philip the Fair, always hard-pressed for funds, had imposed new tolls and assessments on the land route after Champagne became formally annexed to the Kingdom of France. Many merchants simply opted for the sea route through the Straits of Gibraltar to northern Europe.[25] In 1277 the first Genoese ships reached Bruges in Flanders, thus opening a new route that was critical to the further development of commerce in Europe.

Two other factors must be considered in the decline of trade fairs. Sporadic fighting returned to Europe in the 1290s and evolved into the Hundred Years' War, an intermittent struggle between England and France that lasted from 1337 to 1453. The Champagne fairs were also undermined by the Franco-Flemish civil wars (1293-1328), along with wars in Italy, such as the destructive Guelf-Ghibelline wars (1313-43), which brought almost continuous foreign intervention by Catalan, French, German, and Hungarian armies. This round of warfare was complemented by the Genose-Venetian naval wars (1291-99), the Mamluk conquest of Crusader Palestine (1291) and retaliatory papal bans against Muslim trade, Ottoman advances into the Byzantine Empire (from 1303), and anarchic warfare in the Mongol Khanates from the Black Sea to Persia during the 1330s.[26]

With wars come famine and pestilence. The Black Death of 1347-50 struck Europe hard. The plague was introduced to Europe by the Genoese, who, in 1346, had been besieged by a Tatar army in the town of Caffa in the Crimea on the Black Sea. Although the Tatars were hit by the plague, they were plucky enough to turn their problem into a weapon. The Tatars took their dead and catapulted them into Caffa in a concerted effort to spread the infection and weaken the Genoese resistance. As the rain of disease-spreading dead bodies came down on Caffa, the Genoese quickly took to their boats, sailing through the Black Sea, the Aegean, and the Mediterranean, leaving in their wake the spread of the Black Death. During the outbreak of the bubonic plague, it is estimated that in some parts of Europe a half or a third of the population expired.[27] The combination of war and disease decidedly ran against the need for a relatively stable political background for trade and a growing market of consumers. Instead Europe was hit with what has been called a "price scissors" of falling agricultural prices and rising industrial prices. As Professor David Hackett Fischer explains, "The price of food rose sharply during the epidemic years, then began to fall very rapidly as there were fewer months to feed. At the same time prices of manufactured goods tended to rise, partly because artisans and craftsmen could demand higher wages, and also because of dislocations in supply."[28] This condition only helped aggravate socioeconomic differences throughout Europe, leading to peasant revolts, such as those that struck France in 1358 and England in 1381.

The trading fairs in the twelfth and thirteenth centuries played an important role in placing European trade into an international mode. In a sense, the trade fairs functioned as money and commodity exchanges for merchants all over Europe and were a reflection of the Commercial Revolution that shook Europe. The pattern of credit that emerged in the trade fairs was equally important—credit became a key lubricant for trade, a system supported by trust and the rule of law. Furthermore, the spread of trade and credit reflected the emergence of towns and the bourgeois, who came to play a significant role in changing Europe's sociopolitical system as it shifted from the old feudal order to more assertive political units, such as the Italian city-states, the subject of the following chapter.

The Crusades, the Knights Templar, and Credit

The popular image of the Crusades is one of heavily armored Christian knights slugging it out in noble combat with scimitar-wielding Saracens. The knights were usually portrayed as devout men on a mission from God to recapture the Holy Land from the Muslim interlopers. Reality is a bit more sordid. The Crusaders, who hailed from England, France, and Germany, were not always guided by the light of Christian faith. Some were Christian zealots ready to slaughter all unbelievers, including other Christian sects and Jews. Many were adventurers, number two and three sons of noble families with no hope of inheritance at home, seeking fame and fortune in the East. Whatever the nature of the individuals involved in reclaiming the Holy Land from the forces of Islam, the Crusades functioned as a tremendous stimulus to trade between East and West. With that increase in trade came a leap forward in the use of credit throughout Western Europe, something that was also advanced by the trade fairs.

What prompted the Crusades? Very briefly, the Crusades were caused by the Islamic fundamentalism of the Seljuk Turks, who replaced Arab power in the Levant. The Seljuks had a much less tolerant view of Islam than the Arabs and threatened to cut off travel to Jerusalem for Christian pilgrims. The Seljuks also threatened the Byzantine Empire, whose emperors appealed for help from the western European kingdoms. In 1095, the Church rallied Western Christianity to launch a sizeable military expedition against the Turks in order to reclaim the Holy Land. The First Crusade, which began in 1096 and ended in 1102, resulted in the capture of Jerusalem in 1099 and the creation of the Latin states along the coastline of present-day Lebanon and Syria. With military conquest came trade and with commerce came the need for new credit arrangements. Into this gap came the Knights Templar and the northern Italians, sometimes referred to as the Lombards.

On July 18, 1100, Baldwin I succeeded his brother Godfrey of Bouillon and became the King of Jerusalem.[29] Baldwin's hold over the Kingdom of Jerusalem was, to say the least, precarious. The First Crusade had recaptured the Holy Lands from the Seljuk Turks, but this had hardly finished the Moslem threat. As one historian observed, "The Latin Kingdom existed, but there was as yet no stable government, no system of taxation and no reliable defense network either along the coast or around the newly conquered cities. Communications were intermittent and always difficult..."[30] Out of this difficult situation the Knights Templar were to emerge. By the end of the second decade of the twelfth century they arose to protect and assist pilgrims traveling to and in the Holy Land. In time, the Knights Templar were to become an influential European entity in the realm of finance. The rise of this religious order, its business acumen, it involvement in international credit, and the wealth it accumulated are an interesting part of the history of credit related to the fundamental relationship between credit and power. In this case, the drama of the Knights Templar played out between the contending powers of the Roman Catholic Church and the French Monarch.

The Knights were a religious order whose earlier mandate was to keep the roads and highways safe from the menace of robbers and highwaymen, with special regard to the protection of pilgrims. In this, the order fused two ideals of medieval society, knighthood and monasticism, into a code for a community of warrior monks. Over time, however, the role of the Knights Templar expanded. As the order spread throughout Europe, Cyprus, and the Holy Land, it came to acquire castles, farms, and a fleet of ships. The pilgrim traffic, in particular, became a profitable enterprise for the Templars, especially as it was an easy extension of their primary mission. The order, besides having the Templar's fleet to help transport pilgrims, created a financial structure that made it possible for them to extend loans for crusading enterprises.

In the predominantly urban monetary economy in the Holy Land, the Templars quickly adopted the use of gold Arab dinars, Byzantine hyperpera, and silver drachmas. In fact, their feudal income was in cash. As they became more conversant in the monetary-based economy of the East, the Templars were in an advantageous position to anticipate the similar type of economy, which gradually was developing in Western Europe. This also meant that they were ready with techniques to satisfy the demands of customers who needed sophisticated credit services.[31]

The Templar's international network and its close relationship with the papacy provided them with a special position of being at the right place at the right time. The movement of Europeans to and from the Holy Land created the need for credit. Simply stated, the Crusades were wars and wars cost money. Wars also resulted in situations where prisoners were held for ransom. The Knights Templar, as a monastic order, provided an international network capable of moving valuables as well as credits from one end of Europe to the Holy Land. Moreover, as men of God they had the trust of those who used them. Additionally, most Templar convents were heavily fortified, adding to a sense of security.

In time, the Templars became agents for ransom payments and the transfer of funds to the Holy Land for wars and provided loans to crusaders and pilgrims. What this meant was that the order's financial role included the transmission of credit, payment at a distance, and tax collecting activities for popes and kings. As Jack Weatherford stated on the Templar network, "A French knight could deposit money or take out a mortgage through the Templars in Paris but receive money in the form of gold coins when needed in Jerusalem. The Templars, of course, charged a fee for the transaction, and since they paid out in a different currency from what they received, they could take an additional cut of money for the exchange."[32]

As the Templars became a force in international finance, they became active in Italy and competed with the Italians in finance. There remains a degree of speculation about who first mastered the art of international credit—the Templars or the Italians. Edward Burman, a historian on the Templars, commented, "It seems clear that the appearance of such techniques early in the twelfth century antedates the widespread adoption of them by Italian bankers during that century. Eventually the Italian bankers and other secular financiers supplanted the role of the Templars, and have thus come to be seen as innovators when perhaps the techniques they used already existed."[33] Burman also observed, "…it is interesting to note that in the three Italian cities where banking activities developed in the late twelfth century the Templars had already been established by mid-century: in Siena, Lucca (the Church of S. Pietro), and Florence (S. Giacomo)."[34] Although it is not clear who first developed the techniques for international credit, what is certain is that the Templars were active in finance and shipping and that such activities overlapped with those of the Italians. At the same time, there was definitely competition between the Templars and the Italians merchants.

The Templars became the bankers for powerful Popes and monarchs. In particular, when the Holy See did banking in the Holy Land, the Templars were often the bankers of choice. This created a situation within the order in which knights were also trained for banking as well as fighting. At the same time, for much of the thirteenth century the Temple in Paris acted as a treasury for the French kings and loans were made to Aragon as early as the 1130s.[35] With permanent missions in France, England, Aragon, Italy, and the Holy Land, the Templars grew to have considerable power as well as wealth. With those trappings came a degree of arrogance. Wealth and arrogance are two elements of human nature that often lead to downfall.

By the end of the thirteenth century when the Muslims retook Jerusalem, the Templars were pushed out of the Holy Land and had located their main operations in France. Smug in the role as bankers to the Pope and powerful due to their wealth throughout Europe, the Templars soon came to the attention of King Philip IV, also known as "the Fair." Always short of money due to his many wars, King Philip borrowed from the Jews and Lombards (merchants from Italy), and in time he persecuted both and took their property. In 1304 he expelled the Jews from France. Still in need of funds, King Philip was soon ready to turn on the Templars.

The leaders of the Knights Templar were taken entirely unaware by the French king. Most of the leadership in France, including the elderly grand master Jacques de Molay, were arrested and imprisoned in October 1307. It was claimed that during admission ceremonies recruits were forced to deny Christ, spit on the cross, and to engage in indecent kissing; brethren were accused of worshipping idols, and the order was said to encourage homosexual practices.[36] In his quest for more money, King Philip in arresting the Templars had done something beyond making an undignified and greedy swipe at money—a secular ruler had openly charged an order directly responsible to the Pope with heresy, a crime that had fallen within the jurisdiction of the Church. Although Pope Clement V was able to stall the proceedings against the Templars for some time, he eventually was forced to give way to King Philip who confiscated the order's possessions in France. Ultimately the Templar leaders were executed as heretics, by being burnt at the stake, while their order was abolished by Pope Clement in 1312. By that time, however, the Commercial Revolution was a spent force and the great spurt of trade was in decline before the devastating power of the same forces that eclipsed the trade fairs—wars and the concomitant societal disequilibrium.

The demise of the Templars was decidedly to the advantage of the Italians. In the Middle East, this provided more commercial activities for the merchants and financiers of the Italian city-states, who, since the beginning of the thirteenth century, had been very active in this area. There were also chances to grab land and establish outposts, which Venice did with Cyprus and Crete. Elsewhere in Europe, the destruction of the Templars left credit needs to be fulfilled, which the Italians were ready and able to meet.

Notes

1.   The Magyars rolled into Austria and Hungary in the ninth century, mainly intent on looting and pillaging. However, in 935 German forces decisively defeated the Magyars, after which they settled in the central Hungarian plain.

2.   Norman F. Cantor, *The Civilization of the Middle Ages* (New York: Harper Perennial, 1994), p. 277.
3.   J.M. Roberts, *The Penguin History of Europe* (New York:Penguin Books, 1996), p. 153.
4.   Ibid., p. 154.
5.   Henri Pirenne, *Medieval Cities: Their Origins and the Renewal of Trade,*trans., Frank D. Halsey (Princeton, NJ: Princeton University Press, 1969 [1925]).
6.   Ibid., p. 232.
7.   Ibid.
8.   Robert S. Lopez, *The Commercial Revolution of the Middle Ages 950-1350,* p. 90.
9.   Edwin S. Hunt and James M. Murray, *A History of Business in Medieval Europe, 1200-1550* (New York: Cambridge University Press, 1999), p. 25.
10.   John F. Chown, *A History of Money: From A.D. 800* (New York: Routledge, 1994), p. 124.
11.   Robert-Henri Bautier, *The Economic Development of Medieval Europe* (London: Thames and Hudson, 1971), p. 111.
12.   Rondo Cameron, *A Concise Economic History of the World: From Paleolithic Times to the Present* (New York: Oxford University Press, 1997), p. 67.
13.   Hunt and Murray, *A History of Business in Medieval Europe*, p. 29.
14.   Ibid.
15.   Ibid., p. 65.
16.   Chown, *A History of Money*, p. 124.
17.   Ibid., p. 125.
18.   Pirenne, *Medieval Cities*, p. 121.
19.   Iris Origo, *The Merchant of Prato* (New York: Penguin Books, 1963), p. 151.
20.   Chown, *A History of Money*, p. 120.
21.   There appears to be some question as to the actual date of the Hanseatic League's foundation. We concur with the explanation of James Westfall Thompson: "In 1265 one may say that the Hanseatic League, at least so far as the German cities in it were concerned, was formed. For between 1260-65 we have substantial legislation on the part of the concerted cities of North Germany 'which have the law of Lubeck'—a striking evidence of Lubeck's initiative in the whole movement—for the protection of merchants both in person and in their goods 'against robbers, bandits, pirates and feudal war,' together with provision 'to hold a meeting once a year to legislate about the affairs of the cities.' Although the specific word 'hansa' was not to appear yet for a century to denominate this union of North German cities for promotion of their trade, nevertheless by 1260-65 the Hanseatic League was more than half formed. The intra-German element in the league at least was constituted." James Westfall Thompson, *Economic and Social History of Europe in the Later Middle Ages (1300-1530)* (New York: Frederick Ungar Publishing Co., 1931, 1958, 1969), p. 151.
22.   P.H. Sawyer, *The Age of the Viking,* (New York: St. Martin's Press Inc., 1962), pp. 195-96. Else Roesdahl, *The Vikings* (London: Penguin Books Ltd., 1992), p. 188. According to Icelandic literature, some people emigrated from Norway circa 900 because of royal tyranny. Young men left because opportunities were better abroad or because they were exiled. J.M. Roberts, *The Pelican History of the World*, (London: Penguin Group, Pelican Books, 1988), p. 347.
23.   Thompson, *Economic and Social History of Europe in the Later Middle Ages*, p. 167.
24.   John Munro, "Patterns of Trade, Money and Credit," in Thomas A. Brady, Jr., Heiko A. Oberman, James D. Tracy, eds., *Handbook of European History, 1400-*

1600: Late Middle Ages, Renaissance and Reformations, Vol. 1. Structures and Assertions (Grand Rapids, MI: William B. Eerdmans Publishing Company, 1994), p. 153.

25.   Henry A. Miskimin, *The Economy of Early Renaissance Europe, 1300-1460* (New York: Cambridge University Press, 1975), pp. 109-118; Robert S. Lopez, *The Commercial Revolution of the Middle Ages, 950-1350* reprint ed. (New York: Cambridge University Press, 1971, 1976), pp. 85-102, and John L. La Monte, *The World of the Middle Ages: A Reorientation of Medieval History* (New York: Appleton-Century-Crofts, 1949), pp. 362-375.

26.   Munro, "Patterns of Trade, Money and Credit," in Brady, et al, *Handbook of European History*, p. 154.

27.   Roberts, *The Penguin History of Europe*, p. 158.

28.   David Hackett Fischer, *The Great Wave: Price Revolutions and the Rhythm of History* (New York: Oxford University Press, 1996), p. 45.

29.   Steven Runciman, *A History of the Crusades Vol. 1, The First Crusade and the Foundation of the Kingdom Jerusalem* (New York: Pengiun Books, 1986), pp. 146-147.

30.   Edward Burman, *The Templars: Knights of God* (Rochester, VT: Destiny Books, 1986).

31.   Burman, *The Templars: Knights of God*, p. 76.

32.   Jack Weatherford, *A History of Money*, p. 66.

33.   Burman, *The Templars*, p. 75.

34.   Ibid.

35.   Alan Forey, "The Military Orders 1120-1312," in Jonathan Riley-Smith, ed., *The Oxford History of the Crusades* (New York: Oxford University Press, 1999), p. 192.

36.   Ibid., p. 208.

6

The Italians and Credit

While the Knights Templar were an important force in developing credit, they were easily surpassed by the northern Italians, sometimes collectively referred to as Lombards, reflecting that the general region from which they hailed was known as Lombardy. The Italians were highly entrepreneurial, export-oriented, generally structured around family-run businesses and backed by the central authority of the rulers of the city-states that dominated their region. In fact, some of the leadership of those very same city-states came from the merchant-banker class. The northern Italian merchants, above all else, represented the direct link between trade and credit. Without the necessary credit instruments and institutions, trade throughout a revitalized Europe would not have been possible. The Italians contributed to the technical skills associated with credit, such as accounting and billing and in the use of credit in European-Levantine trade relations. As historian Thomas J. Blomquist noted of the Italian contribution, "By the thirteenth century, clearance was apparently a standard function of exchange banking throughout the Mediterranean region. Only in the fourteenth century did northern money changers adopt the techniques of deposit and transfer banking pioneered and carried across the Alps by the Italians." [1]

Italian men of trade and commerce were by that time active in all northern cities. In London, Lombard Street reminds one that this was once the Italian quarter. Additionally, Italian finance helped make some of the earlier voyages of exploration possible, a fact that is often overlooked, but is nonetheless important. It should also be clarified that while the Knights Templar burned out before stronger forces, the Italians enjoyed considerable longevity, weathering the machinations of kings, princes, and popes and surviving the Black

Death. And, while their contribution began before the Renaissance, the golden age of Italian credit bloomed during that flowering of Western civilization.

Venice and Genoa: Credit in the Age of Renewed Trade

Italy in the 1200s was divided into many independent entities. Of these, the city-states of Genoa, Florence, and Venice were dominant players in handling trade throughout the Levant and Black Sea in one direction and throughout the western Mediterranean and Western Europe in the other direction. There was considerable competition in developing trade and the Italians became actively involved in the politics of the Byzantine Empire and the Muslims in seeking to maintain trade links to Asia. Within this complicated international brew of trade and commerce, the power of the Italian city-states was based on a combination of economic, political, and military power. Genoa's and Venice's sizeable fleets, which were used in both war and peace, gave the Italians considerable diplomatic clout in a world of fluid politics in Southern Europe and the Levant for several centuries.

Venice was founded in the turbulent aftermath of the fall of the Roman Empire. Located at the mouth of the River Po, it was composed of a chain of small islands in a protected lagoon. Difficult to reach from the mainland, Venice became a safe harbor for those fleeing the turmoil of barbarian hordes. While blessed with a strategic location, Venice also benefited from its imperial relationship with the Byzantine Empire. In 992, the Byzantines bestowed upon Venice a grant favor as a faithful "subject" of the eastern empire, when they granted free access to Constantinople and a reduction in customs duty—a privilege that few other trade partners had at this time.[2] Although Venice was, in fact, independent of the Byzantine Empire, the imperial relationship provided a shield from the empire building of Charlemagne and his heirs. In return, Venice aided the Byzantines against pirates and Muslim sea raiders and helped to maintain a fiction of it, maintaining an imperial presence in the West. By the eleventh century, Venice emerged as the dominant power in the Adriatic and Ionian Seas and was enjoying a middleman role in trade between East and West.[3] An additional bonus for the Venetians was the Crusades, during which the city-states trading families provided transportation and supplies to the Crusaders. Credit was a natural outreach of these other activities and Venetian merchants made use of bills of exchange.

Another city-state to benefit from the revival of trade and the Crusades was Genoa. Located in northern Italy, with mountains cutting off any prospect of viable exploitation of its hinterland, Genoa was decidedly wed to the sea. During the tenth and eleventh centuries Genoa gradually emerged as a force in the western Mediterranean, actively preying on the Islamic states in North Africa. By the First Crusade in 1096, Genoa was well-established as a force in long-range transport, trading with the Black Sea, the Byzantine Empire, North Africa and Iberia, and finally the Atlantic coast of northern Africa and Western Europe. Like its rival, Genoa also won trading concessions with the Latin kingdoms in the Holy Land.

Between the rivalry of Genoa and Venice and the upswing of trade, the use of credit became more widespread. We have already noted the development of the trade fairs and bills of exchange. The increased demand in trade, stimulated by the Crusades, led to innovation. The Italians were the early innovators in credit as it was their exchange banks that led to the creation of commercial credit and to the clearance of client's obligations by book transfer, something that bankers in Genoa were doing at the close of the twelfth century. According to the oldest Genoese notarian cartology, that of John the Scribe (covering the years 1155-1164), it was likely that money changers, called the *"bancherii"* or bankers, had not yet expanded into the fields of credit, deposit, and transfer banking. The contracts recorded by John dealt with purchase sales and investments. However, as the Commercial Revolution gained momentum and trade fairs commenced, the Italian and, in particular, Genoese money changers expanded their activities into banking proper. Accordingly, the notarial contracts pertaining to the business of some twenty Genoese *bancherii* reveal that changers were granting loans to and accepting deposits from their clients.[4] Genoese *bancherii* also were by 1200 allowing their customers to make in-bank payment by transfer of debits and credits from the account of one client to that of another. The significance of this was noted by Blomquist: "At the same time, interbank arrangements permitted a client of one bank to settle accounts with a colleague who was a client of a second bank by means of a simple oral order of transfer."[5]

Italian lenders also charged interest. Although the Jews were often blamed for charging outrageous levels of interest, their Italian counterparts were hardly shy. Despite the sin of usury, it is known that one Giotto in thirteenth-century Tuscany hired out looms to poor weavers at a profit of no less than 120 percent.[6] Although Giotto was not lending money, his leasing of looms at a high level of interest provides some insight into what could be charged. Not much had changed by the fifteenth century. Short-term loans to the Florentine Republic during a military crisis in the 1430s came with hefty rates of 34 percent.[7]

To generalize, the avocations of banker and merchant were very closely related during the late Middle Ages in northern Italy. Traders in money and, by extension, credit, were divided into three groups. At the low end of social standing were the smaller moneylenders or pawnbrokers, often referred to as *lombardi*. They offered loans at a high interest in return for a pledge (like the Jews), usually to the poor. A second group was the money-changers. They dealt in the actual exchange of coins and the trade in bullion and precious stones. Unlike the lowly *lombardi,* the money-changers held a respectable and authorized position in each city, being largely responsible for the regulation of currency (important to trade and credit) and the detection of counterfeit coins.[8]

The third and final group was the international merchant-bankers, who conducted a multitude of businesses throughout Europe and the Mediterranean, including dealing in goods as well as in bills of exchange. As Origo noted of the incentive to be in the bills of exchange business: "Profits on the purchase and sale of such bills— which always involved an exchange, as well as a credit transaction— were generally recognized to be high, if precarious."[9] Although most merchants preferred the profits from their merchandise, as opposed to exchange dealings, it was the precariousness of the profits that caused these transactions to be approved by the Church. This was done by the Church on the grounds that, since the bills were bought and sold at a fluctuating price determined by the unpredictable variations of the exchange, the banker's profit was not —like interest on an ordinary loan—"a certain gain," and therefore "not usurious."[10]

The Italians also had an advantage over their potential competitors in the north in that they were the first to use gold coins in a meaningful fashion. It was not until the fourteenth century that northern Europeans, such as the Hanse, attempted gold coinage. As already noted, Florence issued gold coins as early as 1252, which were well-accepted as a means of exchange. Venice and Genoa also had gold coins. In Italy, advanced knowledge of credit instruments and the more extensive use of gold coins, tended to economize the metallic currency. What this meant was that in the south, less money was required for a greater volume of transactions and therefore capital costs were lower for the Italian trading northward than for northerners trading southward.[11]

As the Italians marketed Middle Eastern and Asian products in Western Europe, they were forced to establish trading outlets in all major cities of the continent. In 1277, Benedetto Zaccaria, the Genoese naval commander who had fought in the eastern Mediterranean to support the Byzantine emperor, sailed to the British Isles and Flanders. From that point forward, Genoese and sailors of other Italian cities traded with Northern Europe, penetrating the region by ocean routes, which they had already done previously for a time, along the rivers of the Rhone and the Rhine and across the passes of the Alps. Thereafter, Italian merchants began to serve northern ports of call such as London and Bruges through permanent local offices.[12] By establishing an international financial network, they also eventually became the bankers of the European monarchs and financiers of numerous large enterprises, such as the mining of tin in Cornwall, England.

In the first century of the Crusades, Venetians and Genoese also traded with the Arabs in the Levant and obtained many of the products of South Asia that came along the caravan routes to the Persian Gulf and the Red Sea. But, when in 1291, the last stronghold of the Crusaders, the city of Acre, was taken by the Muslims, trade with the Orient was again disrupted significantly. It is perhaps no coincidence that in the same year, the Vivaldi brothers of Genoa tried unsuccessfully to reach the Orient by circumnavigating Africa, but they never returned.[13]

At the same time, the Polo brothers were traveling on the Silk Road overland to China. This route, which connected China and India with Europe and the Mediterranean area, was known to traders and travelers already in the third century B.C. Unfortunately, it was often closed to active commerce for long periods because of wars and unrest in the areas of Central Asia through which the route passed. However, when Genghis Khan established Mongol supremacy in Central Asia and Mongol power came to control Eurasia from Eastern Europe to China and his descendent Kublai Khan became Emperor of China the route was again safe to travel. In 1271 the Polo brothers of Venice, one of whom was Marco Polo's father, started from Trebizond on the Black Sea on an overland voyage to China in 1271. Marco, who remained in China and visited the court of Kublai Khan, did not return until 1295. His book, *The Travels of Marco Polo*, probably helped make the Genoese eager to build up trade with the Far East by sea, so as to better compete with the Venetians.[14]

The business activities of the Genoese in the Iberian Peninsula were in the Christian kingdoms as in the Islamic south. For example, in 1248 when the King of Castille captured Seville from the Moslems, he have Genoese merchants who had contact with the Arabs permission to settle in that city. Moreover, in the following decades the Genoese, followed by the Venetians, sailed regularly past Gibraltar into the Atlantic. From there they went southward along the coast of Morocco where the Genoese already had a trading depot, and northward along Portugal's shores where they also established themselves and become influential. This was evident in 1317 when King Dinis of Portugal appointed the Genoese Manuel Passagno to the position of Admiral in the Portuguese fleet. These Genoese navigators also instilled in the Portuguese the desire to find a sea route to the Far East.

Venice regarded this Genoese-Portuguese aspiration with considerable trepidation: if the sailors of Genoa and Portugal could find a route circumventing the Moslem middlemen, they could obtain Asian products cheaper and crush their Venetian competitors. The Genoese-Venetian rivalry increased in the following century and culminated in the War of Chioggia, 1378-1381. It appeared initially that Genoa was to emerge the victor, but in the final phase of the war, fortune deserted her and she was defeated, beginning the city's decline as a major political and naval power. Soon thereafter Genoa was forced to accept foreign protectors, first Milan and thereafter France. However, Genoa did remain an economic center of prime importance in the following two centuries.

Genoa was also one of the first states to attempt to establish a public bank. As exchange banks often invested a portion of their assets in risky mercantile ventures, many failed, hence raising the perceived need for public banks. The Casa di San Giorgio opened its doors in 1408 and credit was extended to tax farmers and others on security of shares in the public debt. Private bankers also were allowed to open accounts with the Casa di San Giorgio. Despite considerable business, the bank closed its doors in 1444 and another attempt to establish a public bank was not tried until 1586.

Although Genoa's political power was eclipsed by the fourteenth century, its bankers remained a power into the seventeenth century due to their financial acumen, the fortunes of European politics, and their extensive European networks. However, these factors ultimately turned against Genoa, making it a spent force by the seventeenth century, during which time she loaned heavily to the governments of Spain and France. The many bankruptcies of these two nations finally ruined the financial position of the Italian city-state.

Florence and Its Merchant Banks

While we have largely focused on Genoa and Venice, we cannot neglect the contribution made by Florence. The Florentine trading strategy in the thirteenth and fourteenth centuries capitalized on rectifying the chronic imbalance in the flow of funds between Italy and Northern Europe. Significant credit balances accumulated in the branches of the Italian merchant banks in northern towns partly because the value of spice imports exceeded that of local exports.[15] Consequently, Florentine merchants sought to rectify the interregional disequilibrium by first turning to northern wool markets to provide a commodity of adequate volume and value and, secondly, by extending loans to local princes who regulated their sales in northern markets.

The Florentines, like most Italians, were equally active in establishing trade companies, also known as the "super-companies."[16] In many regards, the emergence of the super-companies reflected the interrelationship between the international organization of credit and the growing sophistication in the organization of business. The most well-known companies were the Bardi, Peruzzi, and Acciaiuoli. Medieval historians Hunt and Murray define the super-companies as such: "They were unusually large and qualitatively different, engaged in an exceptional range of activity—general trading, commodity trading, and manufacturing—over a wide geographical area for an extended period."[17] By no means were they a bank; rather a merchant-bank, with a strong international focus. The super-companies were also one of the first business organizations to transcend purely family interests.

Emerging from the traditional societies, the super-companies provided a new capitalist vehicle that attracted capital outside of the old family enterprise. The departure from family-based businesses to super-companies was underscored by structure and organization.

Financing for the company came from equity investments as well as three classes of long-term liabilities—partners' earnings retained in the business, additional money contributed by partners beyond their basic equity, and time deposits accepted from outsiders. This also meant that the super-companies were not permanent entities, but were usually short-term partnerships, which were periodically renewed (which allowed for a redistribution of shares).

Florentine merchant banks also attracted investors who preferred creditor status. This came in the form of deposits from the local political, military, and religious elites. Armed with deposits as well as incremental contributions by partners who wished to limit their equity stakes, the major Florentine companies were well-capitalized to engage heavily in international banking, especially in dealing with bills of exchange.

The Florentine trading companies were initially centrally organized. However the banking crisis of 1345 hit hard among the Bardi, Peruzzi, and Acciaiuoli companies of Florence, leading to a shift to a more flexible decentralized operation that was more akin to a combination of quasi-independent partnerships. This was exactly the type of structure that was evident in the operations of the Medici family in the mid-fifteenth century. Beginning as farmers and evolving into merchants and bankers, the Medici family became one of Europe's most powerful, spanning the period from the mid-1300s to 1748. Led by Giovanni Medici in the early 1400s and then by Cosimo, the Tuscan clan gradually expanded its banking operations beyond the confines of Florence, opening branches throughout Europe. The branch in Rome handled the Pope's account. As Blomquist observed, "In 1458 the Medici family members of the bank were partners in eleven different enterprises, including a cloth manufacturing firm and a silk manufactory as well as branches in Venice, Bruges, London, Avignon, Milan, Geneva, and a bank in Florence. The only common link between these independent entities was that the Medici family controlled the affairs of each subordinate enterprise." [18] For a long time, the Medicis benefited from this structure as it meant that the problems experienced by one branch of the business did not ripple through to the others. In a sense, the combination of quasi-independent partnerships allowed for the containment of bad risks.

The Medici also came to rule Florence, reflecting the powerful combination of finance and political power. This mixture of power was useful when Naples and Venice were at war with Florence. Faced with a threat from the north and south, Cosimo called in the debts from these two enemy cities, making it impossible for them to continue fighting, which was largely conducted by costly mercenaries. Consequently, the Medici were able to blend the power of the purse with that of the sword. For a period they were influential players in Italian politics, while serving the financial needs of the ruling class throughout much of Western Europe.

Papal and Royal Connections

As treated in an earlier chapter, the Church was opposed to usury. This stand was to gradually change. The Italian merchants initially faced competition from the religious orders of Templars and Hospitales, in particular for shipment or transfer of Church funds and as depositories of papal funds (during the thirteenth century). However, these areas of business eventually fell into the hands of Italian merchant-bankers. The other potential source of credit, the Jews, was odious to the Church. After the mid-thirteenth century, it was the Italian merchant banks that transferred papal income throughout Europe to the *camera* (a high-level body in the Church). They also acted as depositories for papal funds, exchanged money, extended credit to ecclesiastics, and frequently lent money to the camera itself. [19] In dealing with the Church, considerable care was taken not to appear to be too greedy and make profits that exceeded the just price.

As the Church required the services of Italy's merchant-bankers, so too did Europe's kings and princes. Italian credit helped finance at least one crusade, while Italian companies were tapped to act as fiscal agents to the English Crown. The credit of Italian merchant-bankers went to keep courts in style and to pay for mercenaries, an essential yet costly factor in Europe's power politics.

Providing credit for the Church and various secular rulers was not without hazard. Overextending credit could translate into devastating blows to Italian banks if a prince opted to default or was tardy in making payments. Unfortunately, this was to happen more than once as exemplified by the failures of Ricciardi of Lucca and the Bardi and Peruzzi of Florence. The Bardi were banished from France at the beginning of the Hundred Years' War because they supported the English king, Edward III. Italian bankers were also hurt when in 1339 Edward III forced the companies to recognize that he owed them a much smaller amount of debt than they had extended after subjecting them to a series of audits. The Medici merchant bank was confronted with the awkward problem of collectability in 1477 when their client, Charles the Bold, the Duke of Burgundy, was killed at the Battle of Nancy.

Those involved in providing credit (and charging interest) had an additional problem. While they were courted by the powerful, they were widely despised by the lower sectors of society. To the common man, all men who dealt in money and credit matters were *lombardi* or pawnbrokers. As Origo noted, "He [the common man] remembered a scene that was often before his eyes: a little man (very often a Jew...) seated from dawn to sundown in the market-place behind a table with a little cloth, noting down his odious accounts in his ledger, demanding an interest of 20, 30, and even 40 percent, and—for a pledge was necessary—taking away from a poor man his patched tunic, from a widow her cloak or bed."[20] Origo also noted that in foreign cities other Italian merchants often would not associate with the Lombards and they were often excluded from the sacraments. In some cases, they were even denied burial in holy ground.

Although the Italian bankers were to seal their loan agreements with contracts and other paperwork, the real issue for collection was the ability and willingness of the borrower to live up to his end of the deal. In the late Middle Ages, most rulers were hard-pressed to remain in power, often being locked in power struggles with their nobles or neighboring kingdoms. Within this rubric of power relationships, the Italian banker, lacking a powerful state behind him, was much lower down the pecking order in terms of urgent attention. While the banker was regarded as an important and influential force in European politics, the power of the purse ultimately was forced to give way to that of the sword. Ultimately, the Italian merchant-banker was vulnerable to default, confiscation of his goods, and, in some cases, the assassin's blade.

Exploring Foreign Shores

One of the roles of the Italians during the Renaissance was to provide both the credit and the talented personnel for the early voyages of exploration into the Atlantic. Indeed, European monarchs were eager to employ the Italians as commanders of their expeditions of exploration and trade. The reason for this is found in the economic and cultural place of the Italian city-states in Europe of the fifteenth century. Simply stated, the Italians city-states during the Renaissance were on the cutting edge of Western civilization, providing artists, engineers, and skilled seamen. The intellectual climate of the early Middle Ages in Western Europe did not favor scientific inquiry, but with the advent of the Crusades, contact with Byzantine culture influenced Western thought profoundly. The coming into frequent touch with Arab and Jewish thinking also broadened Europe's intellectual horizon. And this, as is well known, led to a revival of the old Greek spirit of rational inquiry.

The Italians, traders and strategically located at the crossroads of the pulls of these civilizations, were one of the first peoples in Western Europe thus influenced. At Padua a start was made to study medicine in a scientific manner.[21] New foundations for the study of geography were adopted through the studies of the German scholastic scholar Albertus Magnus and others.[22] Magnus questioned the belief that traveling south one could come to a region where the heat would make all life impossible, and he expressed the opinion that the equatorial belt was probably inhabited. In 1410 the reintroduction in Italy of the works of Ptolemy for study made the concept that the world was a sphere acceptable to most scholars. This, together with the printing of more accurately executed maps, the portolan maps in the following years, shows that there was a significant increase in geographical knowledge.[23] The so-called Medici Atlas in the Laurentian Library in Florence portrays with precision the location of the Azores.[24] The Atlantic was becoming less mysterious. Accepting that the world was round, a Florentine scientist Paolo da Toscanelli, in the middle of the fifteenth century, approached King Alfonso V of Portugal with the project of sailing westward to reach China. The same idea was presented to his son King John II some twenty-five years later by Columbus.[25]

The Italians were also willing to provide the financial means to conduct overseas expeditions. With the surplus capital from successful trading ventures, a willingness to speculate on a maritime gamble and skilled sailors, Italian bankers, merchants, and contractors were almost always involved. The financial contacts, therefore, which an Italian merchant sailor had, made him a preferred choice for arranging an expedition of exploration.

The story of Giovanni di Verrazano illustrates the core involvement of the Italians. A group of Italian bankers and merchants in Lyons wanted to obtain silk and other Chinese products cheaply. Consequently, they became the promoters of Verrazano's voyage and persuaded the French king, Francois I, to let him make a voyage in 1524 across the Atlantic to find the fabled Northern Passage to the Orient. Influential in this group was a certain Bonacorso Rucellia, a relative of Verrazano's, who, furthermore, was the banker of none other than Jean Ango, the leading merchant-ship owner of northwestern France.[26] Although Verrazano did not discover the passage to India, he did begin the exploration of North America's east coast and left his name in the New York area in the form of the Verrazano Straits and a major bridge. Unfortunately, for the explorer, he was later killed and eaten by the Caribs in the Caribbean.

The best known of the Italian explorers was Christopher Columbus, who was well-connected with the wealthy and influential Italian communities in Spain and Portugal.[27] These communities had grown in importance after the capture of Constantinople in 1453 by the Ottoman Turks, because many Genoese at that time transferred their investments from their colonies and settlements in the eastern Mediterranean to the territories and islands of the Iberian monarchies.[28] Retaining the eastern possessions after 1453 became difficult, and they lost them in the following decades. Even if trading with the Ottoman Turks was possible, it was far less profitable and far more troublesome than in the times of Byzantium. Also, the Black Sea trade in Russian and Tartar slaves had come to a halt. Finding a new trade route to India and China became more imperative, as did the desire to have a new source for slaves. The Genoese merchants were especially interested in finding solutions to these problems.

As discovering new sources of income was very much on the minds of many officials at Isabella's court in Spain, because of the expensive wars against Islamic and European rivals, it is not surprising that a project presented by a well-educated member of the Italian community obtained their interest. How willing Isabella was to let Columbus make his voyage can be gleaned from the fact that she quite readily agreed to all his demands for rights in the lands he would discover.

The exploration of Africa and the Atlantic at that time brought the rivalry between the rulers of Spain and Portugal to the Pope, prompting him to issue a Papal Bull stating where each of them had a right to sail. This meant that for the Genoese this meant to travel and trade in the South Atlantic they required the approval of the Portuguese king and to do the same in the north they needed permission from the Spanish king. What brought about this change?

By the end of the fifteenth century, the position of the European monarch was changing as centralizing royal authority was increasing while that of the feudal lords was waning. In France, King Louis XI's crowning success in 1477 was the defeat of his most powerful vassal, the Duke of Burgundy. The kings of France were on the path to becoming absolute monarchs. In Spain in 1469, the marriage of Isabella of Castille and Ferdinand of Aragon, causing the unification of Spain, also brought about a decrease in the power of independent-minded noble Grandees. The authority of this royal couple was further enhanced by successfully fighting the Muslims in southern Spain. In England, a long civil conflict involving the Crown and feudal lords, known as the War of the Roses, ended with the accession to the throne of Henry Tudor as Henry VII in 1485. Under his strong leadership, England became a nation-state where barons could no longer defy the king. Thus, in every one of these three nations, as well as in Portugal, the political power of cities and nobles was being curbed by that of the monarch's centralizing authority. The Europe of a congery of quarreling nobles and cities defending their feudal interests was being transformed into a continent where a few dynastic rulers competed for hegemony.

The Papal Bull of 1481 gave the Pope's blessing to the Treaty of Alcacovas between Spain and Portugal of 1479, through which Portugal saw the Papal Bull of 1456 reaffirmed, giving her the exclusive right of exploring the Atlantic southward along the African coast. Italian sailors could now only sail in those waters under the patronage of the king of Portugal. Should the Portuguese king not grant them the right to do so, they had to find another king as patron. Simply stated, the Italian city states could no longer ignore the will of the monarchs of Europe on the high seas. The Italians who wanted to find an alternative sea route to the overland route to India and China had to do so under the flag of a foreign monarch. The rise of strong monarchs makes it seem understandable why Columbus, Vespucci, Cabot, and Verrazano sailed under the banners of foreign rulers. The power of Italian finance was not enough to compete with the combination of military and ideological power of centralizing monarchs.

Besides being seats of scholarly studies, Italian cities at that period were also places where new inventions were rapidly expanding technical know-how. One witnessed the Genoese innovations in shipbuilding, the use of the magnetic compass, and the fact that Italy's most famous mapmakers at that time were the Genoese Vesconti.[29]

These factors gave rise to the perception in the rest of Europe that Genoese captains were the most knowledgeable and the best instructed of the Western world in the art of navigation. Consequently, they could easily find employment at home and abroad. An additional attraction of Genoese captains was the fact that the accountants of Genoa had been the first to introduce Italy to the new art of double bookkeeping.[30] Besides a knowledge of ships and seas, therefore, many a Genoese captain acquired good accounting skills for trading. It is not surprising that the rulers of Europe had great confidence in the capabilities of Italians as sailors and traders, especially those of Genoa, and were also more apt to lend credulity to the exploration projects of these men than to those presented to these rulers by their own subjects.

What impact did the Italian discoveries have on the New World and how did they affect Italian commercial states in the sixteenth century? Although the new colonies were not under Italian control, the Italians were adept at using economic influence in them for gaining political power. By aligning themselves with the local nobility in Spain, they obtained considerable control over the municipal government of Seville.[31] When in 1503 the Spanish government desired to regulate trade with the Americas and make it part of a monopoly of the crown, the Casa de la Contractación was created. The Genoese of Seville, however, were well-positioned. Consequently, they did not have to fear at that time that it would harm their economic interests. One of their members, Francesco Pinelo,[32] was appointed by the crown as one of the three officials in charge of this institution.[33] For this reason one notices in the early years of the colonization of Santo Domingo, the first place the Spaniards settled in the Americas, that it was the Genoese who introduced the sugar plantation system from the Canary Islands. The Portuguese plantation system in Brazil had the same Italian roots. The Italians had learned about cultivation and production of sugar from the Arabs in Syria in the days of the crusades. From there they had introduced the plantation system to Cyprus and then to Sicily and Southern Spain. Finally, early in the fifteenth century they brought it to the Canary Islands, Azores, and Madeira.[34]

Decline of the Italian Merchant-Bankers

The great discoveries were not to benefit the commercial cities of Italy. The discoveries of new sea routes and continents had transferred international trade from the Mediterranean to the Atlantic—a geographic shift that was to be in the long run detrimental to Genoa, Florence, and Venice. The shift initially favored Seville.[35] The Spanish city, however, was unable to maintain its dominance, which then shifted to the great ports of Portugal and France, and then to the Low Countries, where Antwerp became the commercial and financial center of Europe in the sixteenth century. Political and financial difficulties brought an end to Antwerp's primary stance in the 1560s. At this time, financing the Spanish debt, which the Fuggers and other German financiers had done, ended because several bankruptcies of the Spanish state had caused them to lose much of their capital. Knowing how to handle Spanish problems the Genoese stepped in and until 1627, when yet another Spanish default shook the financial world, Genoa's bankers saw their city as being one of the primary financial centers of Europe. Spain's ongoing financial mismanagement resulted in the kingdom not benefiting from the rich silver mines of the Americas. As the famous Spanish poet and satirist made clear in his poem, "Poderoso Caballero Es Don Dinero," silver that came to Spain from America went straight to Genoa.[36] Here men from the banking family of the Grimaldis and others seemed to be the holders of Europe's financial power.[37] In the seventeenth century, after Genoa lost its financial clout, Amsterdam in Holland, which had succeeded Antwerp as the financial market of Western Europe, became the capital market of a new world order.[38]

Perhaps the end of the Medici financial empire is most instructive of the rise of centralizing monarchs and their greater political-military power. Yet, one should be aware that the Medici were in a highly competitive field. As one historian commented, "they were the largest, but not gigantic, fish in a well-stocked and capacious pool."[39] The Medici star was at its highest under Lorenzo the Magnificant, the grandson of Cosimo. Described as "quite strikingly ugly," with a cracked, nasal and high-pitched voice, he was also strong, virile, clever, and inexhaustibly energetic.[40] According to at least one historian, he also had a strong taste for sexual innuendo and ribald stories as well as boisterous practical jokes. While Lorenzo had his puckish side, he was also regarded as the epitome of the Renaissance man—he was the ruler of Florence, a poet, scholar, and patron as well as a banker. In most of those categories he did well. As a banker, however, he was not so lucky or talented. As the historian Christopher Hibbert commented, "Lorenzo had none of his grandfather's taste or talent for business; he gave far too much scope to his branch managers and relied far too heavily upon the often ill-judged advice of his temporizing, ingratiating general manager, Francesco Sassetti."[41]

Under Lorenzo the fortunes of the Medici as a banking force went into decline. They lent money to Edward IV of England during the War of the Roses, which proved to be a costly mistake. Pressed with many expenses and considerable political intrigue during the War of the Roses, the English king had difficulties in repaying all his loans, greatly contributing to the bank's decision to close its London branch.[42] Mismanagement also played a part in the failure of the London branch. Problems arose in other branches, with Bruges and Milan offices collapsing and other offices in Lyon, Rome and Naples falling into difficulties. By the time of Lorenzo's death in 1492, at the age of forty-three, the Medici star was sinking rapidly.

The final blow came in 1494. Lorenzo's son, twenty-year-old Piero had succeeded him. Unlike his well-liked father, Piero was not well-loved by the Florentines and was seen as ruthless, tactless, unforgiving against his enemies and disloyal to his friends.[43] On top of that he had a violent temper and with age became arrogant. Piero soon got Florence involved in a conflict with the young and eager for glory King of France, Charles VIII. Charles was poorly educated, shortsighted, and distressingly ugly, but he was ambitious. When King Ferrante of Naples died in 1494, the French king decided to reassert his family's claim to the Kingdom of Naples and to the Kingdom of Jerusalem, which went with it. Piero sought to maintain Florence's neutrality and avoid the French army marching through his domains. Charles would not be delayed and advanced his forces through Florence. The Medici were forced to flee.

For the Medici, the invasion meant a loss of their treasures and forfeiture of their palaces and villas, which drove the firm into bankruptcy, even though the family remained the most prominent family in Florence until the eighteenth century.[44] In a sense, the failure of the Medici bank ended an era in the history of credit. As Blomquist noted, "Although the Italians continued in banking in later centuries, their dominance of international commerce and finance was broken. Within a few years before and after 1500, the center of gravity of international finance began to shift northward. By 1520 Italian bankers held only a secondary position in European money markets."[45] Although Genoa would regain some clout after Antwerp's political problems in the 1560s, that position was limited to being an important money market for southern Europe. The Protestant Reformation had caused, to a degree, a spilt along religious lines, between northern and southern Europe. This was reflected in the fact that by 1600 when Italian cities were important financial centers for southern Europe, Amsterdam in Holland was the financial center for northern Europe and the world beyond European shores.

Conclusion

The Italian city-states left a clear mark on history as early innovators and purveyors of credit and key players in the exploration of the New World. The Italians were clearly a catalyst in the development of an international credit system that spanned much of Europe and reached into the Levant. At the same time, their localized political structures, their inability to unify into larger and more powerful bodies, and their incessant rivalries weakened them as the power of centralizing monarchs grew in Spain, Portugal, France, and England. Italian credit initially played a significant role in the expansion of European trade and commerce as well as in the rise of Spanish and Portuguese power, but the inability of cities to cooperate with each other and create strong central political and military power was to mean that the bulk of new colonialists in the New World initially spoke Spanish and Portuguese, not Italian. Moreover, Italy's role as the primary purveyor of credit declined as more players to the north picked up the game as will be shown in the next chapter.

Notes

1.   Thomas J. Blomquist, "European Banking," in Joseph R. Strayer, editor-in-chief, *Dictionary of the Middle Ages: Augustinus Triumphus—Byzantine Literature* (New York: Charles Scribner's Sons, 1982), p. 74.
2.   Robert-Henri Bautier, *The Economic Development of Medieval Europe* (New York: Harcourt, Brace, Jovanovich, Inc., 1971), p. 65.
3.   Peter Lauritzen, *Venice: A Thousand Years of Culture and Civilization* (New York: Atheneum, 1981), pp. 28-31.
4.   Thomas J. Blomquist, "Banking, Europeans," in Strayer, editor-in-chief, *Dictionary of the Middle Ages Vol. 2* (New York: Charles Scribner's Sons, 1983), p. 73.
5.   Ibid.
6.   Iris Origo, *The Merchant of Prato: Daily Life in a Medieval Italian City* (New York: Penguin Books, 1957), p. 152.
7.   James D. Tracy, "Taxation and State Debt," in Brady, Oberman, and Tracy, eds., *Handbook of European History 1400-1600*, p. 563.
8.   Ibid., p. 147.

9.   Ibid.
10.   Ibid., p. 148.
11.   Harry A. Miskimin, *The Economy of Early Renaissance Europe, 1300-1460* (Englewood Cliffs, NJ: Prentice Hall, Inc., 1969), p. 123.
12.   Jonathan Barron Baskin and Paul J. Miranti Jr., *A History of Corporate Finance*, (New York: Cambridge University Press, 1997), p. 33.
13.   L. Boulnois, *The Silk Road* (London: George Allen and Unwin Ltd., 1966), p. 203. Also see Felipe Fernandez-Armesto, *Before Columbus: Exploration and Colonization from the Mediterranean to the Atlantic, 1229-1492* (Philadelphia: University of Pennsylvania Press, 1987), p. 152. As noted by Fernandez-Armesto: "Others ventured, however, south into waters unsailed—so far as we know—for centuries off the west coast of Africa. Record on only one such voyage has survived, that of the brothers Vivaldi, who from Genoa in 1291 departed 'for the regions of India by way of the Ocean', thus apparently anticipating the task Columbus was to set himself exactly 200 years later. The Vivaldi presumably envisaged a circumnavigation of the Atlantic, but the galleys they deployed were hardly suited to either purpose, too low and shallow for rough Atlantic waters, too dependent on inshore sailing for the inhospitable African coast. The Vivaldi were never heard of again, but it is likely that there were other journeys in the same direction, some of them in galleys, albeit with less ambitious aims." Pp. 152-153
14.   From the middle of the thirteenth century Kublai Khan played a prominent role in conquering China. In 1267 he launched his first campaign against the remnants of the Sung Empire, and in 1276 he finally took the Sung capital. Kublai then became the recognized emperor of China. He moved the capital to Peking, where it is still today. By that time he was the sovereign of an empire that reached from Korea in the east to Arabia and Poland in the west. Paper money was the official currency of his realm.
15.   Baskin and Miranti, *A History of Corporate Finance*, p. 36.
16.   Some of the more famous trade companies were the Bonsignori company of the Siena and the Ricciardi company of Lucca.
17.   Hunt and Murray, *A History of Business in Medieval Europe*, p. 102.
18.   Blomquist, *Dictionary of the Middle Ages*, p. 77.
19.   Ibid.
20.   Origo, *The Merchant of Prato*, p. 151.
21.   A.C. Crombie, *Medieval and Early Modern Science* (Garden City, NY: Doubleday & Co. [1952] 1959), p. 25.
22.   B. Penrose, *Travel and Discovery in the Renaissance* (New York: Atheneum, 1962), p. 12.
23.   Silvio A. Bedini, "Portolan Chart," in Joseph R. Strayer, ed., *Dictionary of the Middle Ages*, p. 35.
24.   T.R. Hale, *Renaissance Explorations* (New York: Atheneum, 1962), p. 12.
25.   Miles H. Davidson, *Columbus Then and Now* (Norman: Oklahoma University Press, 1997), p. 39; Gianni Granietto, *Christopher Columbus* (New York: Doubleday and Company, Inc., 1985), p. 58.
26.   Samuel E. Morison, *The Great Explorers* (New York: Oxford University Press, 1978), p. 132.
27.   Paolo Emilio Taviana, *Christopher Columbus—The Grand Design* (London: Orbis Publishing Ltd., 1989), p. 497.
28.   German Arciniegas, *Caribbean—Sea of the New World* (New York: Alfred A. Knopf, 1946), p.13.
29.   Bailey W. Diffie and George D. Winius, *Foundations of the Portuguese Empire*, (Minneapolis, MN: University Press of Minneapolis, 1977), p. 130.

30. Jane Jacobs, *Cities and the Wealth of Nations* (New York: Random House, 1984), p. 157.

31. Ruth Pike, *Enterprise and Adventures, the Genoese in Seville and the Opening up of the New World.* (Ithaca, NY: Cornell University Press, 1966), p. 7.

32. Clarence H. Haring, *Trading and Navigation Between Spain and the Indies in the Time of the Hapsburgs* (Gloucester, MA: Peter Smith [1918] 1964), p. 21.

33. Ferdinand Braudel, *The Wheels of Commerce, Civilization and Capitalism*, Vol. II (New York: Harpers and Row, 1979), p. 393. See also Pierre Chaunu, *Conquette et Exploitation des Nouveaux Mondes* (Paris: Presses Universitaires, 1969).

34. The Arab plantations in the Middle East used slaves. Slavery was an accepted institution for both Moslems and Christians in the Mediterranean area. It was regarded as quite normal to sell captives taken in war as slaves. When in 1453 Constantinople was taken by the Turks, its Christian citizens were sold into slavery by the Sultan. The same happened when the Turks attacked and captured Otranto in Southern Italy in 1480. They turned the city, noted Norwich, "into a flourishing market for Christian slaves." John Julius Norwich, *A History of Venice* (Middlesex, England: Penguin Books, 1983), p. 357. When Sultan Melmet died a year later, his successor withdrew the Turkish forces from Otranto. When the Italians began to establish plantations in their Mediterranean possessions, they also used slave labor. When the Turkish conquests in southern Europe and the Middle East made obtaining slaves from southern Russia and the Caucasus area difficult, the Italians brought African slaves, who had been brought along the Saharan caravan routes to the Mediterranean by Arabs. Later when they sailed south along the west coast of Africa, the Italians, Spaniards, and Portuguese directly brought the slaves from these regions to the Iberian Peninsula and the Atlantic islands. When they arrived in America, Spaniards and Italians had, therefore, no qualms of using American Indians of the Caribbean as slaves and when disease and the evil conditions under which they lived wiped them out in a few decades, the Spaniards imported luckless Africans provided by Italian merchants. The Genoese would see no evil in this trade in humans. Until well into the seventeenth century, the asiento, the contract for obtaining slaves for the Spanish Americas, remained in Italian hands. The institutions on which the plantation system of the new world rested was Italian in origin for they had, as was shown, tested and developed the techniques, finances, administration and labor organization which sustained them and made them profitable in their possessions in the Levant and the Mediterranean. David Brion Davis, *Slavery and Human Progress* (New York: Oxford University Press, 1984), p. 54. The European discovery of America was to a great extent an Italian enterprise, and the first development of the plantation system there also had its Italian roots and was the earliest economic system introduced in Latin America. The institutions which gave Latin America its Spanish character were the hacienda system based on feudal principles of labor and the missions of the church.

35. See Hugette and Pierre Chaunu, *Seville et L'Atlantique 1504-1660*, 8 vols. (Paris: Librairie Arma Colin, 1955-1959). Pierre Chanu, *European Expansion in the Later Middle Ages* (New York: North Holland Publication Co., 1979), p. 156.

36. Francesco de Quevedo, "Letrilla," *Poesia Española* (Vol. 4), Marvin Diego, ed. (Mexico City: Ediciones de Annrea, 1958), p. 213.

37. Ferdinand Braudel, *Civilization and Capitalism 15th and 18th Century (Vol. 2) The Wheels of Commerce* (New York: Harper and Row Publishers, 1979), p. 524. Other Genoa banking families were the Pinelli, Lomellini, Spinola, and Doria.

38. Ferdinand Braudel, *The Wheels of Commerce*, p. 393.

39. David Abulata, "The Impact of Italian Banking in the Late Middle Ages and the

Renaissance 1300-1500," in Alice Teichova, Ginette Kurgan-van Hentenryk, and Dieter Ziegler, *Banking, Trade and Industry: Europe, American and Asia from the Thirteenth to the Twentieth Century* (Cambridge: Cambridge University Press, 1997), p.28.

40.   Christopher Hibbert, *The Rise and Fall of the House of Medici* (London: Penguin Books, 1974), p. 113.

41.   Ibid., p. 158.

42.   One of the ironies in history was that although Edward was unable to repay his Italian loans, he was to die solvent. As Desmond Seward wrote, "Historians vary considerably in their estimate of Edward IV, but it has to be said on balance he was colorful and impressive rather than truly great. Certainly he ended his life in unchallenged occupation of the throne, a fine fighting soldier who defeated all his enemies, while his financial policy was so sound that he died solvent—something no English monarch had achieved for at least two centuries." Desmond Seward, *The Wars of the Roses: Through the Lives of Five Men and Women of the Fifteenth Century* (New York: Viking Press, 1995), p. 254.

43.   Hibbert, *The Rise and Fall of the House of Medici*, p. 177.

44.   Ibid., p. 201.

45.   Blomquist, *Dictionary of the Middle Ages*, p. 78.

Part 4

Modern Credit Period

7

Credit Goes North:
The Road to Amsterdam

The city of Bruges, Belgium, does not exactly leap off the map as an important location in international finance. Indeed, Bruges is usually associated as the place where Flemish painting began its colorful history. The works of Jan van Eyck, Petrus Christus, Hieronymus Bosch and Pieter Bruegel (both the elder and younger) reflect the society of medieval Bruges, which was founded upon trade and commerce. Yet Bruges is regarded as the home of the first modern *bourse* or stock market and then nearby Antwerp, which succeeded it in economic importance by the end of the fifteenth century. Antwerp was until the late 1990s one of the oldest consecutively running *bourses* in the world. Together with the stock market in Amsterdam, the three cities of the Low Countries, today's Belgium, and the Netherlands constituted the forerunners of contemporary major stock markets. Cities such as Bruges, Antwerp, and Amsterdam were the movers and shakers in the newly emerging international credit system in the sixteenth and seventeenth centuries, much as New York, London, and Tokyo are today. Without their contributions, today's global credit system would have taken considerably longer to develop, if at all. The Dutch, in particular, merit special attention, considering the importance of their contribution to finance. As John Steele Gordon in his history of Wall Street, *The Great Game*, commented, "The Dutch invented modern capitalism in the early seventeenth century. Although many of the basic concepts had first appeared in Italy during the Renaissance, the Dutch, especially the citizens of the city of Amsterdam, were the real innovators. They transformed banking, stock exchanges, credit insurance, and limited-liability corporations into a coherent financial and commercial system."[1]

This chapter focuses on the emergence of Bruges and Antwerp as major credit centers, the role of the south German banking groups, and concludes with the rise and decline of Amsterdam as the credit hub of the Western world. The period spans the mid-1500s to the late 1600s. The Reformation, the Protestant Revolution that occurred in the early years of the sixteenth century, divided Europe. Southern Europe remained Catholic and its financial center continued to be Italy, while the north converted to Protestantism, with its financial center ultimately settling in Amsterdam. As Amsterdam became the major financial center in Europe, it developed a sophisticated stock market, which helped finance the flow of global trade, witnessed the rise and fall of joint stock companies, and gave the world "Tulip Madness."[2] It is important to underscore that in the cases of Antwerp and Amsterdam, they became the dominant credit centers in the emerging global economy, overshadowing all others. And in the case of Amsterdam, Dutch credit was to become an important force in Northern Europe's dynamic economic development and in the development of European colonialism. Three critical factors that elevated Amsterdam and the Dutch to a credit superpower were: (1) sound public finance; (2) a strong position in international trade; and (3) a commanding position in capital markets in the form of the *bourse*.

Bruges

During the thirteenth century the sea route along Europe's Atlantic coast emerged as one of the most significant trading arteries of the Western world. For the Flemish cities of the Low Countries ties with the Italian traders who initiated the sea route were significant, which was especially true of Bruges, a city on the Zwyn, a tributary of the Scheldt River. Long before 1277, the city had traded with Italy by overland connections via Champagne in France. When the sea link with Italy was established, Bruges's importance became paramount. At that time, the cloth industry, based on imported wool from England was already a vital industry in this city. What made Bruges particularly attractive was that it had two ports—one where ships could drop anchor and discharge their goods, and the second, a riverport, which was surrounded by a network of canals, linking the city to the European interior, especially the German Rhineland.

Many Lombard traders settled in the city and introduced accounting practices that made the development of credit possible, thus adding impetus for the creation of larger and more inter-European enterprises. The courtyard of the house of the De Beurze Family, used for the exchange of financial papers by the Italians, was the beginning of a stock market, and the French name for a stock market, "La Bourse," is probably derived from Beurze.[3]

Bruges united the two major poles of maritime circulation of Europe, that of the Mediterranean with that of the Baltic and North Seas.[4] Obviously, trade with England and central and southern Germany was also of primary importance. Bruges evolved into a highly prosperous city, with a well-established and comfortable merchant class. With its trade and industry, it was the principal commercial and financial city of Western Europe. One reflection of the city's wealth was to be found in food. In its markets were to be found, and exchanged, products transported from the Near-East and Africa by the Genoese and the Venetians, and goods brought from Russia and Scandinavia through the Baltic by ships of the Hanse. Beyond the local produce of cabbages, carrots, and turnips were pears, apples, and the "lenten" fruits that came from the south and could not otherwise be found in that region in February and March.[5] But that was not all. Oranges came from Africa and Spain, while figs and grapes came from the Mediterranean region. Clearly, Bruges represented a lifestyle superior to much of the rest of Europe at the time and its prosperity was tied to commerce.

Bruges remained the major commercial and financial center of Western Europe until well into the fifteenth century when Antwerp gradually replaced it. The silting of the Zwyn estuary caused Bruges's decline, making its harbor difficult to reach from the ocean. Additionally, Bruges's position as a major credit hub was hurt by the constraints placed on trading by the guilds of Bruges, which hampered commercial activities. Antwerp, further up the Scheldt, had a good harbor and its authorities did not pursue heavy-handed rules restricting trade. This city at the boundary of the provinces of Flanders and Brabant had a rather independent government that granted much freedom to local and foreign business enterprises and banking institutions. In particular, Antwerp levied no heavy taxes and allowed foreigners considerable freedom in trading. In contrast to Antwerp, all sales in Bruges had to be made through Bruges brokers, who charged a commission on each transaction. Considering the close relationship between trade and finance, it is easy to understand why merchant bankers were willing to leave Bruges and set up shop in Antwerp.

Antwerp

Many modern banking techniques and the sophisticated use of a stock market had their beginnings in sixteenth-century Antwerp. In the second half of the fifteenth century Antwerp took off economically, stimulated by an upsurge in international trade. As Bruges declined, Antwerp became the great storehouse through which merchandise flowed, ranging from all kinds of African products such as molasses from the Canary Islands and slaves and sugar from Brazil to English wool and Portuguese pepper from the East Indies. Goods flowed through Antwerp into the European hinterland, including the great southern German trading cities such as Augsburg. Antwerp's rise to a great trading and finance center was accompanied by population growth: about 1440-60, the city had only 3,334 houses; half a century later, the number was 6,800 and in 1500 it had grown to 9,000, compared with only 6,000 houses in another major town at this time, Brussels.[6]

The combination of the immense trade in products and goods from all over the world made Antwerp the most vital business center of Europe. Antwerp's trading system assembled all the necessary ingredients for success—a well-equipped port and key human infrastructure—merchants, bankers, brokers and commercial agents. Much of the financial activity was centered on the bourse.

The Antwerp bourse, which in 1531 was opened "to the merchants of every nation and language," became the place where fortunes were easily gained and lost.[7] The high energy level was linked to the fact that many of those acquiring fortunes in trade were young men, who were more than willing to take a gamble. This gave the bourse a "brisk and bustling atmosphere" and helped make it "a dangerous place where fights often broke out and people were not infrequently killed."[8] Concerned about the violence, local authorities passed a regulation that no person might draw his knife during an exchange session, on pain of a fine of a hundred florins. This regulation was hardly effective. As one Belgian historian noted, "In spite of this there were several deaths each year. In 1551, there was the case of the merchant Alfero, who was murdered by Josepho de Ferrere. In the same year another merchant Deodati, was killed as the result of an affair concerning women."[9] Adding to this wild atmosphere, Antwerp's criminal underworld was actively engaged by those individuals wishing to hire assassins.

The economic ferment in Antwerp gave rise to a culture of speculation in all fields in which rich citizens and foreigners participated. It also helped create a market for the sale of patents and secret processes for manufacturing, many of which were fraudulent.

Antwerp's bourse and the society constructed around it therefore formed a core element of a new type of economy, based in large part on services, including financial services. This helped the bourse develop practices that not only facilitated private financial dealings, but also provided rulers of kingdoms with new means of obtaining money. [10] As Randall Germain stated, "The rise of Antwerp, and particularly its bourse, signaled a shift in the structure of public financing available to sovereigns (American bullion and revenue from the granting of lucrative trading monopolies) and the imperial demands which they assumed."[11] These trends were reinforced by an improving structure of the market, with one Antwerp financier, Paul van Daele, publishing a regular list of exchange rates and buying rates for Italian, French, English, and German commercial bills.[12]

Although the early bourses were dominated by the Italians, Antwerp was to develop a capital market that was open to businesses and monarchs of all nations. As Ehrenberg commented on this development, "...Antwerp created a Bourse for the merchants' from everywhere and, abolished all restrictions on their trade, brought them into immediate daily communication, and created what the Paris jurists in their memorandum of 1530 called the 'Bourse commonalty,' i.e., an assembly of business men of different backgrounds for a common purpose, the transaction of business of a given kind, an assembly whose members accordingly had certain interests in common with one another." [13] In a sense, the Antwerp bourse stretched the boundaries of international credit beyond the dominance of the Italians, opening the door to others, especially the merchants of central and south Germany, where mining and a growing textile industry had developed major cities active in European trade. In fact, over time the major suppliers of credit were large German banking houses, in particular the Fuggers and Welsers of Augsburg.[14] The bourses also offered a new source of money for monarchs and their governments.

Another important factor that elevated Antwerp from other financial centers was that its bourse provided the first sustained secondary market for public debt. An example of this was with the juros and asientos, debt of the royal Spanish government, which were bought and sold by third parties as demand allowed.[15] The development of a secondary market made Antwerp a much deeper market for capital as the trading in foreign government securities broadened the scope of the bourse's activities.

In time, the Antwerp bourse came to be the primary place where capital could be raised in large amounts. For the kings and princes who were busy conducting wars, this became an essential source of funding. In all of this, creditworthiness was a rudimentary concept. The quality of a debt owed by a monarch was not determined by his creditworthiness, but by the kind of security that he offered the creditor, i.e., the nature of the guarantee or the pledged revenues. However, the creditor, usually a merchant banker, had to take into consideration such things as the fortunes of the harvest, the ability to pick the winner in a war, and how to deal with the untimely death of the borrower on the field of battle. Without such things as key man life insurance or credit agencies, even the largest and most sophisticated Italian and south German firms had problems with accurately assessing the full value.

It is important to underscore Antwerp's significance to links between international trade and commerce. As Germain noted, "During its heyday in the sixteenth century, Antwerp facilitated the movement of goods through Europe by providing the necessary credit to finance their journeys. It drew silver from German mines, through the services of German banks such as the Fugger, to Antwerp, and passed that silver on to the Portuguese who required it for their dealings in the Far East. It extended credit to the Spanish crown to finance the exploitation of the New World."[16]

Antwerp's most prosperous years were the last twenty years of the reign of the Hapsburg Emperor Charles V (1535-1556). Charles was born in Ghent in Flanders and, in 1506, had inherited at the age of six, at the death of his father, the overlordship of the Low Countries (present-day Belgium and the Netherlands). When his maternal grandfather Ferdinand II of Aragon passed away in 1516 he became king of Spain and its overseas possessions. Three years later, in 1519, when his paternal grandfather Emperor Maximilian of Hapsburg died, he became ruler of the Hapsburg lands in Austria and Germany. In that same year, with much financial help, primarily from the financially powerful Fugger and Welser families of Augsburg, he was elected Emperor of Germany.

The Age of the Fugger: South German Bankers

The continual need for money to finance his empire brought Charles V repeatedly to seek assistance from the financial families of south Germany, who were early and apt pupils of the Italian bookkeeping systems. Of these, the Fugger and Welser families of Augsburg, Germany were probably the most prominent. However, it was the Fuggers who gave their name to this period, referred to as the Age of the Fugger.

The Fuggers were often regarded as the bankers to the Hapsburgs, a notion that clearly reflected the interplay between the power of the sword and that of the purse. The Fuggers emerged on the historical stage as weavers in the village of Graebn in Swabia in southwestern Germany. Hans Fugger was the first of his family to gain historical note, being a successful textile trader and establishing his family in Augsburg in 1367. His grandson Jakob was highly successful in finance and responsible for developing the Hapsburg relationship.[17]

Although the Fuggers were a family firm, Jakob was the one responsible for developing the Hapsburg relationship. Following an apprenticeship in Venice where he learned accounting, Jakob took charge of the Fugger agency in Innsbruck in 1485. In 1487, Jakob Fugger loaned Sigismund, the archduke of Tyrol, 20,000 ducats. As security to the loan, the Hapsburg lord gave Jakob control of the most productive of the Schwarz silver mines and the revenues of the entire province of the Tyrol. Silver was in high demand for fine ornaments and as the second negotiable currency after gold. Control of such resources was profitable and added to the Fugger's financial power. The power of the Fugger's was not to stop there. Another loan to Sigismund in 1488 gave the Fuggers the management of silver production in its entirety.

When Maximillan followed his cousin Sigismund as archduke of Tyrol in 1490 he inherited the relationship with the Fuggers.[18] Simply stated, he could not do without them. The young archduke promptly turned to his bankers for a new loan which he required for his wars in order to consolidate the Hapsburg holdings. By 1508, the Fuggers had spread throughout Europe, with investments in textiles, real estate and, of course, silver and copper mining. They were also involved in helping finance expeditions to the Americas and emerged as chief papal banker in Germany and Scandinavia, charged with the lucrative monopoly of transferring funds from the sale of indulgences.

The Fugger's extensive international network also allowed them to provide another critical service to the Hapsburgs, whose empire was fragmented throughout the continent. As the vassal states paid money to the Hapsburgs, they provided payment in multiple European currencies. The movement of such payments was slow and fraught with dangers. Consequently, it was easier to rely on the Fuggers who could get their money to Augsburg in as little as two weeks by means of bills of exchange. Simply stated, the Fugger agent in Antwerp received the money due in exchange for a written credit note, which could be quickly sent to Germany and exchanged for cash in Augsburg against Fugger assets.

The rise of the Fuggers represented a change in the world of credit. By the early decades of the sixteenth century, the Italians had been eclipsed by their northern competitors. Northern finance, with a more sophisticated structure of business, emerged during this period with greater influence in the affairs of Europe. Professor Eugene Rice, Jr. made the following comparisons between the Medici and the Fuggers:

> In 1460 the most impressive business organization in Europe was the Medici Bank of Florence. By 1545, the Fugger Company of Augsburg was the largest firm. The Medici Bank (the firm was called a *banco*, but its activities were commercial and industrial as well as financial) had eight branch offices, the Fuggers, twenty-five. The Medici owned three modest textile firms. The Fuggers owned silver mines in the Tyrol and gold mines in Silesia, mined mercury in Spain, and controlled the larger part of copper production in Hungary...Finally, the capital of the Medici Bank in 1451 was 90,000 florins; that of the Fuggers in 1547 was over ten times as great. The larger scale of economic activity in the sixteenth century is clear.[19]

The fortunes of the Fuggers, however, were to become tightly bound to those of their primary customer. Under Charles V, who followed Maximillan as emperor, the heavy costs of fighting wars against the Ottoman Turks, and French and German Protestants put imperial finances under considerable strain. Jakob actually wrote Charles in 1523 to tactfully remind the emperor of his debts, which resulted in a partial repayment. Although the Fuggers believed that they were overextended to the Hapsburgs, they could not refuse their major borrower, who also happened to be one of the most powerful forces in European politics. Jakob died in 1525, leaving his heirs with the legacy of the royal relationship and its debts. Under Jakob's son, Anton, the firm remained active in securing loans for emperors and kings. Although Anton was forced to retreat from some of the company's mining ventures, he was successful in diversifying the firm's activities into the spice trade and cattle importing. Although Anton amassed a considerable fortune for the Fuggers by the mid-1540s, the family business remained sensitive to the financial fortunes of Europe's royal families. In the next half century this meant losing money. Although the Fuggers were to remain in business, they were finally forced to dissolve the company after the Thirty Years War of 1618 to 1648 and had little impact on international credit thereafter.

Another major German banking family was the Welsers, also from Augsburg and a major force in trade and credit operations in Antwerp. After all, Antwerp was the center of the activities of the large ocean fleet of the Welsers. Their ships brought spices and other goods from Asia and America via Lisbon and Seville to the market of this city. Thus the Welsers had access to the then-expanding commerce with the New World, which was largely the preserve of either the Portuguese or the Spanish. And, of course, the Welsers, for the trade and shipping of colonial wares had many contracts with the king of Portugal and Spain.

The Welsers reflected the increasing internationalization of Europe's trade. In alliance with the Ehingers of Constance, the Welsers concluded agreements with the emperor, in his capacity as king of Spain, that allowed them equal footing with Spanish traders in the New World. While this provided them the opportunity of opening factories in Seville and Hispañiola (present-day Dominican Republic and Haiti), it also meant that they received a four-year permission to send German miners to the New World to assist the Spanish colonialists. The concession for trading in Seville was highly significant, considering that the Spanish city was then the mistress of the Spanish Atlantic.

Equally significant, the Welsers were granted the rights to conquer and colonize what was eventually Venezuela—then an unknown region, allegedly the home of El Dorado, the Golden Man.[20] It was this hint of El Dorado's vast fortune of gold that fueled German efforts in Venezuela. Because of this, the Welser forces neglected to make permanent settlements, which ultimately guaranteed their failure in what was to be the first German attempt from 1529 to 1546 at establishing a colony in the New World. Venezuelan historian Guillermo Morón states that the Welsers and their agents "spent most of their time scouring the country," and, "Colonial administration was almost totally lacking."[21] Financially the Venezuela operation was, for the Welsers, costly and unprofitable. For Welser agents in Venezuela the operation was deadly as more than one of them died from Indian arrows or intrigues with their fellow colonialists.

The financially more powerful Fugger family mostly aided Charles V with his expenses in Spain and the German Empire. However, they also participated in financing some of the overseas trade of Spain and together with the Welsers were involved in a colonizing expedition of the Spaniards to Argentina in 1534. Charles V, in 1534, dispatched an expedition to Argentina under the command of Pedro Mendoza, a wealthy Spaniard who was to be the first governor of Argentina and who financed the expedition in part with loans from Charles V's Flemish and Dutch bankers. The Fuggers and Welsers assisted the expedition with ships and equipment.[22]

At the end of his reign, Charles V had ever increasing difficulties in Germany with several Protestant rulers who finally brought about the Schmalkaldic War. This and the aforementioned wars with France and the continual military threats of the Ottoman Empire, caused Charles to be continuously in great need of money to pay his armies. Therefore, he placed great pressure on the Fuggers, the Welsers, and other great German business families for new loans, even though these financiers believed that he lacked the capability of giving them effective securities for such loans. Both the Fuggers and the Welsers felt themselves overextended in their financial dealings, and were highly reluctant to provide more credit. With such problems at hand, the great German bankers were slowly losing their prominent position in the financial world. Thus, in the final years of the reign of Charles V, the Fuggers and Welsers were slowly being replaced by Genoese bankers who regained their former relative importance as the financiers of Spanish loans. For the Welsers, the accusation Charles V had made in the 1540s that in Lyons they had underwritten loans of his enemy, the king of France, put a strain on their relations with the royal court of Spain.[23]

In the end, both the Fuggers and Welsers became hostages to the fortunes of the great princes to whom they lent money. Although both families and their partners had extensive operations throughout Europe with major offices in Antwerp and Lyons, they became vulnerable to sovereign risk. German banking was particularly shaken when Philip II declared bankruptcy in 1577, leaving some to conclude that the Age of the Fuggers had ended.[24] For example, when the financial crisis of 1557 overtook the Welsers, their major exposures were to unpaid claims on the French court, Spanish loans, and Netherlands bonds. Although the financial crisis of 1557 did not finish off the Welsers and other financial groups, the clock was ticking. The early 1560s were tough economically and south German business houses suffered significantly, though the Welsers and Fuggers appeared to weather the situation better than most. However, with the progression of political and social turmoil in the Low Countries in the 1580s and the general credit crisis that emerged, the Welsers and Fuggers became more and more overextended. In 1580, the Welsers sold their Antwerp property and during this period a number of key family members died. By 1620 the fortune of the Welsers had hit bottom, with Paul Welser dying in prison, having earlier declared bankruptcy. The Fuggers had to dissolve their company after the Thirty Years War in 1648.

The Winds of Change in Credit

European credit underwent an important transformation in the 1500s and 1600s. While credit had been the domain of those involved in trade capable of generating cash surpluses, the shift was evident as creditors now functioned more as private bankers. Not only did creditors function as money brokers or commercial agents for long-distance trade, they also increasingly came to take deposits. By the sixteenth century, many of the features of modern finance were solidifying. As Henry Kamen commented, "...where bankers did not charge for the deposit service, they tended to lend the money out in the modern way. A depositor who called for his capital might get it in cash or, as often happened, in credit. He might even be granted an overdraft in order to increase his confidence in the deposit banker." [25]

Henry Kamen, in his *European Society 1500-1700*, also noted that the new private banks were a source of insecurity: "Their capital was small, and deposits were often put into very risky ventures. The practice of credit was shaky, since it needed only a few persistent rumors to cause a run on the bank and hence its collapse." [26] As already noted with the Italian merchant banks in the 1400s, the risks to credit during the 1500s included wars. Moreover, the introduction of mercantilistic rules and laws made shifting assets and refusing loans to kings difficult for financiers and there was little recourse for them when a government default occurred. Private banks were at risk when they lent to the Spanish monarchy as well as to France during the Wars of Religion. The last was particularly bruising for aspiring bankers: in 1575 there were forty-one banks in Lyons, one of the country's major trade hubs. By 1580, there were twenty banks and in 1592 only four survived. In the 1587-89 period in Spain and Italy alone, there were twenty bankruptcies among the large banks.

Considering the risky nature of private finance, two trends soon emerged. As private banks appeared risky, there was a call for the establishment of public banks. Secondly, those seeking speculative credit were forced to look elsewhere for funds, which provided an ongoing niche of business for merchant bankers and, in time, for bourses. The establishment of a public bank meant that the institution was licensed by public authority and that it was open to both private and governmental clients. The largest amount of capital supporting the public bank was "public" or municipal. However, although the public banks were created for financial security, enterprise credit was seldom allowed.[27]

As we have already chronicled, merchant banks provided a source of credit for everything from paying for armies to facilitating the Church's transfers in Europe. At the end of the day, the merchant banks were limited by the amount of capital that could be raised and were often caught overextended and prone to failure. Consequently, as demand for credit grew, the bourse was to emerge during the sixteenth century as an important source of credit. Beginning in the early sixteenth century large financial dealings were largely transacted in Augsburg, Genoa, and Florence. Credit was provided after negotiations with individual firms, without direct competition of one house with another. In a sense, the market system of competition had not yet emerged. The payments from such negotiations were usually made in Antwerp and Lyons. Yet, a bourse where loans could be traded and capital raised did not yet exist. The driving force of change came from the political realm, in that ongoing years of war created a heavy demand for credit. The politically tangled web of war and credit included a nasty conflict between the Hapsburg Charles V and France's Francis I, which began in 1542 and resulted in the fielding of large armies that called not only French and Spanish troops to arms, but also pulled in large numbers of Swiss, German, Swedish, and Danish mercenaries. The Hapburgs also had to contend with the Ottoman Empire pushing up from the Balkans towards Austria. All of this cost money—money for troops, equipment, and allies.

The growing financial need of the kings and princes of Europe forced them to agree to floating loans bearing interest, which soon became a regular means of covering extraordinary expenditure and were soon used for ordinary expenditures as well.[28] The critical change in all of this was that hitherto capital for war had been raised either compulsorily from the subjects of the kingdom or voluntarily from the merchant banks. Now the loans needed were much larger and the demand was more frequent. Fortunately for the warring monarchs, the rise of the bourse was to provide a badly needed fix in providing capital.

Shifting Fortunes

Although the dynamic of European credit was to shift from Bruges to Antwerp at the end of the fifteenth century, religious rebellion and war in the second half of the sixteenth century shifted the financial center to Amsterdam. In 1556, when Charles's son Philip came to rule the Low Countries and the following year in Spain as King Philip II, the Reformation had made the freedom-loving city of Antwerp a haven for Protestants, which Philip, a good Catholic, could not tolerate.

The growing discord between Protestants and Catholics resulted in anti-Catholic riots in Antwerp and other cities in 1566, and in 1568 when Philip sent Spanish troops to eliminate and suppress Protestant opposition. This action sparked a general rebellion in the provinces of the Low Countries. In the southern provinces (present-day Belgium) Philip's government quickly regained control of the situation, but in the northern provinces the Protestants maintained the upper hand. In 1576, the unpaid Spanish troops in Antwerp mutinied and sacked the city, which did little to endear Spain and its royals to the local population. Needless to say, Antwerp soon joined the north in defying Philip II.

Antwerp was not to regain its dominant commercial and credit role. When in 1581 the Northern Provinces gained their independence and became known as "The Dutch Republic," fortune did not smile as kindly on Antwerp or other Belgian cities. In 1585 Spanish troops retook it for Philip, leaving behind a trail of destruction. In fact, the religious wars left Belgium in a state of devastation: once prosperous cities and towns were depleted of their populations, agricultural productivity slumped, and law and order virtually disappeared. While the military campaigns did little to restore calm needed for commerce, the Dutch authorities found it easy to close the Scheldt River, the critical waterway for all ships wanting to go to Antwerp, and the city soon ceased to be a significant port and economic center and was replaced by Amsterdam.

If religion was causing problems between the Low Countries and the Spanish, it must be noted that the mercantilistic policies of Spain did not help to maintain good relations between Spain and its European rivals. As mentioned earlier, monarchs competing for power in Europe viewed enlarging their territory as the major indication of becoming more powerful. The struggle between the Spanish Hapsburgs and the Valois, and later Bourbon kings of France was, therefore, a struggle for land. Trade was good as long as it was pursued by one's own countrymen and facilities. When foreigners were involved the gain went abroad and this had to be prevented.

The mercantilists stressed the importance of trade and commerce as the source of the nation's wealth, and advocated policies to increase a nation's wealth and power by the encouragement of exports and discouragement of imports and thus have a favorable balance of trade. Furthermore, amassing bullion in gold or other precious metals was of prime importance. However, mercantilist practices in trying to achieve this could differ greatly both in time and space. The early practices of free enterprise and market economy which we could observe developing in the late Medieval period were significantly hampered by mercantilist policies which were becoming prominent starting in the sixteenth century.

Portugal's policies regulating colonial control and trade early in the sixteenth century can be regarded as mercantilist as it was a royal monopoly, "organized by royal factors."[29] Spices, the most important product from the country's overseas possessions were sent to Portugal in closely regulated shipments. From Lisbon, the spices were then re-exported to Antwerp and traded through Portuguese factors established in that city. However, the heavy level of governmental and bureaucratic interference made the spice trade of little profit to the Portuguese government. In time, much of this trade fell into the hands of the great bankers of the period, in particular, the Fuggers, who happened to be a major force, as mentioned before, in financing the royal government. The spice trade had, therefore, not really benefited Portugal, but it did help to enrich Antwerp.

The core of Spanish mercantilism was to be found in her colonial policies.[30] The policies adopted by the Spanish government in 1503 saw to it that the Casa de la Contratacion established at Seville regulated all trade with the Americas. The chief instrument of administration, however, was the royal Council of the Indies, which "was not definitely organized until 1524. The council made the laws for the colonies, decided on policies for them and acted as a final court of appeal."[31] Even though Italian merchants living in Spain had been active in helping Columbus and his successors to develop the Caribbean colonies and although the king-emperor Charles V had opened "the trade of the Indies to his non-Spanish subjects" (i.e., the Welsers and Fuggers), the participation of these foreigners was not desired by Spanish merchants and officials. This became more evident as Philip II after his accession to the throne in 1556 made exclusiveness "the permanent keynote of Spanish colonial policy."[32] The monopolizing of colonial trade and making certain that the bullion of the Americas would go to Spain were the major objects of Madrid's policy.

Both Spain and Portugal established conditions that would retard their economic development and pass the leadership of Europe to northern countries. Both Iberian countries had established themselves as military and ideological (i.e., Christian) powers capable of projecting their influence on a global basis, with power being highly concentrated in the person of the king. The mercantilistic economic policies they adopted cut these countries off from outside capital (like the Dutch), while the high costs of military expenditures exceeded revenues, even with the inflow of wealth from the Americas. Another factor was that social mores placed an emphasis on military and religious occupations, which contributed to the development of a strong societal bent to regard land as a measurement of wealth, not the profits earned from more base pursuits such as trade and finance. In fact, the records of rich Spanish merchants in the late sixteenth, seventeenth, and eighteenth centuries demonstrate that they kept only a small part of their capital in continuing trade, with the remainder invested in land and, to a lesser extent, employed in lending.[33] Consequently, while a Portuguese and Spanish merchant class existed, it never developed into a strong economic and political force like its Dutch, English, German, and Italian counterparts. The Dutch merchant class, in particular, benefited from a more decentralized political structure that allowed them to pursue their main interests as capitalists, profits. The Iberians, in contrast, adopted mercantilist policies that did not place an emphasis on individual profits, but on national wealth. Ultimately, this was to mean that Portugal and Spain missed their chances to develop their cities into world financial hubs, leaving the shifting fortunes of credit to move northward to Amsterdam.

The Birth of the Dutch Republic

Before 1568 the Dutch, living in a land that was part of King Philip V's domain, could to a great extent freely transport colonial goods from the Iberian Peninsula to the rest of Europe and were not much bothered by the Iberian mercantilistic policies. However, when hostilities erupted with Spain in 1568, and especially after 1580 when the Iberian kingdoms (of Spain and Portugal) were united, the war and the mercantilistic attitudes of the Spanish royal government forced the Dutch to attempt sailing themselves to East Asia and the Americas. After 1581 Holland and other northern provinces of the Low Countries decided not to recognize Philip as their ruler. The English, who also had their disputes with Spain over sailing the oceans, had the same problems as the Dutch. However, after 1588 when the Spanish Armada sent by Philip to bring England and Holland under his control, was defeated, world trade was open to these two nations, as it was for the French Protestant traders, especially those in the city of LaRochelle. But the French Royal government adopted mercantilist policies in the seventeenth century and ended the free commercial practices of the French Protestants. Historians view British policy in the Tudor and early Stuart periods as being to a high degree mercantilistic. The Dutch remained advocates of free trade, despite certain mercantilistic actions as in granting the East India Company a monopoly on trade with Asia.

What was to make a significant difference in elevating the Dutch as a credit power over the Portuguese and Spanish as well as the French was that the Dutch Republic of the seventeenth century was not ruled by an authoritarian king but by an oligarchy of powerful merchants and businessmen whose base of political power was in being mayors of the important cities or members of cities' councils. They were referred to as the regents. Significantly, they perceived the national interest of the republic not as the great monarchs did in gaining more territory in war, which caused these kings many financial crises, but in gaining more money preferably under peaceful conditions. The regents shared power with the provincial stadholder, but the latter, who in most provinces was the Prince of Orange, had little power in setting economic policy.

The seventeenth-century financial history of the Dutch Republic "contrasted strikingly with the dismal succession of defaults by the rulers of great powers."[34] In part to maintain the principles of free trade the Dutch Republic ended up in wars with England in 1652, in the time of Cromwell (who was not a friend of free trade), and 1665, in the time of Charles II. Through prudent policies these naval wars were not financially ruinous for Holland nor were the land wars fought on the continent. As one historian noted, "A good part of the military success of this small new nation may be attributed to the excellence of Dutch state credit."[35] In fact, it can be argued that one of the key reasons for the rise of Amsterdam as the world's credit center was that the Dutch adopted sound public finances. Sound public finance, which benefited from a solid position in trade, helped give the Dutch Republic good credit, which in turn allowed German mercenaries to be hired for land defense. Moreover, as the country was united and the people trusted their government, the republic could pledge the nation's credit effectively: the entire future surplus of all the people. As Sidney Homer noted,

> Dutch credit was freely used for defense; it was not abjured. The national debt increased during these wars and became large. But it was almost all funded debt; floating debt was only used for emergencies and was promptly funded. The provinces and towns kept faith with their creditors who were their own people. With prosperous trade there was usually more capital seeking investment than there were safe borrowers. Creditor groups several times effectively objected to plans to raise taxes and pay off the national debt. Sixty-five thousand people in one province alone had money in Dutch state annuities. These annuities were advertised and sold by voluntary subscription. There were many kinds of annuities: life, 30-32 year, perpetual bonds, and lotteries. These loans were not, as in France and Spain, secured by specific revenues, but only on the general credit of the issuing provinces or towns. Confidence in the honesty of administration was unshaken.[36]

In the early years of the republic there was a certain degree of rivalry between the provinces of Holland and Zeeland, which frequently caused difficulties for the highest authority of the Seven United Provinces (also known as the Dutch Republic), the States General (the Staten) or parliament. Zeeland resented Holland's predominant political influence on the government of the confederated country, which was underscored by the fact that Holland carried an estimated 58 percent of the republic's financial burden.[37] Zeeland's resentment also stemmed from the initial decades of independence when the war with Spain continued, giving England the right to station troops in Flushing, which limited Zeeland's freedom of action. Furthermore, Zeeland lost an important economic hinterland in Belgium, which was then called the Southern Netherlands and which remained after the Dutch Rebellion under the control of the Hapsburgs of Spain.

Despite the loss of an economic hinterland, Zeeland played, after Holland, the most important role in making the republic the major economic power of seventeenth-century Europe and in creating its overseas empire. A significant, large percentage of the first settlers in the newly established colonies in the Americas were citizens of Zeeland. Many of the Dutch who came to New Amsterdam, now New York, came from Zeeland. One of them, a certain Claes, is said to have been a son of a farmer from the hamlet of van Rosenvelt of the Zeeland Island of Thoelen. Claes is the progenitor of the Roosevelt family of New York that gave the United States two presidents.[38]

The emergence of the Netherlands resulted in the creation of a wealthy new society in Europe. Years of conflict with the Spanish had given way to the development of a highly affluent society in the early seventeenth century. As the historian Simon Schama commented, "The Republic was an island of plenty in an ocean of want. Its artisans, even unskilled workers and farmers (for it seems a misnomer to call them peasants) enjoyed higher real incomes, better diets and safer livelihoods than anywhere else on the continent."[39] Indeed, Dutch shipping plied international waters, playing an uncanny role in riding one consumer trend after another. In many regards, the Dutch were for a period the world's foremost trading nation. The size and strength of the Dutch merchant navy, the ability of its generals to stave off foreign invasions and the wealth generated by international trade elevated Holland to the big leagues as a global power. The combination of these factors stood behind the rise of Amsterdam as the planet's financial hub.

An additional factor was that from 1568 on, many citizens of the Southern Netherlands and especially those of Antwerp emigrated to Amsterdam, which was rapidly emerging as Europe's financial, trading, and intellectual hub. By 1585, the exodus was enormous. In the two following years it was said more than 20,000 people left Antwerp.[40] Those going to the Dutch Republic settled mostly in the provinces of Zeeland and Holland. Many prominent commercial families from Antwerp continued their businesses in the Zeeland at the cities of Middelburg and Flushing, thereby increasing the importance of these cities as trade centers.

In Holland, many of the well-to-do Southern families went to Amsterdam. Though the city was already a prominent commercial center at that time, the fall of Antwerp made Amsterdam by 1600 the financial center of Western Europe. The southerners brought considerable financial expertise, which was reflected by the fact that, in 1610, of the 320 largest account holders in the Amsterdam Exchange Bank over half came from the south.[41] That Amsterdam's economic growth could, in part, be attributed to the new arrivals from the south can also be gleaned from the fact that in the 1630s approximately one-fourth of the city's wealthiest citizens were emigrants from Antwerp and the Southern Netherlands. However, at that time Amsterdam, together with many other cities of Holland, had already a highly developed shipping industry, most of which was with the Baltic. If in the fifteenth century the Baltic trade was carried by ships of the Hanse, the reverse was going to be true in the sixteenth century.

The Dutch Financial Explosion

The advances of the Dutch in global trade and in empire building were paralleled by the advances in credit. In fact, the emergence of the Amsterdam bourse as the Wall Street of the seventeenth century was due to a combination of forces: sound public finances married to a successful position in trade and an ability to control Europe's major capital market.[42] Clearly, trade generated wealth in the Netherlands and was a source of excess capital that became available as credit. The Amsterdam Bourse made that capital available.

The Dutch were the first to establish a public bank in the north in the form of the Wisselbank (Exchange Bank of Amsterdam). Established in 1609, it was well known for its stability and integrity and attracted both Dutch and foreign capital.[43] The bank was created as an instrument to facilitate payments in Amsterdam's rapidly growing foreign trade, as well as to provide a greater degree of stability in the circulation of paper by restricting the circulation of paper credit, which was regarded as unsatisfactory due to the practices of exchanges and cashiers. The Wisselbank, therefore, became a critical component of Dutch power, playing a role in safeguarding a working credit system.[44] Business was a matter of transfer between accounts and the bank maintained a high level of dependability, which made Amsterdam bank money so desirable a form of settlement for business.[45] This situation arose despite the fact that it actually cost depositors to have accounts, rather than paying them interest.

Another element that worked in favor of the Dutch was the evolution of the bill of exchange. As already discussed the bill of exchange was an essential credit instrument used by the Italians. By the seventeenth century, use of this instrument became more sophisticated. With the Dutch, the bill could be assigned by the drawer to others, the successive bearers possessing the same legal rights vis-à-vis the debtor as the original drawer. To add to the protection of the bearer (i.e., the purchaser of the bill), the assignment of bills required an endorsement. The endorsement was the signature of each successive bearer, an act that implicated them in responsibility for the bill in the event of the debtor's default. The significance of the growing sophistication of the bill of exchange was noted by the Dutch economists Jab de Vries and Ad van der Woude: "These practices gave the bill a high degree of transferability, permitting it to act as a form of payment."[46]

While Amsterdam played a critical role in the provisioning of credit for commerce, specifically for that in the Baltic as well as for Dutch overseas trade, it had a significant role in Europe's foremost bourse. While the origin of bourse activities can be traced to the commercial transactions in Italy as far back as the thirteenth century, the roots of the modern stock market are to be found in the Effecten-Beurs of Amsterdam in the seventeenth century.

As early as the mid-sixteenth century, Amsterdam witnessed speculation in grain, which was followed by that in herrings, spices, and whale oil. The actual institution commenced as an open-air market in Warmoestreet. It was later moved to two other locations until 1611 when Amsterdam merchants built their own exchange building. Trading and speculation in shares first appeared in 1602 and were principally of the Dutch East India Company and a number of other companies, such as the Dutch West India Company in 1621.

During the heady ferment of the early 1600s, the Amsterdam stock market became the testing ground for what the British would later call "Dutch finance." The Dutch were to develop the early techniques of stock market manipulation. These included short selling (selling stock one does not own in hopes of a fall in prices), bear raids (where insiders conspire to sell a stock short until the outsiders panic and sell out their holdings, allowing the insiders to close their shorts profitably), syndicates (where a group manipulates a stock price by buying and selling among themselves), and corners (where a person or syndicate secretly acquires the entire floating supply of a commodity, forcing all who need to buy the commodity to do so at their price.[47] According to Joseph De la Vega, a seventeenth-century businessman in Amsterdam and a member of a community of Portuguese Jews whose ancestors had fled to Amsterdam to escape the Spanish Inquisition when Spain and Portugal were united in 1580, there was a wide range of transactions allowed in the market, such as sales of real stock against immediate payment of cash, sales of stock where the money to cover payments was borrowed from individuals, up to four-fifths of its value, and options contracts.[48]

The Amsterdam exchange and other Dutch markets had their ups and downs. Best remembered is the Dutch Tulipmania in 1636, which would clearly be remembered as a major mania and crash.[49] It also involves our story of credit. Although the Dutch are usually associated with the tulip, they cannot claim to be the first Europeans caught up in the beauty of the flower. As Anna Pavord explains in her book, *The Tulip: The Story of a Flower That Has Made Men Mad*, "The first bulbs were probably introduced by a Frenchman. Cargoes of bulbs arrived in Antwerp from Constantinople in 1562 long before they were shipped into Amsterdam. The first known flower bloomed in the garden of a merchant in Augsburg, Bavaria and was recorded by the Swiss botanist and physician, Conrad Gesner."[50] Despite this, the Dutch were enamored with the flower and in the last decades of the 1500s and those of the early1600s, Dutch traders tried to corner the market by purchasing bulbs from Flanders and France to pass on to well-heeled customers. Prices went up accordingly and as early as 1614, Dutch writers were poking fun at those who spent extravagant amounts of money on the tulip bulbs. To put this into perspective, in 1623 the fabled flower "Semper Augustus" was already selling for 1,000 florins a bulb, while the average annual income was about 150 florins.[51]

Between 1634 and 1637, Dutch investors (many of them from the middle class) turned to the tulip market in a frenzy. The driving force was the element of speculation in the game, the possibility that a plain, relatively valueless bulb might emerge one season miraculously feathered and flamed in contrasting colors.[52] If one made the right bet, then one could become a very wealthy man. Accordingly, those involved in speculation included wealthy investors, persistent speculators, the Bank of Amsterdam, persons who loaned money with stock as security, and brokers. It was this cast of characters that got sucked into Tulipmania. As Schama noted, "Unlike other 'decorative' goods, then there was a continuous chain connecting the most prized blooms at the top of the mass trade." The tulip simultaneously retained its associations of precious treasure yet was a prize in some form within the reach of the common man. For a modest outlay he could be drawn into the nexus of buying and speculating which, like all gambles, became quickly addictive.[53] Another force driving up tulip prices was demand from France, where it had become fashionable for women to array quantities of fresh tulips at the tops of their gowns. Wealthy men competed to present the most exotic flowers to eligible women, hence adding to the demand for tulips and pushing up prices.[54]

The great tulip market crashed in 1637. Behind the market boom at the time was an increasing currency, new economic and colonial possibilities. The victories of Gustavus Adolphus, the Protestant king of Sweden, ensured that the Protestant religion would survive, a dramatic reversal of events in 1630 when the armies of the Catholic emperor dominated Central Europe from Bohemia to the Baltic coast, helping to hem in the Dutch. All of this helped to provide a sense of optimism and there remained a sense of confidence about the upward movement of the value of the tulip. In early 1637, that confidence evaporated as public sentiment mounted against the middle men who were making vast fortunes on speculation. In addition, more flowers were coming into the market. At the end of the day, the market only functioned when there was an actual buyer for the product, instead of a speculator. Consequently, by early 1637, there were more sellers than buyers in the market, spelling the end of tulipmania. The bubble simply burst.

The Challenge of Investing Overseas

The Dutch as a surplus credit nation needed to invest their money. While throwing money into the tulipmania was one way, other Dutch investors turned overseas. Although the risks were often higher than at home, the returns were considerably higher as well. In many respects, the Dutch were among the first investors in "Emerging Markets" and were venture capitalists in backing a number of companies that traded in Asia and the Atlantic. The Dutch were also willing to function as a catalyst for the foreign ventures of others.

Important to the Dutch, but less significant than the Baltic trade, was the trade established with East Asia in the early seventeenth century. The first ships of Holland went to the East Indies in 1594 and in 1602. Financiers of the Dutch Republic, primarily under the leadership of those in Amsterdam, established the V.O.C., the Dutch East India Company,[55] whose activities stretched from the Cape in Africa to Japan and the Western Pacific. The unique federal structure of the Dutch state and powerful influence of civic autonomy within the republic made it possible to create a completely new type of commercial organization, a chartered, joint-stock monopoly strongly backed by the state which was, at the same time, federated into chambers which kept their capital and commercial operations separate from each other, while observing general guidelines and policies set by a federal board of directors.[56] The company captured from the Portuguese the important Indonesian spice islands of Ternate, Tidor, and Amboina in 1605.[57] This was the beginning of the Dutch East Indies (modern Indonesia), the base for the financial success of the company for the next 150 years. The Dutch were to monopolize it completely.

Trade established with the Americas at this period was significant, but in no way did it match that with Asia. When sugar plantations were established in Brazil, in part aided by capital from Antwerp in the sixteenth century, there were ships from Holland and Zeeland involved in the transport of the white powder to Europe.[58] In the beginning, Dutch and English enterprises overlapped and reinforced each other. Freebooters from both nations (as well as French filibusters) joined together against Spain and Portugal. The famous explorer Henry Hudson was to work alternately for the English and the Dutch (providing the latter with their title to the New Netherlands, which later, after being taken by the British, was renamed New York). Dutch finance was also to play a role in other facets of English expansionism. As one source commented, "The Pilgrim fathers found refuge and financial support in Holland before they departed for Massachusetts; and Dutch finance, expertise, and maritime resources were vital in the establishment of West Indian colonies, especially Barbados. The first settlement of that island was largely the work of the Anglo-Dutch Courteen company based in Leyden and London."[59]

Dutch credit was also instrumental in the development of the Caribbean sugar industry, which began in Barbados. When Portugal's hold over its colonies was weakened during the Spanish Marriage

(1580-1640), the Dutch aggressively challenged Lisbon's hold over Brazil. From 1630 to 1654 much of Brazil was a Dutch colony with an economy dominated by the production and export of sugar from Pernambuco. The Dutch, however, were unable to maintain their control of Brazil, but they provided credit, machinery, and slaves for the English planters who settled Barbados and emulated sugar monoculture from Brazil.[60] Dutch companies were also heavily involved in the financing, shipping, and European sales of Virginian tobacco.

The activities of the Courteens reflect the growing interdependence between the Dutch and the English. The Courteens had settled initially in Antwerp, but in 1568 they left for Zeeland and England. The son of the immigrant in London was William Courteen, born in 1572. When William came of age he went to Holland to represent his father's silk and linen business in Harlem. Successful in this, he also participated with Jan de Moor, the mayor of Flushing, in significant Zeeland commercial activities.[61] The shipping enterprises in which Courteen took part traded with Europe as well as the Caribbean and Africa, and brought him considerable wealth, which was recognized by the British, who knighted him in 1622. Soon thereafter, Sir William Courteen took possession of Barbados for England and sent colonists.[62] As can be gleaned from the Courteen commercial ventures there were many close links in the business world between the English and Dutch.

In the history of credit it is important to underscore that the Dutch were a major force of change in bringing about the ideas of overseas expansion and the related nature of supplying credit for such endeavors. One important individual in this was William Usselinx, who, like the Courteens, was an emigrant from Antwerp. Usselinx was an ardent Calvinist whose major aim was to create a truly Protestant community in the New World, in particular in the Caribbean. Such a goal was based on his intense dislike of the Spanish, who had destroyed the prosperity of his hometown. His ideas found sympathetic listeners in Zeeland, one of the seven provinces and a commercial rival of Holland. He believed that establishing a company like the East India Company was the answer and drafted a plan for such an enterprise. However, the government of the province of Holland was reluctant to do so. In 1609 the Dutch Republic had established a twelve-year truce with Spain, and it was thought that such a plan would provoke the Spaniards. Usselinx, however, preferred to continue the war, driving the Spanish Catholics out of the

Caribbean and opening up the region for God-fearing Protestant settlers. At the end of the truce with Spain, the Dutch West Indies Company was created, not on the lines of Usselinx's idea of settlement,
but instead based on trade and privateering. Usselinx, not asked to
participate in the new company, left Holland, probably in a huff,
heading to Scandinavia and the Baltic region to propose his plans to
the rulers of the northern nations.

Usselinx went first to Denmark, where King Christain IV was
engaging many men from the Netherlands and using Dutch capital
to modernize his country. Two Dutch businessmen, Jan de Willem
and Herman Rosenkrantz had helped in 1610 in creating the Danish
East India Company. As the position offered to Usselinx was not to
his satisfaction, he went to Sweden to interest King Gustavus Adophus
in establishing a Swedish West India Company. The Danes, however, turned to yet another Dutchman, Johann de Willem, to create
an African company. In 1625, he received a license to operate in the
West Indies, Brazil, Virginia, and Guinea. This venture did not go
anywhere and it would not be until 1651, when the Danes operating
through the Gluckstadt Company, were to become more heavily involved in Atlantic commerce, in particular that of slaves, sugar, ivory,
gold, and palm oil.

In Sweden, Usselinx's suggestion was favorably received by the
king.[63] Gustavus Adolphus authorized the Dutchman to found "a
South Company" to trade with Africa. Although Usselinx was opposed to slavery, the company he helped found eventually ended up
involved in the slave trade.[64] Usselinx (in 1627) also sought to interest Duke Frederic of the Baltic duchy of Courland in colonizing
Tobago.[65] Although the Courlanders sent several expeditions to Tobago, their efforts ultimately failed. [66] There was no mistaking the
fact that part of the financing for Courland's overseas venture came
from Amsterdam.

The Dutch also influenced Frederick William, the Elector of
Brandenburg. Young Frederick William had developed a great interest in naval and colonial affairs during his education in Holland. As
a relative of the Prince of Orange, the Brandenburger had been exposed to the hustle and bustle of Amsterdam. In 1672 his state, which
was to be the nucleus of the Prussian kingdom in the eighteenth
century, was at war with Sweden. To fight this war, he needed a
fleet, which the exhausted exchequer of Brandenburg could not pay.
His Dutch advisor, Benjamin Raule, obtained Dutch credit that pro-

vided Frederick William with a fleet. This fleet was the beginning of the powerful German navy in centuries to come. In 1679, Raule also helped the Elector to establish an African trading company and in obtaining a colony on the gold coast in Africa.[67] It was no mistake that Brandenburg's entry into African commerce was led by a Dutchman, Captain Joris Bartelsen, whose idea was to carry slaves from Angola to Lisbon and Cadiz. The company also acquired from the Danes a trading post on St. Thomas, one of the Virgin Islands in the Caribbean.[68]

One last point on the northern map where Dutch expertise and credit showed up in was Russia. In the late seventeenth century, Tsar Peter the Great visited Holland and involved the Dutch in his schemes for modernizing Russia and building a fleet.[69] Thus, we have observed that it was chiefly the Dutch who were the historical "catalyst" for the Baltic peoples, stirring the Courlanders, Swedes, Brandenburgers, and Danes with the idea that they needed their own colonies to produce and export tropical products such as sugar and tobacco, and it was in Holland and Zeeland that they most often obtained the loans for these colonial exploits.

The use of Dutch credit in overseas ventures was not limited to Scandinavia and the Baltic. In France's efforts to settle and make profits from her colonies in North America, Dutch credit was important. Although the Dutch were unable to dominate the fur trade in New France (present-day Canada) in the early 1600s, they provided much of the credit for the Rouen merchants engaged in the trade.[70] Dutch credit was also critical in 1625 for the survival of the small French colony on St. Kitts in the Caribbean. As historian W.J. Eccles noted, "Despite the efforts of both the English and the Spanish to dislodge the four hundred French colonists, they managed to hang on, supported more by itinerant Dutch traders who extended them credit than by the French company which, through incompetence and inadequate capital, soon went bankrupt.[71] Although France was often at war with the Dutch and the mercantilistic policies adopted by various French governments sought to exclude Dutch traders, credit from Amsterdam also played its own modest role in France's overseas expansion.

The Eclipse of Amsterdam

While Amsterdam was to remain a significant financial hub in the eighteenth century, it was ultimately surpassed by London. The Dutch decline was caused by a number of factors. These included an ongoing Dutch involvement in wars on the continent, which sapped the republic's vigor. Unlike the English, the Dutch were not isolated by nature; rather they shared borders with the lands of the Hapsburgs and often ambitious German princes, some closely allied to France whose ruler, Louis XIV, was eager to destroy the Dutch Republic by war. His minister, Jean Baptiste Colbert, felt that he could improve the French economy by building up the French merchant fleet and take away trade from the Dutch whose fleet consisted of three-fourths of the over 20,000 merchant ships in operation in Europe at that time.[72]

The three Anglo-Dutch wars of the seventeenth century, the War of the Spanish Succession (1702-13), and ongoing conflicts with France were all costly in terms of maintaining armies in the field and a fighting force at sea. These wars, in the final analysis, were economically disadvantageous for the Dutch. The War of the Spanish Succession was particularly damaging. England emerged as the primary sea power in the world for the next two centuries and the Dutch no longer were in first place in world commerce.[73] Indeed, the War of the Spanish Succession (in which Dutch trade with France, Spain, and the Spanish New World collapsed) combined with the severe disruption of navigation in the Mediterranean, was ultimately punishing to a nation like the Dutch Republic, which depended upon trade for its livelihood. Moreover, as the conflict wound down, the Dutch were sidelined by the British and French: the former ally proved willing to allow Philip V to remain King of Spain and Spanish America in return for extensive trade advantages for Britain, including holding Gibraltar, Minorca, and the lucrative slaving *asiento* for the Spanish colonies.

The Dutch deeply resented the separate peace agreement reached between the British and French in 1712. Anti-British riots erupted at The Hague and for a spell there was discussion about the possibility of a fourth Anglo-Dutch war. Nor were the Dutch and their allies, the Austrian Hapsburgs and a number of German princes, in any position to sufficiently bring France to its knees. A critical lacuna was the lack of funds to keep large armies in the field. When the Dutch accepted the Peace of Utrecht of 1713 it had already been tailored by France and Britain, both of which did not necessarily have Dutch commercial interests at heart; seeing those interests weakened was more to their liking. Within the next decade, London would increasingly come to dominate global credit, while the position of Amsterdam, like that of the Dutch, would decline.

Another important factor in the decline of the Netherlands as the dominant credit power was in the structure of the economy. The Dutch, who had dominated industrial production through much of the 1600s, were hard-pressed by overseas competition by the last decades of the century. The Dutch also faced more and more competition from Flanders, Rhenish Germany, Saxony, and Silesia in industry, while its luxury trade with the Levant and Spanish America dwindled.[74] Even the bulk trade of herring, salt, and wine in European waters declined. With industry and commerce under pressure, the Netherlands began to slip behind other competitors. Moreover, many Dutch businessmen opted out of industry and turned to passive investment. Consequently, the Netherlands by the late 1700s slipped into a postindustrial stage. The country's wealth was enough for it to maintain an important position as a source of credit, with large sums of Dutch capital being invested in British and French funds, but, by the end of the eighteenth century, the dynamic of being the world's credit powerhouse had been transferred across the North Sea to London.

Conclusion

The period that roughly covered the sixteenth to early eighteenth century witnessed the shift in the loci of credit to northern Europe, first to Bruges and Antwerp, with the involvement of the southern Germans, and finally to Amsterdam. While each city was of importance in the evolution of credit, ultimately the politics of nation-states came to be a primary catalyst of change. The Dutch were able to remain a dominant force in credit for some time, which was due largely to their ability to establish a highly competitive global trading network and to having a financial institution judged to be the most secure in Europe. Also they seemed to have an uncanny ability to exploit each fad being introduced into Europe. However, the very success of the Dutch also undermined their ability to remain at the apex of what was an emerging global credit culture, piggybacking on the trade network. One problem was that the wealth generated by the Dutch was either put back into trade or used to purchase luxuries, creating an affluence, which Simon Schama has called an "embarrassment of riches." At the same time, the Dutch failed to put money into the development of industry, something that the British did, which we will examine in the next chapter.

Notes

1. John Steele Gordon, *The Great Game: The Emergence of Wall Street as a World Power 1653-2000* (New York: Charles Scribner's Sons, 1999), pp. 22-23.
2. Richard Ehrenberg, *Capital and Finance in the Age of the Renaissance* (New York: Harcourt Brace & Co., 1928) p. 333.
3. Jacques Bernard, "Trade and finance 900-1500," in *Fontana Economic History of Europe—The Middle Ages*, Carlos M. Cipolla, ed. (London: Collins, Fontana Books, 1972), p. 301.
4. Michel Mollat Du Jourdin, *Europe and the Sea* (Oxford: Blackwell Publishers, 1993), p. 102.
5. Adrien de Meuss, *History of the Belgians* (New York: Praeger, 1962), p. 122.
6. Ibid., p. 154.
7. Eugene F. Rice, Jr., *The Foundations of Early Modern Europe 1450-1559* (New York: W.W. Norton & Company, 1970), p. 41.
8. De Meeus, *History of the Belgians*, p. 157.
9. Ibid.
10. Du Jourdin, *Europe and the Sea*, p. 149. However, fluctuation in rates and prices could create new forms of instability as the financial crises of 1562 indicated.
11. Randall D. Germain, *The International Organization of Credit: States and Global Finance in the World Economy* (Cambridge: Cambridge University Press, 1998), p. 36.
12. De Meuss, *History of the Belgians*, p. 159.
13. Ehrenberg, *Capital and Finance in the Age of the Renaissance*, p. 316.
14. Ibid., p.36. Ehrenberg dates the emergence of Antwerp as a financial center to 1510, when bills of exchange were drawn on Antwerp by the House of Fugger.
15. Randall D. Germain, *The International Organization of Credit*, p. 37.
16. Ibid., p. 39.
17. After his death in 1408, his sons Andreas and Jakob, carried on the family business until they dissolved their partnership in 1454. Jakob was the more successful of the two, becoming a member of the merchant's guild. From this base, the family became progressively more international in their orientation. Two of Jakob's sons, Ulrich and Georg, expanded the firm's international trade into Rome and Venice. It was, however, yet another brother, the younger Jakob, who was to make the Fuggers an international power.
18. Sigismund was a cousin of Maximillan and of the Tyrolian branch of the Hapsburg family. He would abdicate control of the Archduchy of Tyrol in Maximillan's favor in 1490.
19. Rice, *The Foundations of Early Modern Europe*, p. 41.
20. Ehrenberg, *Capital and Finance in the Age of the Renaissance*, p. 142.
21. Guillermo Morón, *A History of Venezuela* (London: George Allen and Unwin, 1964), p. 37.
22. Charles V felt that if Spain did not take control of the Rio Plata area, the Portuguese would move southward from Brazil along the coast of South America and take possession of Argentina. The Fuggers and the Welsers assisted the expedition with ships and equipment. See David Rock, *Argentina, 1516-1982* (Berkeley: University of California Press, 1985), p. 88.
23. Ehrenberg, *Capital and Finance in the Age of the Renaissance*, pp. 145-146.
24. Germain, *The International Organization of Credit*, p. 37.
25. Henry Kamen, *European Society 1500-1700* (London: Routledge, 1996), p. 70.
26. Ibid.
27. Ibid., p. 71.
28. Ehrenberg, *Capital and Finance in the Age of the Renaissance*, p. 313.

29.   E.E. Rich, "Expansion and Concern of all Europe," in *The New Cambridge Modern History*, Vol. I (Cambridge: Cambridge University Press, 1957), pp. 445-469.
30.   Shepard Bancroft Clough and Charles W. Cole, *Economic History of Europe* (Boston: D.H. Heath & Co., 1941) p. 206.
31.   Ibid.
32.   Ibid., p. 209.
33.   Ralph Davis, *The Rise of the Atlantic Economies* (Ithaca, NY: Cornell University Press, 1973), p. 238.
34.   Sidney Homer, *History of Interest Rates* (New Brunswick, NJ: Rutgers University Press, 1963), p. 124.
35.   Ibid.
36.   Ibid., pp. 124-125.
37.   Simon Schama, *The Embarrassment of Riches: An Interpretation of Dutch Culture in the Golden Age* (Berkeley: University of California Press, 1988), p. 123.
38.   Karl Schriftgiesser, *The Amazing Roosevelt Family, 1613-19* (New York: Wilfred Freud Inc., 1942), pp. 8-13.
39.   Schama, *The Embarrassment of Riches*, p. 123.
40.   Goslinga, Cornelius Ch., *The Dutch in the Caribbean and on the Wild Coast 1580-1680* (Assen, The Netherlands: Van Gorkum & Co., 1971), p. 26.
41.   Kamen, *European Society 1500-1700*, p. 85. Also see Jonathan I. Israel, *The Dutch Republic: Its Rise, Greatness, and Fall, 1477-1806* (Oxford: Oxford University Press, 1995), pp. 344-351.
42.   Immanuel Wallerstein, *The Modern World System II: Mercantilism and the Consolidation of the European World Economy 1600-1750* (New York: Academic Press, 1980), p. 57.
43.   Violet Barbour, *Capitalism in Amsterdam in the Seventeenth Century* (Baltimore: The John's Hopkins University Press, 1950), p. 43.
44.   Schama, *The Embarrassment of Riches*, p. 345.
45.   Ibid.
46.   Jab de Vries and Ad van der Woude, *The First Modern Economy: Success, Failure and Perseverance of the Dutch Economy, 1500-1815* (Cambridge: Cambridge University Press, 1997), p. 130.
47.   John Steele Gordon, *The Great Game: The Emergence of Wall Street as a World Power, 1653-2000* (New York: Charles Scribner's, 1999), p. 23.
48.   Joseph De la Vega, *Confusion de Confusiones* (reprinted in Charles Mackay, *Extraordinary Popular Delusions and the Madness of Crowds* & Joseph de la Vega, *Confusion de Confusiones* (New York: John Wiley & Sons, 1996), pp. 139-141.
49.   Jonathan I. Israel, *The Dutch Republic: Its Rise, Greatness and Fall, 1477-1806* (Oxford: Oxford University Press, 1995), p. 533. Also see Edward Chancellor, *Devil Take the Hindmost: A History of Financial Speculation* (New York: Farrar, Straus, Giroux, 1999), pp. 14-22, and N.W. Posthumus, "The Tulip Mania in Holland in the Years 1636 and 1637," *Journal of Economic and Business History*, Vol. 1 (1928-29), p. 462. Additionally, De la Vega, *Confusion de Confusiones*.
50.   Anna Pavord, *The Tulip: The Story of a Flower That Has Made Men Mad* (London: Bloomsbury, 1999), p. 137.
51.   Ibid., p. 141.
52.   Ibid., p. 157.
53.   Schama, *The Embarrassment of Riches*, p. 351. For a society as affluent as the Dutch, capital needed to be invested. In fact, it could be argued that too much affluence had led to too much credit being available. The tulip, in imported luxury, which initially came from Turkey, became highly prized by the Dutch.

54.   Peter M. Garber, *Famous First Bubbles: The Fundamentals of Early Manias* (Cambridge, MA: The MIT Press, 2000), p. 43.
55.   For more complete information about the Dutch East India Company, see Kristoff Glamann, *Dutch-Asiatic Trade, 1620-1740*, 2nd ed. (Den Haag: Martinus Nijhoff, 1958, 1981); Femme Gaastra, "The Shifting Balance of Trade of the Dutch East India Company," in Leonard Blusse and Femme Gaastra, eds., *Companies and Trade* (Leiden: University of Leiden Press, 1981); and Larry Neal, "The Dutch and English East India Companies Compared: Evidence from the Stock and Foreign Exchange Markets," in James D. Tracy, ed., *The Rise of Merchant Empires: Long-Distance Trade in the Early Modern World, 1350-1750*, reprint ed. (Cambridge: Cambridge University Press, 1990, 1991), chapter 6.
56.   Israel, *The Dutch Republic*, p. 321.
57.   Ibid., 322.
58.   Stuart Schwartz, *Sugar Plantations in the Formation of Brazilian Society—Bahia* (New York: Cambridge Union Press, 1985), pp. 17-19.
59.   *Encyclopedia of North American Colonies Vol. 1* (New York: Charles Scribner's Sons, 1993), p. 224.
60.   Ibid.
61.   Goslinga, *The Dutch in the Caribbean and on the Wild Coast*, p. 81.
62.   This venture met with little success, as title to the island was claimed by James Hay, Earl of Carlisle, who insisted that it had been given to him by James I of England and that it was his right to colonize the island. Earlier, in 1616, William Courteen had aided Jan de Moore in outfitting the Zeeland expedition of Aert A. van Groenewegen, who established, on the Essequibo River in present day Guyana, the first permanent Dutch settlement in South America, called Frot Kijkoveral. Jan de Moore also dispatched a ship with colonists to the island of Tobago in 1628, but they and their settlement disappeared shortly after their arrival. It is presumed that most of them were massacred when Spain decided to reestablish its authority in this area. See Goslinga, *The Dutch in the Caribbean and on the Wild Coast*, pp. 8, 435.
63.   Catherine Lightenberg, *Willem Usselinx* (Utrecht, The Netherlands: A. Oosthoek, 1914), p. 99.
64.   Hugh Thomas, *The Slave Trade: The Story of the Atlantic Slave Trade, 1440-1870* (New York: Simon & Schuster, 1997), p. 172.
65.   Goslinga, *The Dutch in the Caribbean and on the Wild Coast*, p. 437.
66.   In 1633, Duke Frederic sent his son Jacob to Amsterdam to arrange the finances for the colonization of Tobago. In 1634, Duke Jacob, having succeeded his father, again sent colonists to Tobago under the leadership of another Dutchman, William Mollens. The Dutch also claimed Tobago as their own. A Dutch colony on the side of Tobago opposite to the Courland settlement was established. The difficulties that the Courlanders faced in the following years caused them to surrender to the Dutch. In 1666, when the French were the allies of the Dutch in a war against England, the French occupied Tobago. The Dutch reasserted their claim and in 1668 resettled the island. In the meantime, Duke Jacob of Courland had not given up his claim. He approached King Charles II of England in 1669, who agreed to let the Courlanders develop Tobago, which, according to Charles, was English territory. In 1672, when Holland was at war with England, the island was taken by the English, but when peace returned it was given back to Holland. At this time, the Lampsin brothers, who had maintained the Dutch claim to Tobago, sold that claim to the Dutch government. Before the Dutch could do anything, the French took Tobago and retained it by the Peace Treaty of 1678. In the long run, however, Tobago fell to the English, who controlled it until 1962, when Tobago, together with Trinidad, achieved its independence.

67.   Thomas, *The Slave Trade*, p. 224.
68.   Ferdinand Schevill, *The Great Elector* (Hamden, CT.: Archon Books, 1965), pp. 240-241.
69.   Henry Troyat, *Peter the Great* (New York: E.P. Dutton, 1979, 1937), pp. 99-102, 298.
70.   W.J. Eccles, *The French in North America 1500-1783* (Markham, Ontario, Canada: Fitzhenry & Whiteside, 1998), p. 20. Also see Marcel Trudel, *Histoire de la Nouvelle-France, Vol. I, Le Comptoir, 1604-1627* (Montreal 1967), pp. 66-67, 153; and Thomas J. Condon, *New York Beginnings: The Commercial Origins of New Netherland* (New York 1968), p. 15.
71.   Eccles, *The French in North America*, p. 29.
72.   Rondo Cameron, *A Concise Economic History of the World* (New York: Oxford University Press, 1989), pp. 131-132.
73.   In 1700 the last Hapsburg King of Spain, the hapless and childless Charles II (also known as Carlos II) died. With his passage the throne of Spain and the Spanish Empire in Europe and the Americas was left to the grandson of Louis XIV, who now became Philip V of Spain. Philip quickly received support from the French, who invaded the South Netherlands ruled by the Hapsburgs. For the Dutch it was critical to check France and reverse the Bourbon Succession in Spain. The Dutch elite sought to restore the favorable pre-1700 position that it had enjoyed: an active role in maritime commerce which a close alliance of Spain and France prevented as did the mercantilist trade rules France was adopting. Although France's dominance of Europe was to be checked as a result of the conflict, the problem for the Dutch and their eminent position at the apex of international credit was challenged by the increase of British commercial and financial power. The Dutch dilemma, while it was vital to check France and reverse the Bourbon Succession in Spain, was scarcely less vital to prevent the Dutch Republic's nominal ally, Britain, from making gains outside of Europe: Britain was now rapidly emerging as a faster-growing and more dynamic maritime, colonial, and commercial power then the republic, and rivalry between the English and Dutch, especially in India, West Africa, and the Americas was as acute as ever. See Carlton J.H. Hayes, *A Political and Cultural History of Modern Europe Vol. I* (New York: The Macmillan Co., 1932), pp. 306-312.
74.   David S. Landes, *The Wealth and Poverty of Nations: Why Some Are So Rich and Some So Poor* (New York: W.W. Norton & Company, 1998), p. 445.

8

Finance in the Age of British Power

William, Prince of Orange, who became King William III of England, was regarded as somber and haughty, although some referred to him as determined and aloof. Most of all, William, the Dutch Stadtholder, was strongly opposed to Catholic France, the Netherlands' major national security threat. In 1688, the Netherlands was actively preparing for war against France and William was concerned that Britain, under King James II, would join the French side. The English king was known to have Catholic sympathies and from William's viewpoint he could not be trusted. Aware of this, Protestant factions in Britain invited the Dutch leader and his English wife, Mary Stuart (the daughter of King James), across the Channel to assume the leadership of the country. This William did in the last successful invasion of England, which was facilitated by a joint Anglo-Dutch force. In 1689, after accepting the Declaration of Rights, the Dutch prince and his wife became King William III and Queen Mary II of England in what was known as the Glorious Revolution. Substantial changes were to come for England and indirectly the course of the history of credit.

William, as already mentioned was the Prince of Orange and Stadholder of Holland, which was still the world's major credit power. Not surprisingly, it was under William's reign that England's finances were modernized by the consolidation of a credit system, begun by the creation of the Bank of England in 1694. The bank's assumption over time of managing the long-term national debt with the private money invested in it gave Britain a modern financial system, which also provided its credit system a vehicle with which it developed its world trade system and industrial base. This combination of factors allowed Britain to bypass the Netherlands in the eighteenth century as an economic power and made London the world's financial hub. Like the Dutch before them, the British would rest their credit system upon a foundation of prudent public finance, a strong complementary position in trade, and a commanding position in capital markets via the stock exchange.

England reflects the view that the economic foundations of modern nation-states involved the creation of national debt, public credit, and paper money—all the trappings of a working credit system.[1] Simply stated, the process of nationalism, both the cause and the result of wars and imperial expansion, multiplied national debt and produced crises of public credit resolved through more nationalism and war, as well as the creation of a working public and private credit system capable of allowing the state to function and private enterprise to flourish.

Setting the Stage

During the Middle Ages Britain was on the edge of the European map and with the exception of the fishers of cod, British interest was focused on the continent.[2] As trade gradually resumed in Europe, the English became more actively involved in overseas trade, which increased contacts with the rest of Europe. One of the earliest companies to be involved in trading, the Merchant Adventurers, was chartered in 1407, mainly to export finished cloth from the burgeoning English woolen industry to Antwerp. By the middle of the sixteenth century, as much as three-fourths of English foreign trade was controlled by the London officers of the company, many of whom served as financiers and advisers of the Tudor Kings.[3] Despite the existence of such a company, English finance was not really developed until later due to frequent bouts of political turmoil.

Some of this was to change after the voyage of Columbus, which suddenly gave Europe a new horizon in the West. In the new Atlantic world Britain's geographical position was to give it a great advantage over other European powers. In 1497 John Cabot, a sailor of Italian ancestry, crossed the Atlantic for Henry VII of England and claimed the Canadian coast for Britain.[4] In the following century, British privateers and explorers sailed to South America and the Pacific, ravaging Spanish, Dutch, Portuguese, and French shipping and laying claim to various points on the map. From 1588 onward when the navy of Queen Elizabeth defeated the Spanish Armada, the British ventured into the newly forming Atlantic world with even greater confidence.[5] English merchants created companies for world trade in the seventeenth century. The rise of the English in trade was greatly enhanced when its colonial settlements in the Americas began to produce commodities for sale in Europe, with tobacco and furs from the 1620s and sugar from the 1640s. After 1660 England became the major entrepôt through which much of Europe's supply of tobacco and sugar flowed.[6]

Unstable political conditions, however, were to delay the English development of a financial system to rival Holland's across the North Sea. The companies and their owners made money, but outside of bringing their savings to the goldsmith they could do little else and had difficulty placing their savings at interest on good security. So great was that difficulty that the practice of hoarding was common. We are told that as late as 1689 the father of Alexander Pope, the poet, who retired from business in London, carried to a retreat in the country a strong box containing over twenty thousand pounds and took out of it from time to time what was required for household expenses.[7] The idea of lugging around money in such a fashion did little to instill any sense of credit.

Before the seventeenth century Britain's credit system was rudimentary. In the Middle Ages the Jews had been a factor in this system, but were driven out in 1290. Those who were active in the following centuries' credit were often foreigners, such as the members of the German Hanse and the Italians, supporting the merchants and financiers of Italy's major cities. These foreign communities were usually located in London or another major port. By the seventeenth century, however, both the Italians and the Hanse had declined in their ability to offer credit and a local class of creditors was slowly emerging. Those who began the process of lending money had been involved in trades and had surplus capital. As the British historian Tawney observed, "the vast majority of lenders were, in the rural districts, farmers, yeomen or gentlemen, and in the towns, merchants, shopkeepers, mercers, tailors, drapers, haberdashers, grocers and similar tradesmen."[8] Over time, the trade element of business became less significant and many goldsmiths and merchants opted to become leading moneylenders. At the same time, the English government tapped foreign sources for credit, such as the Antwerp bourse.[9] Kamen noted a critical change in the business pattern: "In the sixteenth century, however, all money-backers, not merely the goldsmiths, took part in coin transactions. The backers not only made loans, they also accepted deposits of cash."[10] This meant that there was an evolution of British creditors, now functioning simply as money brokers and agents of long-distance credit to private bankers.

Credit Takeoff

The seventeenth century was to be a massive takeoff point for the development of British credit.[11] Why the seventeenth century? As historian Mark Kishlansky observes, "The modern business world was born; science came of age; literature matured as never before or after; feudal forms withered; torture, witchcraft and heresy died away."[12] The transformation of Britain was sweeping onward from the 1600s and by the early 1700s Britain found itself to be among the intellectual, commercial, and military powers in the world. The Royal Navy came to rule the waves. Through the Stuart periods and Republican period of Cromwell (1603-1714), the British and Scottish were to form the union of Great Britain, colonies were established in the Caribbean, North America, and other places. Settlers from the British Isles peopled the American colonies, and India became incorporated in the British trading system and finally a British colony in the following century. During this period, trade was a critical component of the expansion of British power, which was in part accomplished through the creation of such organizations as the East India Company and the Royal African Company. Moreover, British merchants traded goods such as sugar, cotton, and rum around the globe in such places as far as Connecticut, Barbados and Calcutta. It should also be noted that the Atlantic slave trade was another significant source of capital for a number of the early merchant banks, in particular those located in Bristol and Liverpool.[13]

A key area in the growing power of Britain was the revolution in government finances, which had an impact on the development of stable credit markets. As John Brewer noted, "The late seventeenth and eighteenth centuries saw an astonishing transformation in British government, one which put muscle on the bones of the British body politics, increasing its endurance, strength and reach. Britain was able to shoulder an ever-more ponderous burden of military commitments thanks to a radical increase in taxation, the development of public deficit finance (a national debt) on an unprecedented scale, and the growth of a sizable public administration devoted to organizing the fiscal and military activities of the state."[14] During the seventeenth century, excise and land taxes were introduced to provide a stable flow of revenues to the British government. In all of this, of course, was a political dimension. Throughout much of the 1600s, the British throne and parliament had squared off against each other, partially due to the monarchy's ongoing need of funds. The low point of such clashes was the English civil war (1642-1651), which resulted in Charles I losing his head on the block. The demise of King Charles resulted in the rise of Oliver Cromwell to absolute power. By the mid-seventeenth century, as a degree of political stability settled the country, political parties took shape in the form of Whigs and Tories. While Parliament had earlier demonstrated its ability to dominate the monarchy, the situation had evolved that the purse was the lever by which Parliament controlled the king, but the party system was the tiller by which the king could steer policy in the direction he wanted. This development led to some degree of political stability. In turn, public confidence in the long-term stability of the monarchy and belief in its bonds and notes allowed for the expansion of credit that financed the European wars.

Britain was involved in wars throughout the seventeenth century, especially following Charles' reign. These conflicts included wars with Spain and France, the wars of the Three Kingdoms, the Commonwealth Wars with Holland and Spain, the Anglo-Dutch wars of Charles II, the two rebellions faced by James II, and constant warfare that marked the reigns of William III and Anne. As Kislansky observed, "War finance was no longer an extraordinary expense that members of Parliament were occasionally summoned to provide: it was central to the workings of the royal budget, and drove the modernization of taxation, credit and finance." [15] By the beginning of the 1700s, London was emerging as a global financial hub and British power was becoming more global in nature. A credit culture, which was closely tied to trade, was also emerging, centering on London. However, much of that credit was not used for developing industrial production and some of it was attracted to the various schemes in the London stock market.

A major factor in improving the state's finance was an improvement in the state apparatus after 1688. Boards and departments were created or overhauled with the intention rewarding full-time employees with salaries rather than fees, offering a career ladder of graded appointments with progressively higher remuneration that culminated in a government pension, and establishing administrative loyalty as well as an ethos of public duty.[16] As Brewer noted of the more efficient civil service and its better standards, "the limited extent of venality meant that the effective departments of state had a lighter financial burden to carry."[17] It is important to understand that these bureaucratic reforms did not stamp out all corruption, but limited the range of activities and probably reduced the damage, especially when compared to other European states. That stated, the reforms also led to an unprecedented expansion in the numbers of government clerks working on tax accounts, inventories, financial statutes, rules governing the borrowing of money, and trade data.

One of the important components of the upgrade in Britain's fiscal regime was that, while it improved the predictability of government finances (as much as possible), the impact of taxation fell upon the level of internal demand in the industries facing mass markets, rather than the sources of savings. Consequently, taxation did not prejudice capital accumulation or investment by competing for investment funds or reducing incentives.[18] What this meant was that capital for investment or accumulation remained outside of the government's grasp. Moreover, as the demand for credit was to eventually grow, the savings of businessmen, merchants, farmers, and land-owners would provide a pool of capital resources.

King William was also in need of capital and, to this end, agreed to charter a national bank that would raise money from private sources and lend to the government. The idea was initially floated by a Scotsman, William Paterson, who became an advisor on the undertaking. Thus, in 1694, the Bank of England became a reality. A year later, the Bank of Scotland was born. Checks, banknotes, and minted coins made possible an economy founded on money. The Bank of England's foundation was an important step forward in the history of credit, and its beginnings came out of the politics of the time. Another significant development was the inauguration of some of the first insurance companies, such as the Sun and Lloyds, which protected against the devastation of fire. In time insurance was to be extended to risk in business ventures.

The ideas behind the founding of the Bank of England had been percolating for a while. The primary influence was the experience of the Dutch. To many commercially minded British, the great economic achievements of the Dutch in the fifteenth and sixteenth centuries were a source of envy. One of the conclusions about the Dutch success was that it was due to a successfully working banking system, constructed around the Amsterdam Exchange Bank (founded in 1609). Sir William Petty and Sir Dudley North in the seventeenth century propounded the formation of a bank in England to issue credit.[19] The financial instability of the time only reinforced such views that Britain required better institutions to provide stability.

The Bank of England was organized as a private enterprise and its early guiding light was William Paterson (1658-1719), who was an advisor to William III on economic, financial, and state affairs. Shortly upon its opening the doors, the new holding company promptly lent King William £1.2 million at 8 percent annual interest. As Weatherford noted, "The investors received stock in the bank in proportion to their investments. Chartered as Governor and Company of the Bank of England, the bank raised money to finance the conquest of the world's largest empire over the coming centuries."[20] In time, the Bank of England came to take deposits and issued paper money, which came to be called pounds.

It is important to underscore that the foundation of the Bank of England represented the modernization of the financing of the British state and helped create more credit for business and for expanding colonization projects. The significance of the establishment of the stock exchange and the national debt made possible an economy based on credit.

As British finance evolved, it was, like the Dutch experience with Tulipmania, prone to a number of missteps. In the 1710s, the "South Sea Bubble" amply demonstrated the British penchant for the misuse of credit. The South Sea Company in 1711 put up a scheme to hungry British investors and backed it with large grants of shares to leading politicians. The South Sea Company provoked a wild outburst of speculation that was clearly a mania. In a world without the legal benefits of transparency and disclosure, the scheme that originated from the celebrated Harley Earl of Oxford was that the monopoly of the trade to the South Seas was granted to the company by Spain. Charles Mackay in his *Extraordinary Popular Delusions and the Madness of Crowds* captured the mood around the South Sea Company: "Everybody had heard of the gold and silver mines of Peru and Mexico; everyone believed them to be inexhaustible, and that it was only necessary to send the manufactures of England to the coast to be repaid a hundred-fold in gold and silver ingots by the natives." [21] Credit and speculation traveled hand in hand, with available credit fueling the fires of speculation. In the end, the investor was pulled into a scam that went belly-up, leaving many people with large losses. In response, Parliament passed the Bubble Act in 1721 that forbade the formation of joint-stock companies without a royal charter. The royal charter was an instrument that was costly and difficult to obtain, which meant that the easiest method of raising capital for large-scale industrial organizations was closely scrutinized.

The rise of London as the world's major credit hub also carried with it a degree of significance in the realm of international affairs. Clearly, Britain's rise to prominence came at the cost of the Dutch. As the historian Landis noted, "In the seventeenth century, England harassed and fought the United Provinces [the Netherlands] at every opportunity: hence a tax on the export of unfinished woolens and Alderman Cockayne's Project (1614-17) to take back from the Dutch the valuable dyeing and finishing process (unsuccessful); two navigation acts, designed to hurt the Dutch in their role as chief carriers and middlemen (they did); and a pair of naval wars that displaced the Dutch as masters of the seas, extruded them from North America, and led indirectly to their containment in India."[22] Although the Dutch were to place William III on the throne and Britain and the Netherlands became partners, the British became the senior of the two. Moreover, as Dutch industry and commerce became less competitive, Dutch investors turned to exporting capital to Britain, which was soon to undergo its industrial revolution. As late as 1776, Adam Smith praised the Netherlands as "a country that had acquired that full complement of riches which the nature of its soils and climate and situation with other countries allowed it to acquire."[23] Despite that praise, Britain was already well advanced in its surpassing of the Netherlands as the world's dominant credit center.

An important component to the rise of London was that the government believed that favorable conditions in the London capital market were critical to its national policy objectives.[24] This was reflected by the experience of Walter Boyd, who, during the 1790s, was head of the major loan-contracting firm of Boyd, Benfield and Company. Working with the encouragement of Britain's Prime Minister William Pitt, Boyd, in 1794, placed a massive £6 million loan for the Imperial Government of Austria. Most of the loan was placed in the hands of British investors. As Samuel L. Hayes III and Philip M. Hubbard noted of the interplay between politics and finance, "...making finance available on reasonable terms to Britain's allies and denying to belligerent France was seen as astute management of wartime relationships. Thus, the level of interest rates and the volume of new securities issues on the financial market were then, as now, a constant preoccupation of both the government and Britain's private sector."[25] Much like the Medicis before, access to credit was used by the British to help allies and denial of credit was used to punish enemies.

The Industrial Revolution and the Growth of International Credit

The Industrial Revolution that was to make England the "workshop of the world," had its roots in the late 1600s, but it was not until the mid-1700s that the process became more pronounced. During the late 1600s and early 1700s a number of developments occurred that gave impetus to the Industrial Revolution. These included the decay of the guild system, the spread of a free labor market, and the introduction of labor-saving machinery. The guild system, which was based on small levels of specialized manufacture, was undermined by the new technology and organized means of production. As for the introduction of labor-saving machinery, such inventions included the steam pump of Savery and Newcomer (perfected in 1712) that helped solve the problem of flooding in the coal mines. Others were John Kay's fly-shuttle loom, James Hargreave's hand-operated spinning jenny, and Richard Arkwright's water-powered spinning frame.[26] The combination of these factors gave considerable momentum to industry. However, British credit had yet to soar and the Industrial Revolution was slowed by an ongoing lack of capital and the appalling state of the country's transport system.[27] The lack of capital was due in part to the fact that many investors were attracted by government funds that provided an attractive return. This meant that industrial undertakings were left without a pool of ready capital. As the historian Plumb observed, "The position was made worse by a scarcity of banks in the provinces, and so the enterprising industrialists were denied the financial facilities so necessary for growth of their business." [28] Another factor working against the advancement of credit was that English banks were small. Moreover, English authorities exerted little control over the banks' extent of their note issues, cash ratios, reserves, check transactions or expansionist credit policies.[29] While this fed expansion, it also maximized the loss of confidence and the collapse of credit in bad years, but did nothing to curb the vigor of booms.[30] Nevertheless, by the end of the eighteenth century the Industrial Revolution took off.

A critical motor for England's coming Industrial Revolution was the development of trade. As already noted, by the 1660s England had become an important trade entrepôt for the rest of Europe. From 1650 to 1760 foreign trade continued to be a significant source for economic momentum, influencing levels of wealth, the size of markets available to the industry of a comparatively small country, sources of savings, the considerable differentiation of the economy and society in England relative to other nations. The coming of the steam engine brought railways and steamships first to Britain. The impact of railways cannot be understated. As rail historian Kevin O'Connor commented, "The railways assisted the growth of education and literacy and thus were unwitting agents in the growth of democracy. Papers and magazines were transported on trains to outlying regions, informing people about the wider world, and fresh food was carried to the cities on the return journeys. The railways also led to advances in science and technology, from metallurgy to the electric telegraph." [31]

The scope of change was sweeping—not since Egyptian times had there been such a change in transportation. By the eighteenth century, when the Industrial Revolution was in full swing, British industrialists were well-situated to benefit from the already established patterns of markets and commercial institutions. Simply stated, as new production techniques came on line, British industrialists were soon able to undercut the handicraft industries of the rest of the planet in price and quality.[32]

An important component of the financing of the Industrial Revolution was the stabilizing role played by the Bank of England. That institution's dominant role in credit was considerably augmented by the Bank Charter Act of 1844 in which Parliament gave the Bank of England a virtual monopoly on the right to issue bank notes in the United Kingdom. What this meant was that the Bank of England's role was greatly enhanced, the printing of bank notes made more uniform, and the Old Lady of Threadneddle Street (as the bank came to be called) had to guarantee the convertibility of all of its paper notes into gold on demand.

The Bank of England had a high level of prestige and gained the trust of industry, commerce and finance. By the end of the 1800s, the Bank of England had emerged as a central and stabilizing institution of the world monetary and banking system. The significance of such an institution cannot be understated. While credit markets had become relatively more national during the 1600s and 1700s, with the exception of Amsterdam, the Bank of England provided a global force for the monetary well-being of British industry and trade, which, in turn, filtered to the rest of the planet, especially after the defeat of Napoleon. Britain's triumph ushered in a period of greater political stability, which was conducive to the consolidation of a global economic order under the guidance of the British. Additionally, the gearing up of the economy with the Industrial Revolution generated capital, further giving impetus to London's rise as the dominant credit hub in the world.

The amazing progress of the Industrial Revolution placed relatively large profits into the British banking system that demanded to be invested.[33] Furthermore, the success of British overseas trade added significantly to the capital stock available in England. Finally, London benefited from the development of a sophisticated banking system that could place the balances deposited in the country's banks to good use with merchants and traders operating out of London. A key factor in the development of the British-dominated credit system was that although the creditors were in the private sector, the expansion of the banks occurred under the supervision of the Bank of England, itself privately run yet representative of the state's interest in providing a safe and sound business environment. What this meant for credit was best described by Brewer: "The ease with which money could be borrowed ensured that few savings lay idle and that the full financial resources of the economy were successfully employed....Indeed, it is hard to imagine the sort of expansion that occurred in eighteenth century markets without the development of a well-articulated system of private borrowing and lending."[34]

A few other factors must also be considered in explaining how the London-dominated international credit system worked. The London banks were closely connected to international trade due to the fact that many of them originally began in merchant activities. Morgan Grenfell began with the establishment by George Peabody of a counting house with desks, chairs, a mahogany counter, and a safe at No. 31 Moorgate in the City of London in 1838.[35] The original line of business was importing cotton and tobacco from the southern United States and in return exporting English textiles and steel rails for the then booming U.S. railway system. Baring Brothers &

Company had its humble roots in a drapery business established in Exeter in the early eighteenth century.[36] Carl Joachim Hambos came from a long line of Jewish merchants. Nathan Rothschild came to Manchester from Frankfurt to trade cotton before he moved to London. Last, but hardly least, Schroders was founded in London during the Napoleonic wars by Johann Heinrich Schroder, who was a member of a prominent and prosperous north German merchant family involved in the trade of wine, spirits, coffee, sugar, salmon, herring, lemons, rye, and cloth.[37]

Related to the involvement of the merchant banks in trade was the same institutions' dominance in the working of the gold standard. Britain was the most powerful country and as it defeated the mercantilistic French by 1815, it had imposed a free trade system on a large part of the world. A cornerstone to the free trade system was the widespread acceptance of the gold standard. Simply stated, the global financial and trade system was founded upon the premise that national currencies were all related to the international price of gold—set by the British. It was no mistake that the London bullion market was where most newly minted gold came into the international market. Consequently, London was where the link between gold and credit was the strongest.

Under the guidance of the Bank of England, the world operated on a single monetary system based on common adherence to the gold principle, which meant that gold, in effect, was the world currency. [38] In gold we trust, therefore, was the credo of the British financial and commercial empire and the merchant banks of London, which were at the apex of the system. The merchant banks financed foreign trade, brought new bond offerings to the market, and sought to provide sound investments for the capital their clients deposited with them.[39]

London—The World's Credit Hub

The ability of the British banks to issue long-term bonds and loans, like the Dutch, elevated London's position head and shoulders over any possible rival's. Although the finance houses of Amsterdam, Paris, Frankfurt, Hamburg, and Vienna (and Berlin after 1870) could offer bills of exchange, none was able to compete with London's ability to fund long-term private and public debt. From about 1850, London became the primary place of issue, initially for railroad investments and eventually for other major infrastructure projects that provided the glue for the international economy of the nineteenth century. The London houses dominated what came to be called haute finance, becoming the mechanism that facilitated the flow of capital from the areas of surplus to areas of demand.

The primary incentive for involvement in infrastructure projects around the world was profit. As Hobson noted, "Britain's surplus of capital was also invested abroad, at first in securing the governments of Europe bankrupted by the French Wars of 1793 to 1815. As the burden of debt of the Napoleonic wars receded, the higher returns available from financing (often speculative) projects aboard attracted investors in London."[40] An important development along this line was the Prussian loan of 1818.

In the aftermath of the French wars, most European governments badly required capital. Until 1818, those loans were conducted in the currency of the country seeking the loan. For example, the French loans raised by Barings to pay for the Napoleonic wars had paid interest in francs in Paris, with attendant inconvenience and exchange rate risks for British investors. This was to change with the 1818 Prussian loan, engineered by Nathan Rothschild. Nathan structured the loan with two conditions: first, the loan was not to be in thaler, but in sterling, with the interest payable (half-yearly) not in Berlin but in London; and secondly, there was to be a British-style sinking fund to ensure the amortization of the loan. (A sinking fund is money accumulated in a custodial account to retire debt instruments according to a predetermined schedule, regardless of pricing changes in the market.) An additional factor was that the loan was issued not only in London, but also in Frankfurt, Berlin, Hamburg, Amsterdam, and Vienna. As Niall Ferguson indicates, "Whatever its significance for Prussian politics, the 1818 Prussian loan was without question a watershed in the history of the European capital market, as contemporaries came to recognize....In other words, it represented a major step towards the creation of a completely international bond market."[41]

The expansion of the pool of British credit was also fed by legislation regarding joint stock companies, which was finally settled in 1862. Joint stock companies were already a powerful force in credit formation in London, but the clarification of the law on the matter helped provide considerable impetus in increasing the numbers of companies with limited liability for their shareholders. By 1880, *The Economist* demonstrated that the annual new capital subscriptions had almost doubled in the preceding three years. The impact of this was captured by Richard Graham: "Because of the rapidity of its accumulation, this capital was frequently directed toward investments abroad."[42]

London's global credit role was central to the economic development of vast tracts of the planet. One of the first places to benefit from the flow of British credit, entwined with the global advance of the Industrial Revolution, was Ireland. Long under the sway of the British, Ireland in the early 1800s had a population of about six million, providing a large market for new industrial goods produced in Britain and other non-industrial products from the colonies. Irish horses and agricultural produce were also in demand in Britain. It was believed that any improved system of transport would make more efficient the delivery of goods and people. A group of merchants and bankers who did business with each other out of parts of Dublin, Liverpool, Cardiff, Bristol, and London threw their support behind the idea of bringing railways to Ireland.[43] One of the leaders of this group, known as the supporters of the "Irish Sea Economic Area," was James Pim, a partner in a stockbroker firm in Dublin. A Quaker, he had ties to his brethren in England, who were also major railroad proponents. This also gave him access to credit. Although the first line would not start until 1835, the ideas and credit were transferred from England, reflecting a process that was to reoccur throughout the British Empire.

Beyond Ireland, in the far-flung reaches of the British Empire, railroads were built, telegraph wires put up, and electricity generators constructed. Much of the financing of U.S. economic development prior to the United States Civil War was funded by London, either through loans from the influential city banks like Lloyds, Barings Brothers, and Morgan Grenfell, or via the stock market in the form of bonds. Although London's role was as the major credit source to the entire planet, the bulk of the investment by the early 1900s was in Europe, North America, and other temperate countries.[44] The possible exception to this was Latin America, in particular Argentina and, to a lesser extent, Brazil.

British credit also spread around the globe in the form of overseas banks. As British industry and commerce stretched into Asia, Latin America, Africa, and Australia, not all of the banking business was done by the merchant banks, such as Barings and Rothschilds. The merchant banks conducted much of their trade finance and other business with correspondent banks in the United States and in mainland Europe. Once beyond those points on the map, local Western-structured banks either did not exist or were in their infancy. Consequently, British entrepreneurs involved in trade and finance moved to fill the gap, creating a sizeable number of overseas banks. In the nineteenth century, a rash of new banks emerged with such names as The Colonial Bank (which was active in the British West Indies), the Bank of South Australia, the Union Bank of Australia, the Chartered Bank of India, Australia and China, the Bank of Montreal, and the Bank of West India.[45] The last-mentioned eventually changed its name to the Oriental Bank and until its demise, ran a network of branches in Colombo, Calcutta, Hong Kong, Singapore, South Africa, and Australia. Other important institutions emerged, some of which are still with us today as with Hong Kong Shanghai Bank, Standard Chartered, and some of the large Australian banks. British overseas banks even penetrated Japan before the Meiji Restoration of 1868. The Oriental Bank acquired an important role as financial advisor to the Japanese government and floated in London the Meiji government's first two foreign loans, in 1870 and 1873.[46]

The significance of the spread of Western-structured banks to Asia and other parts of the planet was that it further established the creation of a Western-dominated international credit system. The dominant credit culture was thereafter to remain solidly Western, in particular Anglo-American in departure. Although local forms of credit were not to be entirely eclipsed, their role in local economies was to decline radically in a global capitalist system pushed by the British.

British Credit in the Americas

British credit for overseas financing was active as early as the first decades of the 1800s in Latin America, where British merchants spearheaded it. One of the more interesting stories was that of the Parish Robertson brothers. Initially opening up a trading operation in Buenos Aires in 1807, the Parish Robertsons were highly entrepreneurial and soon expanded their business into Paraguay and into other parts of Argentina. As business was good and they accumulated a considerable fortune, the brothers decided to go into finance. By 1817, they founded a commercial house at Buenos Aires and simultaneously established an agency in Liverpool, England.[47]

When South America threw off Spanish rule in the 1820s, the Parish Robertsons were in a highly strategic position to expand their economic empire. They were soon active in the issue of foreign loans for the government in Argentina and Peru. Additionally, they promoted mining companies in Argentina and Bolivia and founded ranching and colonization companies in the Rio de la Plata region. As Carlos Marichal noted, "Such a variety of transactions placed them in a special category among Anglo-Argentine merchants. The scope of their activities reflected the advantages of establishing special relationships with leading mercantile and banking firms in Great Britain and with political leaders in Latin America."[48]

Marichal, in his *A Century of Debt Crises in Latin America* affirmed that a similar pattern emerged throughout the rest of Latin America. Well-connected merchants with profits that could be put to work as loans emerged in Colombia, Venezuela, Chile, and Peru. For many new nations in Latin America, independence cost money. Fighting the Spanish required arms and arms cost money. Fledgling governments with weak institutions were not exactly cash-flush, hence their need for credit. Well-connected British merchants with access to London's credit markets were thus attractive options. As Marichal observed, "In summary, independence opened up new and dynamic channels of Latin American trade and rapidly tied the region into a web of international mercantile and credit transactions controlled from London, Glasgow, and Liverpool."[49]

British credit was not only involved in trade in the Americas, but also played an important role in the region's industrialization. As Graham's study of British involvement in Brazil's modernization during 1850-1914 shows, Britishers helped construct the major part of the transport system on which industry was to depend for the receipt of raw material and access to markets; much of the industrial machinery and supplies which were used by Brazilian factories were produced in Britain and sold through a distributive system created by the British; the technicians who installed the equipment, directed its operation, and taught the workers to operate it were usually British; and they invested directly in textile plants, sugar and shoe factories and flour mills. As Graham noted, "...they advanced not only the credits to finance these sales but often provided the loan capital that enabled Brazilians to invest in manufacturing enterprises."[50] Much of the same could be said about the British involvement in other major economies in Latin America.

British credit was also deeply involved in financing U.S. economic development. During the early nineteenth century, the American Mid-

West and the agricultural sector opened up and made substantial advances. This process was reflected by the birth of new cities such as Chicago, built on the Great Lakes, where the construction of the canal system facilitated the industrial expansion of Ohio, Michigan, Illinois, Pennsylvania, and northern New York State. At the same time, the cotton industry in the South was stimulated by the spread of textile machinery, especially in the United Kingdom, France, and Belgium. All of these developments required credit, something that was lacking with the U.S. fledgling financial system and something that was readily available in London. Consequently, British finance went into the U.S. cotton industry, the digging of canals, and the construction of railways.

The risks of extending credit to developing nations such as the United States, Colombia, and Argentina were high because of a multitude of reasons. Needs for funds were extensive throughout the Americas and the British had well-established trade relations that opened the doors to lucrative commercial opportunities. At the same time, political conditions were often unstable and commodity price swings frequently resulted in boom-bust cycles. As capital requirement rose, British-led foreign ventures turned to London's Royal Exchange. The time was ripe for Latin American mining companies. The British government, successful in its war against Napoleon, was borrowing less and the 1817 French reparation loan had produced a capital gain for British investors and whetted their appetites for more foreign loans.[51] Latin American bonds beckoned and those related to the mining sector loomed as the most attractive. In mid-1826 alone, twenty-six different Latin American mining companies had been registered, many having members of parliament sitting on the board. One prospectus proclaimed that "lumps of pure gold, weighing from two to fifty pounds, were totally neglected," and that the company's mines would "yield considerably more than the quality necessary for the supply of the whole world."[52] As in any type of speculation, the mining companies were regarded as sure rides to riches, hence fueling greater investment. The crash of 1825 ultimately brought the number of mining companies down and restored a degree of cold reality about the risks of extending credit to overseas debtors, many of which were of questionable credit quality.

One of the most interesting developments in London's prominence as the global credit capital was the Barings Panic of 1890. Barings had emerged as one of the most prestigious banks in the world during the eighteenth century. Headed by Lord Revelstoke in 1890, Barings was a world player. Loans were extended to finance railways in Canada, the institution was involved in the great reorganization of U.S. railway monopolies that occurred in the late 1880s, and in France, it was engaged in the resolution of the copper corner that caused the collapse of the Paris bank, Comptoir di Escompte in 1889. While Revelstoke presided over a major institution in international credit that was usually highly profitable, the bank stumbled badly in Argentina. Simply stated, it was overextended in Argentine stocks and bonds. When in 1890 Argentina's Banco Nacional suspended debt services payments due to problems in the economy, Barings had big problems.

On November 8, 1890, Lord Revelstoke sat down with William Lidderale, the Governor of the Bank of England, and Everard Hambro of C.J. Hambro and Son, one of London's other major creditors. During that meeting Lord Revelstoke revealed that Barings had a problem, which could soon become everybody else's, especially if assistance was not forthcoming.

On November 10, Lidderale met with Viscount Goshen, the Chancellor of the Exchequer. He requested support in two forms. First, he needed the Chancellor to persuade the Rothschilds to help transfer a large sum of gold from the Bank of France to the Bank of England to help back up payments for Barings. Secondly, he wanted the British government to put pressure on the Argentine government to cover outstanding debts with Barings. Although these actions were taken, the magnitude of Barings' liabilities was higher than expected and Lidderale was forced to unite the entire London banking community into a rescue operation. With the involvement of such firms as C.J. Hambro and Sons, J.S. Morgan, the Rothschilds, and Smith, Payne and Smith, Barings was able to survive the crisis. By early 1891 the situation had been stabilized.

Although the Barings Crisis of 1890 was not a full-blown international meltdown, it reflected the risks of international lending. For Barings being a king of credit had its rewards, but it also had its risks. Sadly, the ripples caused by the incident were further reaching, reflecting the increasing global and interrelated nature of credit markets. As Marichal noted, "The effects of the panic were soon felt in other nations of Latin America, because the panic provoked a marked reduction in the flow of foreign capital. During the 1890s, European bankers were reluctant to extend more new loans for the government of the region, fearing that they would be burned as badly as Barings had been."[53] This was an early case of what is called contagion. The problem of one market, in this case Argentina, overlapped into other, seemingly unrelated markets, i.e., the rest of Latin America. Needless to say, this problem would reoccur with all too much regularity in the future.

London's Decline

On June 22, 1897, Queen Victoria went to the telegraph room at Buckingham Palace. From that office she sent her Jubilee message to every corner of her empire. At the time of Queen Victoria's Diamond Jubilee, the British Empire was the largest in the history of the world, comprising nearly a quarter of the landmass of the planet and a quarter of its population. The maps painted large swaths of Africa, the Asia-Pacific region, and parts of the Americas in red. At home there was strong sentiment that the British were still the top dogs in the global arena. Indeed, the nineteenth century had been dominated by Wellington's defeat of Napoleon at Waterloo in 1815. The French were utterly crushed and the British navy ruled the waves and kept the peace. Yet, despite the affirmation of national pride, British dominance was in decline. The long "slide down the slippery slope from palmy greatness to anxious mediocrity" had begun.[54] In 1871, when the Prussians created the new German empire, they became significant competition for Great Britain and by 1900 Germany became a burden for the British Empire. As the French recuperated from the Franco-Prussian War, they began to actively seek colonies. At the Berlin Conference of 1885 Britain agreed to allow France and Germany to colonize in order to keep the peace and have a greater amount of European cooperation. The trend continued and after 1870 a united Italy started to clamor for colonies too. Between 1837 and 1901 under Queen Victoria, Britain gained many colonies herself in Asia, Africa, and the Pacific to make her a truly worldwide empire. However, the unification of Germany, the deepening industrialization of France, and the advance of U.S. industry represented greater challenges to Britain's dominance in both trade and commerce, which gradually rippled into the credit system. In 1879, British steel makers produced 1 million tons, outstripping the combined European total. That was to change. German production rapidly expanded, surpassing the British total in 1893. The U.S. had already surpassed the British in steel production seven years earlier.

Briefly stated, reasons for Britain's decline included the country's scarcity of natural resources, its unwillingness to risk family capital, its lack of industrial entrepreneurs, its delays in modernizing industrial techniques, and its reluctance to consolidate or rationalize industrial operations.[55] In addition, the growing strength of Germany and France increased competition in business and sparked a naval arms race between the three European powers, which made investments in the U.S. more profitable. This helped the U.S. stock market to grow stronger while the British economy grew weaker. All in all, London's dominance as the global financial center gradually gave way to growing competition from the United States in the 1880s and 1890s and from a number of new competitors in Europe. At the same time, London's decline was neither abrupt nor dramatic; rather it was to be gradual and constructive in the development of the world's next credit superpower, the United States. In much the same fashion as the Dutch had nudged the development of British credit along with capital and a cross-fertilization of personnel, the British were to provide both to their cousins across the Atlantic. British credit was active in the development of the United States' industrial infrastructure as well as providing important Transatlantic financial relationships. British holdings of U.S. Treasuries amounted to over one-half of the amount outstanding in 1803, although it declined to about 25 percent by 1818.[56]

Barings Brothers was particularly active in the United States. As early as 1803 Barings was appointed official agents of the U.S. government and, in 1828, it added an American partner as well as increasing its alliances with other American banking and securities firms.[57] Barings also helped the United States finance the Louisiana Purchase. George Peabody, already mentioned as the founder of Morgan Grenfell, was actually an American who had moved to London. While he is known to have initially sold bonds of the State of Maryland to British investors, he also took on as an American partner, Junius Spencer Morgan, whose son was to be the banking giant, J. Pierpont Morgan. Simply stated, the emerging market status of the U.S. economy offered better returns on investments than in the British economy—despite political risk (such as the War of 1812 and the Civil War) and the lack of a central bank to supervise the financial sector and effect monetary policy. At the same time that the Americans were developing what would become competitive financial institutions and credit markets, competition was also emerging in Germany, France, and Switzerland (as will be shown in the next chapter).

One of the seminal events to reflect London's decline was the outbreak of World War I. As Erik Banks aptly noted, "Having long enjoyed a dominant position in international trade and industrial development for many decades, the country's economic future was now in the balance. Its ability to earn £200 million annually from overseas investments, control more than 60 percent of the world's industrial exports, and command in excess of 70 percent of global shipping, was in jeopardy."[58] That jeopardy would not go away as World War I effectively ended London's clear-cut dominance. That conflict arrested and ultimately broke a long-running period of monetary cosmopolitanism, which based its trust in London's ability to provide the necessary credit to finance global development. It was no mistake that at the beginning of the war, all of the principal stock exchanges in Europe were closed due to concerns about financial panic and that the New York Stock Exchange remained open. Equally significant, the U.S. dollar was the only currency that remained convertible into gold. By the end of the Great Conflict, London was no longer fully able to fulfill that role. This became painfully evident when the global economy slipped into the Great Depression at the end of the 1920s.

The Second World War and the ensuing peace were also difficult on British financial institutions. In many cases, the reduction of the empire to a few small holdings around the world and a return to Great Britain was matched by a sharp decline in London as an international credit center from which recovery would be gradual. At the core of London's changed circumstances was an important shift of the country and its institutions from being the center of international events and credit to becoming a less important player, overshadowed by the United States and the Soviet Union. The financial stress of the global conflict forced the British to refocus their efforts on reconstruction of the home economy. Since the United Kingdom was a net importer, rather than an exporter of capital, it no longer had the power and influence to lead the world as it had done for many decades. Simply stated, the U.K. lacked the resources, trade surpluses and invisible earnings critical to its former role as the provider of the world's credit. This was evident in that the Second World War had lost Britain half of its foreign trade, two-thirds of its overseas markets, and one-third of its merchant fleet.[59] For London, decline meant a long period of restructuring of its economy and its interrelation with the world.

Conclusion

London's rise to global dominance in the history of credit was guided by the coming together of three key factors: (1) the establishment of a well-functioning system of public finance; (2) a dominant position in trade that helped generate capital surpluses; and (3) a commanding position in international capital markets, especially in providing long-term credit. The foundations for these conditions came prior to 1815, but the defeat of Napoleon and the peace it established as well as the demands for credit in Europe, the Americas, Asia, and Africa helped provide a greater impetus to London becoming the superpower as an issuer for the world's development. Between the strong position in trade, the advancement of the Industrial Revolution in the first half of the nineteenth century, and the relative peace that accompanied British dominance, London's financial institutions adapted with considerable flexibility to providing credit for infrastructure. The motivation of the key players was, of course, profit, a factor that drove English investors to risk higher returns overseas. At the same time, the British government found it worthwhile to have London function as the main hub of the global economy, a situation reinforced by the City's role as the major market for the world gold trade and the use of the gold standard in international trade and commerce. It is also important to note that even though the British trade position eroded and other cities challenged London's dominance, the ability of British banks to provide long-term credit helped maintain the city's position at the apex of the global credit system up until 1914 despite the relative decline of British power. Even after 1914, London would not be eclipsed entirely by New York. The total eclipse would only come after the Second World War.

Britain's dominance was to gradually erode in the late nineteenth century and more markedly in the first decades of the twentieth century. Decline as a world credit superpower came from the damage caused by the First World War, the rise of U.S. credit, and Britain's erosion as the world's industrial workshop before American and European competition. The story of the shift of credit leadership from London to New York, however, is in the following chapters.

Notes

1. This view has been advanced by a number of historians. See Patrick Brantlinger, *Fictions of the State: Culture and Credit in Britain, 1694-1994* (Ithaca, NY: Cornell University Press, 1996).
2. As John Brewer noted, "In the fourteenth and fifteenth centuries England was one of the most effective states in Europe, with a much-feared army and the military capability to command a sizable 'empire' on the Continent. But from the mid-fifteenth century, when the artillery of Charles VII won the decisive victory of Castillon and drove the English out of almost all of France, to the year 1558, when England lost her last continental foothold at Calais, British military might underwent a marked decline." *The Sinews of Power: War, Money and the English State, 1688-1783* (New York: Alfred A. Knopf, 1989), p. 7.
3. *The New Encyclopedia Britannica, Volume 8* (Chicago: Encyclopedia Britannica, 1998), p. 28.
4. John Cabot was born Giovanni Caboto in Genoa and was a seasoned traveler in the Mediterranean and the Middle East. For more about him, see Peter Firstbrook, *The Voyage of the Mathew: John Cabot and the Discovery of North America* (San Francisco: KQED Books & tapes, 1997).
5. For information about the formation of the Royal Navy, see N.A.M. Porter, *The Safeguard of the Sea: A Naval History of Britain, Vol. 1 660-1649* (London: Harper Collins Publishers, 1997).
6. Ralph Davis, *The Rise of the Atlantic Economies* (Ithaca, NY: Cornell University Press, 1973), p. 207.
7. Lord McCauley, *The History of England* (New York: Penguin Books, 1986, first published 1848-1861), p. 488.
8. Quoted in Henry Kamen, *European Society, 1500-1700* (London: Routledge, 1996), p. 69.
9. Randall D. Germain, *The International Organization of Credit: States and Global Finance in the World Economy* (Cambridge: Cambridge University Press, 1998)., p. 39. "The Antwerp Bourse even lent funds to the English crown, and provided one of Queen Elizabeth I's counselors, Sir Thomas Gresham, with the blueprint for the nationalization of the English capital market."
10. Kamen, *European Society*, p. 69.
11. Great changes also came in British daily life in the seventeenth century. These included the emergence of newspapers and the introduction of new foods, such as tea, rum, coffee, and chocolate. Personal hygiene took a great leap forward as the water closet appeared in fashionable homes (this also made public thoroughfares safer to walk). As people migrated to cities where jobs increasingly were created, urban life expanded considerably at the expense of rural areas. New recreations were invented: the first cricket club was founded, King James I introduced golf in England and established the Royal Blackheath Golf Club in 1608. At the same time, technology leapt forward setting the stage for the Industrial Revolution in the next century. The prototype of the steam engine was created; coke was produced and then used to manufacture iron; and the cooking hob and the pressure cooker were invented (which relieved people of the tedious chores of turning food on spits for hours or boiling beef for lengthy periods of time). At the same time that technology moved forward, Britain underwent an intellectual revolution. Francis Bacon laid the foundations for scientific experimentation and the inductive method; Robery Boyle posited on the existence of the chemical elements; and Isaac Newton propounded the theory of gravity. The intellectual revolution was no less vigorous in such areas

as literature, medicine, and political theory. It was, after all, in the 1600s that Shakespeare wrote *Romeo and Juliet*, Hobbes, *Leviathan,* and Locke *Two Treatises of Government.*

12.   Mark Kishlansky, *A Monarchy Transformed: Britain 1603-1714* (New York: Penguin Books, 1997), p. 1.

13.   Eric Williams, *Capitalism and Slavery* (Chapel Hill: University Press of North Carolina, 1994), pp. 98-102 and Germain, *The International Organization of Credit,* p. 48.

14.   Brewer, *The Sinews of Power,* p. xvii.

15.   Kishlansky, *A Monarchy Transformed,* p. 340.

16.   Ibid., p. 69.

17.   Ibid., p. 70.

18.   Peter Mathias, *The First Industrial Nation: An Economic History of Britain 1700-1914* (London: Routledge, 1995).

19.   John W. McConnell, *Basic Teachings of the Great Economists* (New York: Barnes & Noble, Inc., 1943, 1956), p. 193.

20.   Jack Weatherford, *The History of Money* (New York: Three Rivers Press, 1997), p. 157.

21.   Charles Mackay, *Extraordinary Popular Delusions and the Madness of Crowds,* (New York: John Wiley & Sons, Inc., 1996, originally published in 1841), p. 70.

22.   David S. Landes, *The Wealth and Poverty of Nations: Why Some Are So Rich and Some So Poor* (New York: W.W. Norton & Company, 1998), p. 448.

23.   Adam Smith, *The Wealth of Nations* (Chicago: Cannon edition, 1976), p. 106.

24.   Samuel L. Hayes III and Philip M. Hubbard, *Investment Banking: A Tale of Three Cities* (Boston: Harvard Business School Press, 1990), p. 13.

25.   Ibid.

26.   Paul Langford and Christopher Harvie, *The Eighteenth Century and the Age of Industry* (Oxford: Oxford University Press, 1988), p. 81.

27.   J.H. Plumb, *England in the Eighteenth Century* (Harmondsworth, England: Penguin Books, 1950), p. 126.

28.   Ibid.

29.   Mathias, *The First Industrial Nation,* p. 36.

30.   Ibid.

31.   Kevin O'Connor, *Ironing the Land: The Coming of the Railways to Ireland* (Dublin: Gill & Macmillan Ltd, 1999), p. 5.

32.   Mathias, *The First Industrial Nation,* pp. 13-14.

33.   Germain, *The International Organization of Credit,* p. 48.

34.   Brewer, *The Sinews of Power,* p. 187.

35.   Dominic Hobson, *The Pride of Lucifer: Morgan Grenfell 1838-1990, The Unauthorised Biography of a Merchant Bank* (London: Mandarin, 1991), p. 10.

36.   See Philip Ziegler, *The Sixth Great Power: Barings, 1762-1929* (London: Collins, 1988).

37.   Richard Roberts, *Schroders: Merchants and Bankers* (London: the Macmillan Press, 1992), pp. 3-21.

38.   Weatherford, *The History of Money,* p. 59.

39.   As Germain noted, "The London merchant banks thus stood at the center of the credit practices which constituted the nineteenth century's international organization of credit. They acted, for example, as the principal conduits through which foreign credits financed the building of infrastructure in Canada, Latin America, and much of Africa, including the development of railroads, ports and utilities." *The International Organization of Credit,* p. 49.

40. Hobson, *The Pride of Lucifer*, p. 12.
41. Naill Ferguson, *The House of Rothschild: Money's Prophets 1798-1848* (New York: Viking Press, 1998), pp. 124-125.
42. Richard Graham, *Britain & the Onset of Modernization in Brazil 1850-1914* (Cambridge: Cambridge University Press, 1972), p. 3.
43. O'Connor, *Ironing the Land*, pp. 5-6.
44. W. Arthur Lewis, *The Evolution of the International Economic Order* (Princeton, NJ: Princeton University Press, 1978), p. 38.
45. For a treatment of British overseas banks, see Geoffrey Jones, *British Multinational Banking, 1830-1990* (Oxford, UK: Clarendon Press, 1993), Chapter 2.
46. R.P.T. Davenport-Hines and Geoffrey Jones, "British Business in Japan since 1865", in R.P.T. Davenport-Hines and Geofrrey Jones, eds., *British Business in Asia Since 1860* (Cambridge: Cambridge University Press, 1989), p. 222-224.
47. For further information on the Parish Robertsons, see John and William Parish Robertson, *Letters on South America*, 3 vols. (London, 1843); and R.A. Humphreys, "British Merchants and South American Independence," in the volume of essays by the same author, entitled *Tradition and Revolt in Latin America* (London, 1972), pp. 113-117.
48. Carlos Marichal, *A Century of Debt Crises in Latin America: From Independence to the Great Depression 1820-1930* (Princeton, NJ: Princeton University Press, 1989), p. 19.
49. Ibid., p. 21.
50. Graham, *Britain & the Onset of Modernization of Brazil*, p. 125.
51. Edward Chancellor, *Devil Take the Hindmost: A History of Financial Speculation* (New York: Farrar, Straus, Giroux, 1999), p. 98.
52. Ibid., p. 101.
53. Marichal, *A Century of Debt Crises in Latin America*, p. 151.
54. Geoffrey Holmes, *The Eclipse of a Great Power: Modern Britain 1870-1992* (London: Longman, 1994), p. viii.
55. Erik Banks, *The Rise and Fall of the Merchant Banks* (London: Kogan Page, Ltd, 1999), p. 149.
56. Charles R. Geisst, *Wall Street: A History* (New York: Oxford University Press, 1997), pp. 17-18.
57. Vincent P. Carosso, *Investment Banking in America: A History* (Cambridge, Mass: Harvard University Press, 1970), pp. 9-10.
58. Banks, *The Rise and Fall of the Merchant Banks*, p. 212.
59. Jacques Attali, *A Man of Influence: SG Warburg* (Baltimore, MD: Adler & Adler, 1987), p. 277.

9

Continental Echoes

The angry, shouting mob watched with morbid fascination as King Louis XVI was brought forth. He was strapped to the small, narrow table on the guillotine, a machine used to behead condemned prisoners by means of an angled blade set in a heavy block that falls freely between upright posts. As the blade fell with a sickening thud, lopping off the King's head, no one would ever have thought that being a bad borrower would have such a dramatic outcome. Yet the story of how poor King Louis lost his head to the mobs of the French Revolution is linked to the tale of the evolution of credit in France.

While considerable attention has been given to the rise of British finance, and rightfully so, at the same time the rest of Europe was not standing still. British power did not come to dominate the globe without political and economic competition from France and eventually Germany. France fought several wars against the English and, certainly, under Napoleon the rest of Europe was rocked by the might of French arms. Germany's later unification in the nineteenth century ultimately led to the creation of one of the world's most industrialized states and a fierce competitor to British power in the early twentieth century, both militarily and economically. In both France and Germany, the story of credit was closely entwined with the expansion of political and economic power. Significantly, the events to shape the modern credit systems in these countries came largely in the nineteenth century. By the 1870s a modern infrastructure existed, encompassing law and finance in Western Europe, a critical fundamental for the Continent's industrial revolution, especially railroad construction.

While Germans and French were involved in establishing credit institutions, part of the story of Europe's continental credit was to involve the well-known Jewish banking dynasties of the Warburgs and the Rothschilds, two families that reflected the ebb and flow of European history. Although both families had their roots in Germany, their banking enterprises became transnational in nature, having an impact well beyond Europe. The story also involved the Swiss, who played a role in France's financial affairs and developed their own set of credit institutions, which over time would become internationally influential. While the British, French, and Germans were able to develop their own credit institutions, Europe's other major powers, the Austria-Hungarian Empire, the Russian Empire, and the Ottoman Empire lagged behind in this area. The weakness of credit systems in the three eastern empires hindered their industrial development and left them at a disadvantage vis-à-vis their rivals, to whom they turned for credit.

Credit in France

The history of credit in France took a decidedly different track from the experiences of Holland and England. Paris evolved as an important financial center, but it never achieved the same prominence of Amsterdam and London. Why? While late medieval France was a significant part of the trade fair network, the autonomous development of local financiers, the creation of a central or state bank, and a thriving bourse were slow in coming. Lyons did play an important role, but it was a hub for Italian financing families that helped elevate that city.[1] This is not to argue that there were no French creditors. Indeed, there was a gradual emergence of a prosperous patrician class in French towns, some of whom turned to moneylending. Most of these creditors emerged outside of Champagne and Paris, where French businessmen did not have to face tough and internationally sophisticated Italian competition. Centers of early French credit were in Gascony (where the local wine merchants backed with loans the wrong side in the war against the English) and Arras.

The most famous of early French creditors was Jacques Coeur, a well-known and wealthy merchant from Bourges. Coeur became the royal *arbegtier* (financial agent) of Charles VII, from 1438 to 1451. The French king was heavily engaged in war against the English, which meant that he was in need of credit to continue these campaigns. Coeur was able to obtain the financing required and became highly important to the kingdom for a period. As an internationally sophisticated trader, Coeur had close contacts with all the main foreign centers of international trade, in particular Aragon and Florence. His most famous act was to obtain the loans that were needed to finance the French reconquest of Normandy in 1450. Coeur made considerable money from lending to Charles, especially as he charged interest at the rate of 15 to 20 percent. Coeur also used his privileged position as the king's creditor to secure large assignments on various crown revenues, while his agents became fiscal officials for the crown. The latter meant that royal funds under Coeur's agents could be placed at the merchant-banker's disposal. The creditor had emerged as one of France's most powerful figures, holding sway over the monarchy by the power of the purse. In the age of kings this naturally caused irritation within royal circles. Moreover, what the king owed Coeur was more than what his majesty wanted to pay back. With the war against the English virtually won, Coeur had outlived his usefulness. In fact, he had become a problem, considering the power that he had gathered around him. The solution was simple—the merchant-banker was arrested on spurious charges, his property confiscated, and the king's debt extinguished.[2]

Coeur's demise was a clear-cut signal to local creditors that doing business with the French king was dangerous. The example of Coeur, not to mention the Jews, Knights Templar, and Lombards in previous days, as well as tough international competition from the Italians, appears to have discouraged local French creditors from developing beyond a certain size. The inability of France to develop lasting and strong local credit institutions was to have a political impact as it weakened the monarchy's ability to wage war, improve the national infrastructure, and augment the national wealth.

The root causes for France's different track in credit rest in the peculiar nature of its political economy. In contrast to the maritime nations of Britain and Holland, where the parliamentary body dominated finance, big finance in France was dominated by the monarchy, which relied upon taxes to raise revenues. However, taxes were sometimes difficult to collect, often stimulated public discontent (as well as revolts), and were usually inadequate in dealing with the state's seemingly endless appetite for funds required to wage war. The situation became only more snarled when a harvest failed and tax revenues were called by creditors well in advance. France's early credit culture was made no better when French kings, hard-pressed to meet their obligations, demonstrated little compunction in turning on their creditors either with a default or trumping up charges against the creditor and confiscating property or canceling state obligations whether owed to Jews, Lombards or Knights Templar. At the end of the day, the survival of the crown was more important than maintaining an excellent credit record—at least for the short term. Besides, at the high rates of interest charged, when the royal government did pay, the profits were handsome. This managed to keep enough creditors in the game despite the high risk.

In the sixteenth century, the fiscal situation was on occasion helped by the spoils of various military campaigns and by the selling of titles and posts to those who could afford them. For example, there is ample evidence that Francois I (1515-47) sold royal offices in large numbers. Yet both options failed to keep the treasury in the black. Another option was to borrow from whomever was willing (and in some cases foolish enough) to lend to the royal government. By the sixteenth and early seventeenth century, both Lyons (in France) and Antwerp, with the help of the Italian merchants, had developed into new money markets.[3] The French monarchy would often tap these markets.

French finances were also helped by the merchants and businessmen from the Atlantic coastal cities, which were predominantly controlled by the Huguenots. The Protestant Huguenots had become powerful in the sixteenth century and King Henry IV had in 1598 with the Edict of Nantes given them greater economic and political freedom. However, during the reign of his son, Louis XIV (1610-43), the French central government under Prime Minister Richelieu sought to curb the autonomy of the free and fortified Huguenots cities. In the religious war that ensued, La Rochelle, was taken by the royal forces and all of its freedom abrogated. La Rochelle had been emerging as a major international trade hub for France. By the end of the conflict the autonomy of Huguenot coastal cities was curtailed, which undermined the ability of the French to adopt a more market-oriented approach to economic affairs as was evident with the Dutch. In 1685, with the revocation of the Edict of Nantes Huguenot power was sharply reduced.

The reign of Louis XIV, the Sun King, did much to provide a lively history of wars and a colorful court, but was a blow to France's fiscal sobriety. During the Sun King's rule France fought four major conflicts—the War of Devolution (1667-68), the Dutch War (1672-79), the Nine Years War (also known as the War of the League of

Augsburg, 1689-97), and the War of Spanish Succession (1701-13). The ability of the French state to constantly maintain large armies in the field was an ongoing drain on the treasury and massive borrowing was required. This unfortunately occurred with periodic defaults on interest payments. France's creaky fiscal machinery also had political implications. With the size of national manhood measured by one's armies, failure to have a smooth flow of war funds could cut one down to size. Clearly, for Louis XIV weakness on the fiscal side of the equation hurt. Simply stated, the military operations did not decide the outcome in the conflict; rather the financial strength of London and Amsterdam enabled the allies to outlast French resources.[4]

It was no surprise that when Louis XIV died in 1715 he left a legacy of debt behind him. The state had borrowed heavily from domestic sources and was forced to raise funds from abroad, including the Protestant bankers of Geneva and other Swiss towns. This heavy debt burden opened the door to experimentation with John Law's Royal Bank during the Regency that followed Louis XIV's death.

The Amorous Scotsman and the Mississippi Land Bubble

John Law is one of the history of credit's more colorful characters. Born in Edinburgh in 1671, he was the younger son of an old established family in Fife. As was the case in much of Scottish banking, Law's father had been a goldsmith and then a banker, a profession that the young Law was steered into for three years. Upon his father's death, Law went to London, where he took up a life of gambling and wanton amorous adventures. Ultimately, his gambling created large debts, while his interest in the ladies resulted in a duel over one lady's honor in which Law's opponent was killed. The young Scotsman was arrested and charged with murder. Law, however, managed to escape to the Continent. Apparently, some time was spent in Amsterdam, where he studied the local stock market in the morning and pursued his gambling in the afternoon, while his nights probably remained free for the ladies. In 1700, he returned to Scotland, where he published *Proposals and Reasons for Constituting a Council of Trade.* This was followed by the publication of a proposal for a "Land-Bank." Scotland had already begun to develop its modern financial situation, most evident by the creation of the Bank of Scotland in 1695, which probably also influenced Law.

Law's land-Bank idea was founded on the premise that the notes issued by such an institution were never to exceed the value of the lands of the state, upon ordinary interest, or were to be equal in value to the land, the right to enter into possession at a certain time. Although his proposal generated interest in the Scottish parliament, it failed to win enough support to become a reality. Restless by nature and with an outstanding charge of murder still against him, Law once again retreated to the Continent. He resumed his old habits of gambling, roaming through Flanders, Holland, Germany, Hungary, Italy, and France. His survival seemed to have been supported by the gaming table.

Law's ideas of a land-bank provoked intense interest in France following Louis XIV's death. Considering the country's shaky financial system, the idea of a land-bank had a certain appeal. Soon finding himself before the Regent, the Scotsman argued that a metallic currency, unaided by paper money, was inadequate to the needs of a commercial nation. He proposed as a means of restoring France's credit, then at a low, that he be allowed to establish a bank, which should have the management of the royal revenues and issue notes both on that and land security.[5] Additionally, he proposed that this bank should be administered in the king's name. Although there was resistance to Law within the ruling elite, a royal edict was published in 1716 authorizing Law to establish a bank, the Banque General.

Law's bank was immediately successful and it soon was extending credit through new branches in Lyons, Rochelle, Tours, Amiens, and Orleans. The bank's notes were payable on sight and in the coin current at the time they were issued. As Charles Mackay observed, "This last was a masterstroke of policy, and immediately rendered his notes more valuable than the precious metals. The latter were constantly liable to depreciation by the unwise tampering of the government. A thousand liras of silver might be worth their nominal value one day, and be reduced one-sixth the next, but a note on Law's bank retained its original value."[6] Consequently, Law's notes were regarded as the best value possible in the French currency market. Critical to Law's notes was the public trust in their value being upheld by the bank and not being tampered with.

In January 1719, the Banque General was taken over by the regent and renamed the Banque Royale, with a note issue guaranteed by the crown. Law remained in control of the new institution. For

France, the Banque Royale as it came to be called, appeared to be heaven-sent. France went from being credit-starved to having credit. The state benefited from this turnaround as its creditworthiness looked better due to having an institution regulating the distribution of its notes and providing liquidity to the economy. However, sound banking practices soon fell by the wayside as the government (not Law) insisted upon lending beyond what the bank had the ability to pay. No doubt greed played a role.

Law's other major venture, the creation in 1717 of the Compagnie d'Occident (also referred to as the Mississippi Company), paved the way for a major financial crisis, which would bring down the Royal Bank and leave a lasting historical legacy. The Mississippi Company, with shares traded on the Paris bourse, was established to have the exclusive privilege of trading on the Mississippi River and in the province of Louisiana (then in France's possession). An easily duped public was convinced that the far-distant land was rich in precious metals, and the Mississippi Company, supported by the profits of its exclusive commerce, was to be the sole collectors of taxes and coiners of money. In a system with virtually no transparency and disclosure, investors had to take claims at face value. Moreover, as there was a rush of investors willing to put their money down, the thundering of a bull market was difficult to resist.

The Mississippi Company's success attracted large numbers of French investors of all classes as well as investors from England, Amsterdam, Hamburg, and northern Italy. There was a frenzy to get shares, as the prices kept going up. One aspect of this was that Law's bank issued increasing amounts of paper currency to provide loans for the purchase of shares. As the Mississippi shares climbed in value, more money was printed, creating an inflationary spiral which pushed the share price from under 500 livres at the launch of the Banque Royale and its system of money to over 20,000 by late 1719.[7] Law's good reputation, the succession of the Banque Royale, and a lack of information available to the investing public set the stage for a major disaster which had strong implications for the slower development of modern credit institutions in France.

Although warnings were given about the Banque Royale's growing inability to meet all its obligations in terms of notes issued and a few individuals in parliament questioned the soundness of the Mississippi Company, France headed into 1720 oblivious to the impending crash. At the same time, Law had reached his political apex. In

January 1720 he was made France's Controller General and Super-intendent General of Finance. He now controlled all government finance and expenditure and the money creation of the Banque Royale as well as being the chief executive officer of a private firm (the Compagnie d'Occident) that dominated France's overseas trade and the development of its colonies.[8]

The unsuspecting investors continued to pour their money into Mississippi stock (as well as other such companies which sought to cash in on the mania). However, once confidence in the Banque Royale and the Mississippi Company came into question, the house of cards came tumbling down. The critical element of trust evaporated. This was helped along by the action of the king, who as an insider, sold his shares in the company near the peak of speculation in February 1720, after which Law ended support for the company's stock in the market. There was soon an angry mob making a run on the bank, which was forced to close. Law and his family, once the heroes of French society, were forced to flee France.

The failure of Law's bank had three lasting effects on France. A lack of confidence in the government to honor and manage its debts was reinforced and made the creation of a central bank on the Dutch or English model impossible. Second, the great financial crash of 1720-21 enabled the government to write off huge debts. Thousand of government creditors were ruined by the declaration of state bankruptcy caused by the Banque Royale's failure. Third, French public opinion developed a deep hostility to breaches of public faith: from 1726 onwards governments had sought to keep public confidence by avoiding any suggestion that they might default on their debts.[9]

The Quest for Stable Credit

Although the 1720-21 crisis was surmounted, France had another acute financial crisis in 1770. During this round of troubles the government once again suspended payment on short-term credits and reduced or deferred payment of other government debts. The 1770s crisis caused a general outcry, the government's creditworthiness was shaken with investors, and, no surprise, it had trouble in obtaining new credit. To subsequent governments leading up to the French Revolution, the lesson seemed clear: bankruptcy was not an option as it destroyed the state's credit and made further borrowing difficult.[10] The French government had already borrowed money on terms decidedly less favorable than either the Dutch or the British, because France continued to lack a publicly supported bank through which credit could be cheaply channeled. Law's bank indeed left a legacy.

Although France lagged behind Holland and Britain, it was not without some development of credit institutions. In 1776, the French credit system took a timid step forward with the establishment of the *caisse d'escompte* or discount bank. While this was to provide a state bank to help provide credit, the institution was quickly dominated by speculators rather than by the investing public. Any help it gave to the government's credit was marginal, though it was a shift in the right direction.[11] Unfortunately, the French monarchy as the major user of credit in the kingdom, continued to rely on other financial intermediaries for raising its loans. Simply stated, terms for the king to borrow were bad, but bodies such as the municipality of Paris, the estates of the provinces that retained them, and the clergy all could borrow at better terms. Consequently, the government was forced to use these intermediaries to borrow from foreign sources as well as the small local financiers.

By the time of the French Revolution in 1789, France's credit culture was still rudimentary, especially when compared to England and Holland. A domestic financier class with considerable clout, an appetite for risk, and a strong capitalistic orientation as in England and Holland did not exist. Whereby commerce and a fondness for money became critical factors in the development and the more dynamic nature of the Dutch and British economies, the French maintained a fondness for land that penetrated all levels of society. Historian G.V. Taylor captures the cultural dimension that underpins the different path France took in its credit history:

> There was in the economy of the old regime a distinct configuration of wealth, non-capitalist in function, that may be called "proprietary." It embodied investments in land, urban property, venal office, and annuities. The returns it yielded were modest, ranging between 1 and 5 percent, but they were fairly constant and varied little from year to year. They were realized not by entrepreneurial effort, which was degrading, but by mere ownership and the passage of calendar intervals. Risk was negligible.[12]

With a highly hierarchical society, an orientation on the part of the ruling class to proprietary behavior, and a weak credit system, France initially lacked the foundations to develop a modern economy. Although a commercial class arose in France, it did not have the same dominance as it did in Holland and England, where a far less powerful proprietary class did not dominate the economy. The Dutch and English were willing and able to assume risk, which in turn allowed them to extend credit in helping upgrade the nature of the national economy.

By 1789, France was in the grasp of yet another severe financial crisis, partially due to the financial strain of supporting the American Revolution. The king's Swiss financial advisor, Jacques Necker, desperately sought to inject a greater fiscal propriety, but the task was hopeless.[13] Although there are many reasons for the French Revolution, the state's inability to establish a smooth-working system of credit was a factor. As the hapless Louis XVI was forced to call the Estates to raise money, the door was opened to a universe of grievances reflecting a polarization of society. The Estates General were thus called for the first time since 1614 in order to raise money for the crown through taxes. This gave the Third Estate to which the non-property, commercial class belonged an opportunity to demand fundamental changes in the governmental structure. The *ancien regime's* inability to finance itself was the reason that it had to submit to the Estates, thus opening the door to revolution, eventually causing Louis XVI to lose his head.

During the French Revolution and the Napoleonic years that followed from 1804 to1815, the national attention did not focus on economic affairs, but on the strengthening of the military and an attempt to conquer the rest of Europe. Nevertheless, a number of small private banking firms functioning at a local level provided credit to a relatively restricted group of clients. An example of this was the firm of Tardeaux Freres. Established in Limoges in 1809, it serviced local porcelain and shoe-making companies.[14]

After Napoleon when the monarchy was re-established, the private sector played a more pronounced role in economic development and demand for credit to finance growing trade and inventories grew. Complementing the local firms were merchants, who provided financial services informally as an adjunct to their principal business activities and what became known as the *haute banque parisienne*. The latter was a group of financial houses largely consisting of a number of Protestant families, mostly descendants of Huguenots who had fled to Switzerland or elsewhere after the revocation of the Edict of Nantes and returned to Paris with the easings of prohibitions in the eighteenth century.[15] Among the members of *the haute banque* were such names as the Mallets, Delleserts, Hottinguer, André Odier, and Vernes families. Although dominated by Huguenots, Catholics were also part of this group and, in time, Jews. The latter were well represented by the Rothschilds, but other Jewish families included the firm of B.L. Fould et Fould-Oppenheim, which originated in 1813 and whose members climbed to the periphery of the *haute banque*.

Toward a Modern Credit System

It is important to underscore that France's shift to a modern credit system remained shaped by the memory of the Royal Bank of the 1720s. This was reflected by a cautious attitude to any expansion of the state into financial matters.[16] Created during the Napoleonic years, what was to become the country's central bank, the Bank of France (*Banque de France*) obtained a monopoly of the Parisian note issue from 1803 and was charged with discounting notes. With shareholders and directors drawn mainly from the *haute banque*, the Bank of France was exceedingly cautious. As one historian observed, they were "only too conscious of the disastrous experience of John Law's experiments in the 1720s."[17]

After the fall of Napoleon and the restoration of the Bourbon monarchy in 1815 there was a highly cautious approach to extending credit and providing other financial services by the Bank of France which left the field open to others. It was no mistake that the liberation loans of 1817-1818, which France agreed to compensate other European nations for the Napoleonic wars, were largely underwritten by the Barings of London and Hope of Amsterdam. It was not until 1821 that a consortium composed of Henri Hottinguer, Benjamin Delessert, and Baguenault obtained the contract to the first French loan underwritten completely by French banks.

By the 1830s, French banks were beginning to think along new lines. One idea was for a bank that provided development capital for industry. One of the key forces for the marriage of banking and industry was Jacques Lafitte, a Catholic and a man of humble origins who rose to head the large *haute banque*. Lafitte accumulated widespread business interests during his career, which convinced him that the expansion of French commerce and manufacturing was constrained by a lack of readily available funds. Along with the Pereire brothers, who were also involved in banking, the ideas generated by these men helped set the stage for the establishment of the Comptoir Nationale d'Escompte de Paris in 1848 and the Credit Foncier and Credit Mobilier in the early 1850s. Lafitte himself presided over the creation of the Caisse Generale du Commerce et de l'Industrie in 1837. This institution accepted short-term interest-bearing deposits and invested some funds in industry in France and elsewhere.

The creation of the Comptoir, Credit Mobilier, and Credit Foncier came from the liquidity panic caused by the 1848 revolution that brought in the Second Republic. France's acute political instability made it a high risk for foreign investors, who in the past had been willing (at high rates of return) to advance money to the French. Consequently, local French credit institutions were now more ready to fill the gap, especially as national economic development continued to move ahead. As railway investment increased, the demand for credit also increased (as it was doing in the United States and Canada).

During the Second Empire from 1852 to 1870, the Credit Mobilier became a powerful institution. The guiding lights for the new institution were Emile and Isaac Pereire, two Jews from Bordeaux, who were able to gain the patronage of Napoleon III. Credit Mobilier was involved in railway finance, short-term commercial lending, and had an active branch in Madrid. Active in many sectors of the economy and close to the emperor, Credit Mobilier expanded its business to be supportive of government loans, corporate finance, and company promotion. By 1856 the Credit Mobilier was handling the finance of sixteen large industrial and financial enterprises, having an aggregate capital of a billion francs, a fifth of the volume of all securities quoted on the Paris Bourse.[18] The advances of the Pereires, however, did not occur without upsetting the political life of European finance, especially as they appeared to be intent on cutting their rivals, the Rothschilds, down to size. As historian Theodore Zeldin wrote of the fall of Credit Mobilier in the late 1860s: "it was faced with the implacable hostility and rivalry of the Rothchilds, so that when it got into difficulties in the late 1860s, it was destroyed."[19]

As elsewhere in Europe, the advancement of institutions like the Credit Mobilier represented a significant evolution in who provided credit. Prior to 1800 the small family private banks had dominated. Their's was an opaque world, one characterized by an ability to wield personal influence and act behind the scenes. Much of the capital to draw upon was family wealth and they were conservative in the selection of their clientele. Business was conducted in a restricted and confidential fashion. Networks of relationships between these financiers, politicians, and business often compensated for a lack of liquid funds. Simply stated, without proper bank supervision it was exceedingly difficult to determine the assets and loan portfolio of these small private banks. In essence, a good reputation and the right connections often were enough to get the loan business and the banker could then turn to other bankers or investors to tap credit.

France's shift to a more industrialized economy changed the banking environment. As already noted, new larger banks emerged to handle heavy capital demand associated with large-scale industrial projects, such as railway construction. For the old banks, the growing industrialization of the French economy meant change or die. Most of the old banks responded favorably to the changes occurring and developed their own industrial interests. For example, the *haute banque*, together with the Rothchilds moved into corporate insurance, a new sector of complementary business. By the 1860s, France's credit system was rapidly evolving along a similar track to the more advanced British system, though it clearly lagged behind as an international hub.

Paris, compared to London, came late to the development of a competitive credit system. By the 1870s, it had become one of the most important financial hubs on the Continent and its capital market was larger than Germany's. At the same time, the outflow of French capital was dictated by French foreign policy. Following the downfall of the Empire of Napoleon III in the 1870 Franco-Prussian War, Paris sought to contain the spread of German influence. This meant that French credit competed with German credit in the Balkans and Russia. While the Germans were to dominate the flow of credit to Romania and were highly competitive in the Ottoman Empire, the French held sway in Serbia. Russia was a point of fierce competition between German and French credit, but after 1890 the latter won out. While Russia's industrialization required large amounts of external credit, the French desired St. Petersburg as an ally against the Germans. The development of a Franco-Russian alliance was no doubt helped by French credit.[20]

As an interesting social note, the perceived power of the purveyors of credit in France had grown considerably since the days before the French Revolution. "The bankers," wrote Stendhal, "are at the heart of the state. The bourgeoisie has replaced the faubourg St Germain and the bankers are the nobility of the bourgeois class."[21] Although the French bankers did arrive at a certain level of power within the national economy and had considerable influence in society, the French ruling class remained suspicious of them and maintained a degree of control over their institutions. That degree of suspicion, no doubt, made a critical difference between the development of British banks as global forces and the lesser stature of French banks throughout much of the nineteenth century.

Germany—Credit, Unity, and Industrialization

While France and Germany were both slow to develop competitive credit systems, they arrived at the same point in the late nineteenth century from very different experiences. At the end of the Middle Ages, around 1500, France was united and Germany was fragmented. The crucial difference was that royal power in Germany failed to achieve the same central position as did the French monarchs, who after a number of long struggles emerged at the head of a strong centralized dynastic state. The German emperors, inheritors of the Holy Roman Empire, maintained a vision of a universal empire, with considerable attention given to Italy, which was a cockpit of influence between the Empire and the Papacy.[22] Consequently, as France moved toward a centralized state, Germany became a group of independent states and cities with an emperor to which the rulers of these states gave dubious allegiance. The emperor was elected by a few (seven or eight) electoral rulers of the prominent secular and religious states. There was also an ineffectual legislature, the Reichstag.

More complicated was the issue of borders. The Holy Roman Empire was composed of hundreds of separate entities. In the words of historian David Blackbourn, the inhabitants of those entities "owed loyalty to an even larger number of people—not just local rulers, but church, guild and feudal lord. In so far as there were clear territorial boundaries in the Empire, they divided it internally as much as they defined it externally."[23]

Germany remained a fragmented patchwork of states and independent cities, with a legacy of having one of Europe's worst conflicts, the Thirty Years War (1618-48), fought on her soil. Needless to say, the Thirty Years War and others (such as the Seven Years War 1756-63) weakened Germany's economic prospects as it was difficult to develop any markets of size or scope. Simply stated, there was no national economy in the same sense that evolved in England and France. By the eighteenth century, the two most important states of Germany were Prussia and Austria. The Elector of the State of Brandenburg (a Hohenzollern prince) became King of Prussia in 1701 and a rival, later in the eighteenth century, of the Habsburgs, rulers of Austria and holders (most of the time) of the imperial crown.[24]

Germany had been the home to entrepreneurial business during the late Middle Ages and the Fuggers and Welsers were known for their financial clout. Yet in the 1500s most Western European countries witnessed the advance of royal power over that of feudal lords, which coincided with the emergence of a strong bourgeoisie. This was lacking in Germany. As the historian Pinson noted, "The economic transformations brought about by the Age of Discovery and the Commercial Revolution, in which Germany, like Italy, did not participate, brought a halt to the nascent capitalist development in these two countries. Until well into the nineteenth century Germany remained predominantly agrarian...without a strong and militant bourgeoisie."[25] This was to change in the nineteenth century and with it, the role of credit.

First, Napoleon's victories on the battlefields against Prussia and Austro-Hungary in the 1790s and early 1800s greatly shrank the number of German states, from hundreds to dozens. After his victory at Austerlitz in 1805, the Holy Roman Empire was dissolved. Secondly, the defeat of Napoleon left two clear-cut contenders for dominance in the German cockpit—Austria and Prussia. Within the German Confederation that replaced the Holy Roman Empire, these two states now squared-off in a long duel for supremacy. Thirdly, the Germans were aware as early as the 1780s that they lagged behind the English in the industrial revolution. As the political situation became more clarified as to Prussian dominance, there was also a push to develop industry. Fourthly, in the 1820s and 1830s the course of major rivers, including the Rhine, Mosel, and Danube, were straightened to make season-round river travel easier, which enhanced national communications. Fifthly, both the Austrians and the Prussians began an overhaul and improvement in the condition of state finance during the second half of the eighteenth century and was paralleled by the establishment of a more professional bureaucracy.[26] Sixthly, there was a move to simplifying and unifying the legal regime as exemplified by the Prussian Civil Code initiated by King Frederic Wilhem II and promulgated in 1794, which sought to increase efficiency and uniformity. Seventhly, international trade began to pick up as Germany in the late eighteenth century and early nineteenth century became much more involved in trade, in particular with the Atlantic.

Consequently, during the nineteenth century, Germany underwent major transformations that allowed it to emerge with greater weight on the map of global credit. At the end of the Franco-Prussian War in 1870, under the auspices of the Prussian Chancellor Bismarck all German states were united into one nation, the Second Reich, with the Prussian Hohenzollern king as Emperor Wilhem I. It lasted until 1918. From 1800 to 1900 Germany changed from being an agrarian society to being an industrial society. At the same time, there was a shift from cosmopolitanism to nationalism, from being a group of small states to being a Great Power, from idealism to materialism. Critical to the development of credit was that with reunification came a turn to developing smooth-running state finances, a difficult task; the expansion of trade; and the emergence of capital markets. The move toward a more integrated economy came with the establishment of a customs union in 1828 by a treaty between Prussia and Hesse-Darmstadt, which was followed by railway construction throughout the region.

Germany's unification under Otto von Bismarck's direction, could not have occurred without credit. Bismarck's quest to remake the German landscape cost money. Prussia was forced to fight and win wars against Denmark (1864), Austria (1866), and France (1870). The fielding of armies was expensive and Bismarck was forced to play politics with Prussia's parliament, which on more than one occasion was unwilling to raise the capital needed under conditions that the Iron Chancellor found palatable. Consequently, Bismarck found the services of private bankers, such as Gerson Bleichroder, highly useful.

Bleichroder was born in Berlin in 1822 and was a Jewish contemporary and associate of the Rothschilds. He entered the world of private banking in 1839 as a member of his father's private banking firm. In the 1850s Germany underwent an economic boom and Bleichroder formed syndicates with other German banks to create new investment companies as well as entering the metallurgical industry and promoting several railroad lines.[27] From 1852 to 1873 the German rail network expanded from 400 miles to 24,000 driving demand throughout the industrializing economy.[28] As his success grew, he came into contact with both the Prussian royal family and the junker nobleman Bismarck. These relationships set the stage for Bleichroder's becoming a co-founder in 1859 of the so-called Prussian Consortium, a syndicate of banks created to raise 30 million taler for the financing of the Prussian mobilization during the Franco-Austrian war. Indeed, there were a number of new banks to draw upon: the Schaffhausensche Bankverein had been established in 1848, Disconto-Gesellschaft in 1851, the Darmstadler Bank in 1853, and the Berliner Handelsgesellshcaft in 1856.[29] During the same year of the Prussian Consortium, Bleichroder became Bismarck's personal banker through an introduction via the Rothschilds. As Bismarck rose to the political pinnacle of German politics in the 1860s and 1870s, Bleichroder's role as a provider for the Prussian government increased, coming to the rescue of his junker partner more than once with a timely loan.

Although the German states were not without banks, as reflected by Bleichroder's role, trade financing of these sovereign and independent states remained largely in the hands of external actors, in particular London banks. Unification, however, aided and accelerated the process of industrialization, which was tempered by a heavy dose of newfound nationalism. While local institutions provided credit locally, the export sector remained a foreign activity. The new German government did not want that to remain the case and soon promoted local groups to provide both trade finance and investment capital. The creation in 1870 of Deutsche Bank in Berlin was a critical development along this path. The new bank's charter reflected the changing nature of German economy as well as the desire to gain greater control over credit: "It is the purpose of the corporation to do a general banking business, particularly to further and facilitate commercial relations between Germany, the other European countries, and overseas markets."[30]

The establishment of Deutsche Bank indicated that the Germans recognized a gap in banking and credit that needed to be closed to make certain that its foreign trade was to remain independent of the British banks. It also guaranteed that Germany's effort to secure a place for its nationals in international trade would not be held hostage to foreign control. The introduction of the gold standard in Germany in 1873 helped the new bank carry out its program as did the establishing of branches at the central points of German overseas trade in Bremen and Hamburg. Deutsche Bank also opened up an agency in London. Later, other German joint-stock banks, in par-

ticular Disconto Gesellschatt and the Dresdner Bank, expanded operations overseas.

By the 1890s German credit became an important force in global
economic development. Although the reach of German finance was
not as pervasive as that of the British, it was competitive with the
French. It is important to emphasize, however, Germany's financial
system could not compete with that of the British. Simply stated, as
the German economy was in the middle of an expansionary boom
throughout the second half of the nineteenth century, what capital
there was went mainly to local enterprises.

Although Germany had lagged behind Britain in its industrial
development, the period between 1870 and 1914 was one of rapid
change. As Blackbourn noted, "By the 1870s Germany had become
a respectable European industrial nation; on the eve of the First World
War it was a major economic power."[31] German banks became a
key force in their country's next round of industrialization. The banks
worked very closely with the large German companies that emerged
in the 1880s. While German corporations generated their own capital, that hardly filled the gap. Consequently, the banks played an
important role in providing long-term financing. The significance of
the bankers' role, their interrelationship with business, and how credit
worked was depicted by one observer as such: "From the 1880s,
industrial and financial capital became increasingly interlocked. It is
sometimes said that the banks directed industry, even that they provided the impetus towards trusts and mergers."[32] Bankers sat on the
boards of major corporations and were involved in making major
decisions pertaining to the direction of business. At the same time,
this heavy involvement in business on the part of German bankers
made them equally vulnerable to the fortunes of their companies.
This also meant that German banks were more apt to provide credit
to their closest customers even when economic conditions deterio-
rated and the natural inclination was not to extend new credit.

What small amounts of capital that remained from national development were earmarked by the dictates of German foreign
policy.[33] German bankers became active in providing credit for the
development of a number of countries in the Balkans, Italy, Russia,
and the Ottoman Empire. German finance exercised considerable
clout in Romania, where it was used to build railways, and in Italy,
where it helped prop up the government. It also was a major means
of gaining greater influence in Istanbul, the capital of the corrupt

and declining, yet geo-strategically important Ottoman Empire. Furthermore, German banks lent money to Mexico and helped, to a limited degree, in the construction of Imperial Germany's overseas empire in Africa and the Pacific.

Although finance had existed prior to German unification, the formation of a well-defined and functioning nation-state provided a solid foundation for local credit institutions to expand their operations both domestically and internationally. Within Germany, Berlin became the financial center, though both Hamburg and Frankfurt were to maintain some degree of significance due to the Warburgs in the former and the Rothschilds in the latter, as well as a number of other regional banks. It is important to add that German credit became an important lever of political power for Berlin, especially in dealing with the lesser-developed and economically weaker states in the Balkans.

Jews and Credit in Modern Europe

The story of Jews and finance in modern credit centers largely around Germany, France and Britain. Germany had provided a comparatively more welcome environment than many other parts of Europe, especially in the aftermath of the Thirty Years War (1618-48), which had devastated much of the country. Even though Germany was more open to the Jews, life was characterized by well-defined parameters with many cities requiring them to live in ghettos. Real advances in the Jewish role in finance, however, came with the modernization of French finance (in which the Rothschilds were an active force), which paralleled, in part, the fortunes of the Warburgs.

The Rothschilds began in Frankfurt Germany.[34] Initially engaged in trading, these activities took them further afield in Europe. The significant move to international banking occurred under the guidance of Mayer Amschel Rothschild (1743-1812).[35] Described as a "studious man," Mayer spent his life traveling between the humble Jewish ghetto of Frankfurt and the mansions of the wealthy and well-to-do Gentiles whom he served.[36] His most famous client was Prince Wilhelm of Hesse. This patriarch of the Rothschilds' banking dynasty was forced to operate with the appropriate servility in the presence of his clients, initially selling rare coins and medals. The situation changed with the disruptions caused by the Napoleonic Wars, which provided Mayer the chance to act first as Prince Wilhelm's agent and to hold a monopoly on the disbursement of the prince's loans. From that position, the Rothschilds moved on to a larger, European stage in banking, conducting business with other Jews as well as well-known Gentile firms, such as the Bethmanns, de Neufvilles, and Brentanos. Fortunately, Mayer had five sons, whom he was able to put into building up a European-wide banking network. The oldest son, Amschel, remained in Germany to manage the German bank, Nathan was assigned to England, Solomon to Vienna, and Karl to Italy. Karl's son James went to Paris, where he became a force in the world of credit. The ability to have bankers throughout continental Europe and London was to be highly useful as well as lucrative. This is amply illustrated by the following set of accomplishments for the Rothschilds.

In 1798 Nathan Mayer Rothschild left Frankfurt at the age of twenty-one and went to Manchester, England. However, by 1809, he had moved to London, settling in at New Court. Although Manchester was a significant industrial hub, London was rapidly emerging as an international financial hub. The move proved fortuitous as, in 1814, Nathan assembled bullion and coin across Europe for the payment of Wellington's army. Considering that James de Rothschild had begun the family's banking activities in Paris during the last years of the First Empire, and that his uncle was financing the anti-French war effort, made the Rothschilds' banking exploits all that more amazing. Nathan followed this success with another in 1815, when he gathered funds to pay English, Dutch, and Prussian forces at Waterloo. He also provided some 10 million pounds during the crash of 1825 to support the Bank of England when 145 banks failed, preventing the collapse of the banking system. To the Rothschild financial empire England was of primary importance, but as the industrial revolution shifted into high gear on the continent, other markets beckoned.

On the European continent, the Rothschilds established an impressive track record. As already noted, James de Rothschild penetrated French banking in the 1810s and following the defeat of Napoleon he was able to make the House of Rothschild into one of the leading financial forces in Paris. By 1830 no one could dispute his wealth, power, and influence. Yet, the Rothschilds remained Jews and this meant that they could be excluded or, on occasion, snubbed. This was indeed the case with the inner circle of the *haute banque*, which managed to keep the family at arm's length. It was not until

1855 that James was able to obtain for his son Alphonse the much coveted seat as regent of the Bank of France.[37]

The power and influence of the Rothschilds was evident in the role the family had in financing Belgium's early independence. In the peace following Napoleon's final defeat at Waterloo, Belgium was put under the rule of the Netherlands. This arrangement was not destined to work. The Dutch were largely Protestant and their appointed officials throughout the predominantly Catholic and Flemish-speaking Belgium were therefore non-Catholic. The Dutch were a decided northern influence, while Belgium had for several centuries been heavily influenced by the Catholic south. Moreover, French investment in Belgium was sizeable. By 1830 the Netherlands and Belgium separated, with the latter becoming for the first time a sovereign nation.

Belgium at birth lacked a solid credit system. Although local financiers had continued to make loans in the seventeenth and eighteenth centuries to the governments of Austria, Spain, Sweden, and Russia, that activity had declined considerably by the early nineteenth century. A local bank, the Société Générale was established in 1822 (still under Dutch rule), but it clearly lacked the financial wherewithal to meet the new nation's credit needs. What was also problematic to Brussels was that although independence was gained, it was not until 1839 that the Dutch King William accepted as definitive the peace agreement arranged by the London Conference.

Enter the Rothschilds. To justify their claims to nationhood and to mitigate the Dutch political risk, the Belgians needed credit. The Rothschilds had credit and, at this stage, had a reputation for making loans to governments. The Belgians needed capital to create and maintain a standing army as well as to launch an ambitious public works program. The Rothschilds, operating out of London and Paris and with the consent of the British and French, began negotiations with the new kingdom. In December 1831 they signed a contract at Calais with a Belgian financial commission for underwriting a loan of 48 million florin. For the first ten years in the life of the kingdom of Belgium, the Paris House of Rothschild was its mainstay in international financial markets in the first fifteen years of its existence. Between 1830 and 1844 the government of Belgium raised five major loans—of the five, the London and Paris branches of the Rothschilds underwrote all but one.[38]

Belgium was not the only Rothschild success story. A Solomon Rothschild-led consortium opened the Nordbahn, the first railway in the Austrian Empire in 1839. These successes were furthered in 1845, with Rothschilds leading the formation of the Compagnie du Chemin de Fer du Nord, France's first major railroad. The shift into railway finance in France was followed by lending to Belgian national railways. Activities that followed included NM Rothschild & Sons assuming control of the operation of the British Royal Mint Refinery, the organization of the repayment of the 2,000 million franc French indemnity to Prussia after the Franco-Prussian War, and in 1875, a 4 million pound loan to Britain to acquire the controlling interest in the Suez Canal.

The Rothschild's story does not end here. Well-established in Europe, the family financial empire parlayed its expertise as the banker and advisor of governments to a more global role. In 1887, Rothschild guaranteed a loan to Cecil Rhodes to fund De Beers' acquisition of its last sizeable diamond-mining competitor in South Africa. In 1912, De Rothschilds Freres swapped Russian oil interests for shares in what became Royal Dutch Shell. In 1931, the English and French Rothschilds played a key role in the rescue of Austria's Creditanstalt.

The Rothschilds represent international finance at its most sophisticated level. An enterprising Jewish family was able to take advantage of an extensive family network throughout Europe at a critical juncture. The Rothschilds were strategically well-placed to take credit from one market and make it available to another. They also had a keen ability to negotiate with key players and were highly regarded for their confidentiality. All of these factors parlayed into a successful family banking venture capable of weathering revolutions, strikes, and world war. Today, the Rothschilds continue to exist as a family-run banking group, with a Swiss holding company, a main bank in London, and operations around the world.[39]

By 1870, the German Jews, in particular, operated at a pivotal time in history, as it was the period that Otto von Bismarck united Germany. Equally important, for the world of Jewish financiers, the compartmentalization of national economies that had existed in the seventeenth and eighteenth centuries due to a number of wars gave way to a new round of international and regional trade and trade required credit. As Ron Chernow commented of the Warburgs in Germany: "The Mittelweg Warburgs also flourished at a transitional moment in economic history, as regional firms expanded into national companies and increasingly exported or produced overseas. They would rise along with the explosive growth of the new global economy, as imperial governments and industrial titans required large-scale financing that only the private bankers could provide."[40]

The Warburgs were no less international players than the Rothschilds. Beginning from humble roots in Hamburg, Germany, this large family was able to create an ongoing financial concern that was part and parcel of the formation and development of Imperial Germany.[41] With family ties in Russia, Sweden, and New York, the Warburgs cast a big shadow over Imperial Germany. In the second half of the nineteenth century Hamburg benefited from the growing industrialization of Europe as well as German unification.

The rise of the Warburgs had many similarities to the Rothschilds. For the Warburgs, a large family spread across Europe and the United States, settling in Hamburg was good fortune, much as it was for the Rothschilds going to London and Paris. Hamburg was a vital port, functioning as a key outlet for German exports as well as being a point of entry for imports. Although anti-Semitism existed, the city was relatively tolerant to the Jews. Hamburg, which had been one of Germany's important Hanseatic cities, had long been a significant trading and commercial hub.

The first major international venture for the Warburgs came in 1857, when an economic crisis shook Hamburg. In 1856 the Crimean War came to an end, setting off a steep deflation in commodity prices. The first casualties were across the Atlantic, in the United States, where a number of banks and railroads went belly-up. The contagion spread into Europe, notably Scandinavia and finally Hamburg. As Ron Chernow observed, "The Warburgs and other local bankers had to redeem a flood of speculative bills they had endorsed and it looked as if many banks and trading firms would collapse."[42] The Warburgs were not deterred: Family relations allowed them to find assistance through Creditanstalt, a Viennese bank recently established by the Rothschilds. A loan arrived from Austria, with the backing of Emperor Franz Josef I, which settled the panic in Hamburg.

From the Austrian loan the Warburgs were not to look backward. In 1863 the firm dropped its official title of Geldwechsler or moneychangers, taking on the more dignified title of Bankiers.[43] In 1870, M.M. Warburg & Co. helped establish the Commerz-und-Disconte Bank, which expanded business into stock trading. By the founding of Bismarck's Second German Reich in1871, the Warburgs were significant players in the new German banking elite. The extension of family ties to the United States opened another door of opportunity. Felix Warburg's marriage in 1875 to Frieda Schiff provided the Hamburg-based family with a crucial tie to the wealthy German-Jewish banking families of New York. By 1881, the Warburgs were actively marketing U.S. railroad securities issued by Kuhn, Loeb to German investors.

Both the Warburgs and Rothschilds as well as other Jewish banking families played a significant role in modernizing Europe's credit systems during the industrial revolution. They were well-placed by history to take advantage of what became a pressing need for credit, especially with the advent of railroads. The creation of new nations, such as Germany and Belgium also opened the door to new opportunities that were readily and lucratively exploited. Although the late nineteenth century and early twentieth century were good times for Jewish purveyors of credit, the advent of the First World War was not kind, while the interwar period was marked by growing anti-Semitism, ultimately leading to the rise of Nazis in Germany. Like other minorities involved in credit before them, such as the Italians or the Knights Templar, the role of being the financier of governments and the high profile that came with it carried high risk.

High in the Alps: The Swiss

Another important component of continental Europe's credit system was Switzerland. Although Swiss financiers were not to stride on the same global stage as their British, Dutch, French, German, and Jewish counterparts, they did play a role in shaping the modern credit system and set the stage for a bigger role for their country in the twentieth century. The Swiss emerged as an independent nation beginning in the fourteenth and fifteenth centuries, fending off Habsburg and French attempts to gain control over the Alpine nation. At the same time, the Swiss became a source of mercenaries for the rest of Europe, earning considerable income for their country. In fact, King Louis XI used Swiss auxiliaries to break the power of Charles the Bold of Burgundy at Muten and Nancy in 1476 and 1477. At home, however, Switzerland was a collection of cantons and cities, each seeking to assert its power, creating a degree of political turmoil, while economic prospects were not great, with the exception of being on one of Europe's most traveled North-South trade routes.

Switzerland was confronted with the stark fact that it had only limited supplies of rich agricultural land and lacked abundant natural resources. This meant that the Swiss were forced to find alternative methods of making their livelihoods. As historian Gordon A. Craig commented, "In the Middle Ages the favored method was the selling aboard of military skills; at a later time this was supplemented and then supplanted by the export of products that Switzerland's neighbors could not themselves produce economically, clocks and watches, for example, and silks and linens of such fine quality that 'Swiss cloth' enjoyed an international reputation."[44]

Switzerland's initial involvement in the credit business was started by foreigners, namely Jewish and Italians moneylenders. They were not to last and by the fifteenth century, they faded away due to a lack of welcome and being subject to periodic violence and expulsions. Into this void stepped local *burgers*, who had made money from trading mercenaries. This coincided with Switzerland's role as the cradle for the birth of the Protestant Reformation. After all, it was from Zwingli's pulpit in sixteenth-century Zurich that the world first began to hear about a revolutionary way of thinking. As Professor Arthur Jones noted,

> No longer was life on earth to be regarded only as a preparation for the hereafter. Protestantism placed at least equal importance on preparing for life on earth. Thus, it rejected the sinfulness of wealth and embraced the nation of commerce as a worthwhile activity. Men were not only free to save and invest, but could do so with the comfort that financial success was nothing less than a confirmation of God's everlasting grace.[45]

By the eighteenth century some of the Swiss moneylenders moved into private banking. Swiss cities were also reinforced in their financial role by the movement of French Protestants, fleeing periodic Catholic backlashes in France. Geneva was notable for its French Protestant community and was a significant source of credit for France, despite religious tensions. Indeed, one of Louis XVI's chief financial advisors was one Necker from Geneva. The French historian Georges Lefebvre wrote of Necker: "This man from Geneva; son of a Prussian immigrant, had come to seek his fortune in Paris, and having made it, had risen in society....He was an adroit, technical man, and, as a banker and a Protestant, he could obtain, up to a certain point, the cooperation of foreign financial interests, not only in Paris, but in Switzerland and Holland. He succeeded in keeping the French state alive for a year in the worst of economic and political circumstances."[46]

One of the movers and shakers behind the birth of a modern Swiss credit system was Alfred Escher, a native of Zurich and the son of a merchant entrepreneur, who had made a sizeable fortune trading in land, cotton, tobacco, dye woods, and colonial wares. By the late 1840s, Zurich had emerged as Switzerland's economic capital. Certainly this gave Escher a strategic vantage point for a career as a leader of Swiss liberal policies as well as finance. He was part of the dominant elite who firmly believed in economic growth and the development of productive forces, with an almost religious zeal.[47] Part of what Escher saw as critical to his nation's development was the railroad. To develop a rail system, along the lines of Britain, France or the United States, it was necessary to have capital. For Switzerland this meant turning to outside sources for credit, as Swiss finance was not yet mature enough to handle the high levels needed. This was to change under Escher's guidance.

One of the first forays into railroad construction occurred in 1838, when a group of Zurich businessmen formed a company to build a line from their city to Basel. Although the company failed, due to difficulties in obtaining local finance and to the opposition of the Basel cantonal government, which owned competing toll roads and passed on the essential documents with critical information about possible routes to another company that was successful. By 1847, Switzerland had its first railways up and running, but much more was needed to make it a fully integrated system. Escher, now a force in the federal government, backed more rapid railway expansion.

The lack of credit, however, remained a nagging problem. Foreign banks were interested in supporting Swiss railway construction, including the Rothschilds in Frankfurt, who provided credit for the Northeast Railway in 1853. For a period it looked as though the Swiss would remain dependent on outside credit—something that did not sit well with the more nationalistic part of the population. Consequently, Escher founded a local Swiss bank in 1856, called Credit Suisse. The primary purpose of creating the bank was to provide a conduit for channeling local savings into construction of what was to be known as the Gotthard line. At the same time, the creation of Credit Suisse cut German financiers out of the action.

Credit Suisse was modeled after France's Credit Mobilier. The idea was that it would be a bank with a large accumulation of capital that was provided by selling public shares on a large scale and which existed not to pay out large dividends but to serve a public interest by investing in the economy.[48]   Although some investments were received from Leipzig, Augsburg and Berlin, the bulk of the capital for the bank and the railway system came from within Switzerland. Under Escher's guidance from 1856 to 1877, Credit Suisse grew to become an important European bank, still playing a role in global finance in the twenty-first century.

Credit Suisse was not the only Swiss credit institution to emerge. Bank Leu was founded in Zurich in 1775 and Swiss Bank Corporation was established in the country's second largest city, Basel, in 1872 to provide a credit institution to handle large international business and local savings and credit. Swiss Volksbank was established in 1869 to provide financial services for the small saver.

Switzerland's early development as the home of what were eventually to become world-class credit institutions came from a combination of political stability in the nineteenth century, rule of law, heavy involvement of the country in international trade, and the pressing need to provide credit to national development in the form of the railways. To this could be added a dose of nationalism that stimulated the Swiss at a critical juncture to create their own competitive institutions. The history of the Swiss was one of closely guarded independence—maintaining independent credit institutions clearly fit into that pattern as it was one of the most secure banking systems and Switzerland was neutral and attracted deposits from all over the world.

Three Empires: Weakness in Credit Development

While the British, Dutch, Germans, French, and Swiss were able to develop functioning credit institutions capable of financing national development, the same success was not evident in Europe's other major powers, the Austro-Hungarian Empire, the Russian Empire, and the Ottoman Empire. With the exception of Bohemia in the Autro-Hungarian Empire, the eastern empires lacked the infrastructure required to develop a modern business class. There was a greater dependence on outside sources of credit to fuel national development, ranging from the construction of railways to promoting local industrialization. The Austrians, Russians, and Ottoman Turks were also usually hard-pressed on the budget front, due to poor revenue collection, weakness of the revenue base, and, in some cases, the poor organization of tax collection authorities. Consequently, Western Europe had emerged as the cockpit for economic development with its sophisticated banking and credit systems by 1870; however, this was not true for the large empires of Central and Eastern Europe, which were therefore dependent on West European credit for industrial and railroad development.

One last point is that the three empires were autocratic regimes, with pyramid power structures. Authority flowed down from above and policy directives were usually more focused on military and other matters related to ruling large and somewhat diverse populations. Commerce was not looked upon highly and there was often little understanding for the need for the development of well-run credit systems. The downward flow of authority also did little to provide an upward flow of new ideas that could have helped refocus the ruling elite as occurred in Western Europe.

The Austro-Hungarian Empire in the eighteenth and nineteenth centuries was more industrialized than Tsarist Russia and the Ottoman Empire. Compared to Britain, France, Germany, and the United States, the Austrians were relatively backward. While the Austrians made selected products of superior quality, such as Bohemian glassware, Stryian steel, and Viennese shawls, generally speaking goods from neighboring Germany were superior and cheaper in greater quantities.[49] Perhaps one of the most glaring reflections of the Austro-Hungarian Empire's relative economic backwardness was evident when compared with Belgium in the 1840s. Belgium, with a population one-fourth of the Austro-Hungarian Empire, had five times the Austrian capacity in stationary steam engines and almost five times her coal consumption.[50]

One of the major forces in Austria-Hungary's relative economic backwardness was what historian Alan Sked has called a "chronic lack of credit." The most significant credit institution was the central bank, the Austrian National Bank, which was founded in 1816. Based on the model of the Bank of France, its role was to be the sole issuer of notes and to discount bills of exchange. Yet, in regard to the Austrian National Bank's overall impact on the credit market, in large part, its terms of discounting were so stringent that only the wealthiest and most respected clients were permitted access to bank funds.[51] The central bank also had branches in main cities, but they were limited in function. Beyond the activities of the National Bank of Austria, there were a number of savings banks. Limited in numbers, they came on the scene in 1818 with the founding of the Erste Oesterreichische Sparkasse, and aimed to promote thrift and industriousness among the lower classes. Unfortunately, the savings banks shifted clientele, becoming the domain of the better-off, while they were not permitted to finance industrial enterprise.[52]

Considering the lacuna in local sources of credit, the role of foreign banking houses was significant. Among those involved were the houses of Rothschild, Schoeller, Geymuller, Sina, Stametz-Mayer, and Arnstein-Eskeles. These banking houses bought and sold government debt, provided long-term loans for the nobility, generated credit for industrial and commercial development and provided discounting facilities to companies outside of Vienna. We know that the relationship between the houses of the Austro-Hungarian government was close. This was indeed the case of the Rothschilds, with Prince Metternich, the dominant political force in the empire during the first half of the nineteenth century, publicly accepting an offer of Rothschild hospitality, "taking soup," with family patriarch Amsel in Frankfurt in 1821.[53] Prince Metternich was to later receive a number of personal loans from the Rothschilds and was to use the Jewish finance house for his government's financing.

By the mid-nineteenth century Austro-Hungary's local credit system was inadequate for the needs of the empire's development. Indeed, in an incident fashion, the paucity of the credit system helped push along the 1848 revolution in Vienna that toppled Metternich and almost ended Habsburg rule. Although the Habsburgs survived the 1848 revolution (with the assistance of Russian troops), they presided over a credit system that continued to lag behind Western Europe, with important consequences for Vienna's standing in Europe's complex power politics.

The Tsarist Empire of Russia in the nineteenth century was more backward in its credit system than Western Europe and the Austro-Hungarian Empire. While the Habsburgs presided over an economy that did have pockets of industrial excellence, those pockets were far fewer in Russia. The Tsarist state, which emerged in the fifteenth and sixteenth centuries, was led by the Tsar, his ministers and certain high-ranking members of the nobility and backed by a troika of the army, the bureaucracy, and the institution of serfdom, a system of labor that tied the peasants to the land in near-slave-like conditions. The economy was largely agricultural, with some industrial development in St. Petersburg and Moscow.

The key conditions for credit to develop were weak. The rule of law was that of the Tsar, an autocrat, and carried out by a corrupt officialdom. The bureaucrats, called *chinovniks*, exceeded half a million and in the Tsar's name, were ready and able to exploit those who came under their scrutiny. According to historian W.E. Masse, the *chinovniks* "for the Russian public, were synonymous with extortion and corruption," while one Russian nobleman, in a memorandum submitted to Tsar Alexander II shortly before his accession in 1855, referred to them as "a savage and greedy horde which has taken possession of Russia and enjoys without inhibition the rights of conquerors."[54] Needless to say, the law courts, staffed by *chinovniks*, left much to be desired. This meant that one of the basic ideas supportive of a working credit system—that a contract is a legal and binding document upheld in a court of law—and the accompanying concept of trust, were lacking. As Masse noted, "In practice, for the mass of the Russian people, the law did not exist."[55]

While credit systems were being installed in depth in the Netherlands in the sixteenth and seventeenth centuries and in Britain in the seventeenth and eighteenth centuries, Russia remained in a condition of semi-feudalism and in a long transition to early capitalism. The machinery of state, with the exception of the security apparatus in crushing dissent, was weak and led to ongoing fiscal problems. As Russian historian Nicholas V. Riasanovsky noted of the situation in the late eighteenth century: "The successors of Peter the Great, not unlike the reformer himself, ruled in a situation of continuous financial crisis."[56] The Russian state's expenditures in 1794 were broke down between 46 percent going to the military, 20 percent to the state economy, 12 percent for administration and justice, and 9 percent to maintain the imperial court.[57] Beginning in 1769, the rulers of Russia began tapping foreign markets, mainly in Holland.

The Napoleonic wars added an additional burden to Russia's already creaky financial structure. In the period between 1803 and 1815, public spending had roughly quadrupled as had the circulation of paper roubles, leading to inflation and currency depreciation. The Tsarist government, with poor tax collection at home and no homegrown major credit institutions to call upon, turned again to Western Europe, first to Barings and Reid in 1820 and the Rothschilds in 1822.[58]

Russia was an ongoing borrower in foreign markets throughout the nineteenth century and its weak credit system would continue to be a key factor in the backwardness of its industrial infrastructure until the twentieth century. Alexander II, who ruled Russia from 1855 until his assassination in 1881, did implement a number of reforms that helped modernize the economy. Of the utmost importance, he emancipated the serfs in 1861, hence making available a force of mobile free labor. This occurred at the same time that railways, financed by foreign credit, were constructed. Although these developments stimulated an expansion of banking and credit facilities and laid the foundations for Russia's "industrial revolution," the land of the Tsars would be a pale shadow of the great institutions that rose in the West and dominated global capitalism.

Europe's other "major" power in the eighteenth and nineteenth centuries was the Ottoman Empire, also referred to as the "sick man of Europe." The Ottoman Turks, initially led by the Sultan Osman (1259-1326), originated from Central Asia and over time conquered most of the Byzantine Empire. During the sixteenth century, they took a large chunk of North Africa and the Balkans. Only in 1683 were they checked at the gates of Vienna, and finally driven from Central Europe. By the eighteenth century, the Ottoman Empire was in decline. However, the collapse would not come until the end of the First World War.

It is important to underscore that the Ottoman Turkish leadership was initially driven by military and religious concerns, not economic management. Moreover, unlike the Austrians or Russians, the Turkish sultans never presided over a unified economy or common market. One drawback was the high cost of transport. Consequently, agriculture was the main occupation for the great majority of the sultan's subjects. At the same time, the Turks established a regular, relatively equitable system of taxation that initially provided ample revenue to support the central government's bureaucracy and military. In this system, political control from the center, in the hands of the sultan (and over time his viziers and eunuchs), was absolute and related to landed property, i.e., his monopoly over granting land to his followers. The Frenchman Jean Bodine commented that the "King of the Turks is called the Grand Seignior, not because of the size of his realm...but because he is complete master of its persons and property."[59]

The Ottoman Empire was decidedly caught between eastern and western influences, but its cultural roots were Asian. Its absolutist state, heavy emphasis on control, relations to the land and agricultural orientation of the economy had much in common with other Asian empires. This also meant that there were no social forces in the Ottoman Empire capable of challenging the ruler's absolutist power. As Professor Ahmad observed,

> In the Ottoman Empire this fact was more pronounced because it was a cosmopolitan, multi-ethnic, multi-religious society in which non-Muslim communities—Greeks, Armenians, Arabs and Jews, to mention the most prominent—played very important economic and administrative roles but were not permitted to exercise political power. Thus there were very wealthy merchants—Muslim and non-Muslim—who carried out economic functions generally associated with a bourgeoisie but who never acquired the political power and influence of that class so as to mould state and society in their own interest and image. The class might have developed as a landed nobility and tempered the Sultan's absolutism was undermined by the *devshirme* system [a system of handing out favors] in the mid-fifteenth century. The Sultan's monopoly of landed property virtually guaranteed that such a class would not emerge in the future.[60]

The Ottoman absolutist system therefore maintained power in a small faction around the Sultan, which did much to stultify new ideas percolating upwards, such as those pertaining to Western economic and financial practices. In the Dutch Republic it had been the merchants, entrepreneurs, and middle class who had come to preside over the political machinery in the seventeenth century to the effect that they advanced policies conducive to creating a highly efficient credit system as well as public trust founded upon the rule of law. In the Ottoman Empire, the Sultan and his clique remained a powerful obstacle to change, a condition to be reflected in the weak local credit system and a dependence on external credit that became highly pronounced during the nineteenth century. Along these lines, wealth was expected to derive from new tax resources in the lands annexed by conquest, not by intensive methods such as maximizing the income from agriculture, industries, and commerce through new technologies.[61]

What fueled the Ottoman Empire's dependence on external credit was a combination of factors. These included the purchase of military equipment from Western Europe, trade finance (to pay for the rise in consumer goods), and the construction of railroads in the coastal regions beginning in the 1850s. External borrowing also became an essential part of Ottoman fiscal policy. By the mid-nineteenth century, the Ottoman state was plagued by a chronic fiscal crisis and budgetary deficits. This situation was largely due to the appropriation of a sizeable portion of potential tax revenues by powerful intermediaries. One offshoot of this was the frequent debasing of the Ottoman coinage, which for a time provided the state with additional revenues to meet its costs. The debasing of gold coins, however, was a stopgap measure as by the 1840s it had become an ineffective and costly method due to its impact on raising inflation. It also increased societal tensions within the empire and did much to undermine any confidence in the state held by the public as well as local creditors.

Local Ottoman banks, led by the Armenian bankers in Galata (referred to as the Galata bankers located in Istanbul) in the early 1800s, were willing to make short-term loans to the state at high rates of interest. However, by the 1840s, the Ottoman state's demands outstripped what the Galata bankers were willing and able to lend. The ranks of the Galata bankers expanded to include other groups, such as the Greeks, Jews, and a number of Europeans who had settled in Istanbul. But this expansion was hardly enough to deal with the heavy demand of the Ottoman state. The Galata bankers turned to their European banking connections, borrowing from them and passing on these short-term funds to the Ottoman government (at a cost of course).[62] Although the Ottoman bureaucracy was resistant to formal external borrowings, this opposition faded in 1854, when fiscal difficulties intensified during the Crimean War in which the Turks had sided with England and France against Russia. This began a period of external borrowing that ended with the default of 1875-76. In the period between 1854 and 1875, the Ottoman Empire borrowed heavily from European financial markets, increasingly at unfavorable terms. In fact, in 1861, a default was narrowly averted. This did not daunt investors (many of them small investors in France). Yet, by 1870, the empire's debt servicing accounted for one-third of treasury income and the percentage was rapidly rising.

As for the Galata bankers, their power peaked in the 1850s.[63] Throughout the early nineteenth century they were critical as financial intermediaries for the Ottoman government. Without them, the government would have been exceedingly hard-pressed to obtain credit. However, as the credit needs of the Ottoman government expanded beyond what the Galata bankers could provide, European competition increasingly displaced them. As the link to credit from Europe became more direct, the Galata intermediary role declined.

Ottoman debt financing became a house of cards by the 1860s. Debt payments exceeded the empire's ability to repay. The only way the process of financing the Ottoman's budget deficit, its large import bill, and interest on external debt, was to borrow even more debt. Naturally, the heavier the debt burden there was the less chance that it could be paid back. What kept the ongoing flow of funds was a misplaced confidence that the Ottomans would repay, based on the flawed assumption that as long as the Turks had access to credit markets they could continue to repay. Greed of investors also played its part, considering the high returns of Ottoman debt.

The Turks, seemingly caught up in a snowball of ever-expanding debt, were also responsible for the ensuing mess. Efforts were made to reform the monetary system, the root of the empire's woes. A general monetary reform was conducted in 1844 and the loan of 1858 was intended to restore stability to the monetary system. Yet these reforms failed due to political opposition and bureaucratic ineptness, both of which were reinforced by a lack of public trust in the government. This meant that the wealthy Armenian and Jewish bankers within the empire showed a marked reluctance to invest in productive enterprises, which required long-term investments.[64] Reforms along the lines mentioned above would have rocked the old political establishment, forcing a realignment of forces not necessarily favorable to the ruling elite. Rather than being the hapless victims of the dominant economies of Europe, the Ottoman ruling classes made a clear decision to structure their fiscal policies with the idea of maintaining an inflow of external credit.

What sank the Ottoman house of debt was a combination of bad news, both foreign and domestic. Within the empire drought and floods led to famine in Anatolia in 1873, which resulted in a fall in tax revenues. The Sultan's government sought to compensate by raising taxes, which did little to relieve the empire's problems. Consequently, the Ottoman government looked to European financial markets for new loans. This time, however, that source of credit had dried up. The beginning of the Great Depression in the United States and Europe in 1873 with a series of stock market crashes, "made it impossible for dubious debtors like the Ottoman Empire to raise money."[65] Consequently, the Ottomans were forced to default on their 200 million pound (English) external debt.

One result of the 1873-74 debt default was that European financial interests gained greater control over the empire's creaky fiscal structure. One instrument of this was the Ottoman Bank, which was established in 1856. Despite its name, the Ottoman Bank was a Franco-British enterprise and its headquarters was in Paris. It did, however, work closely with the Ottoman government to reestablish some degree of fiscal stability and repayment. Moreover, after considerable foot-dragging and negotiations, the Ottoman Public Debt Administration was founded in 1881 with the purpose of managing some of the empire's major sources of revenue to help repay the outstanding debt.[66]

The Ottoman Empire was ultimately unable to reform itself and would collapse at the end of the First World War. The empire's credit problem was never to go away and can be considered as one factor of many which weakened the central government of the Sultan and made its demise inevitable.

The Rest of Europe

Beyond the development of modern credit systems in Western, Central, and Eastern Europe, modern credit systems were also to develop in Sweden and Denmark. As a part of Western Europe, these countries were more closely tied to the new ideas shaping finance and credit. Although not as developed as those in England, France, and Germany, Swedish banks were to emerge to be competitive in their own markets and were competitive in terms of offering trade finance. Indeed, the Swedish central bank, the Riksbank, began operations in 1668, well ahead of the Bank of England and the Bank of Scotland.

Europe's southern tier of countries—Spain, Portugal, and Italy—lagged well behind Western Europe and were dependent on British, Dutch, German, and French credit to advance their industrial development. Spain and Portugal had long since declined as major powers and their credit systems did not provide the infrastructure needed for a modern business class. It was only in 1782 that Spain's first modern bank and direct forerunner of the central bank, the Banco Nacional de San Carlos, opened its doors for business. Portugal did not create a central bank, the Banco de Portugal, until 1846, though the country did have other financial institutions, such as the Banco de Lisboa and the Companhia de Confiança Nacional (which specialized in the financing of public debt). Italy did not unify until 1870 and its central bank was formed only in 1893. Despite the greater size of Italy vis-à-vis Spain and Portugal, Italy was to remain a relatively poor country and dependent on loans from Western Europe to develop its economy. The slowness of Italy to develop a modern financial system was indeed ironic, considering the legacy of Italy's central importance to the early development of credit and banking. Sadly, banking of the free cities of Italy had declined considerably by the end of the seventeenth century and was of little importance by the eighteenth century.

Conclusion

The modernization of credit in continental Europe, excluding Holland, was much different from Britain. The combination of cultural, historical, and political factors guaranteed a lag. Yet, with the Industrial Revolution, Western Europe, in particular France, Germany, and Switzerland, was to catch up (as did the Scandinavian countries). The three empires of the East, the Austro-Hungarian, the Russian, and the Ottoman did not. The means of modernization in Western Europe came from local forces gradually undertaking many of the same transformations in the conduct of business—in a sense becoming more British and Dutch in their ventures into extending credit. This also had a political component as the French, Germans, and Swiss developed political systems based on some form of electoral representation, which in turn allowed the middle class and the purveyors of credit a voice in the process of national development. Naturally these groups sought to advance laws and regulations in their interests, which were conducive to the advancement of working credit systems. This was not the case of the three Eastern empires. Interestingly enough two of the key forces in this process were religious minorities, the Huguenots in France and the Jews in France and Germany. Another significant factor in continental Europe that echoed the British and Dutch experiences was that as France and Germany became, in turn, the sources of credit for other nations, credit emerged as an important tool of political and economic influence in world affairs. This, indeed, was felt in the Ottoman Empire, which became dependent on the inflow of external credit to balance its books.

Notes

1.   The bankers of Lyon were prominent around 1500 due to that city's existence as a big center for trade fairs and money transactions. Despite such prominence, the inhabitants of the city took a limited role in the credit business, leaving banking largely to the Italians who settled there. See Jean-François Bergier, "From the Fifteenth Century in Italy to the Sixteenth Century in Germany: A New Banking Concept?" in *The Dawn of Banking* (New Haven, CT: Yale University Press, 1979), p. 107.
2.   N.J.G. Pound, *An Economic History of Medieval Europe* (New York: Longman, 1974), p. 434.

3.   Robin Briggs, *Early Modern France 1560-1715* (Oxford: Oxford University Press, 1977), p. 4.
4.   Ibid., p. 154.
5.   Charles Mackay, *Extraordinary Popular Delusions and the Madness of Crowds*, (New York: John Wiley and Sons, Inc., 1996), p. 31.
6.   Ibid., p. 32.
7.   Edward Chancellor, *Devil Take the Hindmost: A History of Financial Speculation* (New York: Farrar, Straus and Giroux, 1999), p. 61.
8.   Peter Garber, *Famous First Bubbles: The Fundamentals of Early Manias* (Cambridge, MA: MIT Press, 2000), p. 97.
9.   William Doyle, *Origins of the French Revolution* (Oxford: Oxford University Press, 1989), p. 46.
10.   Ibid., p. 47.
11.   G.V. Taylor, "The Paris Bourse on the Eve of the Revolution, 1781-1789," *American Historical Review*, ixvii (1962): 956-7.
12.   G.V. Taylor, "Capitalist and Proprietary Wealth and Definition of the Bourgeoisie," in James Frigugliette and Emmet Kennedy, eds., *The Shaping of Modern France* (London: Collier-Macmillan Limited, 1969), p. 18.
13.   Jacques Necker was born in Geneva in 1732 and died in 1804. In 1750 he went to Paris and entered banking. He rose rapidly to importance, established a bank of his own and became a director of the French East India Company.
14.   P.L. Cottrell, "Investment and Finance," in Derek H. Aldcroft and Simon P. Ville, eds., *The European Economy 1750-1914: A Thematic Approach* (Manchester: Manchester University Press, 1994), p. 264.
15.   See Herbert Luthy, *La Banque Protestante en France de la Révocation de L'Edit de Nantes á la Révolution, Vol. I* (Paris, 1959).
16.   P.L. Cottrell, "Investment and Finance," p. 264.
17.   Ibid., p. 264.
18.   Rondo Cameron, *France and the Economic Development of Europe 1800-1914: Conquests of Peace and Seeds of War* (Princeton, NJ: Princeton University Press, 1961), pp. 147-148.
19.   Theodore Zeldin, *France 1848-1945: Ambition and Love* (New York: Oxford University Press, 1979), pp. 82-83.
20.   Herbert Feis, *Europe, the World's Banker, 1870-1914* (New York: Augustus M. Kelly, 1930, 1964), pp. 73-80.
21.   Quoted from Zeldin, *France*, p. 77.
22.   Koppel Pinson, *Modern Germany* (New York: The Macmillan Company [1954] 1966), p. 5.
23.   David Blackbourn, *The Long Nineteenth Century: A History of Germany, 1780-1918* (New York: Oxford University Press, 1998), p. xv.
24.   J.M. Roberts, *The Penguin History of Europe* (London: Penguin Books, 1996), p. 308.
25.   Pinson, *Modern Germany*, p. 5.
26.   David Blackbourn noted of the professionalization of the Prussian civil service: "The rise of the Prussian army is, in fact, hard to separate from the larger process of bureaucratic-state-building. The administrative machinery built up by the Hohenzollorns blended the management of military and civil affairs. Under successive rulers who steadily expanded the standing army, in a society where military drill reached down into the villages and officers enjoyed a high status, ways had to be found to pay for and provision the soldiers. That meant maximizing the flow of royal revenue, against opposition from privileged estates and corporations. Institutions designed to achieve this included the General Directory in Berlin and the

provincial War and Domains Chambers, the centerpieces of a growing apparatus of career officials or 'dynastic servants' who concerned themselves with military, judicial and fiscal affairs. These officials were trained and examined (after 1770 all applicants underwent written and oral examinations); they were expected to devote themselves exclusively to their jobs, and they began to develop a marshal esprit de corps." *The Long Nineteenth Century*, p. 22.

27.   Fritz Stern, *Gold and Iron: Bismarck, Bleichroder and the Building of the German Empire* (New York: Vintage Books, 1979), p. 10.
28.   Blackbourn, *The Long Nineteenth Century*, p. 180.
29.   Gustav Stolper, *The German Economy: 1870 to Present* (New York: Harcourt, Brace & World, Inc., 1967), p. 27.
30.   Robert Franz, "The Statistical History of the German Banking System," *Miscellaneous Articles on German Banking*, U.S. State Document 508 (Washington, DC: GPO, 1910), pp. 29-33 on the internet http://www.forham.edu/halsall/mod/germanbanks.html.
31.   Blackbourn, *The Long Nineteenth Century*, p. 313.
32.   Ibid., p. 323.
33.   Randall D. Germain, *The International Organization of Credit: States and Global Finance in the World Economy* (Cambridge: Cambridge University Press, 1998), p. 56.
34.   For more information on the Rothschilds, see Herbert R. Lottman, *The French Rothschilds: The Great Banking Dynasty Through Two Turbulent Centuries* (New York: Crown Publishers, Inc., 1995); and Frederic Morten, *The Rothschilds: A Family Portrait* (New York: Atheneum, 1962).
35.   For more information on Mayer Amschel Rothschild, see the Amos Elon, *Founder: A Portrait of the First Rothschild and His Time* (New York: Viking, 1996).
36.   Naill Ferguson, *The House of Rothschild: Money's Prophets, 1798-1848* (New York: Viking 1998), p. 42.
37.   The first Jewish banker to achieve a seat on the Board of Regents at the Bank of France was Adolphe d'Eichthal, who held that post from 1839 to 1849.
38.   Cameron, *France and the Economic Development of Europe, 1800-1914*, p. 337.
39.   According to the Annual Report (1998) of the Rothschilds Continuation Holdings AG, the financial empire is actively globally, with offices throughout Europe, Asia, North and South America, and Africa (Harose and Johannesburg).
40.   Ron Chernow, *The Warburgs* (New York: Vintage, 1993), p. 32.
41.   Ron Chernow noted, "The Warburgs sometimes claim to be Sephardic Jews and fancifully trace their genealogy back to medieval Italy. But the first certifiable ancestor appears in 1559, when Simon von Cassel moved from Hesse to the Westphalian town of Warburg, which was founded by Charlemagne." Ibid., p. 3.
42.   Ibid., p. 12.
43.   Ibid., p. 13.
44.   Gordon A. Craig, *The Triumph of Liberalism: Zurich in the Golden Age 1830-1869* (New York: Collier Books, 1988), p. 96.
45.   Michael Arthur Jones, *Swiss Bank Accounts: A Personal Guide to Ownership: Benefits and Use* (New York: McGraw Hill, 1990), p. 9.
46.   Georges Lefebvre, *The Coming of the French Revolution* (Princeton, NJ: Princeton University Press, original 1947, reprint 1988), pp. 56-57.
47.   Craig, *The Triumph of Liberalism*, p. 95.
48.   Ibid., p. 117.
49.   Alan Sked, *The Decline and Fall of the Habsburg Empire 1815-1918* (London: Longman, 1994), p. 69.

50. Richard Rudolf, "Economic Revolution in Austria?" in John Komlos, ed., *Economic Development in the Habsburg Monarchy in the Nineteenth Century. Essays* (London: 1983), pp. 165-82, p. 168.
51. Nachum Gross, "Austria-Hungary in the World Economy," in Komlos, ed., pp. 1-45, p. 9.
52. Sked, *The Decline and Fall of the Habsburg Empire*, p. 71.
53. Ferguson, *The House of Rothschild*, p. 158.
54. W.E. Mosse, *Alexander II and the Modernization of Russia* (New York: Collier Books, 1962), p. 19.
55. Ibid., p, 21.
56. Nicholas V. Riasanovsky, *A History of Russia* (New York: Oxford University Press, 1969), pp. 314-315.
57. Ibid.
58. Ferguson, *The House of Rothschild*, p. 127.
59. Quoted in Perry Anderson, *Lineages of the Absolutist State* (London: Routledge, 1974), p. 397.
60. Feroz Ahmad, *The Making of Modern Turkey* (New York: Routledge, 1993), p. 21.
61. Halil Inalcik, "The Economic Mind," in Halil Inalcik and Donald Quataert, eds., *An Economic and Social History of the Ottoman Empire* (Cambridge: Cambridge University Press, 1994), p. 51.
62. Sevket Pamuk, *The Ottoman Empire and European Capitalism, 1820-1913* (New York: Cambridge University Press, 1987), p. 57.
63. For more information on the Galata bankers, see Sevket Pamuk, *A Monetary History of the Ottoman Empire* (Cambridge: Cambridge University Press, 2000), pp. 202-203. This remains a subject in Ottoman history on which further research is needed, at least in English.
64. Erik J. Zurcher, *Turkey: A Modern History* (London: I.B. Taurice Co. Ltd, 1993), p. 68.
65. Ibid., p. 76.
66. Pamuk, *The Ottoman Empire and European Capitalism*, p. 61.

10

The Rise of U.S. Power and Credit

The focus of this chapter is the evolution of credit in the Unites States and its relationship to the rise of U.S. power in the period between the 1790s and 1990s. The process by which New York became the dominant force in global credit had its roots in the colonial economy, gained momentum in the late nineteenth century, and rose to its apex in the decades following World War II. We find the central themes of credit history evident—the direct relationship between credit and power (within domestic U.S. politics as well as U.S. relations with the rest of the world); the development of a working credit system in tandem with the evolution of the nation-state that was democratically oriented, placing an emphasis on economic and political freedom; a history of considerable volatility (i.e., the Great Depression of the 1870s and the bankers' panic of 1907). Also evident, but dealt with in the next chapter, are a cultural predilection towards entrepreneurship, trade, and consumerism and the spread of credit from being the privilege of the wealthy and the powerful to becoming available to a wider societal range of American society. U.S. credit, with New York emerging as the major international hub, evolved from a time of dominant personalities in finance, such as J.P. Morgan, up through the 1920s, to the age of large multinational institutions, with the likes of Citibank, Goldman Sachs, Chase Manhattan Bank, and the Bank of America.

The Rise of Credit in the United States

The United States did not suddenly appear as the planet's dominant power in credit. Indeed, in the early years of its existence the young American republic was regarded as highly risky by international investors as it faced considerable political and economic challenges. As the Earl of Sheffield observed of the United States in the aftermath of independence, "...Great Britain will lose few of the advantages she possessed before these States became independent, and with prudent management she will have as much of their trade as it will be in her interest to wish for, without any expense for civil establishment or protection. The States will suffer—they have lost much by separation. We shall regret the money that has been squandered, but it is certainly not probable our commerce will be much hurt, and it is certain the means of employing and adding to our seamen will be greatly increased, if we do not throw away the opportunity."[1]

At the beginning of the nineteenth century, the U.S. economy was characterized as having a small and scattered domestic market and a foreign market that appeared limited due to a heavy dependence on the production and export of primary goods. Moreover, the price of capital was high and domestic financial intermediaries were limited to a handful of banking institutions in Philadelphia, New York, and Boston. Simply stated, the credit system was underdeveloped and dependent on outside capital for any major development projects.

Despite the appearance that the United States faced hurdles in the shift to a more industrialized economy, the young nation benefited from the policies of Alexander Hamilton, in particular, in the areas of the funding of the foreign, domestic, and state debts and the establishment of the First Bank of the United States. The last was the initial effort to establish a U.S. central bank along the lines of the Bank of England (with public and private ownership). These policies formed the monetary and fiscal underpinnings of the new nation as the former created a sound credit basis and the latter was a significant start of an elaborated capital market.[2] The earliest financial centers were Boston, New York, and Philadelphia and, to a lesser extent, Charleston. Of particular importance for New England was shipbuilding. The northern economy was gradually moving toward industrialization, while the southern economy was dominated by agriculture, in particular cotton. Initially trade finance was in the hands of British banks, though local institutions would grow in significance.

During the early years of the Republic, Wall Street, that is the country's stock exchange, can only be described as rudimentary. Although it had its roots back to the 1650s when Dutch merchants and traders met to buy and sell shares, it was not until 1790 that Wall Street gained any significance. Even then it lacked any set location and was barely supervised and regulated. What helped develop Wall Street into a capital market were foreign investors, in particular the British and Dutch, seeking higher yielding securities than found at home. Both the British and Dutch were big buyers of U.S. Treasuries and infrastructure-related bonds. In fact, when the First Bank of the United States was incorporated in 1791, foreign investors, mainly the British, accounted for $7 million of the original capital of $10 million.[3] Both Britain and the Netherlands functioned as credit surplus nations, with the United States clearly a credit-deficit nation, much of its capital going into its gradually industrializing economy.

Although raising credit in the United States prior to the Civil War was rudimentary, two things happened that reinforced the survival of an entrepreneurial credit culture. The first was that foreign capital, namely British and Dutch investors, believed that despite high risks, the United States was an economy guided by the rule of law. Although state debt defaults would make the United States a sometimes treacherous place to invest, the federal government stood by its direct obligations. When the United States liquidated the First Bank of the United States in 1811 (due to Congress's dislike of foreign ownership as well as an ongoing battle over state's rights), British investors had their subscriptions returned just before the outbreak of the War of 1812. As Wall Street historian Geisst noted, "The return of their funds became an important chapter in American finance because it showed that the government was willing to do business on an impartial basis, and that would influence future British investments for decades to come."[4]

The second element to emerge was the use of underwriting syndicates. In February 1812, the U.S. Treasury sought to raise $16 million to finance the war against the British. With British investors out of the market and other European investors squeamish over the conflict, only $6 million of bonds were sold. As oft stated—necessity is the mother of invention. The government then turned to three wealthy individuals—John Jacob Astor, Stephen Girard, and David Parish (a representative of Barings)—who purchased the remaining bonds. The three men were wealthy and had considerable connections to people with money, which they leveraged to sell the bonds at a profit. Although there were eyebrows raised by populist Jacksonian politicians about the linkage between wealthy merchants and national finance, the underwriting syndicate idea was successful and in one form or another was to remain a fixture in domestic and international markets.

Although Wall Street would grow in significance in the first half of the nineteenth century, its expansion was limited by a number of factors. These included the underdevelopment of the economy. While parts of the country were rapidly industrializing, agriculture still played an important role. Consequently, many Americans remained apart from being fully integrated into the nation's day-to-day economic life. The long taming of the frontier forced many people to be self-sufficient and not dependent on others for their survival. However, in the decades just prior to the U.S. Civil War, the national market was being steadily deepened by the movement of the people out of self-sufficiency into the money economy, a trend in part mirrored by growing urbanization. This occurred as a response either to the demand for labor in the rapidly expanding urban areas or to the higher price of agricultural goods and lower international transport costs. Market forces became more pronounced with the better utilization of ships caused by suspension of the navigation laws, the improvement in the terms of trade with the rise in freight rates, the growing concentration of the South on cotton, and the emergence of a pattern of regional specialization.

The turn to the market economy was to have a profound impact on credit. U.S. credit markets prior to the Civil War remained highly concentrated in the most urbanized and commercialized part of the country—New England and the Middle Atlantic States. New York and Philadelphia had populations in excess of 100,000. Boston and Baltimore were in excess of 35,000. New York and Philadelphia were the primary manufacturers for the nation. The former produced men's clothing, sugar refining, boots and shoes, cabinet furniture, machinery and steam engines, and newspaper printing.[5]

One of the first industries to benefit from the development of local credit institutions was textiles in New England during the early 1800s. With a heavy concentration of people and initial stimulus from foreign trade, New England witnessed the birth of a number of savings institutions and other financial intermediaries. In time, these institutions began to expand their operations outside of shipping and into textiles. With the abundance of water power, Boston capitalists soon demonstrated a predilection for textile manufacturing and shoe production.[6]

The rapid pace of change, the growing urbanization of the country and industrialization in the north, with its concentration of credit institutions, eventually set the nation down the path of civil conflict. The strong agricultural base of the southern economy, its use of slave labor, and lagging industrialization created two distinct visions of the future. These differing perceptions could not be reconciled even with a gradual move towards urbanization and industrialization in the south.

In 1861, the Southern states decided to part company with their Northern brethren with the action of bombarding Fort Sumter. The conflict that ensued lasted until 1865 and left the North triumphant. For the standpoint of credit, this meant that northern banking institutions concentrated in New York, Boston, and Philadelphia remained dominant on the domestic scene. In fact, wealthy bankers, such as Jay Cooke, were experimental in raising bonds for the federal government during the war.[7] Yet U.S. credit continued to be a poor cousin to European, in particular British, finance. In fact, U.S. banks did not have a sterling reputation, with tales about "wildcat banking" in which unscrupulous individuals printed money in a reckless fashion and then went bankrupt, sometimes with their top management skipping town with a large share of the deposits. The era of wildcat banking ended when Congress passed the National Bank Act of 1863, establishing the Office of the Comptroller of the Currency (OCC), which had the authority to print money and provide licenses for nationally chartered banks. The OCC also had the authority to supervise nationally chartered banks.

The poor cousin legacy of U.S. finance was to change with the emergence of big business in the United States following the Civil War, which helped stimulate the development of finance capitalism. Railroads, which ultimately stretched from coast to coast, were the first manifestation of the arrival of big business in the United States. As sociologist William Roy commented, "No economic sector was as important to the rise of large American business corporations as the railroads. Indeed until the end of the nineteenth century, railroad companies and large corporations were synonymous."[8]

The railroad was also a significant agent of change as it multiplied other advances made in the industry. Prior to the advent of railroads most goods consumed by Americans were produced locally. In many regards, the United States before the Civil War and transcontinental rail systems was a nation of farmers, who gave the economy a distinctly agrarian characteristic. After the Civil War rail construction spread across the country to serve the agricultural sector. The mighty seas of wheat and corn produced in the fertile Great Plains were now linked to big markets as in Chicago. For the first time, it was possible to move goods beyond meeting local market demand. This development also meant that economies of scope were coming into reach. Combined with other technological advances, such as the invention of the elevator and breakthroughs in mechanical refrigeration and mass production, the railway became an important catalyst in the industrialization of the United States. While business pioneers, such as Gustavus Swift (in meatpacking) and Adolphus Busch (in beer), came into their own in the late nineteenth century, they had benefited from those who had provided the credit for the initial construction of the railways.

During most of the nineteenth century the United States was a net capital importer, drawing most importantly on the London market. Almost every U.S. Treasury issue, in particular the ones designed to consolidate the massive civil war debt, had to include London houses of issue to be successfully placed.[9] Yet by the 1890s the U.S. economy had matured to the point where it held sufficient concentrated surplus capital to dominate its own investment market.[10] Prior to that period, the growth of heavy industry had depended upon foreign money. English investors alone had placed over $2 billion in American railroad securities by 1890.[11] This was to change following the boom of the 1880s as the total funds of banks and trusts, life insurance companies, some corporate reserves, and a few private fortunes gave the United States a new kind of independence, a relative yet vital freedom.[12]

Another development stimulated by the boom in railroad financing was the further elevation of New York City as the primary credit center in the United States. Although other East Coast cities such as Boston and Philadelphia remained financial centers, New York emerged in the 1850s and 1860s as the gateway to large-scale financing. As railroads developed and needed more capital to become established and expand, the dependence on eastern money, in particular New York, increased.[13] The centralization of the finance capital in New York was associated with two closely related factors: bonds were increasingly the instrument used to capitalize construction and expansion, in part because they were more easily marketed abroad and the city was initially a center of trading government securities.

As to the second point, Roy notes, "Since government financing and infrastructure development were so closely intertwined, New York became the center of railroad financing."[14] This concentration of credit business meant that New York also became the headquarters for the country's great investment bankers. Who were these investment bankers, who held sway over Wall Street, dominated the development of the nation's railroads, amassed amazing fortunes, and earned both the admiration and hatred of the rest of the population?

The Time of Giants

The right to allocate the newfound wealth of credit resources fell to a few men in the United States economy whose companies were so structured that their chief executives could operate with little government regulation and supervision, both nationally as well as internationally. Nevertheless, most of this elite of plutocrats or robber barons lacked a clear idea of how to use the credit surplus. Like many Americans adrift in the shift to a market and industrial economy, they sensed the passing of familiar opportunities without recognizing alternative areas for investment. However, they were most receptive to the strong-willed guidance of an even smaller elite within their own ranks. This tiny elite not only had plans of what to invest, but also had recently acquired the eminence to command a hearing. As Wiebe noted, "Led by J.P. Morgan, whose imaginative policies in railroad cooperation had already won him fame during the eighties, a handful of financiers, almost all of them private investment bankers, took charge of the new surplus."[15]

While Morgan was a major force in putting J.P. Morgan Bank on the map as a global player, the United States produced its own class of world-class capitalists who emerged from industry and came to be the powers to be on bank boards. Others in this elite club included Andrew Carnegie, Henry Clay Frick, Charles Schwab, and Cornelius Vanderbilt.[16] What was significant about this group was that they were an important catalyst in the transformation of the United States into a more industrialized and urban nation and a growing player in the globalization of credit. As biographer Samuel A. Schreiner, Jr. noted of Frick: "Henry Clay Frick was the quintessential capitalist, a truly representative figure of America's Gilded Age. The span of his adult years corresponded almost exactly with that of the fantastic period of explosive growth in material wealth that made the United States of America the richest, most powerful nation on earth. Everything was up for grabs, and the spoils were plucked by those with the greediest grasp. Moneymaking was the national sport."[17]

The giants of the age mostly began in industry. Frick started with coke and steel, Vanderbilt with steamships, Carnegie with steel, and Morgan with banking, but heavily involved in railroads. Relations between bankers and industrialists were close and, in many cases, incestuous in that many of the giants came to sit on boards of banks. One could certainly make the case for the existence of interlocking directorates in which a handful of names dominated the boards of many companies, most of them related, with, of course, considerable political clout. In this era of unbridled capitalism, there was a belief in "trickle down" economies. In a sense, there was an illusion of ever greater wealth raining down on everybody in the United States, which was still not fully explored or exploited.[18] The relationship of wealthy and powerful industrialists and their banker allies had ramifications to the young country's political development. It was the perception and somewhat true that the Republican Party was the party of the wealthy, while the Democrats attracted labor and populists, though they also had their deep-pocketed supporters. At the same time, the wealth of the plutocrats, their involvement in politics (often through bribery), control of the nation's finance, and heavy-handed approaches to dealing with labor did little to endear them to the public.

The case of the notorious Jay Gould is instructive. Of Scots descent, he was born in 1836 in Roxbury, New York. Like many of the big names in finance, Gould started off in industry, beginning as the part-owner of a tannery in Pennsylvania. Allegedly using his co-investor's profits as well as his own to buy a bankrupt railroad—without telling his partner—Gould survived at least one near-bankruptcy and made enough money to eventually establish his own brokerage house just before the Civil War. Casting his eyes on the stock market, he decided to launch a takeover of the Erie Railroad (known as the Scarlet Woman on Wall Street for the shadiness associated with it). After a stock war with Vanderbilt, Gould emerged triumphant, becoming president of the line in 1868. This stunt was followed in 1869 by an effort to corner the gold market. Gould made a hefty profit from his attempt to corner the gold market, though many other brokerages went under and the action caused a severe, national financial panic. He did not escape entirely free, however, as during the panic he was set upon by an angry mob, only narrowly escaping with his life. Gould continued to be active, acquiring several western railroads (one of which was the Union Pacific), bought a major newspaper (the *New York World*) and purchased the Western Union Telegraph Company. He was also active in seeking to prevent unions from developing within the businesses he owned. *The American Heritage Encyclopedia of American History* captured his place in history: "During his life, Gould was one of the nation's most vilified businessmen, a symbol of the speculative greed that many saw as endemic in the Gilded Age."[19]

More significant to the world of credit and the development of the United States as the dominant global player was the career of J.P. Morgan. Born in Hartford, Connecticut in 1837, Morgan's bulbus-nosed caricature came to dominate U.S. credit circles. His father Junius Spencer Morgan (1813-1890) was a successful financier and established a trans-Atlantic business. Julius Pierpont inherited his father's business in 1890 and consolidated its European and American interests. Morgan's London ties were essential in bringing badly needed capital from British bankers to rapidly growing U.S. corporations in the 1870s. Under his guidance, J.P. Morgan and Company was active in financing railroads, steel, mining, and utilities.

Morgan was a major force in the first merger wave of American industry. Morgan began reorganizing railroads in 1885, rationalizing their operations and stabilizing their financial bases. His active involvement in corporate restructurings, which resulted in sitting on the board of more than one company, made him one of the world's most powerful railroad magnates. He also helped consolidate U.S. industry, helping to arrange the merger of Edison General Electric and Thomson-Houston Electric Company to form General Electric. In 1901, he presided over the merger of Carnegie Steel Company and others to form the U.S. Steel Corporation, the world's first billion-dollar company in terms of capitalization. U.S. Steel had a worth equal to seven percent of the U.S. GDP. All told, Morgan was the dominant force in a wave of mergers between 1897 and 1904, which took some 4,277 companies and consolidated them into 257 corporations, greatly reducing chronic excess capacity and instilling greater efficiency.[20]

The rise of powerful financiers reflected the rise of the purveyors of credit over the U.S. economy. J.P. Morgan, Jacob Schiff of Kuhn,

Loeb and George Baker of New York First National Bank took an active role in guiding and directing the allocation of credit to the structures and business organizations that they felt were fit for the new age of American industry. As George P. Baker and George David Smith commented, "As fiduciaries, they guarded the interest of both shareholders and bondholders, while providing informed advice on corporate strategy, policy and financial structure. Such ongoing monitoring by the financiers who had restructured the business was the hallmark of what historians call 'financial capitalism.'"[21]

The Panic of 1907 and Its Aftermath

The power of the plutocrats over finance, or at least their tremendous influence, was made most evident in 1907, when the world tottered on the brink of a serious financial meltdown. After a serious round of speculation in 1903, the stock market began to rise, eventually turning into a bubble. With each movement upward, the banks became increasingly exposed as either underwriters or investors. Trust banks, administrators of trust funds, were particularly exposed as many of them lent directly to market speculators. As Geisst observed, "If stocks fell, the trust banks would be severely hurt, as would their investors. Without a central bank, no one would lend them the money if a depositors run developed or they needed cash to prop up their positions under duress."[22] On October 21, 1907 to a backdrop of falling stock prices, a run occurred at the Knickerbocker Trust. The bank quickly folded and its president committed suicide. The Panic of 1907 was in full swing.

The Panic of 1907 represented a tough challenge to the U.S. government. President Theodore Roosevelt was no friend of the plutocrats, but he recognized that short of a central bank to function as a lender of last resort he would have to rely on the one man with enough clout to turn the situation around—J.P. Morgan. Returning from an Episcopal church convention, J.P. Morgan set up his headquarters in his library and within a few weeks rallied the banks, sought and moved credit to where it was needed, and eventually calmed stock markets.

Since 1836, when President Andrew Jackson had killed the Second Bank of the United States (a second attempt at a central bank), the United States lacked an effective way to regulate the supply of money and credit and had no official lender of last resort. There was a strong historical tradition dating back to Andrew Jackson, which crystallized after the Civil War in the Greenback, Granger, and anti-monopoly movements. This tradition expressed the discontent of a great many farmers and businessmen with the economic changes of the nineteenth century. One of the big bogeymen of the populists was the banker, of which Morgan was the prominent face. Morgan was able to provide a private sector solution to the problem in 1907, though the dependence on him raised concern about his pervasive influence in national finance. As J.P. Morgan biographer Jean Strouse noted, "Market experts regard it as the work of a clearheaded master who grasped the big picture and took decisive action, but off Wall Street it has been seen as yet another example of rich people manipulating events for their own profit."[23] Indeed, in 1910, Robert La Follette, a populist Republican senator from Wisconsin, described Morgan as a "thick-necked financial bully, drunk with wealth and power [who] bawls his orders to stock markets, Directors, courts, governments and nations."[24] Despite that unflattering view, J.P. Morgan was a financial pioneer, helping to advance the U.S. credit system by making it more efficient (through corporate rationalization) as well as broadening the financial relationship with the British.

One offshoot of the plutocrats' long shadows over American politics was the emergence of the Progressive Movement, which sought to cleanse U.S. politics and bring the trusts down to size. It was believed that the changes enacted by the plutocrats (as well as by the advent of new technology) in the form of mass industrial production, urbanization, and ongoing use of the unsavory stock market put the true and simple America at risk from foes of "extraordinary, raw strength—huge, devouring monopolies, swarms of sexually potent immigrants, and the like."[25] Although big business continued to exist in the United States and wield considerable economic clout in political circles, the Progressive movement became a strong enough political force that it could not be ignored. Indeed, the Democratic Party in the 1890s was strongly influenced by the Progressive movement and populism. For its part, populism began during the economic depression of the 1870s, when there was a sharp decline in the livelihood of farmers at a time when their living and operating costs were increasing. Populism took a political form during the next two decades, as large numbers of farmers became members of organizations such as the National Grange and the Farmers' Alliances. The latter organizations were cooperatives that hoped to lower farmer's costs by selling supplies at reduced prices, loaning money at rates below those charged by banks, building warehouses to store crops until prices became favorable, and taking political action to achieve these objectives.[26] By 1891 the populist movement grew strong enough to establish a national organization, the People's Party.

The Populists participated in the election of 1892, advancing James B. Weaver as their presidential candidate. Their platform advocated the free coinage of silver and the issuance of large amounts of paper currency (they were well aware that inflation caused by such actions would raise commodity prices and allow farmers to pay off debt); the reduction of transportation costs through the nationalization of the railroads; a graduated income tax; and an eight-hour work day. Weaver did not win, but gained over a million votes. In the 1896 elections, the Populists backed the pro-silver candidate of the Democratic Party, William Jennings Bryan, who lost. From that point forward, the populists declined.

Progressivism developed into a broader impulse toward criticism and change that was highly conspicuous after 1900, when the already forceful stream of agrarian discontent was enlarged and redirected by the growing enthusiasm of the middle class for social and economic reform.[27] Although it was a vague and not cohesive movement it did find expression in T. Roosevelt's Progressive Bull Moose Party in 1912 and clearly influenced the Congress and presidents: moreover, it helped the U.S. Government emerge as a powerful force of regulation during the late 1890s and early 1900s. This was reflected by the passage of the Sherman Anti-Trust Act, a brief law that outlawed monopoly and was targeted at the power of the plutocrats, and the creation of the Federal Reserve Board in 1913. The latter was established to function as a central bank, operating with a degree of autonomy.

The political rise of Theodore Roosevelt in the 1880s and 1890s reflected the growing concern about the political power of the plutocrats. As his biographer, Edmund Morris, noted, Roosevelt was worried about the "rush toward industrial monopoly": in the twenty-five years between the Civil War and 1890, twenty-six industrial mergers had been announced; in the next seven years there were 156; in the single year 1889 a record $900,000,000 of capital was incorporated.[28] First as governor of New York State and then as resident following the assassination of President William McKinley by an anarchist Leon Czolgosz, Roosevelt moved to deal with what he called the "wealthy criminal class." As Roosevelt stated, it was not until his election as Governor of New York that he could take aim against "the combination of business with politics and the judiciary which has done so much to enthrone privilege in the economic world."[29] Consequently, Roosevelt as president moved to rein in the plutocrats, prosecuting several trusts. However, Roosevelt placed an emphasis on regulation, not the destruction of the industrial-finance groups that had formed a number of trusts. Ironically, Roosevelt's successor, President William Taft made much more use of the Sherman Antitrust Act against the plutocrats.

Under President Woodrow Wilson, who succeeded Taft in 1912, the Federal Reserve Board was created in part to modify the power of bankers and speculators. There were twelve regional central banks under the board, privately owned by the banks in their region that could discount commercial papers with them. Of critical importance to this system was that these banks could regulate the money supply by raising or lowering the discount rate. The apex of the Federal Reserve Board system was the Reserve Board, which consisted of members nominated by the president. The political significance of this was noted by Dietmar Rothermund: "The respective legislation had been introduced in order to tame the powerful New York banks, but it was soon evident that the New York central bank was the most important one and that its governor was more powerful than the Federal Reserve Board."[30] The U.S. credit system was therefore modified in terms of a furtherance of government regulation, though the combination of the Office of the Comptroller of the Currency (OCC) and then the Federal Reserve Board still left the market in force as the primary driver. The OCC was created to end "wild cat" banking, (i.e. setting up banks, taking deposits and then closing) provide national bank licenses, and print the greenback, the first federal dollar.

By 1914, American credit had changed radically. Since the end of the Civil War a slow but steady process of regulation had set in and the United States had made a significant shift from being a credit-deficit nation to becoming a credit-surplus nation, gradually coming to challenge British dominance. U.S. and British banks had become fierce competitors in international markets. Equally important, the time of giants had ended. Although strong individuals would emerge in the annals of U.S. credit in the twentieth century, none would have the same clout and ability to impose their personalities on the shape of industry and finance as had the plutocrats. While they caused considerable human misery, they were also major innovators in the development of credit institutions in the United States. They forced much needed change in U.S. industry, resulting in considerable consolidation of many sectors of the economy, helping develop economies of scale for the first time. The railroad industry, for example, was made to run more efficiently instead of being a patchwork of small lines running across the nation. Over time, however, old age and government regulation caught up with them—Gould died in 1892, Cooke in 1905, Morgan in 1913, Carnegie in 1919, and Frick in 1919. With their passing, the age of giants ended and a new age, born of war and economic volatility, emerged.

The Move to Supremacy

By the outbreak of the First World War, the United States was well-poised to assume the mantle of global credit leadership, especially since its rapid industrialization helped it account for about 33 percent of global GNP, which displaced the United Kingdom as the world's leading industrial power.[31] U.S. banks were active throughout the world, in particular in Latin America and the Caribbean, and often worked closely with European, usually British, banks.

While the age of dominant personalities faded away by the early twentieth century, a more institutionalized cadre of banks emerged to assume the role of credit providers, both domestically and internationally. This meant both through the bond and equities markets and through loans. Among this group of institutions was City Bank, Bank of America, Bank of Boston, Merrill Lynch, Goldman Sachs and Kuhn, Loeb, most based in New York City. While J.P. Morgan and City Bank were the realm of the old Protestant families (sometimes referred to as WASPs or White Anglo Saxon Protestants), a group of Jewish firms emerged on Wall Street to play an important role.

Jewish finance in the United States had its origins in the German-Jewish community, which was to provide the North American country with the Goldmans, Sachs, Seligman's, Warburgs, Schiffs, Kuhns, and Loebs, all prominent on Wall Street. The firm of Goldman Sachs, for example, was established in 1869 by Marcus Goldman, who had arrived from Germany in 1848 in the first great wave of Jewish immigration to the United States.[32] The founders of Kuhn, Loeb were of German origin, though they initially settled in Cincinnati and ran a dry-goods and clothing concern before they opened a New York banking house in 1867. The founders of Siligman Brothers were from Darmstadt, Germany.

The combination of old, established Protestant family-dominated banks and their counterparts from the German-Jewish community provided the United States with considerable business talent and financial muscle to undertake a growing amount of international business. Moreover, this combination was comfortable with both London, where most firms had offices, and on the European continent.

The involvement of U.S. banks in lending to foreign governments also dragged the U.S. government into becoming a territorial loan collector. Both Haiti and the Dominican Republic were unable to repay their loans in the early 1900s, which ultimately resulted in their occupation by the United States for lengthy periods of time. In fact, it was a concern that if the United States failed to reorganize Dominican and Haitian finances, the Germans might be inclined to intervene, much as they had in Venezuela in 1902 with the use of gunboats. With tensions rising in Europe between Germany and Britain, Washington's national interests were to deny the Germans any excuse to possibly develop the two Caribbean nations as bases from which to threaten American shipping (a policy that the British favored). Consequently, the Dominican Republic was occupied by U.S. troops in 1905 at which time a financial receivership was established. Haiti underwent similar treatment in 1915. What this also meant was that the U.S. added a new twist to the Monroe Doctrine, stipulating that no new European power (besides France, Britain, and Holland) was to have a territorial foothold in the Americas—if a country failed to pay its international debts. It was the United States that would do the collecting by occupying the country and collecting taxes.

Although the First World War brought considerable economic dislocation, the conflict helped consolidate the United States as the leading credit power in the Americas and one of the most powerful on the planet. Adding to the United States momentum, new modes of industrial production were being introduced. Henry Ford introduced the Model T in 1908, followed by the advent of assembly-line production in 1913, hence revolutionizing manufacturing. At the same time, the New York Stock Exchange was the only major bourse to remain open during the war, the U.S. economy was untouched by the war, and the U.S. dollar remained convertible to gold. As Germain observed, "The war provided the first real stimulus to New York's potential as an international financial center, by allowing American banks to step into the breach created by the suspension of clearing through London in July 1914."[33] Moreover, New York remained the only major market open to borrow from—something that the British and French did to finance their war efforts going. The combination of new muscle in industrial manufacturing (which was also far from the battlefields of Europe) and finance clearly elevated the military and economic power of the United States, pushing it to the apex of the global credit system.

The end of the First World War witnessed a short, sharp world boom in 1919 and 1920. France, Germany and much of continental Europe did not partake in the boom, lacking the financial resources to participate.[34] In fact, France and Britain had a heavy load of wartime loans to repay the United States, while Germany was stuck with massive wartime reparations under the Treaty of Versailles and racked with astronomical inflation. Unfortunately, this world boom outside of Europe was followed by a downturn in a number of countries.

The U.S. economy shrugged off the cooling of world growth and was soon on to the "Roaring Twenties." While Flappers, Al Jolson, and isolationism dominated American society, the period between 1922 and 1926 was one of rapid economic growth, marked by an upsurge in industrial production, the consumption of luxury goods, and a construction boom. Big business and finance were back. Yet, despite the shift in New York as the world's major credit hub, the United States was reluctant to assume leadership. Powerful isolationist sentiment, in fact, prevented the United States from becoming a member of the League of Nations, sadly the brainchild of President Wilson. The Dawes Plan to reorganize the German Reichsbank under Allied supervision in order to stabilize the German currency in 1924, was one of the exceptions to this. While the Dawes Plan helped re-establish the global credit network, it was an unbalanced system and ultimately flawed in keeping the system above water.

In the United States strong economic growth, an excess of credit, and a booming stock market all fed into a scenario leading to a massive crash. It is important to clarify that in the United States capital did not go back into investment. Investment options were relatively limited, but speculation in the stock market provided a highly attractive option. The enormous discrepancy between investment and speculation is reflected by comparing the following figures: new investment in 1925 was $3.5 billion and in 1929 $3.2 billion; the nominal value of shares traded in the stock market in 1925 was $27 billion and in 1929 it was $87 billion.[35]

The causes of the Great Depression that began in 1929 and continued into the 1930s will be an ongoing point of debate for historians and economists. The reasons advanced include the handling of war debts, the sterilization of gold, a deflationary monetary policy after an expansionist period, protectionism, and the overproduction of wheat.[36] Certainly the decision of the newly created Federal Reserve Board to tighten credit was a big mistake, possibly one of the most critical as it dried up credit when it was most needed. As Rothermund noted, "All these factors were due to long term developments, but they were accentuated by the sudden crash of the stock market in October 1929 which undermined the world credit system and thus was the proximate cause of the depression."[37]

No matter what theory is expounded, an excess of credit leading up to the stock market crash was a factor as was the shortage of it in the aftermath of the crash. It can be argued that the ready availability of credit in the form of bank loans to stock market speculators, who borrowed against the margin (against the collateral value of their stock portfolio) set the stage for a crash once stock market prices plummeted.

As the market climbed to its apex, call money rose from $6.4 billion at the end of December 1928 to $8.5 billion in early October.[38] Funds were diverted from consumption and production and instead went into speculation. However, when stock prices began to fall, the banks held back from lending to the stock market and elsewhere, creating a severe liquidity crunch. When a new infusion of new capital was needed the most, it simply evaporated. This situation was worsened by the government's reaction, which was to dry up credit providing capital to the banks. The ensuing financial crisis was to last through most of the 1930s and credit was to remain scarce.

It is important to clarify that the U.S. government, through the Federal Reserve Board, had begun as early as 1928 in curtailing available credit. Concerned about financial speculation and inflated stock prices, interest rates were raised. By the spring of 1929 industrial production declined. By summer, a recession was beginning to be felt. As was noted in *The Economist,* "In the two months before the Wall Street crash, industrial production fell at an annual rate of 20%. When the crash came, however, it was savage: stunning drops on October 24th, 28th, and 29th, then a rally, then another fall. By mid-November the market had declined by half."[39]

Although the drama of the stock market crash has lived on in American history, the actual numbers involved in trading in the stock market were relatively small and limited mainly to the wealthy, many of whom lived in the greater New York City area. The stock market crash in 1929 did not represent a wide segment of popular involvement, but was most likely limited to well under 400,000 individuals. Yet, because of their wealth and their being overextended in many cases to the banks, the impact of their financial demise was all the greater.

The Great Depression visited economic pain and suffering around the planet. Banks failed, companies closed their doors, and breadlines formed. In the United States alone, more than 11,000 banks out of 25,000 banks had failed.[40] The political impact was no less destabilizing. Faced with rapidly contracting economies, and shell-shocked populations, governments fell around the planet and the door was open to those willing to offer radical solutions to problems. This was most evident in continental Europe with the rise of fascism in Italy, Spain, and Germany and by the rise of militarism in Japan. In Germany, Adolf Hitler and the Nazi Party swayed the voters with calls for national self-sufficiency and a rejection of the decadent Weimar Republic, weakened by the onerous war reparations in the Treaty of Versailles. The Great Depression also had a nasty bite in financial circles in the United States and the United Kingdom. While London remained a highly significant hub in global credit, New York had made considerable strides to overtake it. The global economic crisis, however, made the question of dominance in credit a secondary issue in the 1930s.

The interwar period was another transition period in the global credit system akin to earlier shifts between Antwerp to Amsterdam to London. These earlier shifts were marked by considerable political upheaval and economic advances. As Germain noted, "The interwar years stand as another period of transition in the international organization of credit, similar in outline to the transition from Antwerp to Amsterdam that was occasioned by the Revolt of the Netherlands in the late 1560s, and the transition from Amsterdam to London that was consummated by the two decades of European War beginning in 1763."[41] Within this context, there was no straight line in the rise of the United States as the primary credit power, but with the world undergoing massive structural changes, New York was gradually pushed into a leadership position.

The U.S. Global Credit System: Dominant at Home and Abroad

While the structure of credit in the United States was radically transformed in the first part of the twentieth century, the strength of U.S. banks around the world grew considerably. The Great Depression and the Second World War greatly diminished the power of British and other European banks. In Asia, Japan was occupied by the United States and China fell into a civil war in the late 1940s. Only the Soviet Union had a superpower status comparable to the United States. However, the measurement of power was initially measured by the size of armies, the numbers of missiles, and the development of alliances in what became known as the Third World. In this new postwar balance of power, the United States had a powerful military, but more important over time, a strong and innovative economy, backed by a well-functioning credit system. The Soviet Union relied upon military power and an ultimately flawed economic system, which had little idea as to how to effectively use credit. The United States created an international web of credit that linked to it Western Europe and most of Africa, Latin America and Asia.

Certainly one of the most successful credit stories for the United States in the Cold War was the Marshal Plan, which pumped millions of dollars into the reconstruction of Western European democracies in the late 1940s. As the conflict against Nazi Germany came to an end in Europe and the Cold War commenced, most of Western Europe was either devastated by the destruction of its industrial infrastructure or lacked adequate credit to restart production or purchase the necessary raw materials. In some cases, even having the necessary food to feed local populations was a concern in 1946 and 1947. The Marshal Plan helped pump U.S. dollars into the allied European states, which stimulated reconstruction of local economies. Clearly, U.S. power was overwhelming, but if Washington was to maintain its European allies it was essential to use its economic power to guarantee the survival of ideologically compatible governments.

Another success of the emerging U.S. global credit system was the creation of the Bretton Woods international monetary regime in 1944, which was buttressed by the establishment of the International Monetary Fund and the World Bank in 1947. The IMF's primary mission was to maintain cooperation and orderly currency arrangements between member nations, with the objective of promoting international trade and balance of payments equilibrium. Moreover, if countries were hit by short-term liquidity problems, the IMF could provide assistance. The World Bank, in contrast, was created to help deal with long-term economic development issues, in particular to assist in making structural changes in economies. Both the IMF and the World Bank represented a strong U.S. and Western imprint in terms of the emphasis on capitalist approaches to international economic issues.

The Bretton Woods system was created because of the recognition that one of the causes of the Second World War was the breakdown of the international monetary system, a point that was underscored in 1931 when a financial crisis in Europe caused a run on gold in London which the British were unable to cover, leading to the suspension of gold payment. By 1936, all Western currencies had opted off the gold standard. Consequently, the idea behind the Bretton Woods system was that domestic monetary stability should have the highest priority, which the monetary authorities of the major industrial countries should pursue to ensure stable prices. With stable prices, exchange rates were to be predictable and economic cooperation made more probable.[42]

The Soviet international network had its own system of credit, but that was largely a set of linkages based upon coercion (in Central and Eastern Europe) and mutual interests (India, Vietnam, North Korea, China, and Cuba). In a sense, the world was offered two options, one founded upon a market-driven economic system characterized by a functioning global credit network and the other a closed economic system dominated by a heavy-handed state bureaucracy that sought to control the commanding heights of the economy and channel the flow of credit through narrow and over-regulated networks. The Soviet system regarded capitalism as a system that promoted the exploitation of workers (resulting in alienation) and in general, a wasteful, inefficient and irrational system.

The competition between the Soviet Union and the United States and the two economic systems they represented was ultimately won by the later. Credit clearly played a role. The U.S. economy was far more powerful, much more open to technological innovation than the Soviet economy. Although the Soviet Union appeared to offer military parity in the 1950s, 1960s, and 1970s, the Reagan administration had few qualms about starting a new high-tech arms race that was exceedingly costly. It was also willing to spend more on upgrading conventional arms. The point should be made that the Soviet economy was already deeply troubled before the Reagan administration came into office. Although efforts were made to reform the system starting in the mid-1980s, the decay was too entrenched and pervasive for remedial efforts to be successful. In fact, the weakness of the Soviet economy was evident as the USSR increasingly turned to foreign banks for credit. By the end of the 1980s, external debt was heading in the direction of $100 billion. With the collapse of the Soviet Union in 1992, one of the great ideological challengers to U.S. dominance in the global credit system was vanquished. The United States prevailed as the world's remaining superpower and still the center of the credit universe.

While the new round of the Cold War was reflected with greater red ink in the United States, it did not hamper the United States, with its more than adequate credit system, from moving forward. The Soviets, in contrast, could not compete. The closed nature of Soviet society, the difficulties in the free flow of ideas necessary to make technological advances, and inadequate credit resulted in the downfall of communism in the Soviet Union and its transformation into a new group of nations, each struggling to adopt market-oriented economic policies and working class.[43]

Conclusion

The course of U.S. dominance of the global credit system was largely a twentieth-century phenomena, though the foundations were established in the late nineteenth century. Clearly, credit played an important role in the transformation of the United States from becoming an agrarian-based economy to being an industrial giant, in the creation of a transcontinental rail system, and in raising the political and military power of the North American republic in global circles. This process did not occur without some degree of volatility in the stock market (caused by both greed and inefficiencies) and societal upheaval (as with farmers). Yet, as the U.S. nation-state evolved, the government role expanded to regulate industry and eventually the markets in order to provide the majority of its citizens with certain safeguards from the forces of unbridled capitalism in the form of the plutocrats. At the same time, there was an evolution to democratize credit in the United States, which is the subject of the next chapter.

Notes

1.   John Baker Holroyd, First Earl of Sheffield, *Observations on the Commerce of the American States*, as quoted in Guy S. Callender, *Selections from the Economic History of the United States, 1765-1860* (Boston: Ginn & Co., 1989), p. 210.

2.   Douglas C. North, *The Economic Growth of the United States 1790-1860*, (New York: W.W. Norton & Company, 1966), p. 46.

3.   Charles R. Geisst, *Wall Street: A History* (New York: Oxford University Press, 1997), p. 16.

4.   Ibid., p. 17.

5.   As North noted, "The heritage of rapid growth in international commerce and shipping prior to 1807 was evidenced by the Northeast's preeminence in the development of a capital market, marketing and transport facilities, insurance companies, and other social overhead facilities connected with shipping and external trade. With the decline of the re-export trade, merchants in the Northeast had become closely tied to cotton. New York in particular became both the center of the import trade and the financial center for the cotton trade." North, *The Economic Growth of the United States*, p. 63. Also see Margaret Myers, *The New York Money Market* 2 Vols., (New York: Columbia University Press, 1921). Myers contends the expansion in the pursuit of trade acceptances derived largely from their widespread use in financing the cotton trade.

6.   See Edgar M. Hoover, Jr., *Location Theory and the Shoe and Leather Industries* (Harvard Economic Studies LV (Cambridge, MA: Harvard University Press, 1937), p. 268.

7.   Jay Cooke was appointed the primary government agent to sell war bonds for the Union. He raised millions of dollars. After the war, he turned to railway finance, which proved to be his undoing.

8.   William G. Roy, *Socializing Capital: The Rise of the Large Industrial Corporation in America* (Princeton, NJ: Princeton University Press, 1997), p. 78.

9.   Randall D. Germain, *The International Organization of Credit: States and Global Finance in the World Economy* (Cambridge: Cambridge University Press, 1998), p. 52.

10.   Robert H. Wiebe, *The Search for Order 1877-1920* (New York: Hill and Wang, 1967, 1995), p. 24.

11.   Ibid., p. 25.

12.   Ibid.

13.   Roy, *Socializing Capital*, p. 109.

14.   Ibid., p. 110.

15.   Wiebe, *The Search for Order*, p. 25.

16.   Vanderbilt began in the shipping and steamship business, but moved to railway finance when he realized that it offered greater chances of accruing wealth. He made a considerable part of his fortune before the Civil War and was to die in 1877.

17.   Samuel A. Schreiner, Jr., *Henry Clay Frick; The Gospel of Greed* (New York: St. Martin's Press, 1995), p. x. Milton Rugoff noted of the plutocrats: "The men who made their fortunes between 1850 and 1890 were rarely prepared for their power their wealth conferred on them. Nevertheless, their success set them apart: they were the fittest. Applying Darwinism to society with godlike assurance Herbert Spencer had declared that progress was made possible by the elimination of the 'unfit', among them he included the incapable and the idle. Presumably a hopeful vision of mankind's future, it seems only to have justified the view that life was a jungle." *America's Gilded Age: Intimate Portraits from an Era of Extravagance and Change 1850-1980* (New York: Henry Holt and Company, 1989), p. 41.

18.   Schreiner, Jr., *Henry Clay Frick*, p. 116.
19.   John Mack Faragher, ed., *The American Heritage Encyclopedia of American History* (New York: Henry Holt and Company, 1998), p. 365.
20.   George P. Baker and George David Smith, *The New Financial Capitalists: Kohlberg Kravis Roberts and the Creation of Corporate Value* (New York: Cambridge University Press, 1998), p. 6.
21.   Ibid., p. 7.
22.   Geisst, *Wall Street*, p. 118.
23.   Jean Strouse, "Annals of Finance: The Brilliant Bailout," *The New Yorker*, November 23, 1998, p. 62.
24.   Quoted from Strouse.
25.   Wiebe, *The Search for Order*, p. 53. Along a similar vein Thomas Watson, a commentator during the late nineteenth century, captured much of the apprehension about the industrialization of America, which included a surge in immigration. According to Watson: "We have become the world's melting pot. The scum of creation has been dumped on us. Some of our principal cities are more foreign than American. The most dangerous and corrupting hordes of the Old World have invaded us. The vice and crime which they have planted in our midst are sickening and terrifying. What brought these Goths and Vandals to our shores? The manufacturers are mainly to blame. They wanted cheap labor; and they didn't care a curse how much harm to our future might be the consequence of their heartless policy." Quoted from Richard Hofstadter, *The Age of Reform* (New York: Vintage Books, 1955), p. 83.
26.   "Populism," Microsoft Online Encyclopedia 2000 *http://encarta.msn.com* c 1997-2000 Microsoft Corporation. All rights reserved.
27.   Richard Hofstadter, *The Age of Reform: From Bryon to F.D.R.* (New York: Vintage, 1955), p.5.
28.   Edmund Morris, *The Rise of Theodore Roosevelt* (New York: Ballantine Books, 1979), p. 694.
29.   Ibid.
30.   Dietmar Rothermund, *The Global Impact of the Great Depression 1929-1939* (London: Routledge, 1996), p. 52.
31.   Zbigniew Brzezinski, *The Grand Chessboard: American Primacy and Its Geostrategic Imperatives* (New York: Basic Books, 1997), p. 4.
32.   For a comprehensive story of Goldman Sachs, see Lisa Endlich, *Goldman Sachs: The Culture of Success* (New York: Simon & Schuster, 1999).
33.   Germain, *The International Organization of Credit*, p. 13.
34.   John Kindleberger, *The World in Depression, 1929-1939* (Berkeley: University of California Press, 1986), p. 15.
35.   Rothermund, *The Global Impact of the Great Depression, 1929-1939*, p. 50.
36.   Ibid., p. 48.
37.   Ibid.
38.   Kindleburger, *The World in Depression*, p. 61.
39.   "A Refresher on the 1930s." *The Economist*, September 19, 1998, p. 95.
40.   Ibid.
41.   Germain, *The International Organization of Credit*, p. 58.
42.   C. Pass, B. Lowes, L. Davies, and S. J. Kronish, *The Harper Collins Dictionary of Economics* (New York: Harper Collins, 1991), p. 266.
43.   Jack Weatherford, *The History of Money* (New York: Three Rivers Press, 1997), p. 224.

11

The Democratization of Credit

The process whereby credit was "democratized" in the United States began in the late nineteenth century and gained considerable momentum in the decades to follow. By the 1920s, credit, to a large extent, was a rich man's prerogative. Credit in limited amounts was available to the rest of society, but usually at very high rates of interest. Yet there arose in the United States a culture of consumerism that maintained a steady demand for credit and ultimately helped stimulate financial innovation in the new rules for pawnbrokers and in the form of credit unions, credit cards, and eventually Wall Street (the world of investment banks and securities trading). In the first half of the twentieth century this was to produce an explosion in credit. According to one measure, that of consumer credit, the U.S. Federal Reserve recorded in 1928 that some $6.5 billion of consumer credit existed; by 1958 it had multiplied to $45 billion.[1]

Three key themes of our study of credit are at play in this chapter. The first is a cultural predilection towards entrepreneurship, trade, and consumerism, which made the embrace of credit acceptable within society. The second theme is the spread of credit from being the privilege of the wealthy and the powerful to becoming available to a wider range of American society. The third is the volatility factor: Throughout the twentieth century, the steady progression of U.S. credit institutions as integral parts of the economy and as everyday parts of the life of millions of citizens was accompanied by the ups and downs of credit markets, in particular, capital markets orbiting New York, especially Wall Street.

The Culture of Consumerism

A considerable mythology exists about the thriftiness of Americans during the early days of the Republic. This has been depicted as a part of the hardy nature of the roughed individualists who settled the original thirteen colonies, pushed out past the Appalachian Mountains, crossed the Mississippi River, and conquered the West. In his *Financing the American Dream: A Cultural History of Consumer Debt,* historian Lendol Calder observes that although we remember nineteenth-century Americans as living in a golden age of thrift, savings, and economic self-discipline, the reality was different. As he states: "It is generally recognized that nineteenth-century producers—farmers, say, or shopkeepers, or entrepreneurs—floated on a vast sea of credit....But nineteenth-century consumers depended on credit, too—credit obtained from a subterranean network of formal and informal lending sources."[2]

Realizing the pressing need for credit to do such things as buy land, conduct business, put in a crop, and start new enterprises, let alone get by with enough food to feed a family, allows us to better understand how a culture of credit became integrated into American culture. It paralleled the development of the related culture of consumerism, which was dependent on consumer credit defined as "short- and intermediate-term credit extended to individuals through regular business channels, usually to finance the purchase of consumer goods and services or to refinance debts incurred for such purposes."[3]

How do we define the culture of consumerism? In a very simple sense, it refers to the ability of people to go out and buy whatever they want, backed by credit, which means buy now and pay later. Calder noted that Americans were very much oriented to the culture of consumerism, which he defined more thoroughly as "a particular way of living that attempts to make sense of the nexus of selling, buying, using and disposing of commodities in which most people today conduct their affairs. It defines the 'good life' not primarily in terms of satisfying work, or economic independence, or devotion to God or commitment to the group, or any other ideal honored by people past and present, but rather is dedicated to the proposition that 'good living' means having lots of goods—goods bought in the market and made by unknown hands, more goods this year than last year, the 'things' as one of the advertisers once promised, 'that make life worth living!'"[4]

Consumer culture took root in the United States during the nineteenth century, but became much more pronounced after the 1920s and especially after 1945, when the combination of credit unions, credit cards, bank lending, and government largesse fueled the quest for the good life for the bulk of Americans. The ideal of upward social mobility, facilitated by easy credit, made it appear that the good life was within reach. This consumer culture was later reinforced by the supply-side economic policies of the Reagan years (1980-88) that penalized savings, seeking to get people to spend to generate demand and eventually economic growth.

Furthermore, the growth spurt begun in the early 1990s and carried through into the early 2000s on the back of the Internet and high-tech related technology, continued the culture of consumption. This was reflected by the low level of savings in the United States, the second lowest within the most developed G-7 countries, and the heavy level of private sector and personal debt (at 134 percent of GDP) at the end of 1999. An image of the era was perhaps best captured by the cover of *Red Herring* magazine of January-February 2000, which had a naked man sitting on a crown-like chair, covered only by a coat of dollar bills. That particular issue dealt with greed in the Silicon Valley, the rise of money managers in the high-tech business, and the decline of engineers. Conspicuous consumption was part of *Red Herring's* concern about America's new gilded age.

While we have briefly discussed the cultural dimension of consumer culture and its relationship to credit, it is now time to turn to those groups that helped democratize credit in the United States.

The Pawnbrokers: Sharks, Leaches, and Remorseless Extortionists?

The great banking dynasties were closely involved with the emerging and credit-hungry corporate America, but the bulk of the population was without such access. Yet the need for credit clearly existed. Two options stood out: either getting credit on an installment plan, which initially meant going to a loan shark or a pawnbroker (sometimes there was little difference between the two), or joining a credit union. According to Calder, "when money is lent or a good is sold it is on the condition that the borrower or purchaser repays the loan with fixed payments to be made at regular times over a specified period."[5] Related to this was a cultural dimension that Americans have demonstrated a long-standing willingness to get ahead by acquiring debt. Consequently, in many cities, people turned to the local pawnbroker, who was more than willing to take someone's possessions, value them, and advance money, while holding those same possessions as collateral. Payments were made in installments.

The first American pawnbrokers appeared in the early decades of the nineteenth century, with New York City legally recognizing them in its 1803 city charter. By 1911, there were 2,000 pawnshops operating in 300 cities, with 400 owners.[6] Rounding out the world of small creditors were a number of loan agencies, usually not legal and often charging annual interest rates in the range of 20 percent-300 percent, sometimes up to 1,000 percent (for the truly desperate).[7] It was estimated in 1907 that there were 70 small loan-offices in New York City and 37 in Pittsburgh, while there were 139 in Chicago by 1916. The outrageously higher rates of interest charged by these small loan agencies earned them the opprobrium of being "sharks, leaches and remorseless extortioners."[8]

The installment plan was to gain considerable momentum in the second half of the nineteenth century, in part, due to the efforts of peddlers and boraxhouses. Peddlers were small-time traders, working door-to-door, often to immigrant families. Calder explains the dynamics of peddling and the link to credit:

> An immigrant wanting to break into the retail trade, but lacking previous trade or professional experience, would arrange with a store or a wholesaler for credit. A line of credit would then be used to finance a stock of items known to be in high demand in the immigrant's own neighborhood, including furniture, housewares, sewing machines, clothing jewelry, and assorted ornamental wares. Now the immigrant was in business. He peddled his goods within a network of customers that over the years, if everything went well, would be built up into the hundreds and even thousands.[9]

The most successful of the peddlers pushed some of the retail stores to adopt installment plans. These retail stores came to be known as boraxhouses, based on the cheap, shoddy goods (referred to as borax) that were pushed on customers. As the retailers became more involved in the sale of goods through installment plans, they began to conduct background checks based on employment and character. While a sizeable portion of the buyers of goods from the boraxhouses were working class, the middle class also was attracted to this means of credit, especially in acquiring such products as furniture.

The middle class also had a limited access to credit via building and loan associations. These savings banks were first organized in Philadelphia in 1831, but had a rather complicated structure that did not open the door to broader application. However, credit unions did offer another option.

The Credit Unions: Give the People Credit!

In Europe, the same problem existed, which had given rise to credit societies founded upon the idea that people could pool their money and make loans to each other. The guiding principles of what began the credit union movement were, (1) only people who were credit union members should borrow from the union; (2) loans would be made for "prudent and productive" purposes; (3) a person's desire to repay (character) would be considered more important than the ability (income) to repay.[10]

The first European cooperatives were established in 1844 in Rochdale, England, and in Germany in 1852. Other credit unions were established in Italy. The German credit societies and their Italian counterparts were the forerunners of the large cooperative banks that continue to exist in Europe. In the United States credit needs existed for large projects, but also smaller, personalized needs. Although the concept was discussed in the United States, and credit union legislation was even considered in Massachusetts in 1871, the idea did not take root until the turn of the century. The first actual move to establish a credit union in North America, however, occurred in another developing country, Canada. As in the United States, credit was something available to Canada's rich and powerful—the working and middle classes were usually left to their own devices. In 1900, Alphonse Desjardin organized a credit union (*caisse populaire*) in Levis, Quebec. As one source noted, "The reasons were the same as those in Germany 50 years before. People were poor, interest rates were financially crippling, and the credit union offered a way out."[11] The first savings deposit in the new Caisse Populaire was a modest ten cents and the first collection from all members totaled only $26.

Desjardins, a firm believer in credit unions, continued to advance the idea in North America, establishing other credit unions. Of particular interest, the Quebecker founded the first credit union in the United States in 1909 in New Hampshire. While the torch of providing credit to the lower classes in North America was lit by Desjardins, Pierre Jay, a Massachusetts banking commissioner, and Edward A. Filene, a Boston merchant were to significantly expand the network.

Filene had first come across credit unions in 1901 when he observed one during a trip to India. Profoundly impressed by what he saw, upon his return to Boston he devoured as much literature on the subject as possible. Filene could be regarded as a "progressive" thinker at the time: the owner of the department store chain that bore his family name, he had started profit-sharing plans for his employees and instituted other than novel fringe-benefit programs. He also started the "bargain basement" idea in department store operation, allowed his employees to engage in collective bargaining and arbitration, established minimum wages for women workers, and advocated a five-day, 40-hour work week. Additionally, Filene was a founder of the U.S. Chamber of Commerce.

Filene was approached by Jay, who as the banking commissioner, had become aware that several groups of employees in the Commonwealth had established their own savings and loans organizations. As the banking commissioner regarded these small associations as providing a needed service, he wanted to make certain that they functioned within the rubric of the law and were properly supervised. Consequently, Jay turned to Desjardins for advice. In 1908 Jay presided over a conference that involved Desjardins, Filene, and other prominent citizens. From this conference came legislation for what was to become the first general state credit union act in the United States in 1909.

The credit union movement, however, did not take off as its initiators had hoped. By 1921, Filene turned to Roy F. Bergengren to help him seek federal legislation and increased state legislation. The Credit Union National Extension Bureau was soon created with the mandate of establishing a nationwide association of credit unions to provide leadership and services to existing credit unions and to organize new credit unions.[12] Bergengren was highly successful in advancing the cause: by 1925, sixteen states had passed credit union laws and 419 credit unions were serving 108,000 members; by 1935, thirty-nine states had credit union laws and 3,372 credit unions were serving 641,800 members. The Great Depression also helped the spread of credit unions as many banks failed, leaving the field even more open to any institution willing and able to provide credit.

What helped cement the credit union as one means of democratizing credit was the establishment of the Credit Union National Association (CUNA) in 1934. This confederation of state credit leagues replaced the Credit Union National Extension Bureau, but Bergengren became the new body's first managing director. Equally important to the creation of CUNA was the passage in Congress in 1934 of a federal credit union act. This allowed the establishment of credit unions anywhere in the United States and provided such bodies the choice of incorporating either under state or federal law.

Although the Second World War brought a halt to the growth of credit unions, the post-war period witnessed a boom. According to the Credit Union National Association, in 1945 there were 8,683 credit unions in the country; by 1955, there were 16,201; and by 1969, the U.S. movement peaked at 23,876 credit unions. Since 1969, the number of credit unions declined due to the merger of many smaller credit unions with larger ones as well as to growing competition from commercial banks and other non-bank financial institutions. At the same time, the number of credit union members has continued to grow, reaching 67.4 million Americans in the late 1990s.

The process of democratizing credit was not entirely left to credit unions. In 1928, National City Bank of New York offered to make small loans to working-class people. This experiment was prompted by problems with loan sharks in New York. The state attorney general decided that if banks were to provide adequate credit, the loan sharks would be put out of business. Consequently, National City Bank was pressured to begin lending to the working class. Although the bank's management was dubious about the activity, it soon demonstrated a profitable side, ensuring the continuation of such lending activities.

The wider distribution of credit received an additional push during the 1930s. While private sources of credit dried up during the Great Depression, the Roosevelt administration took an active role in encouraging banks and other financial institutions to lend more money to the general population for the purchase of homes and automobiles. Encouragement came in the form of government-backed and guaranteed low-interest loans. The government's involvement increased in the aftermath of the war as home loans for veterans were provided. As credit became more readily available, the American public became increasingly more comfortable with borrowing, using the newfound access to credit to purchase homes, cars, and education, as well as televisions, kitchen appliances, boats, and vacations. Within a generation, debt became not only the norm but the expected right of virtually the entire middle class and a good section of the working class.

Opening the Spigot: The Banks

In 1928, the access to credit in the United States underwent a substantial transformation. City Bank, under pressure from the New

York state attorney general to strike a blow against loan sharks, began to provide consumer lending. Although the pressure came as a plea to all banks to curtail loansharking activities, only City Bank (then known as City National Bank) answered the call. It cannot be said that the move to lend to the masses was done strictly out of good will. Charles E. Mitchell, the bank's president, understood that there was considerable potential to such a market. As he stated, "Our contact with this great number of small depositors has brought us to an understanding of their problems [and] their periodic necessitous financial requirement..."[13]

Citibank calculated that despite the perception of frugality and aversion to debt many Americans were indeed willing to borrow to buy those consumer goods they felt denied in achieving the good life. Moreover, the bank was to find this a lucrative enterprise, as it was able to fund loans at 3 percent, but using an interest cost to the borrowers of 12 percent.[14] On opening day for personal loans at City Bank, the response was overwhelming, while the media proclaimed City Bank's decision as a milestone in the democratization of credit and a blow to the nefarious activities of loan sharks. City Bank's success in this field was soon noted by many of its rivals, who followed suit, greatly adding to the momentum to democratize credit in the United States.

From the beginning of loans from City Bank in the 1920s, consumer credit from banks became a part of the American economic landscape. Although the Great Depression dampened consumer credit for a number of years, demand returned as the economy slowly recovered in the late 1930s and took off following the Second World War. Two important factors were at work with the banks—an effort by the government to maintain what it called "fair lending practices," i.e., that all citizens have an equal opportunity to obtain credit from a bank and are not discriminated against, and the volatility factor.

The volatility factor in U.S. credit history is evident in the Savings and Loan (S&L) debacle during the 1980s and the credit crunch that hit the U.S. economy in the early 1990s—also a period of considerable difficulty for U.S. commercial banks. Although much has been written on these matters elsewhere, a brief review of the S&L scandal is instructive from the standpoint of what lessons were learned, especially from institutions involved in providing credit.

Savings and loans banks were originally established to give people a safe way to save their hard-earned money while earning a relatively modest interest. In the early twentieth century people pooled their money to make it possible for members of the S&L association to get mortgages on their homes without falling into the clutches of loan sharks. To help bolster the standing of S&Ls as safe harbors for personal savings in the aftermath of the Great Depression, deposits were insured by the Federal Savings and Loan Insurance Corporation (FSLIC), a federal agency. S&Ls were, before the 1980s, tightly regulated, with regular audits. Lending was generally restricted to homebuyers under rules calculated to prevent excessive risk-taking. The bottom line was that the S&Ls borrowed short (paid interest for deposits that could be withdrawn at will) and lent long (wrote thirty-year mortgages). As economist Paul Krugman noted, "It was an exchange of a privilege (deposit insurance) for a responsibility (low-risk investing). And until the mid-1970s it worked well."[15]

In the late 1970s the ground under which S&Ls provided credit to the public changed. Inflation shot up. S&Ls lost deposits as the interest rates they paid were increasingly less competitive with those offered by commercial banks and money market funds. By 1980, the S&Ls were in a precarious position. Instead of lending money at a higher rate than they paid on deposits, they found themselves paying more on deposits than they were earning in their assets. This mismatch meant that bankruptcy for the industry loomed on the horizon. As the Reagan administration entered office in 1981, the S&L industry was in a bad shape. As Martin Mayer observed, "Even by the highly permissive accounting standards of federal regulators, the S&Ls were supporting $650 billion of assets on a net worth of $32 billion—and would lose more than $4.5 billion of that net worth in Reagan's first year."[16]

A solution to the problem was found—at least some thought in the S&L industry and their allies in the U.S. Congress who passed enabling legislation. A number of measures were taken to deregulate the S&L industry, the most significant of which allowed the banks to purchase higher yielding (yet riskier) securities. If the purchase of high-yielding securities (such as junk bonds, then all the rage) was successful, the industry could grow its way out of its troubles (which it appeared to be doing in the early 1980s). If this gambit failed and the S&L with it, deposit insurance would pay back the depositors with taxpayers dollars.

One example of deregulation pertained to what was called "appraised equity capital." As Mayer explains, "An S&L owned commercial property, as increasing fractions did, either through foreclosure or because some important states permitted direct investment of S&L deposits, could credit itself with any increase in the appraised value of that property and take that credit in capital (allowing, once again, the recruitment of $33 in insured deposits for each $1 of appraised equity increase)."[17] And as Mayer observes, "Given the low professional and moral state of real estate appraisal, this was a direct invitation to cheating."

The ultimate price tag to all this cheating, which occurred in a grand scale in such states as California, Texas, Florida, Arizona, and Arkansas, was enormous, estimated at over $300 billion as to the cost to the U.S. taxpayer. Consequently, the very same institutions charged with providing a safe harbor for people's money and a source of credit for the housing industry, underwent deregulation to allow those very same institutions to go and purchase high-risk and high-yielding assets, many of which failed to lead to new riches and an option to grow out of past difficulties. By the early 1990s, the S&L industry was rapidly becoming a piece of American credit history as an example of good intentions having gone bad.

Not all aspects of bank lending of consumer and other credit to the public have been as sordid as that of the S&Ls. The U.S. government took measures to guarantee (as much as possible) that lending practices were non-discriminatory. Consequently, fair lending practices were passed by the U.S. Congress to ensure that commercial banks did not ignore entire neighborhoods or particular socioeconomic groups, such as African-Americans, from lending. Laws were also passed to stop what has been referred to as predatory lending, that is the practice of seeking low-income borrowers and charging them unfairly high fees and interest. Predatory lending, historically akin to loan sharking, periodically became an issue in the United States. For example, in March 2000, the U.S. Federal Reserve chairman, Alan Greenspan, publicly announced that his institution was concerned about "abusive lending practices that target specific neighborhoods or vulnerable segments of the population and can result in unaffordable (mortgage) payments," loss of homeowners' equity and foreclosure.[18] Greenspan's comments were also echoed by the Comptroller of the Currency John D. Hawke Jr.

Bank lending in the United States to the public continues to play an important role. Billions of dollars are lent on a yearly basis to the public through a myriad of credit institutions, including commercial banks, mortgage and home-equity loan companies. Over time, this access to credit has become what many Americans have become to regard as a natural right. Despite the sometimes-negative perception of the banker in U.S. history, his role has been largely constructive and has been essential to the democratization of credit.

The Credit Card Enters the Scene

Another key element in the democratization of credit in the United States was the advent of the credit card. The original idea of the modern credit card was probably that of the journalist Edward Bellamy. In his *Looking Backward: 2000-1887*, written in 1888, he envisioned a utopian world where there were no coins, notes, or other currency circulated. Although there was no buying or selling, people settled accounts by means of "pasteboard credit cards." These were issued to all citizens and used to acquire all needed goods at large central warehouses. What was stunning was that Bellamy's prediction came well before credit cards came into use and were a form of installment payment. Credit cards first emerged in the United States with retailer Cooperwaite and Sons of New York just before the turn of the century. In 1905, the retailer Spiegel began offering credit terms on everything in its catalog. This was followed in 1906 by Sears, which began to sell washing machines for installments of forty-four dollars a month. In essence, these were installment plans with interest charges built in. The first real credit card, however, was offered by Western Union. In 1914, this company offered the first charge-and-settle-up-at-the-end-of-the-month plan with identification in the form of metal dog tags. The process by which people in the United States turned to credit cards only gained momentum. In 1924, General Petroleum, a chain of California gas stations, was the first to actually use the term "credit card" in its General Petroleum Credit Card. Mobil Oil and Shell soon did the same.

It is important to underscore that the initial developments in the credit card came from the retail sector, i.e., the merchants who recognized the need to reward good customers and provide that little extra to keep them coming back. As one observer noted, "Retailers once held the power in the consumer credit business. They developed the revolving-credit concept, which evolved into metal charge plates and later plastic cards, decades ahead of the banks."[19]

One of the more interesting as well as significant stories in the development of the credit card is the early history of the Diners Club.

As told by Matty Simmons, one of the original players in the drama, the concept of using a credit card at New York's swank restaurants was originated by Frank MacNamara.[20] Described as someone whose appearance would have been ideal for the "part of a traditional used-car salesman," MacNamara invented the Diners Club card in 1950, with the simple idea of "One card. Many restaurants. One monthly bill." Although the initial reaction to Diners Club on the part of the restaurants was dubious, the concept soon became very popular and quickly expanded into other areas such as hotels and rent-a-car franchises. By the spring of 1951 membership exceeded 100,000; by the end of the decade Diners Club cards were held by over a million people. A number of competitors such as Trip-Charge, the Duncan Hines Signet Club, and the Esquire Club failed to make it, but in 1958 American Express came on the credit card scene.

American Express was founded in 1841 by Henry Wells, well before the advent of credit cards. Wells lived in Buffalo, New York, which was then one of the more western U.S. towns. He envisioned that as the United States continued to expand across the continent, there would be a need for a company that could make deliveries. Considering the state of national communications during the first half of the nineteenth century—few major roads, horse-drawn wagons, and canals—the idea was sound, but the challenges were many. Wells, however, made a go of the business and in 1850 merged his company with two rivals, Livingston and Fargo and Butterfield, Wasson and Company. The new company was known as American Express and dominated the express business.

American Express was to benefit from the opening up of the American West and the linking of the United States by railroad. Accordingly, by 1862, the company had nearly 900 offices and more than 1,500 employees.[21] Eventually, American Express opened a new line of business for which it is still famous, travelers checks and money orders. The company flourished in the post-World War I era, survived the Great Depression and boomed in the post-World War II era. As Americans began to travel overseas in ever-growing numbers, American Express was there offering services throughout Europe and Asia. By 1956, American Express had expanded into the world's largest service company, with check sales at $1.6 billion and rising quickly.[22]

The turn to credit cards was a natural progression for American Express. The company had already been in the business of extending credit in the form of travelers checks and money orders and had a national as well as an international network of offices. In the world then being shaped by a revolution in communications and transport, American Express found the move to the credit card a logical next step. After a brief bid to purchase Diners Club, American Express opted to go it alone and officially entered the business in 1958. With American Express joining the ranks of the credit card world, the planet took one more step in the direction of a globally linked credit system, upheld by symbols.

Further momentum in the use of the plastic card and the advance in instant credit came with the entrance of banks into the business. Bank of America was one of the first banks to launch its own credit card, Bank Americard, in 1958. Although Bank of America lost millions of dollars in its first four years on bad debts, start-up costs, and poor management, it turned a profit in 1964. Other banks were soon to follow. Interbank, a cooperative based on the West Coast of the United States, developed a new credit card system called Mastercharge. Over time this non-profit cooperative owned by a number of banks would evolve as a major force in the global credit business. By 1979, it changed its name to Mastercard and was second only to Visa, which had been founded earlier.

The global credit card business made enormous strides in the 1970s, 1980s, and 1990s. It became a regular part of daily life for many North Americans, Europeans, Japanese, and growing numbers of people in the developing world. In 1989, 187 million people worldwide held Visa credit cards. Some 6.5 million businesses of all varieties accepted Visa cards in lieu of cash for sales amounting to $570 million per day, 365 days a year.[23] By 1993, total charges on cards issued worldwide by credit card companies were $1,025 trillion, with Visa leading the way with a volume of $527.62 billion, followed by Mastercard at $320.62 billion, American Express (Amex) at $124.06 billion, JCB (Japanese Credit Bureau) at $32.18 billion, and Diners Club at $20.1 billion.[24] In terms of worldwide ownership at year-end 1993, Visa boasted of 333.1 million cardholders, Mastercard 210.3 million, American Express 35.4 million, JCB 27.8 million, and Diners Club 20.81 million.[25] The continuing penetration of credit cards was further evidenced in 1998 when nearly $1.4 trillion in products and services were purchased using Visa Cards and there were over 800 million Visa (and Visa-related cards such as Interlink, Plus and Visa Cash) in the market.[26] In the same year,

Visa-brand cards were accepted at more than 16 million locations in 300 countries and territories.

Credit cards now function as a form of currency and thus are often referred to as plastic money. In the most basic of transactions, a cardholder purchases a product at a store, the credit card company's computers credit the store account with the appropriate amount, deduct an amount from its own books, and increase the amount the cardholder owes the credit card company.[27] Each month the credit card company requests payment from its cardholders.

The simple credit card, however, is becoming passé. A new "smart card" is increasingly becoming the plastic currency of choice. As futurist Alvin Toffler noted, "With what is called a 'smart card,' the very act of handing it to a cashier who runs it through an electronic device would result in the price of dinner being instantly debited from your bank account. You don't pay at the end of the month. Your bank account pays right away."[28] The smart card is representative of an economy that is rapidly shifting to instantaneousness.

The credit card industry has emerged as a major component of the global credit system. It provides short-term credit that, for a generous interest charge, can be rolled over for a long time. As in any part of life where a large amount of credit is shifted in and out of various parts of the economy, politics plays a part. By the end of the 1990s, the credit card industry was dominated by Visa and Mastercard, which, working through their bank networks, have permeated much of the North American, European and part of the Asian economies.

The Role of Wall Street and the Democratization of Credit

Any discussion about the rise of U.S. credit and its democratization would be remiss in omitting the role of Wall Street in the 1980s and 1990s. Considerable changes occurred in the stock exchange and how business was conducted during these two decades, which had clear ramifications for the organization of credit both within the United States and internationally. The rise of junk bond traders, corporate raiders, the market crash of October 1987, the Orange County derivatives debacle, and the long bull market of the 1990s are well-known, mirror a revolution in popular expectations for wealth and the structure of credit. Part of this change was brought on by innovation in financial markets that pushed for a major shakeup in the traditional intermediary role played by bankers between depositors and borrowers. The process of disintermediation, in which non-bank actors sought and succeeded in drawing funds from deposits and putting them into higher returning securities, many of them in the stock market, provided a massive surge of credit into the U.S. stock market. It also forced conservative commercial banks and invest-ment houses to become more competitive and innovative and opened the door to the spread of wealth to those willing to take the risk. At the same time, there was a steady decline in the level of household savings in the United States, indicating that the shift to wealth-gen-eration in the stock market has made credit a more speculative force in the United States and ultimately in the global economy. No matter how much widespread stock ownership became in the United States, money in the stock market is always more risky than money in the bank, all of which means that while credit has become more democ-ratized, it has also become more speculative in nature as well.

When the Reagan administration came into office following the 1980 election, it sought to pull the country out of an economic mess inherited from the Carter administration. High inflation, a recession, and a decline in U.S. power were clear at the end of the Carter years. With Ronald Reagan in the White House, the U.S. was back and the good times were to roll on in. The undergirding forces to the stock market boom in the early mid-1980s were the supply-side stimulus of the Reagan administration (taxing savings to get people to spend), foreign investment and "merger mania." Taming inflation was also a concern. An important technical change also occurred in the mar-ketplace, allowing a significant breakthrough in financing for cor-porations. The United States Securities Commission under Rule 415 allowed companies to preregister their financing needs through a shelf registration that had a life of two years. This change was sig-nificant for two reasons. First, it greatly reduced the amount of time a company required before going to the market to issue equity or debt. The only thing required was it updated its financials before issuing. Considering the environment of mergers and acquisitions that gripped the corporate world at the time, speed in raising addi-tional capital was critical—sometimes to survival. Secondly, Rule 415 disrupted the old gentlemen's syndicates used to raise bonds and equities. As time became a more precious commodity in credit, there was room for brash newcomers like Michael Milken, who rec-ognized the inefficiencies in corporate America as well as the slow pace of many traditional firms in structuring finance and opening up

the doors of credit. Companies that wanted to expand found themselves in a difficult position, as building new businesses from scratch
was expensive due to new assets reflecting the earlier rise in inflation. Existing assets could be bought more cheaply.[29]

The combination of these factors led to an amazing round of mergers and acquisitions within corporate America, much akin to the
1890s. In 1987 merger activity reached almost $300 billion. At the
same time, the savings and loans industry was deregulated in the
United States, which opened a door to relatively unsophisticated,
but aggressive buyers to the new world of junk bonds. Junk bonds
initially were regarded as "fallen angels," companies that had fallen
on hard times, but had the potential to return to investment grade
status (based on ratings supplied by rating agencies such as Moody's
Investor Service and Standard & Poor's). In the 1980s, junk bonds
became the stamp for up-and-coming companies and companies
fighting off corporate raiders.

The U.S. corporate world in the 1980s was also undergoing significant changes in regard to its role internationally, its relationship
to credit and, most of all, to new technologies. In many cases, corporate America suffered, much as Dutch and British business before
it, a relative decline to the competitive nature of the rest of the planet,
in particular Japan and Europe. As new technologies poured into the
marketplace, many companies were not flexible enough to deal with
change. The large U.S. auto makers wrestled with stiff competition
in both overseas markets and at home and were forced to either
change or perish. Chrysler even had to turn to the U.S. government
for help.

Survival in corporate America meant restructuring, which entailed
eliminating certain areas of production, closing plants, and firing
people. While corporate raiders made millions by attacking and breaking up companies, thousands were tossed into the unemployment
line. The sentiment emerged that the pushing of paper around had
become much more important than producing anything. Connie
Bruck, the author of *The Predators' Ball: The Inside Story of Drexel
Burnham and the Rise of the Junk Bond Raiders*, made two observations about the world created by Michael Milken and his ilk. First,
"It would introduce terror and mayhem into countless corporate
boardrooms. It would cause frightened managements to focus on
short-term gains and elaborate takeover defenses rather than the research and development that make for sustained growth. It would

cause the loss of jobs, as companies were taken over and broken up."[30] She also admits that the threat of corporate raiders brought back the owner-manager to American business and helped "accelerate the trend toward restructuring, as once-placid managements hastened to take measures—such as selling low-earning assets, pruning work forces, renegotiating labor contracts, closing hundreds of older, outmoded plants—before others did it for them."[31]

The go-go period of the 1980s came to an end in the last years of the decade. The October 1987 stock market crash signaled that the party was over. Junk bond traders and corporate raiders fell out of favor, while the savings and loan industry imploded under the weight of bad investment decisions and poor supervision.[32] The late 1980s also witnessed a large number of bank failures, creating considerable doubt about the future of the United States as the world's leading credit power. As already noted, the developing world's external debt crisis had also hurt U.S. banking. Additionally, the United States ran a string of budget deficits, rapidly accumulating debt in the 1980s, with public sector debt climbing from 36.2 percent of GDP in 1981 to 54 percent in 1989. [33] Already noted as well was the Japanese buying of U.S. Treasuries.

The situation changed in the 1990s, with the revival of the stock market. From the early 1990s to 1999, the stock market became an engine of growth, posting record numbers, with the Dow Jones Industrials index breaking 9,000 in 1998 and 11,000 in 1999. The NASDAQ stock exchange was one of the major beneficiaries of the creation of a new economy based on high-tech. The corporate consolidation that began in the 1980s produced more competitive companies, low interest rates stimulated growth (by making credit more available), a relatively cheap dollar helped exports, and foreign investors were attracted to the country's political stability, relatively strong economic growth, and low inflation. Moreover, an aging population in the most developed countries increased investor interest in equities for their retirement savings and financial deregulation and innovation created greater investor choice, improved intermediation and made markets more efficient and global.

Technology was another major factor opening up new options for investors in the stock market. The sweeping nature of tech-driven changes was caught by Andrew Sheng, chairman of the Securities and Futures Commission, in a speech to the Hong Kong Securities Institute on March 18, 2000:

But there is no doubt in my mind that technology has become a major driver of change. The Silicon Valley has been described as "the greatest legal creation of wealth in the history of the planet." Through changes in telecommunications, media and the Internet, and changes in capital raising capabilities via venture capital and markets such as Nasdaq, entrepreneurs are now able to tap increasing resources for new ideas and new investments in technology. At no time in history have the financial markets been so friendly to small entrepreneurs with big ideas.[34]

Another key factor was the explosion in mutual funds. Many families in the United States had traditionally relied on banks to place their savings. The only problem was that the rate of returns from commercial bank savings was well below what people were getting from the stock market. Most Americans, however, did not have the sophistication or training to follow the gyrations of the stock market, track the management of corporations, or examine the particular sector of interest in detail. The solution to connecting the vast pool of personal savings and the stock market, including companies looking for capital, was the mutual fund company. Companies, such as Fidelity, Vanguard or Scudder, offered the small investor an opportunity to have their hard-earned money moved into a country, region or sector, with the attraction of having an army of analysts who did nothing else but cover their particular corner of the market. Considering the ongoing expansion in the stock market and the higher rate of return that wise investors could make, many Americans decided to deplete their savings and play the market—albeit in the hands of a large mutual fund investment company. The three largest funds—Fidelity, Vanguard, and Capital Research—collectively totaled $850 billion worth of assets under their control by the end of 1996.[35]

What the combination of financial and technological innovation and the shift of funds from savings institutions to the stocks resulted in was an unprecedented movement of capital into the U.S. stock market. The substantial upward momentum that marked the NASDAQ in 1999 and 2000, as the market climbed past 4,000 to 5,000, reflected the carnival-like atmosphere. In many regards, the stock market replaced banks as a place to put savings and a place from which to draw credit. The sheer magnitude of U.S. involvement in the stock market was evident by the fact that in 1999 more than 70 million Americans were directly involved in the U.S. equities market and 130 million were indirectly involved (through pension funds, etc.), numbers that tripled in the last two decades. At some point, there was a shift in the nature of these funds from being credit to finance productive enterprises to becoming speculative capital put down on the gambling table. When the Internet stocks crashed in April 2000, the pain felt was widespread, but it did not sink the economy. It would be a year later in 2001 that the Internet or dot.com bubble fully deflated, which did cause a slowdown, yet not a crash.

Conclusion

The path of credit development in the United States was long and it took many decades to establish a truly national system, accompanied by a strong international component. It is significant to underscore that the conditions of credit found in the Dutch and British experiences were evident here. In particular, these were the relationship between power and credit (i.e., the plutocrats and their opponents within the progressive movement) that ultimately resulted in a rule of law through the creation of a system of federal and state regulatory agencies. Also evident was that the democratization of credit, i.e., increased access to credit for broader elements of society—something pushed along by consumerism—reinforced the representative nature of political institutions in the United States and, through this, the concept of the American nation-state. Moreover, this process of credit development entailed considerable ups and downs, especially as it was linked to the development of the stock market as well as international markets. These letter trends, however, are more the subject of the following two chapters.

Notes

1.   Lendol Calder, *Financing the American Dream: A Cultural History of Consumer Credit*, (Princeton, NJ: Princeton University Press, 1999), p. 9.
2.   Ibid., p. 38.
3.   This is the term used by the Federal Reserve Board, which reports monthly statistics on consumer credit. See Douglas Greenwald, ed., *The Encyclopedia of Economics* (New York: McGraw-Hill, 1982), p. 184.
4.   Calder, *Financing the American Dream*, p. 9.
5.   Ibid., p. 17.
6.   For more information on pawnbrokering in the United States, see Samuel W. Levine, *The Business of Pawnbrokering: A Guide and a Defense* (New York: D. Halpern, 1913), pp. 8-25; and "Pawnbrokers and Loan-Offices," *Harper's New Monthly Magazine* 39 (June 1869): 125. The statistics are from W. R. Patterson, "Pawnbrokering in Europe and the United States," in U.S. Department of Labor, *Bulletin* 4 (March 1899), p. 268.
7.   Calder, *Financing the American Dream*, p. 51.
8.   Ibid.
9.   Ibid., p. 55.

10. Credit Union National Association, "History of the Credit Union Movement," (New York, 1996), p. 1.
11. Ibid.
12. Ibid., p. 2.
13. Quoted from James Grant, *Money of the Mind: Borrowing and Lending in America from the Civil War to Michael Milken* (New York: Farrar, Straus & Giroux, 1992), p. 306.
14. Ibid., p. 307.
15. Paul Krugman, *The Age of Diminished Expectations* (Cambridge, MA: The MIT Press, 1997), p. 158.
16. Martin Mayer, *The Bankers: The Next Generation* (New York: Truman Talley Books/Dutton, 1997), p. 375.
17. Ibid., p. 381.
18. Marcy Gordon, "Greenspan Criticizes Unfair Lending to Poor Borrowers," *The Journal News*, March 23, 2000, p. 10.
19. Jennifer Kingson Bloom, "The Old Store Card Is Making a Comeback," *American Banker*, September 4, 1998, p. 6.
20. Matty Simmons, *The Credit Card Catastrophe: The 20th Century Phenomenon That Changed the World* (New York: Barricade Books, 1995).
21. Ibid., p. 59.
22. Ibid.
23. Alvin Toffler, *Powershift: Knowledge, Wealth, and Violence at the Edge of the 21st Century* (New York: Bantam Books, 1990).
24. Simmons, *The Credit Card Catastrophe*, p. 150.
25. Ibid.
26. Information from Visa website—http://www.visa.com/au/who/main.html.
27. Toffler, *Powershift*, p. 64.
28. Ibid.
29. Charter R. Geisst, *Wall Street: A History* (New York: Oxford University Press, 1997), p. 338.
30. Connie Bruck, *The Predators' Ball: The Inside Story of Drexel Burnham and the Rise of the Junk Bond Raiders* (New York: Penguin Books, 1989), p. 19.
31. Ibid.
32. Although the U.S. government was initially slow in responding to the growing crisis in the savings and loan industry, in 1989 it took decisive action, ultimately involving more than $130 billion in public funds, to resolve the long-standing insolvency of Savings and Loans institutions. Insolvent institutions were temporarily placed under the supervision of federal authorities, old management was removed, goods assets were separated from bad assets, which were to be sold or collected by the new supervisory body (the Resolution Trust Corporation), and institutions were restructured, often with public money.
33. Organization for Economic Cooperation and Development, *OECD Economic Outlook June 1998* (Paris: OECD, 1998), p. 254.
34. Andrew Sheng's speech to the Securities and Future Commission, at the Hong Kong Securities Institute, March 18, 2000, provided by the *South China Morning Post Internet Edition*, p. 4.
35. Geisst, *Wall Street*, p. 366.

12

Challenges to the U.S.-Dominated Credit System

Although the United States emerged as the dominant power in the global credit system following the Second World War and defeated the Soviet Union during the Cold War, U.S. dominance over the flow of international credit did not ensure a stable and smooth-running credit regime. Rising competition within the capitalist bloc and the developing country debt crisis in the 1980s guaranteed that the U.S.-dominated credit system would be rocked by periodic volatility. Despite the claims of economists, markets did not always run in the most efficient ways. Both cases reflect that the United States was number one, but primacy did not mean that New York, as the financial hub, and Washington, D.C., as the political hub, always got their way in the various battles pertaining to who got credit and why.

All of this returns us to one of the central themes of our book—the volatility factor. While the late 1940s and 1950s were clearly dominated by the entwinement of U.S. power and credit, the 1960s through the 1980s—the period discussed here—were not so clear-cut. In fact, the U.S. began a relative decline as both Europe and Japan rebounded from the war. The gradual reduction in U.S. dominance added a new factor of uncertainty in international credit markets, which provided a consistent and nagging sense of unease, especially as new innovations hit financial circles.

The Revival of Europe

One of the first erosions in the dominance of the United States in the world of credit came in 1963. In that year, Autostrade, an Italian toll road authority, issued the first Eurobond worth $15 million. Although the issuing of a $15 million bond per se was hardly revolutionary, what was of significance was that it was the first debt issued in dollars outside of the United States. Moreover, the bonds were listed outside of the United States on the Luxembourg Stock Exchange. This was the initial tapping of the vast pool of dollars that existed outside of the United States. The U.S. dollar dominated world trade and, in this case, the financing of trade to Europe. In the 1950s and 1960s, a large amount of those dollars stayed in Europe, hence being called Euro-dollars.

Why did the issuers pick the tiny Luxembourg Stock Exchange and not the vastly larger and more liquid New York Stock Exchange? In some ways it appeared as if Luxembourg's stock exchange was mimicking the story of *The Mouse That Roared*, in which the tiny Duchy of Grand Fenwick, desperate for money, decides the best bet is to declare war on the United States and lose. With the loss, of course reasoned the Duchy's leadership, the generous Americans would provide considerable aid, thus solving the tiny state's financial problems. Was the Grand Duchy of Luxembourg playing the same game? The answer is, of course, no, though tones of the giant battling the Lilliputian remained.

What the Autostrade issue in Luxembourg represented was a significant change in global finance and a challenge to U.S.-based credit dominance. As Europe was regaining its economic strength and the United States was beginning to feel the costs of being a superpower (as well as the world's credit hub), there was growing concern about the large amounts of U.S. currency effectively outside of U.S. monetary control. Part of the problem was that the Bretton Woods system presumably never foresaw that any one country could run a persistent current account balance-of-payments imbalance from one decade to the next as the United States did from the mid-1940s through the 1950s and into the early 1960s. Political and technical factors allowed this situation to continue. The dollar's reserve currency status meant that foreign countries were legally able to accumulate the exported dollars in their central bank, but as the United States was also their military protector, the allies felt constrained in demanding gold for their dollars.[1] This situation would not last.

At the same time that the United States grappled with its current account problem, Europe was undergoing important political and economic changes. At the end of the 1940s Europe had been torn asunder by the Cold War, with Eastern Europe and parts of central

Europe falling to Soviet-dominated hegemony. Western Europe, backed by the United States, was not in great shape. The war had left much of Europe's industrial base in ruins, its credit system near-death (except for Switzerland and, to a lesser extent, Sweden) and political systems in flux. The political right was largely discredited and weak in most countries, while the socialist left faced a strong challenge of Communist parties backed by the Soviet Union, as in the cases of Italy and France. The Holocaust also damaged Europe's credit system as it greatly reduced the financial capabilities of such Jewish financiers as the Warburgs and Rothschilds. From the standpoint of 1949, Western Europe was weak and divided, its economic prospects dim. Credit was scarce and dominated by the United States.

Conditions gradually changed in the 1950s. The North Atlantic Treaty Organization (NATO) provided strong trans-Atlantic counterweight to the Soviet bloc, giving the West a military and political shield behind which to begin economic reconstruction. And, as already noted, the U.S.-backed Marshal Plan helped Europe's economic revitalization. Moreover, Europe's move to economic integration, started by the creation of the Benelux customs union and advanced by the European Coal and Steel Community (ECSC), which was created by the Treaty of Paris in 1951. The signatories were France, Italy, West Germany, Belgium, the Netherlands, and Luxembourg. This movement gained greater momentum with the Rome Treaty of 1957, which brought into being the European Economic Community (EEC). The EEC officially came into existence on January 1, 1958 and was a common market in which member states were to remove the customs duty or tariff protection that applied to goods sold to each other. Ultimately, the EEC would evolve into the European Union, with a membership including most of Western and Central Europe. Europe's economic integration helped provide greater stability which gradually began to help its credit institutions begin to recover and compete with U.S. institutions.

Europe's political and economic decline and the rise of U.S. power were not entirely appreciated. Indeed, the dominance of U.S. economic muscle raised concerns that Europe's economy, and eventually its political systems and culture would fade before the wave of "Americanization." This was a reflection that if European economies and businesses needed credit to recover in the late 1940s and 1950s they had little choice but to go to U.S. markets or, in the case of governments, either to the U.S. government or the International

Monetary Fund and World Bank, both dominated at this time by Washington. Probably one of the best examples of European apprehension about U.S. economic power was Jean-Jacques Servan-Schreiber, a French academic. In his *The American Challenge* (1968), Servan-Schreiber made the dire prediction that within fifteen years the world's third largest economy after the United States and the Soviet Union would not be Europe, but American industry in Europe. U.S. economic dominance was so powerful, with its credit institutions of course playing a part. U.S. companies, he argued would "continue to carve up Europe at their pleasure," but, "If tragedy is upon us, the final act has not yet been written."[2] Although Servan-Schreiber was to be radically wrong, his views did represent the concerns of many Europeans about the economic, political, and military power of the United States.

Despite the views of Servan-Schreiber and others, Europe's revival in the world of credit began in the 1960s, partially caused by actions in the United States. The U.S. government in 1963 imposed an interest equalization tax (IET) in an effort to dissuade foreign governments and corporations from borrowing in U.S. bond markets. It also imposed Regulation Q on the markets, which was passed to curb the outward flow of U.S. dollars by prohibiting the payment of interest on short-term deposits and capped payment of interest on long-term deposits. Moreover, the U.S. Commerce Department ruled that U.S. companies investing abroad had to raise money outside of the United States. The result of these U.S. regulations was the birth of the Eurobond market. As Smith and Walter noted, "So a supply of borrowers—Europeans who could no longer borrow in the United States and U.S. companies that now had to borrow outside the United States—met with a growing supply of funds in the form of Eurodollars."[3]

The Eurodollar market was created prior to the passage of U.S. regulations, but was also an offshoot of politics and economics. The Eurodollar market began in the late 1940s when the Soviet Union, apprehensive that dollar deposits held by U.S. banks might be frozen or restricted, re-deposited dollar funds with a Soviet-controlled bank in Paris, the Banque Commerciale pour l'Europe du Nord (BCEN). This institution was used extensively by the Soviets to facilitate international transactions within the communist bloc. Despite the ideological rhetoric from the capital of Marxist-Leninist thought, Moscow, the Soviets and their allies were forced to earn and pay for their trade in dollars. This trend gained further momentum in 1950 when the bank of China used BCEN to safeguard its dollar deposits after Beijing had become enmeshed in fighting the Korean War against the United States. Over time this base of U.S. dollars, held outside of U.S. jurisdiction, expanded especially as trade and commerce in Europe recovered. The use of offshore short-term deposits paying a rate based on the London Interbank Offered Rate (LIBOR) became a widely used financial vehicle for European banks in the 1950s. As this pool of capital expanded and U.S. regulations were passed, the Eurodollar market became an important force in the development of a new credit market, the Eurobond market. All of this also helped revive the fortunes of London.

Since the end of the Second World War, London's fortunes as a significant international credit center had sunk. The United Kingdom had fallen on hard times. In the aftermath of the war, the process of decolonization witnessed the end of the Empire as India, Pakistan, Malaysia and many other former colonies in Africa and Asia gained their independence. As the historian Eric Hobsbawn noted, "After 1931 Britain ceased to be the hub of the international economy, after 1945 it ceased to be even a formal Empire of substantial size, and comparisons with other industrial countries became increasingly unfavorable."[4] The UK's position as a power in credit circles was further diminished as the country shifted from being a credit exporter to a credit importer. In a sense, London, once the global credit center and capital of free trade, now became the capital of a country forced to look inward. Although London was eclipsed and the power of the British Empire gone, the birth of the Euromarkets provided a new chapter.

In many regards London was well-situated to become the major center for the Eurodollar and Eurobonds. To its advantage, the city on the Thames had a considerable number of credit institutions, such as centuries-old investment banks with long involvement in international markets. There was little formal regulation of the new markets by the Bank of England or the Treasury. Equally important, there were no tax barriers, reserve requirements or foreign exchange controls to impede capital flows. London was ready-made for any new international-type market, which the Eurobond market rapidly became. In 1963, the year that the interest equalization tax was passed, London benefited from New York's decline. In the first half of the year $1 billion in foreign securities was floated in New York; by the second half of the year, after the enactment of the IET, foreign issuance was only $250 million.[5] While New York's issuance of foreign securities (especially for bonds of foreign governments, excluding Canada) plummeted and would not revive in a meaningful manner until the removal of the IET restrictions in 1974, London reaped the benefits. As a contemporary London *Times* article noted, "if this move was primarily designed to protect the American balance of payments, it has already thrown up desirable side effects in the revitalization of European capital markets—particularly London."[6]

Although London was not to regain the dominance it enjoyed in the nineteenth and early twentieth centuries, it made a return as a key component in the post-war international credit system. It still lacked the economic and military power the United States had, which helped maintain New York's role as the global credit hub. Foreign borrowers returned to New York in the 1970s, with issuance rising from $1 billion in 1973 to $10.6 billion in 1976.[7] U.S. dominance, however, was far from complete and London was decidedly back as a credit center. London's position was also helped by the advent of petro-dollars. The old story of surplus capital going to those areas needing capital was the same, but the dynamic behind it became more complex, involving a cast of characters including New York bankers, Arab leaders, and African dictators. The situation was further complicated by the collapse of the Bretton Woods system.

In the early 1970s, the Nixon administration was having considerable problems in bringing inflation under control. Treasury Secretary John Connelly, one of Nixon's closest economic advisers, strongly advocated a devaluation of the U.S. dollar and cutting its convertibility to gold. This would also reduce the pressure on U.S. gold reserves, especially as the French were using their dollars to request convertibility into gold. In a presidential address to the public on August 15, 1971, President Nixon followed through with those recommendations. The result was chaos in foreign exchange markets, a fierce round of inflation in industrialized countries, and a major crisis in the British banking system as the pound plummeted with the dollar. But the fun did not stop there. Other forces were at work in the global economy which were to wreck havoc with the international organization of credit and challenge U.S. dominance.

The Slide into the Developing Country Debt Crisis

Early in the 1970s commodity prices enjoyed a boom. It was believed at the time that the boost in commodity prices was not a one-off event, but signaled a steady future trend. This view was given considerable credence by a report of the private think tank, the Club of Rome, in its 1972 report in which it warned of a rapid depletion of global natural resources. At the same time, bankers in the United States and Europe were beginning to look offshore for new lending opportunities, while the Eurocurrency markets were starting to gather momentum as an option to U.S. dollar debt market. The thinking about commodities coincided with the re-emergence of international banking seeking profits overseas. As Richard O'Brien noted of this situation: "At the same time developing countries' creditworthiness was being given a tremendous boost by the commodity price boom, which was not thought to be a one-off phenomenon—unlike the 1950s boom following the Korean War. Rather, it was seen as a long overdue correction in favor of the producers of raw materials."[8] Consequently, those with credit sought out those who they felt needed credit and who were to be creditworthy in the future due to their prominence as major commodity exporters, especially in the minerals area—Zaire (copper), Morocco (phosphates), and Peru (copper). It didn't hurt matters that these countries were also part of the Western camp in the struggle against the Soviet bloc. U.S. and French military support was used to help prop up both Zaire and Morocco against external security threats as well as internal threats.

Oil was to add an additional element into this mix of banking and the perception of creditworthiness. When oil prices shot upwards in 1973, the industrialized nations discovered their vulnerability to oil prices, but those with this precious commodity gained almost immediate gains in their creditworthiness as well as their clout in the international credit system. Oil, after all, was a commodity akin to credit: without it functioning as a key lubricant to global industry, the world economy could come to a halt. Although oil had been used for industrial purposes in the early twentieth century, it was in the post-WWII era that its use accelerated. Major oil reserves were located around the planet, but the Middle East had a large concentration. Oil prices remained at relatively low prices in the 1950s and 1960s, but underwent a radical upward shift in the 1970s. The catalyst for the upward price momentum was the Arab-Israeli War of October 1973, also called the Yom Kippur War as the Arabs launched an assault on the Israelis on the Jewish holy day of the same name.

Unlike earlier Arab-Israeli wars, Israel did not walk over its enemies. In 1973, the Arabs were highly motivated, well equipped, and initially had the element of surprise on their side. After tough fighting, the Israelis were able to regain the upper hand and within a short period of time drove back the Arab advances. The United States promptly provided military assistance to Israel, activating an air bridge of equipment and ammunition. This helped Israel rapidly replenish its arsenal. This action, however, angered the Arabs, who regarded the United States and the West as allies to their enemy. Using a different means of power at their disposal, the Arabs decided to declare an oil embargo. While this was a retaliatory action against the West, the result was to raise oil prices to hitherto unseen heights. The formation of the Organization of Petroleum Exporting Countries (OPEC), which included major Arab oil producers of Saudi Arabia, Kuwait, Iraq, and Libya as well as Iran, Nigeria, Indonesia, Ecuador, Gabon, and Venezuela, furthered concerns about high oil prices.

The opinion that governments never go bankrupt was attributed to a banker as he assessed the billions of dollars of loans pumped into what was in the 1970s known as the Third World, but now referred to as Emerging Markets. By the late 1970s, oil money was rapidly being recycled out of the United States, Western Europe, and Japan in the form of loans and into Latin America, Africa, and Asia. While the OPEC nations were awash with funds, other developing nations suddenly found that their import bills had increased hugely. To maintain the pace of rapid economic growth, nations like Argentina, Brazil, and Korea turned to borrow those recycled oil funds. The offshoot of all this was that during the late 1970s and early 1980s most developing countries embarked upon a binge of external borrowing. This was particularly the case in Latin America, where the region's long-term debt quadrupled between 1975 and 1982, expanding from $45.2 billion to $176.4 billion, with total external debt standing at $333 billion at year-end 1982.[9]

Up to 1982 it appeared that there was plenty of credit available for everyone and that even if problems occurred, governments would never go bankrupt or default on their debt obligations. Reality was a cold shower. The momentum toward the debt crisis was picking up. In 1975, Zaire was forced to seek a rescheduling due to a fall in international copper prices and mismanagement of its economy. In the same year, the state-owned Indonesian oil company, Pertramina, collapsed amid massive corruption and mismanagement, forcing the government to reschedule its obligations.[10]

The descent towards the global debt crisis was in some ways best caught by Turkey's economic crisis in the late 1970s. After a period of rapid economic growth, easy access to credit, and a flawed strategy of import substitution, the Turkish economy began to have problems with a widening current account deficit. The hike in oil prices aggravated the situation, as Turkey was a net oil importer. A substantial amount of the borrowing was short term and interest payments mounted rapidly. Turkey's current account balance of payments shifted from a surplus in 1973 of $660 million to a whooping deficit of $3.1 billion in 1977. While the economy overheated, the pressure on the country's resources to meet its international debt obligations increased substantially.[11]

In the 1977-79 period, the civilian government responsible for leading the country found the situation increasingly beyond its control. Although two large parties, the center-left Social Democrats and the right-wing Justice Party, rotated in and out of office, they were dependent on the support of a bewildering assortment of small-party alliances. The fragmentation of political parties in Turkey during the 1970s led to a situation in which the major parties were largely ineffective in forming governments that could provide sustained policy direction. The parliamentary parties remained more concerned with political survival, hidden agendas and the destruction of foes than in resolving the country's growing array of economic problems.

Turkey was also hit by the steady increase in interest rates in the late 1970s, which added to its external debt-servicing burden. As the international creditor community began to have doubts about Turkey, difficulties with further borrowing made debt management increasingly problematic. Foreign creditors, in large part, were growing apprehensive about Turkey because of the country's increasing political instability. Lending became increasingly short term. In early 1977, Turkey's foreign exchange reserves ran out, revealing the damaging extent of short-term debt—a debt well beyond the government's ability to repay. By 1978, Turkey had drifted into an acute economic and debt crisis and was forced to seek a rescheduling. While Turkey signaled that not all was well with providing credit to developing countries, its fall from grace as a star borrower did not dissuade international banks from pursuing new opportunities.

On the other side of the world there were more dark clouds on the horizon. In 1979, the United States raised interest rates to quell inflation, which also effectively raised the cost of borrowing in international credit markets. The U.S. economy was beginning to slow, another negative for many developing countries, in particular those in Latin America. By 1982, the clouds of a major debt crisis were moving rapidly in the direction of the global credit system.

When high-ranking Mexican officials knocked on the door of the U.S. Treasury in August 1982 seeking assistance in meeting its debt payments, the U.S.-dominated credit system was confronted with a major systemic challenge. The United States and other industrialized countries had watched the problems with external debt in Zaire, Poland, and Turkey with concern, but the scope of these crises was not systemic in nature, threatening to pull the global credit system down. Mexico's crisis at the start did not appear to be systemic, but once such a major debtor nation crossed the border from being a good prospect to deadbeat, sources of credit soon dried up for other developing countries. Soon, Argentina, Brazil, Chile, and Venezuela were to follow, seeking to reschedule their large external debts. Noted economist Sebastian Edwards noted, "Latin America was severely hit by the sudden drying up of commercial bank loans. Starting in 1982, the net transfer of resources turned negative, and between 1982 and 1986 the annual net transfer averaged -$26 billion, compared with a positive average net transfer of more than $12 billion a year between 1976 and 1981."[12] As the crisis spread to other parts of the globe, banks in the United States, Europe, and Japan were forced to take substantial losses.

One of the major problems that dogged Latin America during the 1980s was the difficulty creditor countries had in reconciling the conflicting interests of commercial banks, foreign policy, and manufacturing. This applied especially for the United States, Latin America's major creditor nation. As already discussed in this book, U.S. banks had a longstanding interest in Latin America that was reinforced by trade relations. In the past, there had been an easier resort to gunboat diplomacy to get results. In the 1980s, gunboat diplomacy fortunately was not in vogue. Yet, ready solutions to the debt crisis were not on hand. Consequently, the creditor countries initially "muddled" through the crisis, regarding it as a short-term liquidity crunch, which could be resolved through austerity and import compression. By mid-decade it was painfully evident that the nature of the problem was structural and long term. Within Latin America flawed economic strategies (i.e., import substitution) and the refusal of U.S. and most European bankers to extend credit meant that the crisis was far from being resolved. This stimulated the first official U.S. effort at a debt policy, the Baker Plan, named after Secretary of Treasury James Baker III (1981-88). The plan acknowledged that sustained, export-driven economic expansion was required if Latin America was to grow out of its debt problem. At the same time, new capital was perceived as necessary from creditor governments, commercial banks, and multilateral institutions like the World Bank and Inter-American Development Bank.

The Baker Plan despite its good intentions, failed to pull Latin America out of the external debt quagmire. By 1989, economist Rudiger Dornbusch critically concluded, "Baker's 'muddling' through remains the Reagan administration's strategy, a treadmill of pretense and make believe in which both debtors and creditors are falling behind."[13] Part of the problem was that commercial banks did not actively open the books to new loans in Latin America. In the commercial bankers' perception, there was no need to throw good money after bad. And, while the international banks dallied, many Latin American governments balked at implementing draconian and politically unpopular cuts in spending and jobs.

While the Baker Plan took considerable heat for its "failure" to address the problems and overreliance on the magic of the marketplace for solutions, the International Monetary Fund and World Bank became important actors in the breaking drama. Teams of Fund and World Bank experts visited Latin American seeking to find a solution. The "cure" was usually a stabilization program, in which the balance of payments deficits would be brought under control through import compression and austerity in government spending. New funds were made available, but only if certain macroeconomic targets were made. This was referred to as "conditionality" under which Latin American governments promised to meet these targets in order to unlock new IMF and World Bank.

Conditionality soon became a dirty word in many nationalistic circles because dictating terms was regarded as demeaning. For both the far left and far right, it was another example of industrialized countries dominating the developing world. On the other hand, many industrialized-country leaders and international bankers felt that conditionality was the only way to encourage Latin countries to make the necessary reforms. The reforms would be beneficial in creating strong and more diversified economies in the Southern Hemisphere that would be capable of meeting their external obligations. However, the mere fact that conditionality was a form of dictating by one party to another left bad feelings and led to a certain amount of resistance on the part of Latin American leaders who did not want to become smeared as a toadies or puppets of the IMF and the industrialized nations. Although the democratic order was able to maintain its hold over the region's political systems, by the end of the decade, there was no shortage of politicians who offered simple solutions to complicated problems. Anti-IMF riots took place in Argentina, the Dominican Republic, Venezuela, and Brazil during the 1980s in protest of harsh conditions that many poor people felt were imposed upon them unfairly. Resentment toward the outside world developed and sizeable elements of the Latin American population grew estranged with a capitalist world order that appeared to have forgotten them except to squeeze them dry of their last pesos.

The slide into the debt crisis in the 1980s established new terms of creditworthiness for developing countries seeking credit. Clearly, countries such as Argentina, Brazil, Mexico, and the Philippines went through a lengthy period of economic restructuring and rehabilitation in the eyes of creditors. The inability of a number of nations to resolve the debt issue in the first round only reinforced the reputation of many Latin American countries as "dead-beat" debtors, incapable of living up to terms of any agreement. Yet, the process of regaining creditworthiness had begun. By the end of the decade the new creditworthiness entailed the following: the dismantling of the import substitution model and protectionist barriers and a move to more open economies and an emphasis on export-driven growth became part of the so-called Washington consensus. Foreign investment was made more welcome and the size of the state was to be downsized through privatizations and reductions in personnel. The running of the government was also to be conducted in a more cost-efficient basis, with an eye to reducing budget deficits and overall public sector red ink. These measures showed up in the early 1990s in improved budget balances to GDP, stronger economic growth, higher exports, a major inflow of foreign direct investment and a return to access to international credit markets as reflected by a substantial upswing in new bond issues from both sovereigns and corporations.

The shift to greater creditworthiness was also pushed along by political considerations on the part of the United States. In the mid- and late 1980s the outcome of the Cold War was still in question. Although Communist attempts to make inroads into the Western Hemisphere beyond Cuba had been blocked, the ongoing debt-related economic difficulties in the Americas and the Philippines was a growing concern, especially as most of these nations now had elected governments which were increasingly committed to market-oriented reforms. Consequently, the Bush administration in 1988 advanced the Brady Plan, named after then U.S. Treasury Secretary James Brady. This program provided a framework under which debtor countries and their commercial bank creditors could renegotiate a reduction in the debt burden. Usually, the creditors agreed to writing down the value of debt as well as the conversion of the commercial bank loans into tradable longer-term bonds, secured in part by U.S. Treasury zero coupon bonds. It is important to underscore that only those countries that had implemented substantial reforms and were deemed as increasingly creditworthy were permitted to negotiate a Brady Plan deal.

While the debt crisis of the 1980s rocked the U.S.-led credit system in one direction, the rise of other capitalist rivals offered a challenge from another direction. Both the economies of Europe and Japan made a substantial recovery from their wartime destruction and by the 1970s and 1980s their financial institutions became competitive with those from the United States. In fact, as we have already observed, Europe began to challenge U.S. dominance in the 1960s. In the 1980s, pressure came from Japan. Although the global credit system remained dominated by the United States as the major political and military power, hence the guarantor of the international rule of law, it was no longer the sole major provider of credit, with local European and Japanese institutions regaining control of their home markets and expanding overseas.

The shift from outright U.S. dominance in global credit was partially evident in the slippage of U.S. banks in terms of being in the top twenty in terms of assets. In 1974, the top three banks— BankAmerica Corp., Citicorp, and Chase Manhattan Corp.—were American, with two others rounding out the top twenty. By 1984, the top two were American, but total U.S. representation had fallen to three banks, while Japanese bank representation went from five to eight over the same period.

The rise of Japanese banks in the 1980s was perceived as a particularly difficult challenge for the U.S. credit community. During that decade it became painfully evident that the King of Credit had become a debtor nation and was dependent on Japanese and, to a lesser extent, European investors to finance a long string of budget deficits. Additionally, the Plaza and Smithsonian accords to devalue the dollar and appreciate the yen appeared to shift the loci of power in the credit universe to Tokyo. The shape of the Japanese "threat" was evident to many in the following statistics:

- By 1992, eight of the world's top ten banks, ranked by assets, were Japanese; Citibank was the world's twentieth.

- By 1989 Japanese banks held almost 11 percent of U.S. banking assets, up from 2.3 percent in 1974.

- By 1989 Japanese banks were providing 20 percent of all credit in California.

- Between 1981 and 1989 Japanese banks increased their share of the assets of the world's top 100 banks from 25 to 46 percent, while the share of U.S. banks declined from 15 percent to 6 percent.[14]

The undercurrent of alarm in U.S. financial circles about the rise of Japanese banks and finance houses was soon picked up as part of a longer and more tense debate over Japanese trade practices that were causing a large trade imbalance in Japan's favor, while putting U.S. companies out of business. Japan's new muscle as a creditor nation also raised concerns that they would soon be buying out U.S. institutions as they consolidated their grasp at the commanding heights of the credit universe. Japanese banks did, in fact, purchase U.S. banks, making the "threat" from Tokyo more tangible. The following paragraph by Daniel Burstein in 1988 captures U.S. apprehension and the links to the world of credit: "Hidden behind the glittering façade of the 'Roaring Eighties' in American business lies the reality that the United States has lost control over the central features of its own economy, thereby foreclosing many of the potential solutions to current dilemmas. Interest rates, the value of the dollar, the financing of U.S. government operations, the flow of imports and exports—none of these areas of fundamental importance to national well-being can be fully controlled any longer by American policymakers, even in those rare moments they can agree on policy."[15]

Although U.S. dominance was challenged by the Japanese in the 1980s, that threat receded drastically in the 1990s, which will be discussed in more detail in the next chapter. At this point though it is important to note that Japan's economic rise did not carry with it a political or military element. Japan was not going to ensure the rule of law around the planet, it was not going to emerge as the major force in challenging the Soviets, and it was not going to send troops to the Persian Gulf to defeat Iraq in 1991-92. Consequently, Japan's gambit at the heights of the global credit pecking order was a historically limited effort, created in part by a temporary weakness in the U.S. economy, the growing competitiveness of Japanese industry, and the yen's appreciation. One offshoot of this was the development of a bubble economy in Japan that was to burst in the early 1990s, making the ups and downs on the Tokyo stock exchange a point of concern for Washington's economic policymakers in the 1998-1999 period.

The shift to a single European market in 1992 and the movement to a single European currency within the borders of the fifteen-member European Union in the second half of the decade, clearly preserved the dominance of European financial institutions on their own turf. Large European banks, such as Deutsche Bank, Socieite Generale, Dresdner Bank, and Barclays Group managed to remain competitive throughout the 1970s and 1980s. In the 1990s, many of these European banks were actively competing with the U.S. and Japanese institutions in everything from international equities and bonds to derivatives and lending. As international credit markets became more complex and the number of products expanded, firms from the United Kingdom, Germany, the United States, France, Switzerland, Canada, and Japan began to encroach with greater frequency on each other's turf. By the end of the twentieth century, U.S. dominance remained at the core of the global credit system. However, being the lead credit power, responsible for maintaining the international flow of credit had serious problems. The Bretton Woods system based on such multilateral institutions as the IMF and World Bank—in some ways the guardians of international credit flows— was showing severe limitations by the 1990s, throwing into question how international credit flows would be managed in the early twenty-first century.

Notes

1. David P. Calleo, *Beyond American Hegemony: The Future of the Western Alliance* (New York: Basic Books, 1987), p. 84.
2. Jean-Jacques Servan-Schreiber, *The American Challenge* (London: Hamish Hamilton, 1968).
3. Roy C. Smith and Ingo Walter, *Global Banking* (New York: Oxford University Press, 1997), pp. 244-245.
4. E. Hobsbrawn, *Industry and Empire* (London: Penguin, 1972), p. 273.
5. Erik Banks, *The Rise and Fall of the Merchant Banks* (London: Kogan Page Ltd, 1999), p. 309.
6. Ibid., p. 310.
7. S. Hayes and P. Hubbard, *Investment Banking: A Tale of Three Cities* (Cambridge, MA: Hardvard University Press, 1990), p. 50.
8. Richard O'Brien, "Introduction—A Perspective on Debt," in Scott B. MacDonald, Margie Lindsay, and David L. Crum, eds., *The Global Debt Crisis: Forecasting for the Future* (London: Frances Pinter Publishers, 1990), p. 1.
9. Sebastian Edwards, *Crisis and Reform in Latin America: From Despair to Hope* (New York: Oxford University Press, 1995), p. 17.
10. See John Bresnan, *Managing Indonesia: The Modern Political Economy* (New York: Columbia University Press, 1993), pp. 164-193.
11. Turkey's debt service ratio increased from 14 percent in 1974 to 33 percent in 1977. Scott B. MacDonald, "Southern Europe," in MacDonald, Lindsay, and Crum, eds., *The Global Debt Crisis*, p. 143.
12. Edwards, *Crisis and Reform in Latin America*, p. 24.
13. Rudiger Dornbusch, "The Latin American Debt Problem: Anatomy and Solutions," in Barbara Stallings and Robert Kaufman, *Debt and Democracy in Latin America* (Boulder, CO: Westview Press, 1989), p. 7.
14. Data in this paragraph comes from Richard J. Barnet and John Cavanagh, *Global Dreams: Imperial Corporations and the New World Order* (New York: Touchstone Books, 1994), p. 405.
15. Daniel Burstein, *Yen! Japan's New Financial Empire and Its Threat to America* (New York: Simon & Schuster, 1988), p. 25.

13

Globalized Markets

The Western credit system has come to encompass the rest of the
world. In many cases credit systems existed prior to the advent of
Western traders, soldiers, and administration. Yet the introduction of
modern credit techniques and markets often came with the creation
of European overseas empires, some of which stretched from the
Atlantic into the Indian and Pacific oceans. Although the creation of
a global credit system dominated by the West has many positive
factors, the system is hardly without problems, as exemplified by
the Asian contagion in 1997-99, which spread beyond the confines of Southeast Asia and Korea to engulf Russia and Ukraine
and threaten Latin America. In particular, globalization represents a tidal wave of change, carried by technological advances,
with political and socioeconomic ramifications. The interrelationship between credit markets and politics was evident both in the
demise of Indonesia's President Suharto in 1998 and as a contributing factor in Boris Yeltsin's early retirement as Russia's president in
1999.

Global Embrace

By the late 1990s the global credit system was truly international,
reaching into almost every corner of the planet. It came in the form
of the World Bank, the International Monetary Fund, commercial
and investment banking, credit card companies, insurance firms, and
investors looking for better rates of return on their investments. It
also came in the shape of venture capital firms as they arrived at
ground zero of the Internet revolution in Asia and Latin America.
Although the credit systems of the past were transnational in nature,
especially since the British period of dominance, the scope was not

the same. Even within the 1990s change was massive. In 1990, net long-term resource flows to developing countries totaled $98.3 billion.[1] Official development finance amounted to 57.4 percent of that total, with foreign direct investment accounting for another 24 percent. Commercial bank loans represented only 4 percent of the total. By 1996, the year before the Asian crisis, the total flow of long-term funds soared to $282 billion, with private flows climbing to $247 billion or 24 percent of the total. Foreign direct investment leaped to $119 billion or 42 percent. The growing pool of institutionally managed funds invested outside of the United States expanded from only 5 percent of the $2 trillion available in 1980 to 20 percent of the $20 trillion available in 1995.[2] The purpose of these numbers is not to make one's eyes glaze over, but to demonstrate the massive nature of credit flowing out of the credit-surplus countries to credit-deficit countries.

Another reflection of the globalization of credit was the expansion of the global bond market in the late twentieth century. In 1970, the total amount of publicly issued bonds in all currencies was $785.2 billion, 65.6 percent of which was issued in North America (the U.S. and Canada), with 25.5 percent issued in Europe and the remaining amount in the rest of the world.[3] By 1998, that number had grown to a whopping $25.5 trillion, with North America accounting for 50.7 percent, with 33.1 percent for Europe, 15.4 percent for Asia, and a little under 1 percent for Oceania and Africa.

A number of developments explain the explosive nature of globalization of credit: substantial changes in technologies for collecting, processing, and disseminating information; the liberalization of financial markets in Asia, Latin America, and Eastern Europe; and substantially increased pools of retirement savings.[4] The combination of these developments helped stimulate greater financial innovation and established a multi-trillion dollar pool of internationally mobile capital. If someone needed credit, it existed.

Two other interrelated factors must be considered—the global banking industry underwent a massive consolidation during the 1980s and 1990s and the role of nonbank financial institutions grew. All of this meant greater competition for profits. Many of the nonbank financial institutions, such as mutual and hedge funds, were lured to the international financial arena by prospects of greater returns on their investments. A World Bank study noted that the above-mentioned trends "accelerated in the 1990s, expanding investment opportunities for savers and offering borrowers a wide array of sources of capital."[5]

The same study also noted that since 1993 the amount of outstanding international debt issued by all companies around the planet rose by 75 percent, reaching $3.5 trillion in early 1998. Although firms headquartered in industrial nations issued most of this debt, companies in developing countries such as Brazil, Mexico, Malaysia, and Thailand also began to tap global credit markets.

The massive surge of credit availability was highly attractive for both participants in the credit-supply and credit-deficit countries. Simply stated, those with too much credit needed to make it available in such a fashion that those without it could make use of it yet provide a return on that investment. For those on the credit-deficit side of the equation there was and remains a critical need of capital to improve hard infrastructure such as roads, railroads, and harbors, and soft infrastructure, such as education, environment, and public health. Although there has been a tendency by some to paint the globalized credit market as the instrument of greedy U.S. capitalist fat cats (many of whom are portrayed as retired and living in Florida), the push for liberalization of capital flows that was undertaken in the 1990s was done by local governments, most of them democratically elected. It was clearly understood in Mexico City, Brasilia, and Seoul that in the global game of economic competition, access to credit—if properly applied—helped augment one's ability to compete, hence improve the living standards of the overall population. Certainly in Asia, people now live longer and live better than ever before, despite the 1997-98 crisis. To say that all of this was pushed by large corporations, who pulled the strings of the World Bank and IMF, misses the fundamental point that development is a two-way street. While the globalization of credit markets has offered much to human civilization, there are also risks.

The Asian Challenge

In 1997 the idea that the twenty-first century was Asia's collided with the grim reality of massive currency devaluations, steep and wrenching contractions in economies, a revolution in Indonesia, and a near meltdown of the financial systems in Thailand and Korea. Even Japan, the world class economy once perceived to be a force capable of buying out America threatened to wobble out of control because of a weak financial system and a plunging currency. Out went books like Jim Rohwer's *Asia Rising* and Ezra Vogel's *Japan as Number One* and in came books like Callum Hendrickson's *Asia Falling* and Victor Mallet's *The Trouble with Tigers: The Rise and Fall of South-East Asia*. Asian aspirations of the dynamic East assuming the leadership of the global economy from a decaying West were nowhere better served than in Malaysia.

On June 30, 1998, amid considerable fanfare, the Malaysian government opened for its first full day of flights, at what was touted as the world's biggest and most modern airport, the Kuala Lumpur International Airport. Malaysia, after all, under the leadership of the pugnacious Prime Minister Mohammed Mahathir had sought to build the world's tallest building, the world's largest building, a high tech corridor, and one of Asia's biggest dams.

The airport's opening was not a raging success. Baggage and check-in computers stopped working. Overhead monitors went dead. Escalators ground to a halt. Hundreds of increasingly grumpy passengers were forced to wait up to four hours, sometimes in the dark, for their bags. Searching for airport officials was fruitless. Opening day for the $2.3 billion airport was frustrating for passengers and an embarrassment to the Malaysian government. Yet for much of Asia 1997 and 1998 were years of just that—frustration and embarrassment. Before 1997 an ocean of credit had flowed into the region spanning India and Pakistan in the west and Korea and Japan in the east. Throughout the 1980s and into the mid-1990s the region's growth was dynamic, the upswings in the standard of living impressive and hopeful, and the new economic power thought-provoking in terms of how such developments shaped the post-Cold War international political system.

While a new sea of ink has flowed explaining Asia's economic rise and fall in the late twentieth century, one word provides a broad gauged answer—credit.[6] Asia had for a long time lots of credit, in retrospect too much. Rapid growth, impressive government programs, praise from multilateral lending organizations, and the need to generate new business on the part of international banks and investment firms made Asia look, feel and touch creditworthy. A critical lacuna, however, was the lack of transparency and disclosure that obscured weakly regulated financial systems through which flowed a massive wave of global liquidity. Behind the glitz of new glossy skyscrapers towering over the grimy, bustling streets of Bangkok, Shanghai, and Jakarta was another story of hidden debts, cronyism, and power. This opaque way of doing business in much of Asia provided secrecy for the rich and powerful to move credit in and out of one country and into another. At the same time, the opaque nature of the Asian credit game meant that governments, multilateral lending banks, rating agencies, and other foreign creditors lost track of how much debt was actually incurred. Additionally, too much credit was available. Annual growth of loans in the 1990-96 period was 20 percent in Indonesia, 17 percent in Korea, and 24 percent in Thailand, compared to 9 percent in Germany, 2 percent in Japan, and 6 percent in the United States.[7] These blistering rates of loan growth were reflected in an increase in domestic debt, which in Indonesia shot up from 45 percent in 1990 to 55 percent in 1996, 68 percent from 79 percent in Korea, and 84 percent to 130 percent in Thailand. When Thailand devalued the baht in July 1997, and much of Asia soon followed, the amount of dollar-denominated debt soared and what was soon revealed as a financial house of cards came tumbling down.

Asia's Past Defining Its Future

Asia traditionally did not fit neatly into the Western credit system. With the advent of European imperial expansion, nations such as India, China, Thailand, and Japan were gradually became a part of the Western credit system. However, that process was largely through the establishment of European banks in various Asian locations, not necessarily a helping hand for the development of local credit institutions. Even in Japan, Western banks played a dominant role in trade finance during the early years of the Meiji Restoration that occurred in 1868. Asian banking, through the end of colonialism, assumed many of the trappings of Anglo-American credit culture, including a penchant for secrecy.

As the West developed what was to become the modern global credit system, Asia was not without its own methods of credit. China, for example, was the home to some of humankind's earliest civilizations and it was there that printing, papermaking, and paper money were probably first invented. Beginning in either the first or second century A.D., paper money was supposed to have been made from the bark of the mulberry tree. In time came the knowledge for making paper and by the Tang dynasty (A.D. 618-907) paper money was decidedly in use.

It is important to underscore that whereas credit and the idea of market forces helped shape Western development, China's development was shaped by a powerful state buttressed by an all-pervasive bureaucracy and a strong military. Additionally, the Confucian cultural and political system rewarded only the learned and studious, not necessarily the entrepreneurial or those seeking to develop major technological inventions. With commerce usually controlled by state forces rather than market forces, gold and silver coins rarely had any role.[8] Consequently, the state issued tokens, which functioned as cash. As these tokens were often made of brass or copper they were heavy to carry, which helped the turn to paper money. The political-economic significance of this was noted by Weatherford: "The invention and dissemination of paper money in China marked a major step forward in government control of the money supply, a development that could have occurred only in a great empire with a ruler powerful enough to impose the will of the state on the economy—even to the point of executing those citizens who dared to oppose its monetary policy."[9]

The use of paper money continued until the Ming dynasty (1368-1644). According to Chinese historian Lien-Chêng Yang this system allowed the government a monopoly over gold and silver: paper flowed from the capital to the provinces and precious metal flowed from the provinces to the capital.[10] Paper money and the rudimentary credit system that went hand in hand with it, functioned as part of the tribute system and stifled the development of healthy commerce.[11] One significant offshoot was that it helped drive out of China many of its more entrepreneurial citizens into other parts of Asia, where they soon demonstrated a keen acumen for commerce. Even in Ch'ing China the most powerful control over the economy was exerted by the state, through the bureaucracy. As Ping-Ti Ho noted, "Even in the late Ch'ing and early Republican periods the few new industrial enterprises launched by the Chinese were almost invariably financed by bureaucratic capitalists."[12] Consequently, China's credit system was to remain relatively rudimentary as a key component in developing business until the advent of Western banks. Even today, China's banking system remains problematic: although in the process of reform in the late 1990s, the legacy of credit, through financial intermediaries like banks, continues to be weak.

The development of modern Japanese banks was more akin to the West and began in the 1860s. Prior to that period, Japan had long been closed to the outside world. After the battle of Sekigahara in 1600, the Tokugawa Shogunate dominated Japan. The Tokugawa system was a type of centralized feudalism that sought to preserve the nominal self-government of feudal lords while, in fact, reducing them to a satellite existence. Under this system the population was divided into four classes: samurai, peasants, artisans, and merchants. Each class had its own proper, well-defined role. Peasants as well as samurai were prohibited from involvement in trade, which became the exclusive reserve of the artisans and merchants. The four-class system was highly rigid and was to last in one form or another until the 1860s. Needless to say, the Tokugawa system was not highly conducive to developing a modern system of credit. An added detriment was that the first Tokugawa Shogun, Ieyasu, adopted and maintained a policy of national seclusion to exclude any disturbing influences from the outside.

Japan during the Tokugawa era was generally an agricultural economy, with pockets of semi-industrial development. The central government was largely financed from the income of the Tokugawa House domain, which came from a rice tax. Additionally, the Tokugawa owned all the mines, issued coin money, and directly controlled the large cities of Kyoto, Osaka, Sakai, and Nagasaki. Yet, Tokugawa shogunate's main contribution was the universal peace that the first shogun's force of arms established and his successors enforced.[13] That peace allowed the transformation of the samurai into a huge bureaucracy in charge of administering the various feudal domains. Hence, the Tokugawa system evolved an efficient administration due to the pressures of rising costs of government and the maintenance of a sizable army of samurai. All of this contributed to the development of an honest, duty-conscious officialdom without which the Meiji's modernization effort would have been more problematic.[14]

The Japanese economy was not static under the Tokugawa shogunate. Trade developed in the country with the merchants of Osaka, Edo, and Kyoto. Rice cotton, oil, iron, tatami surfaces, pottery, paint, tea, and other goods were traded. For over a century, Japan was to prosper, helping to raise the lowly *shonin*, the merchants. Although merchants were the low men on the societal totem pole, many of them were to emerge richer and more powerful than the samurai. Names such as Mitsui emerged during this period.[15] The real development of a modern credit system had to wait until the end of Tokugawa shogunate, which occurred with the Meiji Restoration in 1868. The group of nationalistic modernizers that ended the inward-looking Tokugawa regime understood early in the game the necessity of financial institutions that would serve industrial growth. Indeed, it has been suggested that the Tokugawa shoguns were never quite able to deal with the money economy that was emerging and superseding the feudal economy of rice subsidies upon which the shogunate's economy relied.[16] While they looked to the U.S. and British banking models for inspiration and foreign banks opened up operations in the country as early as 1863, what evolved in Japan bore a distinctly Japanese imprint.[17]

The Japanese government entered the financial business through the creation of the postal savings system, which was followed by the foundation of a number of special banks. These institutions were assigned a particular area of business as per government needs. In the early Meiji period, the government under the guidance of Finance Minister Matsukata Masayoshi was concerned that Japan should have a financial system capable of funding foreign trade and modern enterprise.[18] The Bank of Japan, the central bank, was his creation. Established in 1882, much of the inspiration for the central bank came from Belgium's central bank. Designed to regulate the banking system and the national economy, the Belgian model was attractive because it was a new institution and reflected the many changes that had occurred in finance in the mid-1800s. As the Belgian central bank was partially influenced by the French central bank and there was a pressing need in the European country to centralize control over the monetary system, Japan's central bank fit what was to be more of a dirigiste approach. This was especially the case as the postal savings system averaged about 20 percent of all banking assets in the private sector, hence giving the government a free hand to support, through loans, specific projects deemed in the national interest.[19]

A number of special banks were created to compliment the Bank of Japan. These included the Yokohama Specie Bank (founded as a commercial bank in 1880), which served the needs of foreign trade; the Japan Hypothec Bank (Kangyō Ginkō) created in 1897, and the Japan Industrial Bank (Kōgyō Ginkō) in 1902. The latter two banks were designed along the lines of the French Bank, Credit Mobilier, having the privilege of issuing long-term bonds up to ten times their capital and supplied long-term credits to industry.

Japan's special banks were complemented by the Banks of Agriculture and Industry (Nōkō Ginkō), and the special colonial banks.

The Nōkō Ginkō system provided a bank for each of the forty-six perfect uses. They were later amalgamated with branch offices of the Hypothec Bank. The special colonial banks were the Bank of Taiwan and the Bank of Korea, both reflecting Japan's overseas expansion in the aftermath of the Sino-Japanese War of 1898 and the Russo-Japanese War of 1904-05. Together with the Industrial Bank, these banks were the instruments of colonial expansion.

The Meiji reformers' early moves to gain mastery over the national credit system stemmed from a keen desire to maintain national independence in an age of European dominance. Unlike many countries, like Egypt, the Ottoman Empire, and much of Latin America, Japan did not fall into a debt trap that eroded its sovereignty. Japan's long isolation during the Tokugawa era left the country relatively inward-looking and in need of catching up in terms of technological development. Yct farming and commerce in the Tokugawa period led to an accumulation of capital in private hands, which proved sufficient to fund the first stages of growth, once the government had provided an infrastructure and established a system by which to channel investment in appropriate directions.[20] Consequently, Japan did not require heavy capital inputs from overseas and had not acquired considerable debt before the Russo-Japanese War of 1904-05.

Although the large state banks were major players in the credit system, the private sector was not inconsequential. Three types of credit institutions were to emerge: the insurance companies, the instrumental banks, and commercial and savings banks. It is important to underscore that even in the private sector, the purveyors of credit were involved in the promotion of industrial development, much more than commerce. Considering Japan's precarious position in the late nineteenth century as a newly industrializing Asian nation on a planet of powerful European powers and the United States, industrial development was regarded as essential to national security. The government consequently had few qualms about channeling credit to target sectors. This also meant that bankers actively engaged in several different ways to foster industry and help in the establishment of new enterprises. One offshoot of this as noted by one Japanese economist was that "the officials of banks became themselves directors of industrial enterprises, or company presidents or advisers, and in order to make their money circulate more effectively, they themselves became industrialists."[21] Hence, in Japan the relationship between credit and business was blurred at an early stage.

Japanese bankers faced a major problem in the development of credit. By law the commercial banks were not allowed to make long-term loans for industrial investments. Consequently, Japanese bankers embarked upon a path of least resistance. Operating in a world not driven by transparency and disclosure, but a well-crafted opaqueness, lender and borrower collided to overcome regulatory hurdles. Borrowers often resorted to the expediency of borrowing short term and kept renewing their loans as constantly revolving capital loans. Inove Junnosluke, later the governor of the Bank of Japan observed in 1912: "When managers are seeking funds for capital investments they approach banks with false documents of commercial transactions making them believe that they need only short term credits."

Another offshoot of the prohibition for commercial banks making long-term loans was that a number of businesses created their own banks, hence the establishment of the *zaibatsu* system. Out of relatively humble beginnings, the Big Five—Mitsui, Mitsubishi, Yasuda, Sumitomo, and Dai Ichi—were to emerge in the second half of the nineteenth century as dominant players. Of these, Mitsui was the oldest having been established in the seventeenth century and engaged in domestic retailing and financing. During the Meiji period Mitsui was reorganized by a group of able ex-samurai, who added a general overseas trading company and a bank in 1876. Mitsui also branched out into coal mining, textiles, paper manufacture, sugar refining, and shipping. By the 1920s, Mitsui's business extended its operations into 120 separate concerns, either directly owned and managed, or controlled through stockholding and the appointment of directors.

The second largest *zaibatsu* was Mitsubishi. This combine began with shipping interests and over time added foreign trade, mining, shipbuilding, and a variety of other investment in heavy industries. In the period before the World War II, Mitsubishi's industrial empire stretched to encompass aircraft and automobiles. And, of course, Mitsubishi needing an ever steady flow of credit created its own bank in 1880.

The rise of the zaibatsu in pre-World War II Japan was a critical factor in the shaping of the country's credit culture. Japanese banks and industries had many similar characteristics to their Western kin, especially the French. The close relationships between national objectives and where credit was allocated was apparent. At the same time, the close interrelationship between big business and its creditors was similar to certain European cases. For example, the Warburgs as bankers to German big business were well represented on many industrial boards. In Japan, the relationship was even closer, especially as the banks were part of the zaibatsu. The zaibatsu, as vertically and horizontally integrated combines, wielded considerable power over the capital of the nation. Not only did the zaibatsu hold sway over the commanding heights of the economy, by 1930 it is estimated that Mitsui, Mitsubishi, Sumitomo, and Yasuda banks held 27 percent of the bonds issued by non-Zaibatsu firms.[22]

The dominance of the zaibatsu system in Japan lasted until the Second World War. The major industrialists and their banks were actively involved in the expansion of Japan's overseas empire and took full advantage of the creating of colonies in Taiwan and Korea. During the Second World War credit operations were geared for the war against the Allies. In 1945 Japan surrendered and was occupied by the United States. Initially the U.S. occupation authorities were keen to dismantle the zaibatsu system and replace it with a more open and competitive system, more akin to the United States. However, Cold War politics were to impinge on the dismantling of Japan's zaibatsus. Although the formal structure of the zaibatsu system was dismantled by the U.S. occupation, the old pattern of relationships, especially between major industrial houses and the banks, was to remain largely intact. Additionally, many of the individuals involved in leading the economy before and during the war remained in place, having considerable clout in shaping postwar Japan.

The postwar political economy that took shape in Japan was defined by the eventual emergence of the conservative Liberal Democratic Party (LDP) in 1955, which soon became the cornerstone of political stability. Japan in the late 1940s and early 1950s was marked by a gradual move back to elective government, a jockeying for dominance by newly created political parties, including the Socialists, and efforts to reconstruct the economy. The advent of the Cold War, manifested by the victory of the communists in China's civil war (1948-49) and the Korean War (1950-53), made securing Japan as an ally important to the United States. This meant diluting the anti-zaibatsu reform effort as well as being more supportive of the conservative wing of Japanese politics. Considering that the Socialists won the first postwar election, it became critical to have a strong enough conservative party to curtail the power and influence of the Socialists as well as the Japanese Communist Party. Many of the well-intentioned democratic reforms were jettisoned by the Occupation authorities and, in some cases, reversed.

The LDP developed close ties to the bureaucracy and big business, which gave birth to a system of well-entrenched patronage. LDP legislators would seek public works for their districts, something that for a long time appealed to the electorate. At the same time the bureaucrats helped the politicians, they received in return cash or support for a political career once they were retired at fifty-five years of age. The LDP being conservative and pro-business hustled to receive donations from the corporate sector, in particular from construction companies that benefited from the ongoing cycle of new public works programs.

Japan's postwar political economy was constructed around the *keiretsu* system of interlocking relationships between companies and financial institutions. As Declan Hayes noted, "Keiretsu, kigyo shudan, or kigyo group are interchangeable terms to mean both horizontally connected groups and vertically connected groups in Japan. The Keiretsu were the postwar reincarnation of the prewar *zaibatsu*, whose slogan Sangyo Hokoku (Promote Industry to Save the Country), lived on, in spirit, if not in name through them."[23] In this system, the banks (often led by main banks, usually the largest and most-connected citibanks) played a central role. Their primary function was to allocate scarce credit resources and help pull the Japanese economy behind it, in a convoy-like fashion. It is important to clarify that while the Japanese economy was capitalist, it was not laissez-faire—the approach was neo-mercantilist, aiming at the maximizing of Japan's profitability at the expense of others. This model was to be adopted widely in the rest of East and Southeast Asia.

While Japan's political system has been likened to New York City's Tammany Hall or Huey Long's apparatus in Louisiana, the LDP political machine did manage economic policy with considerable consensus and efficiency.[24] Japan enjoyed a strong economic boom in the 1960s and despite a temporary downturn in 1973-74 because of the oil shock, growth was relatively strong through the rest of the decade. In fact, Japan's average real GDP growth in the 1970-80 period was 4.4 percent, the fastest of the major seven industrial countries. Over the 1980-90 period, the pace slackened marginally to 4

percent, but still remained at a faster pace than the other G7 economies. Japan's economic clout was reinforced by the depreciation of
the U.S. dollar and appreciation of the yen in the 1980s. With the
mighty yen Japan could now afford to invest around the world, which
it did. Japanese credit quickly emerged as a major force in helping
the United States pay for its recurrent fiscal deficits. At the same
time, the heady prospects of being a global economic superpower
were felt at home as considerable speculation went into the Tokyo
Stock Exchange and property markets. By the late 1980s Japan was
living with a bubble economy.

The post-war Japanese economic miracle began to slow in the
late 1980s, but the real problems came with the collapse of real-
estate prices in 1990, followed by a slow and steady decline in stocks.
The nub of the problem was the mountain of bad debt that had been
accumulated throughout the 1980s. As Japanese banks had expanded
into global giants, they accrued massive new assets—often with only
a cursory glance at creditworthiness. Greater credence was given to
relationships rather than creditworthiness. As credit flowed out of
the banks and into the corporate world and eventually into the high-
flying stock market, the seeds of the crisis were sown. As Richard
Katz noted, "If the stock market ever fell—or even stopped rising—
the boom would end. Japan's companies would be forced to repay
all their loans in real money, not paper shares. They would be bur-
dened with a mountain of debt that could threaten both them and
their banks."[25] Real GDP growth slid from 5.1 percent in 1990 to
3.8 percent in 1991 and finally to 1 percent in 1992. Japan's good
times were over. More importantly, this was not just the garden-vari-
ety recession, it was as Katz noted, "a downshifting of the whole
economic trajectory compounded by a financial crisis."[26] Although
the yen remained high and exports like autos and electronics continued to carry weight in international markets, the domestic economy
ground to a halt, growing an average of 1 percent a year between
1992 and 1997.

The problem blocking Japan's recovery was that the banks and
the government were slow to face the scope of the problem. Japan's
commercial banks did not cut off their borrowers in real-estate companies, and government regulators refused to close insolvent banks.
In many regards the issue was political: for the necessary legislation
to pass, the ruling LDP had to enact new bank legislation or allow
the authorities to be more empowered in enforcement of existing

rules and regulations. Yet, by forcing the banks to take a tougher stance against troubled debtors, a number of companies, in particular in the construction, retail and agrarian sectors, would be forced to declare bankruptcy. Considering that many of the same companies as well as a number of the large banks were major donors to the LDP election campaigns, the resolution of Japan's banking crisis was postponed by LDP legislators. Furthermore, the money system that had become dominant in Japanese politics through the 1960s to the 1980s also permeated much of the opposition. Consequently, it was difficult for the government to deal with the problem even though the LDP was ousted from power for the first time in 1993 by a weak coalition of opposition parties.

Japan's financial sector remained troubled and the massive bad debt problem festered throughout the 1990s. Economic growth, though meager, was fueled by rising public sector debt and helped stave off any major collapse. When the rest of Asia was hit by the so-called Asian Contagion in 1997, Japan's bad debt problem worsened considerably, plunging the country into one of its deepest economic crises in the post-war era. This situation caused Moody's Investor Service to downgrade Japan's vaunted Aaa standing to Aa1, a blow to the prestige of the country as well as a reflection on the deterioration of the country's creditworthiness. Clearly, too much credit in the 1980s followed by denial of a burst bubble in the early 1990s was exacerbated by public spending in the mid-1990s, which ultimately led to a severe credit crunch late in the decade. The process of economic restructuring belatedly begun in the late 1990s continued into the 2000s. Indeed, Japan has set itself down the road to what could be sweeping changes with its Big Bang financial deregulation by 2002. Although the Big Bang should be successful, considerable forces remain opposed, which could hinder a return to a more economically viable Japan.[27]

A growing point of concern is the growth of public sector debt to close to 120 percent in 2000, with projections of even greater debt for 2001 and 2002. Although Japan's economic crisis developed apart from the problems in the rest of Asia in 1997-98, the weak performance of Asia's largest economy was a major worry to policymakers throughout Southeast Asia, East Asia, and the United States. It was feared that Japan would fall into a depression, which would be catastrophic for the rest of Asia. Fortunately, the Obuchi government, which came into office in 1998, was able to stave off another substantial economic downturn. Though Prime Minister Keizo Obuchi had been described as having all the charisma of "cold pizza," he presided over an extensive round of structural reforms that began to restructure the banking system, stimulate small and medium-term businesses, and provide a better environment for the establishment of Internet businesses. Yet even in 2000 considerable problems remained, especially as Japanese banks remained reluctant to extend credit to customers beyond the large corporations.

For Japan, one of the critical tests for the country's future direction came in July 2000 with the problems surrounding the Sogo department store chain.[28] Sogo had opened its doors in 1830 and had developed into a nationwide chain. During the bubble economy years it had wracked up a considerable debt, which it was unable to reduce during the slow-growth 1990s. By 2000, it had around $17 billion in debt and was threatening to fail. The company's management was seeking to restructure the company and needed a break on their debt. In this, they appealed to their main banks, which included Shinsei Bank. Shinsei Bank itself was newly re-emerged. As Long-Term Credit Bank, Shinsei had failed and was bought out by a U.S. firm, Ripplewood, in 1998. As part of the agreement to purchase Long-Term Credit Bank, the Japanese government promised to buy portions of the old bank's loans at book value if they declined in value by more than 20 percent within three years. Accordingly, the bank sold its Sogo debt to the government.

What complicated matters was that Sogo requested seventy-three of its 151 credit institutions to forgive its debt. Consequently, when Shinsei sold its debt to its debt to the government, the government initially opted to forgive Sogo of its debt. In essence, this meant that the government was willing to use taxpayers dollars to bail out a department store. Considering that Japan's public sector debt had already climbed over 100 percent of GDP, giving the Asian country one of the highest levels of public sector debt in the industrialized group of nations, the decision to bail out Sogo created a massive public uproar. Members of the ruling LDP party and the opposition parties were also critical as were the major rating agencies, Moody's and Standard & Poor's. Sogo was forced to declare bankruptcy.

Although the pace of change in Japan has been slow in regard to economic reform and in particular in the credit system, change is gradually taking place. A flood of foreign companies, such Ripplewood, GE Capital, and Vanguard (one of the world's largest mutual fund companies) have entered the Japanese market and are forcing local firms to compete. To compete Japanese firms must introduce changes, which means the adaptation of Western ideas about credit, the management of companies and the development of more flexible systems capable of dealing with globalized credit markets.

The Asian Contagion

Although the Asian contagion appeared to sweep in from nowhere like an angry cyclone leaving much of Asia in financial and economic ruins, the root causes for this humbling existed prior to 1997. Although many reasons exist for the Asian financial crash, the underpinning weakness in the credit system was a major contributor. In particular, Asian banks and finance companies generally operated in environments that lacked strong regulatory authorities and promoted opaque business transactions. Internal credit controls were often weak and lending practices were guided by political expediency as opposed to sound business practices.

On top of this, Asia's strong levels of economic growth left many within the region as well as foreign investors with a sense that all was well. After all, there was considerable discussion about the Asian economic miracle. Thailand's average annual real GDP growth was 7.6 percent in the 1980-90 period, followed by an even faster 8.4 percent spurt in the 1990-95 period.[29] Indonesia, the largest nation is Southeast Asia, moved along at 6.1 percent and 7.6 over the same periods. The most dynamic economic expansion, however, came out of Korea and China, with the former roaring along at 9.4 percent and 7.2 percent and the latter an even more impressive 10.2 percent and 12.8 percent. Considering these fast rates of economic expansion in comparison to the much slower pace of growth in North America and Europe, it was difficult to make the case that Asia was on the wrong track and that the foundations of the miracles in East and Southeast Asia were weak.

Thailand became the first Asian tiger to have substantial problems. An ongoing stream of credit had flowed into the country since the 1980s, constantly threatening to overheat the economy. In the process, property prices spiraled upwards, construction companies boomed, and both the country's banks and finance companies lent a considerable amount of money into the sector. At the same time, there was a considerable amount of speculation in the Bangkok Stock Exchange, much of it fueled by finance companies borrowing from banks. Complicating matters was that the Thai currency, the baht, had been closely linked to the U.S. dollar in the early 1990s. As the dollar appreciated in value in the mid-1990s, the Thais did not delink their currency with the U.S. currency, hence gradually losing a degree of competitiveness in their exports which started to become evident in 1996 and much more pronounced in early 1997. The property bubble burst in late 1996 and fallout in terms of troubled finance companies and banks mounted thereafter. International currency speculators were drawn to Thailand, believing that the Southeast Asian nation's currency was overvalued, which was partially reflected by three years of large and widening current account balance of payments deficits. As the currency came under attack, the Thai central bank almost depleted the country's foreign exchange reserves, which stood at $37 billion at the end of 1996. By July 1997, the Thai central bank threw in the towel, stopped defending the baht and devalued. The ensuing economic chaos that engulfed Thailand ultimately caused the government to fall, the closure of the majority of finance companies, and the government takeover of a number of insolvent banks. Thailand was forced to turn to the IMF for assistance, a humiliating turn of events dictated by the very real threat of sovereign debt defaults.

The problem with the Thai devaluation was that the negative turn of events was not limited to that country's borders. Like a contagious disease, the problem spread throughout the neighborhood, engulfing Indonesia and battering Malaysia, Singapore, the Philippines and Hong Kong. By late in 1997, it spread to Korea. Korea, which had recently become the second Asian nation after Japan to gain membership in the Organization for Economic Cooperation and Development, often regarded as the industrialized club of nations, was regarded as a much more economically developed economy than those in Southeast Asia. However, Korea's credit foundations were to prove equally ill founded.

At the close of the Korean War (1950-1953), the Republic of Korea was devastated. The capital, Seoul, had been a battlefield more than once and it was little more than ruins when the firing stopped. Hunger and starvation existed and a weak central government faced a tough foe in the north, while presiding over an economy that was on a par with some of the poorest nations in Africa. By the late 1990s, South Korea had emerged as the eleventh largest economy on the planet, an industrial workshop producing everything from automobiles and ships to electronic components. Yet, not all was well in Korea. In late 1997, the Asian contagion caught up with the Land of Morning Calm. As *The Economist* observed, "Few countries have grown so rich so fast. Nor have many experienced such an abrupt humiliation. After weeks of denial, the government of South Korea, the largest Asian tiger, said on November twenty-first that it would after all need the IMF's billions to set its finance in order."[30] What went wrong?

The root causes of Korea's 1997-98 economic crisis go back almost half a century and involve credit. After the Korean War, South Korea was a wrecked nation, with little prospects for the future. However, from the early 1960s, a mixture of hard work, rigorous education, state-enforced austerity and imported technology caused a substantial transformation in the nation. Korea's leadership clearly understood the importance of economic development as the most effective means of combating the influence and strength of North Korea, both on the peninsula as well as in the developing world.[31] Under Park Chung-hee, who ruled with an iron fist from 1961 to1979, the banking sector was nationalized, almost all officers in the banks were appointed by the government, and lending was made to government-guided strategic sectors. The state controlled access to credit. In this regard, credit was power, though its allocation was not always efficient.

The relationship between the government, the banks, and the local industrial conglomerates known as *chaebols* was close. Although the chaebols were largely privately owned, they depended on credit from the government-controlled banks, which, in turn, gave the government technocrats whip hand in directing to which sectors Korean companies went. This state-bank-chaebol combination has been called Korea, Inc. The result of Korea, Inc. was as one observer noted, "A nation of muddy subsistence farmers was transformed, in a single generation, into the world's largest producer of ships and memory chips, its fifth-largest car maker and its eleventh-largest economy."[32] Added to this, life for the average Korean improved considerably, with life expectancy soaring from forty-seven years in 1955 to seventy-one years in 1997.

While Korea's rapid expansion was amazing in many regards, the foundations were built on clay. In particular, the system of credit allocation proved to be a critical lacuna as the economy matured. Korea as a developing economy benefited from government direction, which was usually pragmatic. However, in the 1990s, the system slowly eroded. The political system became more open and democratic, diluting some of the power of the bureaucrats. At the same time, the chaebols also gained power at the expense of the civil servants. In 1997, the top four chaebols (Hyundai, Daewoo, LG, and Samsung) accounted for over half of the country's exports. As the Korean economy became an international player, the global range of operations provided new opportunities and risks for Korean business managers. Many chaebols expanded into areas in which they had little experience. With more influence than before, not controlled by the government as much, and rapidly expanding into new businesses, the Korean business sector was heading for problems.

An additional part of the looming crisis was the traditional system of government-guided lending on the part of the banks. Simply stated, most Korean banks by the 1990s still lacked any prudent credit culture that could discern between good and bad credits. Although slowly changing, political considerations still overrode credit concerns and bad loans were made to many of the chaebols that were expanding into areas where they lacked expertise. Profits were not always a consideration for Korean companies. However, when the domestic economy slumped in 1996 and 1997, many of the highly indebted companies were unable to meet their debt repayments. This, of course, rippled back into the banking system. In 1997, more than 15,000 Korean companies filed for bankruptcy protection, including five major chaebols, such as Hanbo Steel, Jinro, Kia Motors, and Sammi.[33]

By November 1997, Korea's currency, the won, came under severe attack. The Korean central bank's defense of the won was short-lived, but greatly reduced usable foreign exchange reserves to under $10 billion. Like Thailand before it, Korea was forced to turn to the IMF for help. By late December, the IMF-led rescue package was $60 billion, the largest ever mounted.

Unfortunately, the Asian contagion did not stop with Thailand and Korea, but also hit Indonesia in October 1998. After some initial success in resisting the crisis, Indonesia was also forced to go to the IMF, but the package failed to stabilize the situation because of the political situation. The Suharto regime, in power since 1965, had in the mid-1990s clamped down politically, leaving no avenues for the venting of popular discontent over such issues as corruption, socioeconomic imbalances, and the blatant greed exhibited by President Suharto's family and close cronies. This was to leave the pot of public discontent simmering beneath the surface, waiting for a crisis to boil over.

In May 1998, the Suharto regime sought to phase out food and fuel subsidies to appease the IMF's demands. On one side, Indonesia's international creditors were pressing the Suharto regime to cut costs and make politically painful adjustments. One the other side, the implementation of IMF measures broadened the ranks of the disenchanted. Higher fuel prices translated into more expensive bus fare for workers already squeezed by the economic downturn. The removal of food subsidies meant more expensive daily staples, including food and cooking oil. The action resulted in a massive outburst of public discontent, which gave way to a move-ment to oust President Suharto. Although the Indonesian leader fought hard to remain in control, on May 21, 1998, Suharto resigned and his vice president, B.J. Habibe, became only the third individual to assume the presidency. Indonesia's economy, however, contin-ued to slide, with real GDP contracting by over 20 percent for the year.

Hong Kong was not immune from the Asian contagion as it hit property and stock markets, plunging the economy into its first steep recession in years. Although China, Taiwan, Singapore, and India weathered the storm relatively well, the problem came back to Ja-pan in the form of bad loans and securities losses. Japanese cross-border exposure in Asia at year-end 1997 was $114.7 billion, with the largest exposures in order of significance being Thailand, Indo-nesia, and Korea.[34] The threat of losses incurred in the international lending side of the business did little to ensure Japanese lenders that new loans should be made at home. After all, the Japanese economy's performance was anemic in 1997 and heading into a recession in 1998. By mid-1998, Japan was in a severe credit crunch, unem-ployment was reaching record postwar numbers, corporate bank-ruptcies were on the rise, and the IMF forecast a 2.5 percent contrac-tion in the economy for the year. While the Asian contagion poked a sharp stick into the soft underbelly of Japanese finance, falling Asian demand for imports reduced global trade with a severe impact on the already-shaky Japanese economy.

While the Japanese banking system spurted in 1998, hit by a com-bination of longstanding domestic economic problems and the ill-effects of the Asian contagion, the storm rapidly spread around the planet into Eastern Europe, Turkey, and Latin America. However, the Russian crash of 1998 was probably the most dramatic event, considering the geo-political repercussions of the economic collapse.

It is important to underscore that the Asian contagion spread beyond the region because of two reasons. The collapse in Asian economic activity led to a sharp drop in commodity prices, hurting a broad range of commodity dependent countries, including Russia, Saudi Arabia, and much of Latin America, as well as Australia, Canada, and New Zealand. Additionally, the brutal downturn in Asian demand sparked a general retreat from risk in international capital markets that pushed up the cost of capital for almost all borrowers with the exception of governments in the industrialized world.

The Russian Collapse

On August 27, 1998, any trading floor in New York, London, and Tokyo was not a happy place to be. After a major devaluation and a forced debt rescheduling, the government of President Boris Yeltsin opted to impose some type of currency controls in place. Having fired one cabinet over the weekend, serious questions were being asked as to whether the Russian leader was mentally competent. By the end of one of the worst days in Wall Street trading, it was even rumored that a coup had occurred and that the Russian president had been ousted from the Kremlin. A flurry of denials quickly followed from the Kremlin. Was Yeltsin still in power? If not, who was in power? Did it matter? The bottom line for August 27, 1998, was that in a globalized credit market, the pain was shared with everyone around the planet.

At some stage in the afternoon, a Bloomberg article came out, entitled, "Russian Damage Report: Tally of Losses from a Plunging Market." If it were not for all the carnage of people's lives and that of hedge funds that failed due to the economic meltdown, the entire affair had almost a tragi-comedy side to it. As Martin Quintin-Archard, head of London-based Emerging Markets Bond & Asset Trading Company, stated of the Russian crisis: "This is the biggest, the most, the quickest so far. Look out the window for a plummeting of bankers." [35] The report went on to provide the following nuggets of information: investors who paid $12.93 billion for Eurobonds sold by the Russian government in the past two years suffered losses of more than $8.4 billion; from the beginning of 1998 to late August investors who held some of the $17 billion in Russian government debt that was restructured in October 1997 lost $13 billion; George

Soros's $22 billion group of funds lost about $2 billion on its investments in Russia; Credit Suisse Group indicated that losses during June and August, mostly from Russia, cut year-to-year profits by $254 million; and Republic New York Corp. announced that it would take a $110 million charge in the third quarter of the year for losses on Russian government bonds. Added to this list were concerns about German banks, which lent $30.5 billion, or 42 percent of all commercial bank loans in Russia, and U.S. banks, which were owed about $6.8 billion by Russian companies or the government.

Beyond the financial losses, the Russian summer meltdown also forced many governments to rethink the possibility of a return of governments in the Kremlin who could be less than friendly to the global capitalist system. This, in turn, raised questions about the security of the three Baltic states of Estonia, Latvia, and Lithuania, Russia's immediate neighbors in Central Asia and Ukraine, as well as Central European nations like Poland, Hungary, and Slovakia. Prospects for unsettled politics in Russia further raised concerns about the security of the Central Asian republics, in particular those sharing borders with Afghanistan, where a radical Islamic government under the Taliban had finally reunified the country in August 1998.

How did Russia fall into the mess it was in August 1998? Credit certainly had its place in this story, especially from the standpoint of the country's historical development. Russia under the Tsars was comparatively underdeveloped with the rest of Europe. Long an agrarian-oriented nation, it was only in the late nineteenth century that industrialization commenced in a meaningful fashion. However, Russia did not have a well-developed financial system capable of supplying the necessary credit to help construct railways, upgrade harbors, and purchase capital equipment. Consequently, Russia became dependent on foreign credit to finance its economic development. As already depicted in this book, French and German banks were active in Russian markets and their involvement also had political tones from the standpoint of gaining those countries' influence in the Tsarist court. By the end of the Tsarist period, Russia had a few banks and a fledgling stock exchange, but it remained dependent on outside credit. The downfall of the Tsarist regime did little to develop the Russian credit system.

The rise of Lenin and Stalin eventually provided a degree of political stability to the newly formed Soviet Union, but the credit system was non-capitalist and state-guided. Banks existed, but they were the organs of the state, mandated with the channeling of credit to government favored sectors of the economy. Under communism, credit controls did not exist nor was there a concept of being credit-worthy. By the time the Soviet Union came to an end in 1992, the legacy left behind was one in which there was little comprehension of how credit functioned in a capitalist economy. Additionally, in the new Russia experienced bankers, accountants, and bank regulators were in short supply. The new banks and finance houses had little experience and no historical memories to draw upon. Bank regulation was initially almost nonexistent and rules and regulations either did not exist, were being written or were holdovers from the Soviet Union.

With the end of the Soviet Union and the communist approach to the economy, Russia looked to a brave new world, one that was to hopefully develop into a functioning market economy. The process was not easy with the economy contracting through much of the 1990s, with the low point being in the 1992-94 period, when real GDP contracted on average by 11.9 percent. Hyperinflation also hit the country hard, standing at 2,526 percent in 1992, before falling to more manageable numbers in the following years. Despite both political and economic challenges, the Yeltsin administration appeared to have stabilized the economy in 1995 and 1996, bringing inflation down to 11.8 percent by year-end 1997, which was the first year of the decade to register positive economic growth of 0.4 percent. This period of reform was marked by the privatization of a large number of state enterprises, a settlement with both the Paris and London clubs on rescheduling the former Soviet Union's debt, and stabilization in the value of the ruble.

There were two problems that put Russia's new era of reform on weak foundations—corruption and the condition of the banks. Following the departure of acting Prime Minister Yegor Gaidar and Deputy Minister Boris Fedorov in early 1994, Russia's reform process came under the influence of the "industrial lobby." While there was a flow of privatizations, most were unfortunately a disgraceful state giveaway of lucrative natural resource enterprises to a handful of well-connected industrial leaders.[36] This round of privatizations lasted from 1994 to 1996 and largely privatized the economy, but left it concentrated in the hands of a few parties, who were not particularly concerned about such trivial Western concerns as transparency and disclosure, competition or shareholder rights. They also regarded their newfound economic power as political clout. None of this helped reinforce the movement to a market economy or support the rule of law—two things critical for a working modern credit system.

The hinge in the system was obviously to be the banks, which were supposed to manage the flow of credit. As one source noted, "Russian entrepreneurs rushed to open banks in the post-Soviet era, but few ever established a solid financial footing or offered Western-style retail services."[37] Consequently, it was not surprising that Russia's banks were not up to the challenge, though the problems inherent within these institutions would not become manifest until the late 1990s. An additional problem was the weakness of institutions in Russian society in the post-communist period, which fostered a business environment of greed, the exploitation of profits for consumer binges, and a certain degree of lawlessness. As John Thornhill in the *Weekend FT* captured Russia in the late 1990s, "Fuelled by fast money, a hunger for fresh sensations, loose morals and a whiff of millennial danger, Moscow has turned into the world capital of conspicuous consumption—a kind of 1980s New York mistranslated into Dostoyevskian extremes."[38]

The problem with Russia's new capitalist elite is that they did not re-invest in the country. Only a relatively small section of the population benefited from the years of brutal structural adjustment throughout most of the 1990s as Russia underwent the transformation from economic stagnation under the communists to a more market based economy. Russia's failure to develop a credit culture and the lack of democratization of credit helped open the door to the dark days of 1997. Although Russia did not have a large current account imbalance like Thailand, international investors began to have doubts about the viability of the Russian government to maintain its payments on the country's $165 billion external debt, especially in light of problems in meeting IMF guidelines with the fiscal situation. In late 1997, Russia survived one round of the Asian contagion, but was forced to seek assistance from the IMF. Although more foreign money came into Russia in the first quarter of 1998, investor confidence flagged in June and July and money poured out of the country. By August, the Russian government threw in the towel, opting to reschedule domestic debt and imposing currency controls.

A major part of the problem for Russia was the lack of domestic sources of credit and an ongoing dependence on foreign capital.

The weakness of Russian credit institutions was further underscored by the banks' involvement in forward foreign exchange contracts. The collapse of Tokobank, one of the country's twenty largest banks, reflected the danger of having unhedged forward contracts. At the same time, most Russian banks were characterized by a sharp deterioration in their loan portfolios due to poor risk management and excessive lending to connected companies. Moreover, a number of Russian banks suffered from a maturity mismatch between assets and liabilities. As Russian banks grappled with these problems in 1997 and 1998, the rest of the economy, cut off from outside credit, was hard hit by an acute credit crunch.

By August 1998, Russia had slid into a new major crisis. Yeltsin's presidency was deeply troubled, and the economy was in a state of near-collapse. The great experiment with "capitalism" as defined by Russian circumstances was increasingly seen as a dismal failure. The banking system was largely insolvent, debt obligations transfixed by reschedulings, and productivity stalled.

The political side of Russia's economic meltdown was most evident in the weakening of the Yeltsin administration and the sharp and vocal criticisms of the capitalist experience. As Gennady Zyugorov, the head of the Communist Party, stated to the Russian Duma on August 31, 1998: "I address businessmen, entrepreneurs and nascent bourgeoisie. Your predecessors, in the first 15 years of this century, were unable to share power and property. In the west, they understood the need to share 200 years ago—those who didn't share either had their crowns or their heads removed. Now you are acting in the same way."[39]

In a sense, the advent of credit culture was the imposition of a Western idea on a Russian society still in the throes of seeking a new identity, which meant any adherence to Western ideas of transparency and disclosure were superficial at best. Although the impact of this superficiality was not felt in the mid-1990s, it was harshly felt in 1998 as the Asian contagion spooked investments and creditors into taking a closer look at the precarious nature of Russia's reform effort. Globalization which had allowed the extension of credit to Russia and helped stamp a form of capitalism on Russia also was the force that helped stampede the very same investors and creditors from the Eurasian country.

What the developing world experienced in the late 1990s was a severe credit crunch. While considerable credit flowed into Emerging Markets in the early part of the decade, by 1997 the flow slowed considerably: according to the Institute of International Finance, in 1995-96 private flows amounted to $535.7 billion, while the number fell in 1997 to 241.7 billion and was estimated to be around $158.2 billion in 1998.[40] In fact, in the five most stricken Asian economies—South Korea, Indonesia, Malaysia, Thailand, and the Philippines—there was actually a credit outflow of $6 billion in 1997 and an estimated $24.6 billion in 1998.

The savage economic downturn in Asia, the crash of Russian and Ukrainian economies (with debt defaults), and Brazil's precarious position, forced a serious rethink on the part of global policy-makers vis-à-vis the free flow of capital. Although many reasons can be advanced for the Asian contagion, an overabundance of credit was a major factor. A complicating factor was that the credit flowed into a number of countries that lacked institutions capable of properly using such credit in a productive fashion. Instead, in a number of cases international loans and bonds were used to finance speculation, buy consumer goods, and, as in Indonesia and Russia, enrich those with sticky fingers. A joke during 1998 in financial circles was that the IMF program disbursements were not a complete waste of money for the global economy: though the money given to the Russian government did little to help the Russian people or the economy, it did help real estate prices in the French Riviera. The sad fact is that although the crisis ended by 1999, the legacy of problems was still dogging countries such as Indonesia and Thailand, years later. As *The Economist* noted in late 2000: "Indonesia's debt problems are legendary, and its bank restructuring agency has collected only a sliver of the bad debts that it acquired. Nor, despite much huffing and puffing, has Thailand made much progress."[41]

By the October 1998 annual IMF-World Bank meetings held in Washington, D.C., it was evident that whatever was left of the Bretton Woods system was badly damaged and probably terminal. It was also acknowledged that in taming inflation, the longer phases between recessions have come with a buildup of excessive leverage. As Christopher Mahoney, head of Moody's Banking & Sovereign Group, observed, "The malign aspect has been that the buildup of excessive leverage characteristic of the bull-phase and the resulting asset bubbles have been able to grow uncorrected due to the absence of periodic rate-spikes and credit crunches. The longer the period between rate spikes, the greater the buildup of uncorrected financial excesses."[42] Moreover, despite considerable discussion about creating a new international financial architecture and a move to put up a $41.5 billion support package for Brazil, a replacement for the Bretton Woods system remains nonexistent and the instability of credit markets is likely to be a constant feature for countries in the developing world. This was proven accurate when Argentina, one of the world's leading debtors, ran into problems in 2000 and was forced to seek the support of the IMF to help maintain access to international credit markets.

Chipping Away at the Nation-State

As the world grasps for a post-Bretton Woods system, one development that clearly exists and is not likely to go away any time soon is that the emergence and growing influence of regional groups. This ranges from the role played by regional development banks, such as the African Development Bank and European Bank for Reconstruction and Development to regional trading blocs such as the European Union, NAFTA (North American Free Trade Agreement) and Mercosur (encompassing Brazil, Argentina, Uruguay, and Paraguay, with Chile and Bolivia as associate members). Each of these institutions has an impact over the creation and flow of credit beyond the control of national governments.

The development of regional lending institutions and common markets was stimulated largely in the 1950s by the ultimate goal of improving the livelihood of people in each region involved. The regional or multilateral development banks functioned in such a manner as to channel credit to key sectors or projects. The common markets were to function to maximize trade opportunities for member states, a development that would increase demand and employment opportunities as well as grow the national wealth. The Inter-American Development Bank is the oldest and largest regional multilateral development institution, being established in 1959. Its mission is to help accelerate economic and social development in the Caribbean and Latin America. The Asian Development Bank was created in 1966 and its principal goal is to reduce poverty, with the related objectives of economic growth, human development, improvement in the status of women, and protection of the environment. The newest such organization is the European Bank for Reconstruction and Development, which came about in 1991 to help development in the former Communist bloc countries.

The creation of regional banks and trade organizations accelerated in the second half of the twentieth century. The European Union,
which had its roots in Benelux customs union formed in 1948, at the
beginning of the twenty-first century is experimenting with a single
European currency, the euro. Clearly, the emergence of this currency unit raises significant questions about credit formation as
bonds, equities, and loans are now conducted in euros. It also raises
major questions about the role of the nation-state in contending with
a currency backed by a regional central bank, the European Central
Bank. The apprehension over loss of control over one's national
currency, hence a degree of power over economic policy and credit
formation, has been one factor for opposition to the euro in the United
Kingdom, Sweden, and Denmark, three countries that initially opted
not to join.

The role of regional development banks and trading blocs clearly
impinges on the domination of the nation-state and its related importance to credit. For example, the European Union has fifteen
members. In a number of these countries, such as the United Kingdom, France, and Spain, there are sub-regions that would prefer less
national control over their affairs within the context of a stronger
European Union. Hence, Scotland could become "independent" of
the United Kingdom by shifting "federal" responsibility to Brussels,
the European Union's headquarters. With the euro, Scotland would not
have to be tied as much to the English economy. Credit formation
would not be with the UK pound, but with the euro. The same could
be said for Corsica's ties to France or the Basque region with Spain.

One of the difficulties of the euro and like experiments is the problem of separating financial policy with politics. If a country loses
control over its currency, how does that play out in terms of other
economic policies that are being adopted for labor, education, taxes,
environment, and national finance? The short answer is that the role
of the regional institution can over time, as observed in Europe, over-
shadow the nation-state in many key areas of policy formation. Consequently, the existence of organizations that function beyond the
realm of national governments will continue to somewhat erode the
power of the nation-state. It is also important to emphasize that the
process of regional organizations as well as globalization, while having
a major impact on the nation-state, also reach a point where resistance
is incurred and people back way. The European Union's experiment
with the euro will indeed be closely watched in this regard.

One more dimension of the linkage between the erosion of the nation-state and credit to consider is South Africa during the apartheid regime. Apartheid was a system of racial segregation that was the brainchild of Hendrik Frensch Verwoerd and was adopted by the white racist regime that emerged in the post-World War II era. There were four key elements of apartheid: the population of South Africa was made up of four "racial groups," whites, colored, Indian, and African; whites, as the civilized race, were entitled to have absolute control over the state; white interests should prevail over black interests as the state was to provide equal facilities for the subordinate races; and the white racial group formed a single nation, with Afrikaans- and English-speaking components, while Africans belonged to several distinct nations or potential nations.[43]

The apartheid system was not well received internationally and over time a number of governments adopted sanctions against South Africa. Part of the strategy was to cut South Africa off from sources of credit. Although there had been some disinvestments in the 1960s and 1970s, the nationwide political turmoil in the 1980s, led to more fulsome anti-apartheid actions. Between 1984 and 1990, around 400 foreign companies left South Africa. One of the biggest blows came in 1985 when Chase Manhattan Bank decided to call in its South African loans as they fell due and to freeze all further credit.[44] Worse was yet to come, when other U.S. banks, feeling pressure at home from shareholders and the public, decided to halt any new credit. South Africa was soon put in a position of being forced to reschedule its external debt. Although the external embargo on credit from the United States and most of Europe hurt, it did not fully sink apartheid. The end of that system came from within and was conducted in a smooth and democratic fashion.

One thing that is observable in the South African case is the impact of globalization on the economy. If in 1850 international forces would have told the United States that it would have to give up slavery, Washington would have argued that it was an issue of its sovereignty in which no other nation had the right to interfere. It is questionable that an international coalition would have been able to end slavery in the United States. In the 1950s and following decades, South Africa could not as forcibly make that argument. The world was more globalized and South Africa was vulnerable to both access to trade and the need for credit. Although South Africa sought for several decades to go it alone, the economic cost, especially the lack of international credit, hurt. In a broader sense, this represented the importance of a globalized credit system and the weakening of the nation-state.

Conclusion

Globalization of credit has changed the world. On one side of the equation it has opened the door to credit for millions of people around the planet, helped stimulate economic development and improve the standard of living, and reinforced the post-Cold War turn to capitalism. This is the positive side of globalized credit in which everyone wins—the bankers, credit card companies, governments, individuals applying for home mortgage loans for the first time, and businesses looking to conduct trade across international frontiers. The negative side of the globalization of credit is characterized by the Asian contagion. On this side of the equation nobody wins as investors stampede and take losses, creditors face painful reschedulings or no payments, individuals seeking credit are denied (or slip below the poverty line as in Asia and Russia), and governments face disgruntled populations as austerity measures are taken to counter the loss of credit. Globalization also underscores the pressing need for greater transparency and disclosure in international financial transactions. If nothing else one of the major weaknesses throughout Asia was while government finances were relatively above board and transparent, banks, finance companies, and corporations were secretive in their transactions and activities to the point that the central governments often lost sight of the levels of dollar denominated debt being incurred.

What was lacking in the international credit system at the end of the twentieth century was balance between the negatives and positives inherent in globalization. As we will see in the final chapter, the Bretton Woods financial system and its institutions were unable to handle the strains caused by new technologies and many new players in the credit game, both in terms of government and nongovernment players. The most critical issue facing credit at the end of the century is the pressing need to find a balance between the free flow of capital and the chaos that such a free flow of capital can cause if not supported by the right national frameworks. All of this points to the argument made earlier in the book that though the nation-state is under pressure, it remains the major force left at the end of the day to contend with the rapid pace of changes in the world of credit.

Notes

1.   World Bank, *Global Development Finance* (Washington, DC: World Bank, 1998), p. 9.

2.   Ibid., p. 71.

3.   Christopher J. Wiegand, *How Big Is the World Bond Market?*, Economic & Market *Analysis, Salomon Smith Barney*, April 7, 2000, p. 4.

4.   World Bank, *Entering the 21st Century: World Bank Development Report 1999/ 2000* (New York: Oxford University Press, 2000), p. 70.

5.   Ibid.

6.   One such book that made it to market quickly was Callum Henderson, *Asia Falling: Making Sense of the Asian Crisis and Its Aftermath* (New York: McGraw Hill, 1998). Others followed: Peter Mallet, *The Trouble with Tigers: The Rise and Fall of South-East Asia* (New York: Harper Collins Publishers, 1999); Philippe F. Delhaise, *Asia in Crisis: The Implosion of Banking and Finance Systems* (New York: John Wiley & Sons, 1998); Karl D. Jackson, *Asian Contagion: The Causes and Consequences of a Financial Crisis* (Boulder, CO: Westview Press, 1999), and Mark L. Clifford and Peter Engardio, *Meltdown: Asia's Boom, Bust and Beyond* (Paramus, NJ: Prentice Hall Press, 2000).

7.   World Bank, *Global Development Finance: Analysis and Summary Tables* (Washington, DC: The World Bank, 1998), p. 37.

8.   Jack Weatherford, *The History of Money* (New York: Three River Press, 1997), p. 125.

9.   Ibid., pp. 125-126.

10.   Lien-chêng Yang, *Money and Credit in China* (Cambridge, MA: Harvard University Press, 1952.

11.   Weatherford, *The History of Money*, p. 128.

12.   Quoted in Franz Schurmann and Orville Schell, eds., *Imperial China: The Decline of the Last Dynasty and the Origins of Modern China, the 18th and 19th Centuries* (New York: Vintage Books, 1967), p. 78.

13.   Ryotaro Shiba, *The Last Shogun: The Life of Tokugawa Yashinobu* (New York: Kodansha International, 1998), p. xi.

14.   Johannes Hirschmeier and Tsunehiko Yui, *The Development of Japanese Business, 1600-1973* (Cambridge, MA: Harvard University Press, 1975), p. 13.

15.   It is important to clarify that Japanese merchants did not evolve along the track of the Italians, Flemish, or Dutch, who enlarged the scope of their operations, diversified them, and evolved into creditors to kings and other members of the upper class. As we have witnessed in earlier chapters, the European merchants gained control over the production process of the goods they tracked, dominated the crafts in urban centers and reinvested their capital in increasingly larger scale manufacturing, notably in spinning and weaving. Moreover, they also were pioneers in mining and the rising metallurgical industries. The story was different in Tokugawa Japan. As Johannes Hirschmeier and Tsunehiko Yui, two economists, noted, "In Tokugawa Japan the successful city merchants could not proceed on this forward looking path, because here conditions were different from Europe of the outgoing Middle Ages. Feudal control was not declined and was not multi-central, hence the merchants lacked the freedom and self-assurance of the European counterparts." Hirschmeier and Yui, *The Development of Japanese Business*, p. 34.

16.   Shiba, *The Last Shogun*, p. xi.

17.   Norio Tamaki, *Japanese Banking: A History, 1859-1959* (New York: Cambridge University Press, 1995), p. 17.

18.   W.G. Beasley, *The Rise of Modern Japan* (London: Weidenfeld & Nicolson, 1995), p. 105. Tamaki provided some interesting background information about Matsukata Masayoshi. Born in 1835, the son of a lower ranking and poor Satsuma samurai, he began his career as an accountant. Having been brought up in circumstances of extreme poverty, he was exceedingly conscious of the value of money and developed keen insights into finance that would serve him well. In 1871 he was appointed deputy head of the Finance Ministry and by 1878 he was head of his department. He was initially put in charge of land tax reform which transformed the system based on rice tax to one based on a money tax. In 1881 he became Finance Minister. *Japanese Banking*, pp. 51-54.

19.   Hirschmeier and Yui, *The Development of Japanese Business*, p. 183.

20.   Beasley, *The Rise of Modern Japan*, pp. 114-115.

21.   Sakatani Yoshiro, *Nihan Keizai ran* (Theory on the Japanese Economy), Tokyo, 1912. Pp. 44-45, as quoted in Hirschmeier and Yui, p. 184.

22.   Beasley, *The Rise of Modern Japan*, p. 119.

23.   Declan Hayes, *Japan's Big Bang: The Deregulation and Revitalization of the Japanese Economy* (Rutland, VT: Turtle Publishing, 2000), p. 26.

24.   Jacob M. Schlesinger, *Shadow Shoguns: The Rise and Fall of Japan's Postwar Political Machine* (New York: Simon & Schuster, 1997), p. 13.

25.   Richard Katz, *Japan the System That Soured: The Rise and Fall of the Japanese Economic Miracle* (Armonk, NY: M.E. Sharpe, 1998), p. 8.

26.   Ibid., p. 6.

27.   See Declan Hayes, *Japan's Big Bang: The Deregulation and Revitalization of the Japanese Economy.*

28.   See "Sogo Closes Three Branch Stores." *The Japan Times Online*, July 14, 2000 (*http://www.japantimes.co.jp/cgi-bin/getarticle.p15?nb20000714a1.htm*; Hanabusa Midori, with Tetsuji Inoue and Norinko Tsutsumi, "Sogo Files for Court Protection at LDP's Prompting," *Bloomberg*, July 12, 2000; and Tom Grove, Japan: Sogo Bankruptcy," *Thomson Financial BankWatch*, July 13, 2000.

29.   World Bank, *World Development Report 1997* (New York: Oxford University Press, 1997), p. 235.

30.   *The Economist*, "South Korea: The End of the Miracle," December 1, 1997, p. 21.

31.   Robert E. Bedeski, *The Transformation of South Korea: Reform and Reconstruction in the Sixth Republic under Roh Tee Woo, 1987-1992* (New York: Routledge, 1994), p. 34. Also see A.H. Amsden, *Asia's Next Giant: South Korea and Late Industrialization* (Oxford: Oxford University Press, 1989).

32.   Ibid.

33.   Bill Austin and Yoolim Lee, "South Korea, IMF at Odds Over Bailout," Bloomberg, December 1, 1997,.

34.   Bank for International Settlements, "Press Release: Consolidated International Banking Statistics for End-1997," May 25, 1998, p. 9 in statistical index. Japanese bank exposure to Thailand was $33 billion, $22 billion to Indonesia, $20.3 billion to Korea, $19.6 billion to China and $8.6 billion to Malaysia.

35.   Ted Merz and Brian Rooney, "Russian Damage Report: Tally of Losses from a Plunging Market," Bloomberg, August 1998.

36.   Jeffrey D. Sachs, "Tainted Transactions: An Exchange," *The National Interest* (Summer 2000), p. 98.

37.   Leslie Shepard, "Fraction of Russian Banks Predicted to Survive Crisis," *The Journal News*, October 24, 1998, p. 8D.

38.   John Thornhill, "Russia's New Kleptocracy," *Weekend FT*, September 1998, p. 7.

39.   Quoted from Andrew Higgins and Mark Whitehouse, "Russia Crisis Deepens as Duma Rejects Premier," *Wall Street Journal*, September 1, 1998, p. A14.

40.   Institute of International Finance, Capital Flows to Emerging Market Economies, September 29, 1998, (Washington, D.C.), p. 3.

41.   *The Economist*, "Asian Economies: Stragglers," August 5, 2000, p. 70.

42.   Christopher T. Mahoney, *The Credit Cycle Turns for the Emerging Markets*, Moody's Investors Service, Global Credit Research, Special Comment, December 1998, p. 1.

43.   Leonard Thompson, *A History of South Africa* (New Haven, CT: Yale University Press, 1990), p. 190.

44.   Sebastian Mallaby, *After Apartheid: The Future of South Africa* (New York: Times Books, 1992), p. 44.

14

Conclusion: New Frontiers

In September 2000 the history of credit witnessed an important watermark. One of the banking industry's more venerable institutions, J.P. Morgan & Company, announced that it was being bought by the much larger Chase Manhattan Bank. History will record that the 16,000 Morgan employees and the unique corporate culture based on a business strategy focused on sovereign states, the rich and blue-chip companies were swallowed by Chase, with its 80,000 employees and an emphasis on corporate finance, car loans, mortgages, and mutual funds (and other securities).[1] Although it is not entirely just to depict Chase as a bank for the masses, J.P. Morgan had a long tradition of banking the wealthy, the elite few. Ron Chernow, the author of *The House of Morgan*, was to note correctly that Morgan failed to survive because it was "blindsided by two stunning developments, both of which ran directly counter to its heritage: the democratization of Wall Street and the advent of the New Economy."[2] As one distraught J.P. Morgan employee commented to one of the authors, "J.P. Morgan must be turning in his grave."

Yet, the history of credit has had a long trend line of how innovative new products and new technologies have forced change in the financial world, changing relationships and uprooting the old order. J.P. Morgan, in a sense, was a revolutionary in his own day as his actions brought sweeping changes to U.S. and eventually global credit markets. It can be argued that Morgan and his fellow bankers of the day created more efficient credit markets, which helped U.S. industry become a world power. Over time, many of the same characteristics that ushered in radical change at the end of the nineteenth and beginning of the twentieth century became inadequate to deal with a new round of changes. Ultimately, the end of J.P. Morgan reflects one of the major themes of this book, the democratization of credit. Certainly from the days of the Italian merchant bankers to the sale of J.P. Morgan there has been a relentless spread of credit and its availability to increasingly larger circles of people.

Through the course of our story about the development of credit in the Western world we have emphasized and sought to uphold the following points. First and foremost, there is a direct relationship between credit and power. Secondly, different kinds of political power promote different kinds of economic behavior. Related to this is the third point that certain societal groups were and continue to be able to embrace the relationship between credit and trade in a much more fulsome way than others. Fourth, the Western credit system evolved in tandem with the development of the nation-state. Fifth, the development of a Western-based, but ultimately global credit system occurred with considerable volatility. Crises occurred periodically and often represented a cycle of too little credit, followed by growing access to credit and strong economic growth, too much credit, and eventually the bursting of the bubble. The sixth and last point is that over time the spread of credit went from being the privilege of the wealthy and the powerful to being available to vast numbers of North Americas, Japanese, Europeans and to the citizens of a handful of other relatively developed economies, such as Singapore, Hong Kong, Taiwan, and Israel. While these themes define the history of credit, they will also define the future of credit.

Change, Adaptation, and Volatility

The global credit system at the beginning of the twenty-first century can be characterized with three words—change, adaptation, and volatility. The global economy is undergoing profound changes that are shrinking the role of some players and expanding the role of others. As the process accelerates, adaptability becomes a question of survival for individuals, banks, and corporations, and ultimately countries. Implicit in this view is that those countries that remain linked mainly to the sale of basic commodities will be increasingly at a disadvantage to those economies that have evolved to knowledge-based (also called Information Technology or IT) economies. Simply stated, knowledge-based economies, like the United States and Canada, most of Western Europe, and Japan have built-in advantages for the future as they remain on the cutting edge of technology that will reshape the global economy.

At the cutting edge of the new global economy, credit plays an essential role.

Research and development is critical for technological advances. It is also usually costly. Without trial and error in expensive laboratories the new generation of miracle drugs, which deal with everything from impotency to hair loss, will never make it to the market. The ongoing quest for cures for cancer, aids, heart disease, and the common cold have large price tags attached. Part of those costs will be covered by credit, either through commercial bank loans or the issuance of securities such as bonds and stocks. The boom in Internet stocks in the late 1990s reflects the huge pouring of money into this sector, much of it based on research and projected earnings. Added to this newly shaping credit order is the imposition of the Western bias to transparency and disclosure. In the aftermath of the Asian crisis, transparency and disclosure is gradually becoming more common in such places as Japan, Thailand, and Korea and to a lesser extent in China. Yet, we are far from complete dominance by the Western credit culture as many pockets will continue to resist this as another form of globalization.

What are the new technologies shaping the future of credit? Certainly the Internet is opening up access to credit as never before. The buzzwords of the early 2000s were "ecommerce," "b-to-b" (business to business relations), and "eretail." As technology continues to transform human society, the distribution of credit is also undergoing a revolution. The credit card represents one part of the picture. Another dimension of this is cyberbanking (also called ebanking). One of the first cyberbanks was Security First Network Bank, which was up and running on October 18, 1995, and others were soon to follow, such as the United Kingdom's oddly named Egg. Older banks, such as Wells Fargo, Bank One, and Citicorp, have also moved quickly to adapt to cyberbanking and more efficient use of the Internet for payments systems and online stock trading.[3]

How does one do cyberbanking? With a few clicks of the mouse you are in! Before you on the computer screen is your cyberbank. A small window provides you access to information, customer service, interest rates, and anything else that you need at a bank. A history of Interbank banking explains cyberbanking:

> The old way of banking, going to the branch and waiting in line is slowly dying. People no longer have the time to do banking. They would rather be somewhere else! As peoples' needs change so do the banks. They are willing to help customers in anyway

possible to meet their needs. And that is what is happening. We have entered the age of computer banking. Resistance is futile![4]

The advent of cyberbanking reflects a fundamental change—at the end of the twentieth century, the global economy had made a significant shift away from the physical exchange of money to electronic credit. Credit cards, ATMs, and direct banking all advanced the tendency to rely on new technologies. Why carry large amounts of cash when small plastic cards open gateways of consumerism in the global shopping mall. One additional step takes you into the ethos of the Internet, where sitting at your home in Rye, New York, or Bogota, Colombia, you can purchase carpets from Turkey, fine wines from France and books from Japan. Amazon.com's rise as a hot stock was based on its ability to offer books and music in a rapid and secure fashion. As publisher Rich Karlgaard notes of the Internet: "Free trade is inevitable. When people can shop around the world, they will buy around the world. Government will be overwhelmed by the volume of web-inspired trade. They will be powerless to stop it."[5]

All of this mirrors the rise of technology, a new route for the ebb and flow of capital, and the changing dynamic of global politics. Simply stated, if you don't have a computer linked to the Internet, you can't play. If you can't play, your options for consumerism and for information are more limited than your competition. Moreover, this shift to electronic credit reflects the "commodification" of information. Information has become a hot commodity, a major factor in determining creditworthiness in an age of global business.

The advances in technology that gave us the cyberbanking and credit and debit cards also are providing an improvement in terms of timing. As time itself has become a commodity, technology has vastly sped up the process by which credit transactions can be undertaken. It has allowed the movement of billions of dollars on a daily basis around the world, without anyone having to physically touch a dollar, yen or mark. As Jonathan Williams noted in his history of money: "In some Western countries the use of cash itself had already been superseded in large-scale commercial and financial transactions by the use of various credit facilities and cheques, and this development also began to affect the use of money in daily life, as bank accounts became more common for a larger proportion of the population and the accessibility of credit from banks and retail outlets became much more widespread."[6]

Advances in technology will continue to change the relationship between credit and cash as well as credit and power. Whoever has the technology to rapidly access credit will be in a stronger position than those who must proceed along a slower track. This has implications for business as well as politics. In business, it boils down to the old idea that the fleet-of-foot survive. In a Darwinian sense, rapid access to credit can mean the ability to launch a hostile takeover or beat one off. In politics, it can mean the survival of a government facing huge cash restraints or the winning of a war.

Credit use continues to undergo transformations in the early twenty-first century. In many regards the use of the credit card and cyberbanking reflect the cutting edge of how business and commerce will be conducted in the years to come. They also represent the great divide in the human race. Those with technology and plugged into the global Internet will have opportunities to become wealthy, have access to better health and living facilities, and probably live in a brave new world reaching to the stars. Technological advances also pushed along a significant concentration of financial activity in a clutch of cities, almost entirely in the post-industrial countries led by New York, London, and Tokyo. By year-end 1997, twenty-five cities controlled 83 percent of the world's equities under institutional management and accounted for about half of global market capitalization (around $20.9 trillion), while London, New York, and Tokyo combined held a third of the world's institutionally managed equities and accounted for 58 percent of the global foreign exchange market.[7] Additionally, the shrinking of the commercial marketplace, the globalization of the credit system, and instantaneous communications have stimulated a new wave of cross-border mergers within the technologically advanced countries as reflected by the Ford-Volvo, Deutsche Bank-Bankers Trust and Daimler Benz-Chrysler mergers. Credit markets in the post-industrial world will continue to consolidate, as fierce competition will drive more strategic collaboration.

On the other side of the divide are those that have rejected the global grid—the concept of globalization and all it represents. In some cases, those on the other side of the divide are simply too poor to even consider the Internet and cyberbanking. Instead, the primary concern may be standing in line for food or whether to flee across the border as in the cases of Sierra Leone, the Democratic Republic of the Congo (former Zaire), or Kosovo. What credit there is goes to other areas—arms and food. Some of it also is siphoned into the pockets of the corrupt. There is no rule of law to guarantee the flow of credit into well-established institutions that have the trust and confidence of the population to put their money to work. It is no accident that most Internet users live in the more developed countries. At the end of the day all of this technology has costs—big costs that are not affordable to all. Moreover, as the Internet elite reconceptualize how human society should be structured, those not in the global grid are increasingly having greater difficulty in meeting basic human needs, let alone being competitive in international markets. At the core of this development is credit. More than money in the form of legal tender like the dollar, access to credit will determine winners and losers in the international market economy and within particular national economies.

Not Everyone is Thrilled

Not everyone is thrilled by globalization and its impact on credit. As the world has shrunk and the problems of people in distant parts of the world impinge on daily life, fear and loathing has its place. This is particularly the case of many people in large parts of Asia, Latin America, and Africa who deeply resent "markets" telling them that their national economies are being mismanaged and that bond traders in Manhattan may not get $1 million bonuses because of a debt default. To many, especially on the political left, the trends of technological change, globalized credit, and accelerated means to move money in and out of an economy represent a form of financial casino of stock markets and currency trading that dissipates savings worldwide, a particular concern in developing economies.[8] There is considerable trepidation that if the Western-dominated credit system continues to evolve in the same fashion as it did during the 1990s, the world will become one of worsening inequitable income distributions and insurmountable barriers to upward social mobility.

Concerns about the new credit order are not limited to the political left in developing countries. Similar concerns about the creation of two societies within a single country have their echoes in the most developed countries. Professor James Laxer of Canada's York University's Atkinson College provided an interesting critique of the new credit order in his *In Search of a New Left*. His book captures some of the angst found in Europe, the United States, Canada, and Japan. According to Laxer, a new capitalism based on finance and technology is overcoming the old capitalism based on manufacturing. The finance-technology driven capitalism is heavily involved in global stock markets and its mavens prefer a low inflation environment that is positive for their inflation-sensitive rate of return bond holdings. Those who benefit from the new credit order are a loose confederation of wealthy Americans, bankers, financiers, money managers, rich foreigners, executives of life insurance companies, a highly educated technoprofessional "new class" of university and college professors, technicians, accountants, lawyers, and others doing knowledge-based work, and non-profit organizations, pensioners and people who buy mutual funds. According to Laxer, "The hallmark of the new global capitalism at the end of the twentieth century is the novel freedom and dominance of the financial sector in relation to all the other sectors of business and with regard to the state and society in general. The ability of those who control large pools of capital to move assets freely and to acquire and sell firms at will has given them immense new economic and political leverage."[9] To this he adds, "Today, creditors are in a stronger position to impose their will on the global economic system than ever before."

Laxer is hardly alone. Indeed, a "globalization sucks" school has arisen to deal with the new world order.[10] Academic Louis W. Pauly at the University of Toronto sums up the feelings of many people: "For the vast majority of us who are not Wall Street coupon clippers, not thrilled by the prospect of changing employment fields six or seven times in the course of our lifetime, and not particularly interested in moving to Singapore, this news about 'globalization' engenders a deep sense of disquiet."[11] These fears were manifested in 2000 by the outbursts against globalization that occurred at the World Trade Organization's meeting in Seattle and at the IMF/World Bank's annual meetings as well as the Davos international summit in January 2001. Although the impact of the message of discontent with globalization was conveyed, the messengers (including mask-wearing anarchists) did little to generate widespread public sympathy for such acts as trashing McDonald's and Starbucks. In general, the demonstrations were regarded as a chance for a vocal fringe minority to conduct violence.

The "globalization sucks" school points to something often overlooked in the sterile arguments of investment bankers, economists of large financial services firms and the economists and technocrats at the World Bank and IMF. The missing link is the human factor.

Not everyone, especially the people in rural Indonesia or Honduras, is going to have access to the Internet. This serious disconnect between the technologically advanced and technologically challenged was painfully evident in the IMF's approach to Indonesia in 1997.[12] The Suharto regime had to swallow the IMF austerity program despite the very high political risk that the population would not stand for it. Never stated, but implied, was the belief that if the Suharto government could tough it out – contain social unrest – the economic stabilization program would work. Societal discontent with deep cuts in subsidies for cooking oil and fuel were not really given much weight. After all, in economic planning there is little room for political risk. The combination of harsh economic programs and the corrupt and authoritarian nature of the Suharto regime ultimately brought the downfall of Indonesia's tyrant. Needless to say, the Southeast Asian nation's political turmoil did not abate in 1998 and 1999, while the economy underwent a steep contraction in which the banking system collapsed, companies went out of business, and some $70 billion in private sector debt was left to be sorted out between Indonesian companies and their foreign creditors. Failure to take into consideration political factors resulted in an inability to stabilize the Indonesian economy or restore foreign investor support for Indonesia.

Although the "globalization sucks" school has a degree of validity in how the new credit system is impacting society, it is somewhat short on solutions. No one has advocated a return to Albanian-style self-sufficiency. The calls for the creation of a neo-Luddite life-style appear to have little appeal to the vast multitude of people. There are voices, however, advocating the adoption of more mercantilist approaches, including capital controls. Indeed, the two big countries in Asia that were not hit by foreign currency problems in 1997-98 were China and India, both of which have currencies that are not freely convertible. Russia and Malaysia also adopted currency controls in an effort to stem the flow of currency.

For all the discussions about the creation of new financial architecture by the G-7 countries and the IMF, the most likely path to be taken by the planet will entail an informal, but increasingly more coordinated approach to international monetary policy by the leaderships of the major industrialized countries and China. This was already evident in the lowering of interest rates in the United States and Europe in the second half of 1998. Such actions reduced the price of borrowing money and were meant to keep credit flowing in local economies. While national leaders will be forced to better coordinate their policies, the IMF will be forced to reform itself. As a child of the defunct Bretton Wood system, it exhibited a considerable inability to get its arms around the problem in Asia, threw good money after bad in Russia, and repeated its mistakes in Brazil. The IMF's leadership and responses to the meltdowns in Asia, Russia, and Brazil were inadesquate and in some aspects aggravated the situation. Clearly, the institution needs to develop greater awareness of political factors, must learn to terminate support before the ship sinks, and must provide greater transparency and disclosure about its operations.

We find ourselves at the beginning of the 2000s in a period of great change. A massive shift is occurring in the way we conduct our business and daily affairs. The combination of technology and credit touches almost every aspect of human society around the planet twenty-four hours a day. The danger is the globalized credit system becomes a runaway train waiting for a great collision much like pre-Depression free market capitalism. Unstable capital flows, mainly short-term in nature, have clearly added a highly volatile element into the global credit system in the 1990s. As economist Paul Krugman wrote in the January/February 1999 issue of *Foreign Affairs,* "The answer is that the world became vulnerable to its current travails not because economic policies had not been reformed, but because they had. Around the world countries responded to the very real flaws in post-Depression policy regimes by moving back toward a regime with many of the virtues of pre-Depression free-market capitalism. However, in bringing back the virtues of old-fashioned capitalism, we also brought back some of its vices, most notably a vulnerability both to instability and sustained economic slumps."[13]

This is not a problem solely limited to American investors and Wall Street firms, but also to the local wealthy in countries as diverse as China, Russia, and Brazil. As cities such as São Paulo and Bombay become part of the global credit system, they run the same risks as their more developed counterparts. As the *New York Times* noted in late January 1999, "Wealthy Brazilians, many of them already moving chunks of capital abroad, hold more than $150 billion in their Government's debt and rushing this money out of the country would quickly exhaust Brazil's dollar reserves."[14] This is precisely what happened in early 1999. At the end of the day, emerging market economies are learning a critical lesson—hot money flows are not the most prudent and consistent path to finance development.[15]

In all likelihood, humankind will continue to stumble along, with accelerated changes in the global order, which will be characterized by further technological breakthroughs, the ongoing rise of a class linked to the health of stock and bond markets, the counterbalancing rise of neopopulists, clashes between governments and big credit, and cyclical booms and busts. Certainly we have witnessed these events before in the history of credit. There was no well thought out plan to shift the hub of global credit from Antwerp to Amsterdam to London and to New York. Those historical shifts were accompanied by considerable market volatility, a good dose of warfare, and economic dislocation. To avoid further disequilibrium or to brake a slipping down the slope back to a 1930s-style Depression, measures, such as those advocated by Krugman, are worth implementing. These entail limited capital flows for countries that are unsuitable for either currency unions or free floating of their currencies, re-regulating financial markets to some extent, and seeking low but not too low inflation rather than price stability at all costs.[16] There may be some slowing of the process of an increasingly integrated credit system, but the convergence of basic interest within a widening array of states indicates the momentum will continue. Moreover, the emphasis for real policy making will remain with the nation-state. After all, much of the economic and financial crises that hit in the 1990s were rooted in policy blunders by individual governments, not the international credit system.

What about the Nation-State?

The nation-state has been a key force in the development of a global credit system. It has provided a rule of law and inspired confidence in the free flow of credit. Yet, the very same phenomenon has eroded the power of the nation-state in two ways—it is exceedingly difficult to control global credit flows, and the results of those flows in creating the IT economy have raised forces that increasingly impinge of the role of the nation-state. As James Wolfensohn, president of the World Bank, stated in September 2000, "Today you have 20 percent of the world controlling 80 percent of the gross domestic product. You've got a $30 trillion economy and $24 trillion of it in developed countries."[17] The World Bank head also warned of a "systemic breakdown" due to the social inequities that have developed.

The impending breakdown is not so impending and there have

always been socioeconomic inequities in history. In the same sense, there have always been countries with credit surpluses and countries with credit deficits. Different economic policies have been followed and different economic results have been made. What pushed the Dutch along in the late sixteenth and early seventeenth centuries did not catch on in Africa, India or China. Moreover, credit is now more available—lots of it—in the billions of dollars. Nevertheless, the World Bank's chief is correct in noting that the massive flow of credit often does have an unsettling effect. Indeed, the problems of socioeconomic inequities are more acute in places such as Africa, Central Asia, and Latin America than they are in the United States, Canada, and France. It is in such countries as Sierra Leone, the Democratic Republic of the Congo, and Pakistan that the fate of the nation-state has sagged the most. These are countries where borders mean little and the state's writ has little meaning beyond the confines of the capital. The idea of the rule of law, essential for credit, does not exist. Yet, globalization is not the bulk of the problem—in many cases there is a lack of local responsible leadership willing to make self-sacrifices to create some form of civic society. All too often it is easy to blame the legacy of imperialism or globalization (the new rant) for all the ills that befall local governments. It is also easy to pilfer state finances, as exemplified in the late twentieth century by Suharto's Indonesia and Daniel Arap Moi's Kenya. At the end of the day these are dysfunctional polities, presiding over fragile societies and weak economies. They reflect the weak link in the nation-state and have become a no-go zone for global credit. Sadly, global credit is needed to help provide better lives for the citizens of these states, but credit, as determined by the market, opts not to put itself to work in Kinshasa and Freetown, but gravitates to Shanghai and Singapore.

Credit also gravitates to the creation of IT economies and other efficient sectors of the global economy, not to protecting grossly inefficient agriculture. Yet, in many countries there is public support for protecting certain sectors of the economy from outside competition. In this the nation-state functions on the behalf of its citizens. This is often a difficult problem as protectionism ultimately hurts the home consumer market, raises costs, and complicates international economic relations. With the flow of credit seeping into every corner of the world, national borders are easily transited. Moreover, as credit plows into the IT sector, even nation-states in the most developed countries are facing an erosion of their core functions.

Throughout the upcoming period the nation-state will continue to be challenged. Will the flow of credit between porous national frontiers continue to erode the state's prerogative of calling the shots when it comes to national development policies? In all probability, the nation-state will continue to fight a rearguard action in dealing with the "forces of the market." At the same time, the nation-state is not going to disappear. In fact, the global credit system requires the working of nation-states to guarantee political stability, to coordinate policies with other governments, and to make certain the surplus of capital goes to those places that have deficits. However, in this credit system the message has been sent—get your house in order before you look to the outside to attract new credit from the marketplace. This also applies to many companies in the IT sector, who failed to create business models capable of generating profits. In Wall Street speak this can be translated into—if you want a friend buy a dog. If you want someone else's money to invest, then you had better provide an environment that is guided by Western concepts of transparency and disclosure in corporate and financial transactions, corporate governance, accounting standards, and bankruptcy laws. The message is simple and brutal: if these conditions are not met, then don't expect credit. This naturally makes the need to reform the IMF and related institutions, such as the European Bank for Reconstruction and the African Development Bank, all the more important. It also means that the call for a new financial architecture, with greater efforts to control the flow of credit, is a poorly conceived approach to the challenges of the 21st century.[18]

Conclusion

The history of credit is far from complete. At the beginning of the twenty-first century, the history of credit is undergoing another massive change, stimulated by new technology and the globalization of business. As we have observed through the course of credit history from the late Middle Ages to the late 1990s, such changes have correspondent political and societal ramifications. In the Middle Ages, the advances made by the Knights Templar and the Italian merchants helped revolutionize commerce within Europe, which, in turn, helped stimulate the impulse to venture further afield, eventually to the New World. As we have also witnessed, the advances in credit played an important role in the development of the nation-state, especially in the aftermath of the Treaty of Westphalia in 1648.

Through each turn in history, there have been those with credit and those without. In the era of nation building, the Dutch and British ability to create credit and maintain government access to it, were key elements in their becoming world powers, eclipsing Spain and Portugal on the world stage. No doubt, the entrepreneurial bent of Dutch and English cultures and the respect for the rule of law helped the development of cultures that were willing to use credit, assume risk and take leverage. In time, the United States' superior ability to create and democratize credit helped elevate it into the global center of finance in the twentieth century.

As we noted in our introduction, globalization and technological breakthroughs are increasingly putting the nation-state under pressure. This was made most evident in the late 1990s as the Asian contagion forced a radical change of government in Indonesia, helped usher constitutional changes of government in Korea (through the ballot box), Thailand, and Russia, and put governments under pressure throughout Latin America. Yet, for all the strains on governments, not a single nation-state has come unhinged in Asia, Latin America, Eastern Europe, and the Middle East. Even in Africa, the nation-state remains the dominant force, though pressures clearly exist, though more related to ethnic tensions. All of these factors are part of the process of globalization. The long stretch of time from the end of the Second World War to the 1990s was a period of U.S. dominance of the international credit system, defined by the politics of the Cold War and the economics of industry and services. However, as the Cold War ended and the economic balance in major economies slipped away from industries and more to services, the world suddenly found itself forced to adjust to new sets of relationships. The Asian contagion and the Russian meltdown signified that the post-Cold War order was far from being fully defined and that there was a pressing need to re-design what some have called the "new international financial architecture."

The global system has changed considerably since the trade fairs in the late Middle Ages. There has been a steady progression from the Italian city-states to the Low Countries, ultimately Amsterdam, and then across the Channel to London. The last chapter was the shift in the hub of international credit from London to New York, a passing of the torch from the British to the Americans. The Americans are the keepers of the flame, but the domination of the system is not as clear-cut as it was during the second half of the twentieth century. And that is the challenge for the future. Nothing is clear, expect the historical track record that indicates that credit and the state will continue to function together, mutually dependent on each other. Politics and credit will continue to march hand in hand in shaping economic and societal development. Hopefully the process of democratization of credit will continue to gain momentum and help create a better life for the majority of the planet's population. The historical trend is in the right direction.

Notes

1.   Ron Chernow, "The End of 'High' Finance," *Wall Street Journal*, September 14, 2000, p. 20.
2.   Ibid.
3.   *The Economist*, "Internet Payments: The Personal Touch," August 5, 2000, p. 70.
4.   History of Internet Banking, http://www.ganymade.com/e_commerce/project/e. bank/ HIST/.HTM
5.   Rich Karlgaard, "Digital Rules: Technology and the New Economy," *Forbes*, September 21, 1998, p. 43.
6.   Jonathan Williams, ed., *Money: A History* (New York: St. Martin's Press, 1997), pp. 224-225.
7.   Saskia Sassen, "Global Financial Centers," *Foreign Affairs*, (January/February 1999), p. 77.
8.   See Lucy Conger, "A Fourth Way?: The Latin American Alternative to Neoliberalism," *Current History* (November 1998), pp. 380-384.
9.   James Laxer, *In Search of a New Left: Canadian politics After the Neooconservative Assault* (Toronto: Penguin Books, 1996), p. 66.
10.   See Richard J. Barnet and John Cavanagh, *Global Dreams: Imperial Corporations and the New World Order* (New York: A Torchbook, 1995).
11.   Louis W. Pauly, *Who Elected the Bankers?: Surveillance and Control in the World Economy* (Ithaca, NY: Cornell University Press, 1997), p. ix.
12.   "IMF Admits Errors in Asia but Defends Basic policies," *New York Times*, January 20, 1999, p. A5.
13.   Paul Krugman, "The Return to Depression Economics," *Foreign Affairs* (January/ February 1999), p. 71.
14.   Louis Uchitelle, "A Crash Course in Economics," *New York Times*, January 29, 1999, p. C5.
15.   Sassen, "Global Financial Centers," *Foreign Affairs*, p. 75.
16.   Krugman, "The Return to Depression Economics," p. 74.
17.   Quoted in Roger Cohen, "Growing Up and Getting Practical Since Seattle," *New York Times*, September 24, 2000, Section 4, p. 16.
18.   For a similar view, but with a rigorous economist approach to the issue of capital flows, see David F. DeRosa, In Defense of Free Capital Markets: The Case Against a New International Financial Architecture (Princeton, NJ: Bloomberg Press, 2001).

Bibliography

Andrews, Kenneth R. *Trade, Plunder and Settlement: Maritime Enterprise and the Genesis of the British Empire 1480-1630* (Cambridge: Cambridge University Press, 1984).

Bagehot, Walter. *Lombard Street: Description of the Money Market* (New York: John Wiley & Sons, Inc. 1999). Reprint of the 1873 publication.

Baker, George P., and George David Smith. *The New Financial Capitalists: Kohlberg Kravis Roberts and the Creation of Corporate Value* (New York: Cambridge University Press, 1998).

Banks, Erik. *The Rise and Fall of the Merchant Banks* (London: Kogan Page, 1999).

Barber, Benjamin. "Three Scenarios for the Future of Technology and Strong Democracy," *Political Science Quarterly* (Winter 1998-99): 573-590.

_____. *Jihad vs. McWorld* (New York: Time Books, 1995).

Barbour, Violet. *Capitalism in Amsterdam in the Seventeenth Century* (Baltimore, MD: The Johns Hopkins University Press, 1950).

Barnet, Richard J., and John Cavanagh. *Global Dreams: Imperial Corporations and the New World Order* (New York: A Torchbook, 1995).

Baskin, Jonathon Barron, and Paul J. Miranti, Jr. *A History of Corporate Finance* (New York: Cambridge University Press, 1997).

Beckman, Robert. *Crashes: Why They Happen—What To Do* (London: Grafton Books, 1988).

Bedeman, Robert. *Crashes: Why They Happen—What to Do* (London: Grafton Banks, 1990).

Bedeski, Robert E. *The Transformation of Korea: Reform and Reconstruction Under Roh Tae Woo 1987-1992* (New York: Routledge, 1994).

Belsen, Ken. "Will the Bang Be Big Enough? Japan's Postbubble Troubles." *Bloomberg* (October 1997): 8-25.

Bernard, Jacques. "Trade and Finance 900-1500." In Carlo M. Cipolla, ed., *Fontana Economic History of Europe—The Middle Ages* (London: Collins, Fontona Books, 1972).

Bloom, Jennifer Kingson. "The Old Store Card Is Making a Comeback." *American Banker*, September 4, 1998: 6-7.

Boulnois, L. *The Silk Road* (London: George Allen and Unwin, Ltd., 1966).

Brantlinger, Patrick. *Fictions of the State: Culture and Credit in Britain, 1694-1994* (Ithaca, NY: Cornell University Press, 1996).

Braudel, Fernand. *The Structures of Everyday Life: Civilization & Capitalism 15th-18th Century, Volume 1* (New York: Harper & Row, Publishers, 1981).

_____. *The Wheels of Commerce: Civilization & Capitalism 15th-18th Century* (Berkeley, CA: University of California Press, 1992).

Brewer, John. *The Sinews of Power: War, Money and the English State, 1688-1783* (New York: Alfred A. Knopf, 1989).

Briggs, Robin. *Early Modern France, 1560-1715* (Oxford: Oxford University Press, 1977).

Bruck, Connie. *The Predators' Ball: The Inside Story of Drexel Burnham and the Rise of Junk Bond Raiders* (New York: Penguin Books, 1989).

Brzezinski, Zbigniew. *The Grand Chessboard: American Primacy and Its Geostrategic Imperatives* (New York: Basic Books, 1997).

Boxer, C.R. *The Dutch Seaborne Empire 1600-1800* (London: Penguin Books, 1965).

Burstein, Daniel. *Yen! Japan's New Financial Empire and Its Threat to America* (New York: Simon & Schuster, 1988).

Calder, Lendol, *Financing the American Dream: A Cultural History of Consumer Credit* (Princeton, NJ: Princeton University Press, 1999).

Cameron, Rondo. *A Concise Economic History of the World: From Paleolithic Times to the Present* (New York: Oxford University Press, 1997).

_____. *France and the Economic Development of Europe 1800-1914: Conquests of Peace and Seeds of War* (Princeton, NJ: Princeton University Press, 1961).

Cantor, Norman F. *The Civilization of the Middle Ages* (New York: Harper Perennial, 1993).

Carosso, Vincent P. *Investment Banking in America: A History* (Cambridge, MA: Harvard University Press, 1970).

Chancellor, Edward. *Devil Take the Hindmost: A History of Financial Speculation* (New York: Farrar, Straus, Giroux, 1999).

Chavna, Pierre, *Conquette et Exploitation des Nouveaux Mondes* (Paris: Presses Universitaires, 1969).

_____. *Finance and Financiers in European History 1880-1960* (Cambridge: Cambridge University Press, 1992).

Chown, John. *A History of Money: From AD 800* (New York: Routledge, 1994).

Chernow, Ron. "The End of 'High' Finance." *Wall Street Journal*, September 14, 2000: 22.

_____. *The Life of John D. Rockefeller, Sr.* (New York: Random House, 1998).

_____. "Sayonara to Japan Inc.," *Wall Street Journal*, December 3, 1997: 22.

_____. *The Death of the Banker: The Decline and Fall of the Great Financial Dynasties and the Triumph of the Small Investor* (New York: Vintage Books, 1997).

_____. *The House of Morgan: An American Banking Dynasty* (New York: Simon and Schuster, 1990).

Cipolla, Carlo M. *Before the Industrial Revolution: European Society and Economy 1000-1700* (New York: W.W. Norton & Company, 1976).

Clifford, Mark L., and Pete Engardio. *Meltdown: Asia's Boom, Bust, and Beyond* (New York: Prentice Hall Press, 2000).

Clough, Shepard Bancroft, and Charles W. Cole. *Economic History of Europe* (Boston: D.H. Heath & Co., 1941).

Cobb, William T. *The Strenuous Life* (New York: Wm. Rude & Sons, 1946).

Collins, Michael. *Banks the Industrial Finance in Britain, 1800-1939* (Cambridge: Cambridge University Press, 1991).

Conger, Lucy. "A Fourth Way?: The Latin American Alternative to Neoliberalism." *Current History* (November 1998): 380-384.

Crosby, Alfred W. *The Measure of Reality: Quantification and Western Society, 1250-1600* (New York: Cambridge University Press, 1997).

Davis, Ralph. *The Rise of the Atlantic Economies* (Ithaca, NY: Cornell University Press, 1973).

Davis, R.H.C. *A History of Medieval Europe: From Constantine to St. Louis*, revised ed. (New York: David McKay, 1957, 1970).

de Cortázar, Fernando García, and José Manuel González Vesga. *Breve historia de España* (Madrid: Alianza Editorial, 1944).

De La Vega, Joseph. *Confusión de Confusiones* (new edition edited by Martin S. Fridson) (New York: John Wiley and Sons, Inc., 1996).

de Roover, Raymond A. *Money, Banking and Credit in Medieval Bruges: Italian Merchant Bankers, Lombards and Money Changes—A Study of the Origins of Banking* (Cambridge, MA: Medieval Academy of America, 1948).

DeRosa, David F., *In Defense of Free Capital Markets: The Case Against a New International Financial Architecture* (Princeton NJ: Bloomberg Press, 2001).

Diffie, Bailey W., and George D. Winius. *Foundations of the Portuguese Empire, 1415-1580* (Minneapolis, MN: University Press of Minneapolis, 1977).

Du Jourdin, Michel Mollat. *Europe and the Sea* (Oxford: Blackwell Publishers, 1993).

Eccles, W.J. *The French in North America 1500-1783* (Markham, Canada: Fitzhenry & Whiteside, 1998).

The Economist. "Indonesia: Abracadabra." August 12, 2000: 65.

_____. "Asian Economies: Stragglers." August 5, 2000: 70-71.

_____. "Latin America Seeks Shelter." August 29, 1998: 63.

_____. "Russian Banks: Three's Company." August 29, 1998: 65.

_____. "Asia: The Shoguns in the Shadows." July 18, 1998: 35-36.

Edwards, Burt. *Credit Management Handbook* (Aldershot, England: Gower Publishing Company, Limited, 1997).

Edwards, Jeremy, and Klaus Fischer Banks, *Finance and Investment in Germany* (New York: Cambridge University Press, 1996).

Eichengreen, Barry. *Golden Fetters: The Gold Standard and the Great Depression* (New York: Oxford University Press, 1995).

Ehrenberg, Richard. *Capital Finance in the Age of the Renaissance* (New York: Harcourt Brace & Co., 1928).

Elliott, J.H. *Spain and Its World 1500-1700* (New Haven, CT: Yale University Press, 1992).

_____. *Imperial Spain 1469-1716* (London: Penguin Books, 1963,1990).

Eichengreen, Barry. and Albert Fishlow, *Contending with Capital Flows: What Is Different About the 1990s?* (New York: A Council on Foreign Relations Paper, 1996).

Endlich, Lisa. *Goldman Sachs: The Culture of Success* (New York: Simon & Schuster, 1999).

Ewing, Terzah. "Bridge/CRB Index Hits 12-Year Low, Raising More Concerns About Deflation." *New York Times*, August 27, 1998: C17.

Ferguson, Naill. *The House of Rothschild: Money's Prophets, 1798-1848* (New York: Viking 1998).

Fernandez-Armesto, Felipe. *Before Columbus: Exploration and Colonization from the Mediterranean to the Atlantic, 1229-1492* (Philadelphia: University of Pennsylvania Press, 1987).

Finley, M.I. *The Ancient Economy* (Berkeley and Los Angeles: University of California Press, 1973).

Firstbook, Peter. *The Voyage of the Matthew: John Cabot and the Discovery of North America* (San Francisco: KQED Books & Tapes, 1997).

Friedman, Thomas L. "Techno-Nothings." *New York Times*, April 18, 1998: A-13.
_____. "Where's the Crisis." *New York Times*, May 23, 1998: A15.

Garber, Peter, *Famous First Bubbles: The Fundamentals of Early Manias* (Cambridge, MA: The MIT Presss, 2001).

Germain, Randall D. *The International Organization of Credit: States and Global Finance in the World Economy* (Cambridge: Cambridge University Press, 1998).

Geisst, Charles R. *Wall Street: A History* (New York: Oxford University Press, 1997).

Gleeson, Janet, *Millionaire: The Philanderer, Gambler, and Duelist Who Invented Modern Finance* (New York: Simon and Schuster, 1999).

Gomez, Edmund Terence, and Jomo K.S. *Malaysia's Political Economy: Politics, Patronage and Profits* (Cambridge: Cambridge University Press, 1997).

Goslinga, Cornelius Ch. *The Dutch in the Caribbean and the Wild Coast, 1580-1680* (Assen, The Netherlands: VanGarken & Co., 1971).

Graham, Richard. *Britain & the Onset of Modernization in Brazil 1850-1914* (Cambridge: Cambridge University Press, 1972).

Gray, Cheryl W. "Reforming Legal Systems in Developing and Transition." *Finance and Development* (September 1997).

Greif, Avner. "Reputation and Coalitions in Medieval Trade: Evidence on the Maghribi Traders." *Journal of Economic History* (December 1989): 49, 857-82.

Grove, Tom. "Japan: Sogo Bankruptcy." *Thomson BankWatch*, July 13, 2000.

Haring, Clarence H. *Trading and Navigation Between Spain and the Indies in the Time of the Hapsburgs* (Gloucester, MA: Peter Smith, 1918, 1964).

Harris, Clay. "Pyramid Scheme Operator Is Jailed." *Financial Times*, August 25, 1998: 10.

Hayes, Carlton J.H. *A Political and Cultural History of Modern Europe Vol. I* (New York: The Macmillan Co., 1932).

Hayes, Samuel L,. and Philip M. Hubbard. *Investment Banking: A Tale of Three Cities* (Boston: Harvard Business School Press, 1990).

Hefferman, Shelagh. *Modern Banking: In Theory and Practice* (New York: John Wiley and Sons, 1996).

Henderson, Callum. *Asia Falling: Making Sense of the Asian Crisis* (New York: Business Week Books, 1998).

Hobson, Dominic. *The Pride of Lucifer: Morgan Grenfell 1838-1990, The Unauthorised Biography of a Merchant Bank* (London: Mandarin, 1991).

Hofstadter, Richard. *The Age of Reform: From Bryan to F.D.R.* (New York: Vintage, 1955).

Homer, Sidney. *History of Interest Rates* (New Brunswick, NJ: Rutgers University Press, 1963).

Horseman, Matthew, and Andrew Marshall. *After the Nation-State: Citizens, Tribalism and the New World Disorder* (New York: Harper Collins, 1994).

Hourani, Albert. *A History of the Arab Peoples* (New York: Warner Books, 1991).

Hunt, Edwin S., and James M. Murray. *A History of Business in Medieval Europe, 1200-1550* (New York: Cambridge University Press, 1999).

Hunt, Edwin S. *The Medieval Super-Companies: A Study of the Peruzzi Company of Florence* (New York: Cambridge University Press, 1994).

Israel, Jonathan I. *The Dutch Republic: Its Rise, Greatness and Fall, 1477-1806* (Oxford: Oxford University Press, 1995).

Jackson, Karl D., ed. *Asian Contagion: The Causes and Consequences of a Financial Crisis* (Boulder, CO: Westview Press, 1999).

James, Lawrence. *The Rise and Fall of the British Empire* (New York: St. Martin's Press, 1997).

Jenkins, Holman W., Jr. "A Lost Waah? for Japan's Crybabies." *Wall Street Journal,* December 3, 1997: A23.

Jones, Geoffrey. *British Multinational Banking 1830-1990* (Oxford: Clarendon Press, 1993).

Joslin, David. *A Century of Banking in Latin America* (London: Oxford University Press, 1963).

Judd, Denis. *Empire: The British Imperial Experience from 1756 to the Present* (London: Fontana Press, 1997).

Kamin, Henry. *European Society, 1500-1700* (London: Routledge, 1996).

Karlgaard, Rich. "Digital Rules: Technology and the New Economy." *Forbes,* September 21, 1998: 43.

Katz, Jacob. *Tradition and Crisis: Jewish Society at the End of the Middle Ages* (New York: Schocken Books, 1971).

Katz, Richard. *Japan The System That Soured: The Rise and Fall of the Japanese of the Japanese Economic Miracle* (Armonk, NY: M.E. Sharpe, 1998).

Keen, Maurice. *The Pelican History of Medieval Europe* (London: Penguin Books, 1975).

Kindleberger, Charles. *Manias, Panics and Crashes: A History of Financial Crises* (New York: John Wiley and Sons, Inc., Third Edition, 1996).

_____. *The World in Depression, 1929-1939* (Berkeley: University of California Press, 1973, 1986).

Kishlansky, Mark. *A Monarchy Transformed: Britain 1603-1714* (New York: Penguin Books, 1997).

Krause, Lawrence. *The Economics and Politics of the Asian Financial Crisis of 1997-98* (New York: Council on Council Relations, June 1998).

Kristof, Nicholas. "Japan's Full Story: Review Essay." *Foreign Affairs* (November/.December 1997): 140-145.

_____. "Seoul Plans to Ask the IMF for a Minimum of $20 Billion." *New York Times*, November 22, 1997: A1, A5.

Krugman, Paul. "The Return to Depression Economics." *Foreign Affairs* (January/February 1999).

_____. *Pop Internationalism* (Cambridge, MA: MIT Press, 1997).

Kuttner, Robert. *Everything for Sale: The Virtues and Limits of Markets* (New York: University of Chicago Press, 1999).

Landes, David S., *The Wealth and Poverty of Nations: Why Some Are So Rich and Some So Poor* (New York: W.W. Norton & Company, 1998).

Landes, Peter, and Dan Biers. "This Will Hurt." *Far Eastern Economic Review*, December 4, 1997: 74-78.

Lane, Frederic C., and Jelle C. Riemersana, eds. *Enterprise and Secular Change* (Homewood, IL: Richard D. Irwin, 1953).

Langford, Paul, and Christopher Harvie. *The Eighteenth Century and the Age of Industry* (Oxford: Oxford University Press, 1988).

Lardy, Nicholas R. *China's Unfinished Economic Revolution* (Washington, DC: Brookings Institution Press, 1998).

Laxer, James. *In Search of the New Left: Canadian Politics After the Neoconservative Assault* (Toronto: Penguin Books, 1996).

Lee, Yean-ho. *The State, Society and Big Business in South Korea* (New York: Routledge, 1997).

Lewis, Michael. *Liar's Poker: Rising Through the Wreckage on Wall Street* (London: Penguin Books, 1989).

Lewis, W. Arthur. *The Evolution of the International Economic Order* (Princeton, NJ: Princeton University Press, 1978).

Lightenbert, Catherine. *Willem Usselinx* (Utrecht, The Netherlands: A Oosthoek, 1914).

Linter, Bertil. "South Pacific: Paradise for Crooks." *Far Eastern Economic Review*, November 6, 1997: 31-35.

Little, Jeffery B., and Lucien Rhodes. *Understanding Wall Street* (New York: Liberty Hall Press, 1991).

Longworth, Richard C. *Global Squeeze: The Coming Crisis for First-Worst Nations* (Chicago, IL: Contemporary Books, 1998).

Lopez, Robert S. *The Commercial Revolution of the Middle Ages 950-1350* (Cambridge: Cambridge University Press, 1976).

_____. *The Birth of Europe* (New York: J.B. Lippincott Co., 1967).

MacDonald, Scott B. "The Asian Contagion and the 'Madness of Crowds'." *Looking Ahead* (National Policy Association) August 1998: 17-20.

_____. "Transparency in Thailand's 1997 Economic Crisis: The Significance of Disclosure." *Asian Survey* (July 1998): 688-702.

MacDonald, Scott B., and Georges A. Fauriol. *Fast Forward: Latin American on the Edge of the 21st Century* (New Brunswick, NJ: Transaction Publishers, 1997).

Mackay, Charles. *Extraordinary Popular Delusions and the Madness of Crowds* (new editions, Martin Fridson, ed., New York: John Wiley & Sons, Inc., 1996).

Marichal, Carlos. *A Century of Debt Crises in Latin America: From Independence to the Great Depression* (Princeton, NJ: Princeton University Press, 1989).

Marjolein, Hart, Joost Jonker, and Jan Luiten van Zanden, eds. *A Financial History of the Netherlands* (New York: Cambridge University Press, 1997).

Mathias, Peter. *The First Industrial Nation: An Economic History of Britain 1700-1914* (London: Routledge, 1995).

McCauley, Lord. *The History of England* (New York: Penguin Books, 1986, first published in 1848-1861), p.488.

McConnell, John W. *Basic Teachings of the Great Economists* (New York: Barnes & Noble, Inc., 1943, 1956).

McCormack, Gavan. *The Emptiness of Japanese Affluence* (Armonk, N.Y.: M.E. Sharpe, 1996).

Morici, Peter. "Managing the Global Economy's Managers." *Current History* (November 1998): 374-379.

Morón, Guillermo. *A History of Venezuela* (London: George Allen and Unwin, 1964).

Nemato, Naoko. "Trends in Banking: The Big Bank Accelerates (Japan)." *Standard & Poor's Bank System Report* (November 1997).

Norris, Floyd. "As Profits Soar, Corporate America Takes on More Debt." *New York Times*, July 7, 2000: C1.

North, Douglas C., and Robert Paul Thomas. *The Rise of the Western World: A New Economic History* (Cambridge: Cambridge University, 1973).

Ohmae, Kenichi. *The End of the Nation-States: The Rise of Regional Economies* (New York: The Free Press, 1995).

Organization for Economic Cooperation and Development. *Japan 1997* (Paris: Organization for Economic Cooperation and Development, 1998).

Pauly, Louis W. *Who Elected the Bankers?: Surveillance and Control in the World Economy* (Ithaca, NY: Cornell University Press, 1997).

Pavord, Anna. *The Tulip: The Story of a Flower that Made Men Mad* (London: Bloomsbury Publishing, 1999).

Penrose, B. *Travel and Discovery in the Renaissance* (New York: Atheneum, 1962).

Pike, Ruth. *Enterprises and Adventures: The Genoese in Seville and the Opening Up of the New World* (Ithaca, NY: Cornell University Press, 1966).

Pinson, Koppel. *Modern Germany* (New York: The Macmillan Company, 1966).

Porter, N.A.M. *The Safeguard of the Sea: A Naval History of Britain, Vol. 1 660-1649* (London: Harper Collins, Publishers, 1997).

Postan, M.M. *Medieval Trade and Finance* (New York: Cambridge University Press, 1973).

Power, Eileen. *The Wool Trade in English Medieval History*, reprint edition (Oxford: Oxford University Press, 1942, 1955).

Powicke, Sir Maurice. *The Thirteenth Century 1216-1307* (New York: Oxford University Press, 1991).

Quinn, David. *North America from the Earliest Discovery to First Settlement* (New York: Harper & Row, 1977).

Radelet, Steven, and Jeffrey Sachs. "Asia's Reemergence." Foreign Affairs (November-December 1997): 44-59.

Rich, E.E. "Expansion and Concern of all Europe." In *The New Cambridge Modern History, Vol. I* (Cambridge: Cambridge University Press, 1957).

Rippy, J. Fred. *British Investments in Latin America, 1822-1949* (Hamden, CT: Archon Books, 1966).

Roberts, Richard. *Schroders: Merchants and Bankers* (London: Macmillan Press 1992).

Roberts, J.M. *The Penguin History of Europe* ((London: Penguin Books, 1996).

Roberts, Richard. *Schroders: Merchants and Bankers* (London: Macmillan Press, 1992).

Rock, David. *Argentina, 1516-1982* (Berkeley: University of California Press, 1985).

Roover, Raymond de. *Money, Banking and Credit in Medieval Bruges: A Study in the Origins of Banking* (Cambridge, MA: Medieval Academy of America, 1948).

_____. *The Rise and Decline of the Medici Bank, 1397-1494* (Cambridge, MA: Harvard University Press, 1963).

_____. *Business, Banking and Economic Thought in Late Medieval and Early Modern Europe* (London: University of Chicago Press, 1974).

Rosenberg, Nathan ,and L.E. Birdzell, Jr. *How the West Grew Rich: The Economic Transformation of the Industrial World* (New York: Basic Books, 1986).

Roth, Cecil. *A History of the Jews: From the Earliest Times Through the Six Day War* (New York: Schocken Books, 1971).

Rugoff, Milton. *America's Gilded Age: Intimate Portraits from an Era of Extravagance and Change 1850-1890* (New York: Henry Holt and Company, 1989).

SaKong, Il. *Korea in the World Economy* (Washington, DC: Institute for International Economics, 1993).

Sanger, David E. "Case No. 3: Asian Illness Threatening Vital Organs." *New York Times*, November 22, 1997: D1,D2.

Sarel, Michael. *Growth in East Asia: What We Can and We Cannot Infer* (Washington, DC: International Monetary Fund, 1996).

Sassen, Saskia. "Global Financial Centers." *Foreign Affairs* (January/February 1999).

Sawyer, P.H. *The Age of the Viking* (New York: St. Martin Press, 1962).

Schama, Simon. *The Embarrassment of Riches: An Interpretation of Dutch Culture in the Golden Age* (Berkeley: University of California Press, 1988).

Schevill, Ferdinand. *The Great Elector* (Hamden, CT: Archon Books, 1965)

Schlesinger, Jacob M. *Shadow Shoguns: The Rise and Fall of Japan's Postwar Political Machine* (New York: Simon & Schuster, 1997).

Schriftgiesser, Karl. *The Amazing Roosevelt Family 1613-1942* (New York: Wilfred French Inc., 1942).

Schubert, Aurel. *The Credit-Anstalt Crisis of 1931* (New York: Cambridge University Press, 1992).

Schwartz, Stuart. *Sugar Plantations in the Formation of Brazilian Society—Bahia* (New York: Cambridge University Press, 1985).

Smith, Adam. *The Wealth of Nations* (Chicago: Cannon Edition, 1976).

Smith, Patrick. *Japan: A Reinterpretation* (New York: Vintage, 1997).

Sobel, Robert. *The Pursuit of Wealth: The Incredible Story of Money Throughout the Ages* (New York: McGraw Hill, 2000).

Soyeda, Juichi. *History of Banking in Japan* (Richmond, VA: Curzon, 1993).

Stares, Paul B. *Global Habit: The Drug Problem in a Borderless World* (Washington DC: The Brookings Institution, 1996).

Stern, Fritz. *Gold and Iron: Bismark, Bleichroder and the Building of the German Empire* (New York: Vintage Books, 1979).

Strayer, Joseph R., ed. *Dictionary of the Middle Ages Vol. 2 Augustinos Triumphis—Byzantine Literature* (New York: Charles Scribner's Sons, 1982).

Tamaki, Norio. *Japanese Banking: A History 1859-1959* (Cambridge: Cambridge University Press, 1995).

Tawney, R.H. *Religion and the Rise of Capitalism* (New York: Harcourt, Brace & Co., 1926).

Teichova, Alice, Ginette Kurgon-van Hentenryk, and Dieter Ziegler, eds. *Banking, Trade and Industry: Europe, American and Asia from the Thirteenth Century to the Twentieth Century* (Cambridge: Cambridge University Press, 1997).

Tett, Gillian. "Big Bang or Big Bust-Up?" *Financial Times*, November 14, 1997: 11.

Troyat, Henry. *Peter the Great* (New York: E.P. Dutton, 1979, first edition 1937).

Trudel, Marcel. *Histoire de la Nouvelle-France, Vol. I, le Comtoir, 1604-1627* (Montreal, Canada: 1967).

Usher, Abbott Payson. *The Early History of Deposit Banking in Mediterranean Europe*, reprint eds. (New York: Russell & Russell, 1943, 1957).

Valdez, Stephen. *An Introduction to Western Financial Markets* (London: Macmillan Press, Ltd., 1998).

Vatikiotis, Michael. "Pacific Divide." *Far Eastern Economic Review*, November 6, 1997: 14-16.

_____. "Southeast Asia: Face the Music." *Far Eastern Economic Review*, September 25, 1997: 91.

Wade, Robert. "The Asian Crisis and the Global Economy: Causes, Consequences, and Cure", *Current History* (November 1998): 361-374.

Wallerstein, Immanuel. *The Modern World System II: Mercantilism and the Consolidation of the European World Economy 1600-1750* (New York: Academic Press, 1980).

Weatherford, Jack. *The History of Money* (New York: Three Rivers Press, 1997).

Williams, Jonathan, ed. *Money: A History* (New York: St. Martin's Press, 1997).

Witt, Louise. "Banking Reform: A Look Through the Loopholes." *Bloomberg*, November 1997, pp. 6-16.

World Bank. *World Development Report 1997: The State in a Changing World* (New York: Oxford University Press, 1997).

Wriston, Walter. "Bits, Bytes and Diplomacy." *Foreign Affairs* (September/October 1997): 172-182.

Yang, Lien-Cheng. *Money and Credit in China* (Cambridge, MA: Harvard University Press, 1952).

Yashiro, M.Y., and Thomas B. Lifson. *The Invisible Link: Japan's Sogo Shusha and the Organization of Trade* (Cambridge, MA: MIT Press, 1986).

Weatherford, Jack. *The History of Money* (New York: Three Rivers Press, 1997).

Williams, Eric. *Capitalism and Slavery* (Chapel Hill: University Press of North Carolina, 1994).

World Bank. *Global Development Finance 1998* (Washington, DC: World Bank, 1998).

WuDunn, Sheryl. "Japan Presses Banks to Give Koreans Time." *New York Times*, December 26, 1998: 02.

Ziegler, Philip. *The Sixth Great Power: Barings 1762-1929* (London: Collins, 1988).

Index